JADĪD AL-ISLĀM

Principal publications by Raphael Patai:

Shire Yisrael Berekhya Fontanella (In Hebrew: *The Poems of Y.B.F.)*
HaMayim (In Hebrew: *Water: A Study in Palestinology and Palestinian Folklore)*
HaSappanut ha'Ivrith bIme Qedem (In Hebrew: *Ancient Jewish Seafaring)*
Adam wa'Adama (In Hebrew: *Man and Earth in Hebrew Custom, Belief, and Legend)*
Mada' ha'Adam (In Hebrew: *The Science of Man: An Introduction to Anthropology)*
Man and Temple in Ancient Jewish Myth and Ritual
On Culture Contact and Its Working in Modern Palestine
Israel between East and West
Annotated Bibliography of Syria, Lebanon and Jordan
The Kingdom of Jordan
Current Jewish Social Research
Cultures in Conflict
Sex and Family in the Bible and the Middle East
Golden River to Golden Road: Society, Culture and Change in the Middle East
Hebrew Myths (with Robert Graves)
Tents of Jacob: The Diaspora Yesterday and Today
Myth and Modern Man
The Arab Mind
The Myth of the Jewish Race (with Jennifer Patai)
The Messiah Texts
Gates to the Old City
The Vanished Worlds of Jewry
The Jewish Mind
Robert Graves and the Hebrew Myths
The Seed of Abraham
Ignaz Goldziher and His Oriental Diary
Nahum Goldmann: His Missions to the Gentiles
Apprentice in Budapest
The Hebrew Goddess, third enlarged edition
The Jews of Kurdistan (with Erich Brauer)
Between Budapest and Jerusalem
Journeyman in Jerusalem
The Jewish Alchemists: A History and Source Book
The Jews of Hungary: History, Culture, Psychology

A listing of the books edited by Raphael Patai can be found at the back of this volume

JADĪD AL-ISLĀM

The Jewish "New Muslims" of Meshhed

Raphael Patai

Wayne State University Press
Detroit

Jewish Folklore and Anthropology Series

A complete listing of the books in this series can be found online at wsupress.wayne.edu

Manufactured in the United States of America.

ISBN-13: 978-0-8143-4075-2 (paperback)

Library of Congress Cataloging-in-Publication Data

Patai, Raphael, 1910–
Jadīd al-Islām : the Jewish "new Muslims" of Meshhed / Raphael Patai.
p. cm. — (Jewish folklore and anthropology series)
Includes bibliographical references and index.
ISBN 0-8143-2652-8 (alk. paper)
1. Jews—Iran—Mashhad—History. 2. Muslim converts from Judaism—Iran—Mashad. 3.Mashad (Iran)—Ethnic relations. I. Title.
II. Series.
DS135.I652M377 1997
955′.54—dc21 97-2527

Dedicated
to the memory of
Āqā Farajullah (Yonathan) Nasrullayoff,
head of the Meshhed Jews in Meshhed and in Jerusalem,
who was my chief informant in my early studies of the Jadīdīm,
and
to his son, *yibbadel l'ḥayyim*, Yoḥanan (Ne'matollah) Livian,
for his invaluable help
in Jerusalem in the 1940s and in New York in the 1990s

Contents

Illustrations *9*
Introduction *11*

I. History and Traditions

1. Early Times *25*
2. Before the Allahdād *29*
3. The Ṣūfī Lure *41*
4. Allahdād! *51*
5. After the Allahdād *65*
6. Conversions to the Bahai faith *76*
7. A Decade of Blood Libels and Other Incidents, 1892–1902 *79*
8. Zionism and Early *'Aliya* *86*
9. Disturbances in the 1940s *92*
10. A Picture of Jewish Life *101*
11. Emigration, *'Aliya*, Dispersion *108*
12. A Meshhed Jewish Family: Āqā Farajullah's Memoirs *112*

II. Tales and Legends

Introductory Note *151*
13. A Popular "Life of Nadir" *154*
14. Three Tales about Mullah Siman-Tov *168*
15. Two Stories about the Jews of Kalat *173*
16. How the Herāt Jews Were Saved *178*
17. The Story of the Woman Gohar *182*
18. The Death of Ḥājj Ḥasan Eṣḥaq *189*

III. Customs and Institutions

Introductory Note *195*
19. Birth Customs *198*
20. Jewish Names and Origins *202*
21. The Secret School (Hebrew Education) *205*
22. Girls' Games *222*
23. Ritual Observances *228*
24. Marriage *231*
25. Burial Customs *265*

Conclusion *273*
Notes *279*
Judeo-Persian Vocabulary *299*
Bibliography *311*
Index *317*

ILLUSTRATIONS

Following p. 136:
General view of Meshhed
Meshhed: street in the 'Êdgāh, the Jewish quarter
Street with stores in the 'Êdgāh
Street in the 'Êdgāh
A room in the 'Êdgāh serving as synagogue
Wall in the Jewish cemetery with inscription in Persian and Judeo-Persian
Tombstone in Persian and Hebrew
Members of the Ḥakimian Family, ca. 1900
Āqā Farajullah and wife, ca. 1905
Karbalā'ī Nauruz with men and children of the Kalati family, 1905
Pupils of the Mulim boys' school in the 'Êdgāh, ca. 1920
Young *Jadīdī* couple in traditional garb, ca. 1920
Pupils of the Talmud Torah school, ca. 1920
Karbalā'ī Aghajan Raḥmani with his wife and son, ca. 1921
The *Jadīdī* midwife M'shateh, ca. 1922–25
Ibrahimoff family, ca. 1925
Āqā Aharonoff with his wife, daughters and grandchild, ca. 1925
Male members and children of the Ḥakimian (Mortezaoff) family, 1925
Āqā Jabar Ḥakimian with his son and son's fiancée, 1925
Passover gathering in the home of Āqā Yusef Levi, 1927
Three nephews of Āqā Farajullah Nasrullayoff in India
Wife of Āqā Farajullah, with her son and son-in-law, ca. 1930
Āqā Ibrahim with his wife, ca. 1930
Opening of the gallery of stores built by the 'Azizullayoff family, ca. 1935
Āqā Yusef Aminoff and family in front of their residence, ca. 1935
Students of the *Jadīdī Arz Agdaz* girls' school in Meshhed, 1936
Boy students and teachers of the *Otzar haTorah* school in Meshhed, 1930
At the wedding of Yoḥanan Livian, Jerusalem, 1942
Group of *Jadīdī* amateur actors performing in Meshhed, 1943

Hebrew marriage contract from Meshhed, dated 5544 (1784) *248*

Introduction

Since the Jews of Meshhed, who are the subject of this book, lived in a Shīʿī Muslim environment, and their entire existence depended on how their Shīʿī Muslim neighbors treated them and related to them, this introduction begins with a brief comment on the nature and character of Shīʿī Islam and, in particular, its relationship to members of other religions.

Shīʿa (in its full form Shīʿat ʿAlī, or "the party of ʿAlī") is the name of one of the two major branches of Islam, which differs from the other, that of the Sunnīs, in several important respects. Perhaps the most fundamental feature specific to Shīʿī Islam is its concept and institution of Imāmate (Arabic *Imāma*), meaning the "supreme leadership" of the Muslim community after the death of Muhammad. The Shīʿīs (or Shīʿites) recognize only ʿAlī ibn Abī Tālib, the cousin and son-in-law of the Prophet Muhammad, and his descendants as the sole legitimate Imāms, charismatic leaders of the Muslim community. The Shīʿīs hold that an esoteric knowledge of true Islam is vested in the Imām by a divine spirit, that the Imām has perfect knowledge of everything, including "what has been and what will be," and that thus he is the ultimate source of the true meaning of Islam. All this is denied by the Sunnīs, who consider the Caliphs (Arabic *khalīfa,* "successor" or "vicar") the true religious heads of the Islamic nation.

While the Shīʿīs as a whole constitute a minority within Islam, they are comprised of numerous sects, including the Ismāʿīliyya (in Yemen and India), the Zaydiyya (in Yemen), and several smaller groups. By far the most important Shīʿī sect is that of the Ithnā ʿAshariyya (or "Twelver") Shīʿīs, to which some 90 percent of the population of Iran belongs.

The Twelvers believe in a succession of twelve Imāms, whose veneration is much greater than that of any saint or pope in Catholicism. They believe that the twelfth (last) Imām, who lived in the ninth century, was "occulted," that is, became concealed from the world, but nevertheless continues to live on earth and fulfill the essential functions of the Imāmate. He will return before the end of the world as the Mahdī, the divinely "guided" redeemer, to end all oppression and institute an age of justice, reminiscent of the Jewish Messianic age. Until that time, all secular government is intrinsically illegitimate, and the *mujtahids*,

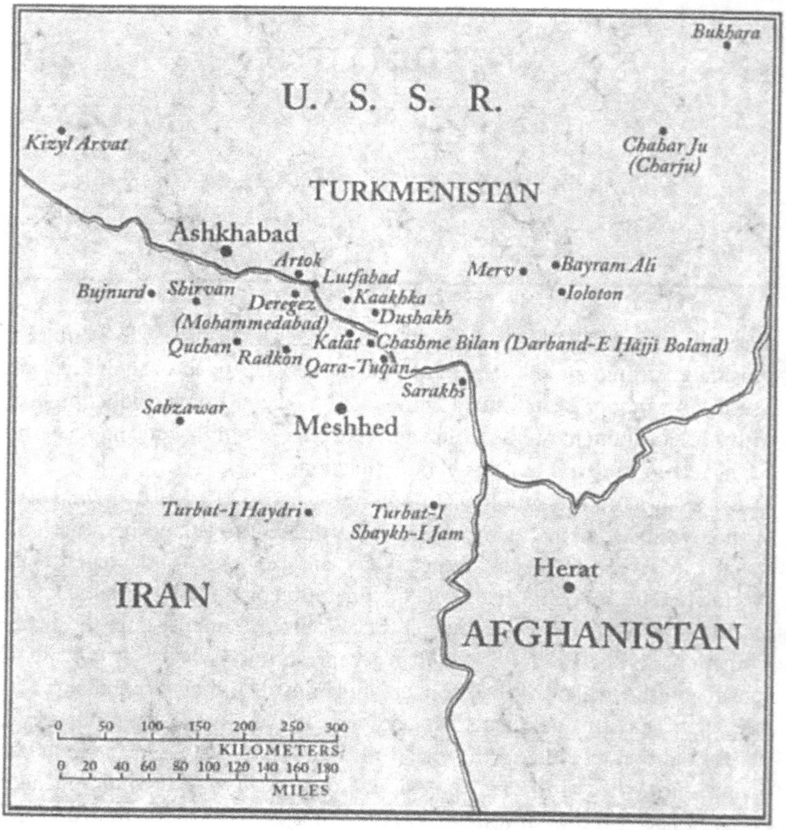

Map of the Iran-Turkmenistan (U.S.S.R.)–Afghanistan border area showing the localities that figure in the life of the Jadīd al-Islām.

clerics trained in Islamic law and theology, are the true leaders and guides of the Muslim community. The *mujtahids* recognized by the community as the most important leaders are given the honorific title of Ayatollah (literally, "sign of Allah").

Apart from doctrinal divergences, a major difference between Sunnīs and Shī'is is the much greater emphasis put by the latter on self-sacrifice for the faith, in emulation of Ḥusayn, son of 'Alī, whose death in battle at Karbala on the tenth of Muḥarram 61 H. (680 C.E.) is considered martyrdom by Shī'ī tradition and is commemorated annually in passion plays and bloody self-flagellation by religious enthusiasts in huge ritual processions. This readiness to become martyrs was a contributing factor in the much greater number of Iranian than Iraqi casualties in the Iran-Iraq War of the 1980s.

Other significant differences include the recognition of *muṭ'a* (temporary or term) marriages by the Shī'īs and the greater role ritual impurity plays in Shī'ī than in Sunnī religion. A Shī'ī man can contract marriage with a woman for a period of time defined in advance, such as ten years or as little as a few hours. Impurity for the Shī'īs is an ever-present danger, against which they have to be constantly on guard. Ayatollah Khomeini, the undisputed supreme religious-temporal leader of Iran from 1979 to his death in 1989, published a tract containing guidance in ritual matters, in which he listed eleven things that make a Muslim unclean: urine, feces, sperm, carrion, blood, a dog, a pig, an unbeliever, wine, beer, and the sweat of a camel that eats unclean things. That these rules concerning sources of pollution have nothing to do with physical uncleanliness but are exclusively a matter of ritual impurity becomes evident from what Khomeini adds in explanation of the eighth point: "When a non-Muslim man or woman is converted to Islam, their body, saliva, nasal secretion, and sweat are ritually clean."[1]

For the Jews (and other non-Muslims), this obsessive concern with the danger of pollution had dire results. Since the "unbelievers" (that is, non-Muslims) were considered as unclean and polluting as a dog or a pig (not to mention urine and feces), contact with them was shunned, because their mere touch was apt to render a Muslim ritually impure; purity could be restored only with elaborate ritual ablutions. Although these avoidances were observed primarily by the Muslim clergy and the religiously learned and scrupulous persons, they created in the population at large an attitude of contempt toward the Jews that was much more pronounced than what the Jews had to put up with in Sunnī Muslim environments. Thus, the position of the Jews as *dhimmīs,* tolerated non-Muslims—not enviable in the Sunnī world, either—was much worse in Shī'ī lands. One manifestation of this was the repeated occurrence of forced conversons of Jews to Islam in Shī'ī Iran, the most recent one of which, the Allahdād in Meshhed in 1839, is of special interest for us. (See below, chapter 4.) First, however, a few words must be said about the history of the Jews in Iran and, in particular, about the conversions to Islam that were forced upon them in former times.

The beginnings of Jewish history in Iran date back to late biblical times. The books of Isaiah, Daniel, Ezra, Nehemiah, Chronicles, and Esther contain references to the life and experiences of the Jews in Persia. In the book of Ezra, the Persian kings were credited with permitting and enabling the Jews (or, rather, some Jews) to return to Jerusalem and rebuild their Temple: its reconstruction was effected "according to the decree of Cyrus, and Darius, and Artaxerxes king of Persia" (Ezra 6:14). This great event in Jewish history took place in the late sixth century B.C.E., by which time there was a well-established and influential Jewish community in Persia.

The apocryphal book of Tobit (possibly from the fourth century B.C.E.) takes place among Jews in Persia, but for several centuries after Ezra and Nehemiah practically nothing is known of the Jews in that country. The hiatus is filled, to some extent, by legends which found their way into the writings of early Islamic scholars, among them Yāqūt, Muqaddasī and al-Qazwīnī, who claim that Nebuchadnezzar (the conqueror of Jerusalem in 586 B.C.E.) settled Jews in Isfahan and that the city was called al-Yahūdiyya ("the Jewish city"). A rare historical document is the edict issued by Darius II in 419 B.C.E., in which he commanded that all the Jews in his kingdom strictly observe the Feast of Unleavened Bread.[2]

The story told in the book of Esther is fiction, but it may be built on some historical event that may have taken place under King Ahasuerus, who possibly is none other than Artaxerxes II (r. 404–359 B.C.E.). If so, it shows that in that period, the Jews in Persia were able to mount self-defense against inimical attacks and were an influential population element in the country.

Historical sources on the Jewish presence in Iran trickle in dribs and drabs throughout the twelve centuries that passed between the establishment of the Achaemenid empire (549 B.C.E.) and the Muslim conquest of Iran (642 C.E.), but they are sufficient to show that Jewish communities did exist, and at times did thrive, in many Persian cities. Toward the end of the second century C.E., the Parthians created the office of the Jewish Exilarch (*Resh Galutha* in Aramaic), who was given considerable powers over the Jewish community and became, under the Sassanids, one of the highest ranking officers of the empire. Throughout this long period, and beyond it, Persian Jewry was intellectually eclipsed by the neighboring Jewish community of Mesopotamia, which produced the Babylonian Talmud (completed ca. 500 C.E.), followed by the religious writings (the Responsa) of the Babylonian Geonim (heads of the Talmudic academies, from ca. 600 to ca. 1200 C.E.).

After the Arab conquest of Iran (642 C.E.), the situation of the Jews in the country became similar to the one the young religion of Islam accorded the Jews and the other "people of the book" (Christians, Sabians, and later also Zoroastrians and Hindus) in all the countries that came under Muslim rule. They became *dhimmīs,* that is, protected people, whose position was regulated by a pact, *dhimma,* under which they were accorded a low-rank status: they were permitted to practice their religion and enabled to pursue their occupations, provided they recognized the supremacy of the Muslims and Islam, paid the poll tax (*jizya*) imposed upon them, and were willing to submit to the routine humiliations involved in every contact between them and Muslims. Muslim historians ascribe the formulation of this pact to the caliph 'Umar I (r. 634–644), but Western scholarship inclines to see in it the codification of later developments: in its complete form, the so-called Pact of 'Umar is not attested before the eleventh century.

Among the limitations imposed by this pact on the *dhimmīs* are rules regarding the clothes they are allowed to wear, the mounts they can ride, the dwellings they can build, houses of worship they can use. The *dhimmīs* must behave humbly and defer to Muslims in every respect. They are not allowed to wear arms, but, on the other hand, they must wear badges (in the case of the Jews, of yellow color) to make them recognizable from afar. They must not try to convert a Muslim to their faith; he who does so, and the Muslim who converts, incurs the death penalty. A *dhimmī* man cannot marry a Muslim woman, but a Muslim man can marry a *dhimmī* woman; the children of such mixed marriages are Muslims. A Muslim can own a *dhimmī* slave, but a *dhimmī* cannot own a Muslim slave. In addition to the poll tax, the *dhimmīs* were subject to other financial burdens. These limitations were not applied with equal stringency in every place and period, but, on the whole, they were followed much more severely in Iran (and in other Shī'ī countries) than among the Sunnīs.[3] On the whole, under the rules of the Pact of 'Umar, the *dhimmīs* were granted safety of life and property (except on the not infrequent occasions when they became victims of mob attacks, as was the case in Meshhed in 1839) and were allowed to practice their religion, to be sure modestly and in a manner the Muslims did not find offensive.

In Khomeini's listing of "unbelievers" among the sources of defilement, the Ayatollah was no innovator; he merely restated and succinctly formulated rules that were on the books and followed in the streets for centuries. For Shī'īs, all contact with non-Muslims was defiling; contact with their clothes, food, and utensils caused ritual impurity requiring purification before undertaking religious or ritual duties. *Dhimmīs* were not even allowed to use the bathhouses of the Muslims. (As we shall see later, the establishment and maintenance of a separate bathhouse for the Jadīd al-Islām played an important role in the family of Farajullah Nasrullayoff.) A set of rules dating from the later nineteenth century even forbade Jews to go out of doors when it rained, since the contagion of impurity was enhanced by wet bodies or substances.[4]

Iran is a big country, with many cities at great distances apart among which there was little contact. As a result of this, the situation of the Jews varied greatly from place to place. These conditions add to the difficulty inherent in trying to present a brief general history of the Jews of Iran in the long centuries that followed the Arab conquest. The difficulty is illustrated by the choppy nature of the best available brief résumé of the history of the Jews in Iran, written by that lifelong student of Iranian Jews, Walter J. Fischel, in the *Encyclopaedia Judaica*,[5] to which we refer the reader.

To turn now to the forced conversions of Jews to Islam in Persia, the first such event took place under Shah 'Abbās II (r. 1588–1629), at a time when the total number of Jews in the country was estmated at nine thousand to ten thousand families or thirty thousand to thirty-five thousand persons.[6] In 1656, the Shah ordered all Jews in his kingdom to become Muslims. After the forced conversion, the newly Islamized Jews became known as Jadīd al-Islām (literally, "New of Islam"), or briefly Jadīdīm (with the addition of the Hebrew plural suffix *-īm,* that is, "New Ones"). Many of them, however, remained faithful to Judaism and lived a life of crypto-Jews, secret Jews, not unlike the Marranos in the Iberian Peninsula after their forced conversion to Christianity in 1492.

The sufferings of the Jews in seventeenth- and early-eighteenth-century Persia were graphically described by two eyewitnesses, the Judeo-Persian poet-chroniclers Babai ibn Luṭf and his grandson Babai ibn Farḥad, both of whom lived in the city of Kashan. The elder Babai began to compose his chronicle in Judeo-Persian poetic form in 1656, in his book *Kitāb-i Anusi* ("Book of the Forced Converts"). His grandson continued chronicling the story of the persecution of Persian Jews and the troubled times they experienced until 1725. The writings of the two Babais are important sources for the lives and tribulations of the Jews of Persia as seen by eyewitnesses who lived through them.[7]

Toward the end of Shah 'Abbās II's reign (in 1661), the Persian authorities allowed the Jadīdīm to return to their old religion, and for about two decades, they were able to practice their Judaism without disturbance. However, the respite was short-lived, and under the later years of Shah Suleiman (r. 1666–1694) and under Shah Sultan Ḥusayn (r. 1694–1722), oppression and persecution were renewed. Only the succession of Nadir Shah (r. 1736–1747), who was an adherent of Sunnī Islam and opposed to Shī'īsm, brought an improvement in the position of the Jews of Iran, who by that time seemed to be condemned to total annihilation. In chapter 1, we shall hear more about the life of the Jews under Nadir Shah; here, I wish only to mention that under his rule the Jews had greater freedom to practice a pious custom that had great importance in their religious life: making the pilgrimage to the Jewish holy places in Persia. They visited the tombs of Mordecai and Esther in Hamadan, of the Prophet Daniel in Susa, of Serah bat Asher in Pir Bakran near Isfahan, and of other biblical heroes believed to be buried in Persia.

After the assassination of Nadir Shah, the persecution of the Jews was renewed under the Kajar dynasty, and it was only from the 1870s that, under the impact of European Jewish intervention, the position of Persian Jews began gradually to improve. Still, the situation of the Persian Jews, even in the late nineteenth century, was so dismal tht it shocked the European travelers who became acquainted with it. Thus, George N. (later Lord) Curzon had this to say about them in 1892 in his classic *Persia and the Persian Question:*

> Usually compelled to live apart in a ghetto, or separate quarter of the towns, they have from time immemorial suffered from disabilities of occupation, dress, and habits which have marked them out as social pariahs from their

> fellow creatures. The majority of the Jews of Persia are engaged in trade, in jewellery, in wine and opium manufacture, as musicians, dancers, scavengers, pedlars, and in other professions to which is attached no great respect. They rarely attain a leading mercantile position. In Isfahan, where they are said to be 3,700, and where they occupy a relatively better status than elsewhere in Persia, they are not permitted to wear the *kolah* or Persian head-dress, to have shops in the bazaar, to buld the walls of their houses as high as a Moslem neighbour's, or to ride in the streets. In Teheran and Kashan they are also to be found in large numbers and enjoying a fair position. In Shiraz they are very badly off. At Bushire they are prosperous and free from persecution. As soon, however, as any outburst of bigotry takes place in Persia and elsewhere the Jews are apt to be the first victims. Every man's hand is then against them; and woe betide the luckless Hebrew who is the first to encounter a Persian street mob.[8]

These words, and many similar references from the pens of contemporary travelers, reflect the reaction of Europeans, who were the products of the West and of central European liberalism in the second half of the nineteenth century, to the treatment of the Jews in Iran, which struck them as cruel, inhuman, and inexcusable. The Iranian Jews themselves, however, had developed a different attitude toward the treatment accorded them through several centuries and to which they became inured in the course of time. In fact, they developed adjustments and defense mechanisms, which enabled them to live, if not precisely happily, at least without suffering undue psychological damage, in the oppressive Shī'ī Muslim environment, and which remained unobserved by and unknown to the European travelers. They were in sore need of such inner defenses, since, as observed by modern students of the Persian Jews, under the Qajars (1796–1925), the situation of the Persian Jews "could rightfully be characterized as 'an uninterrupted sequence of persecution and oppression.'"[9]

Nevertheless, under Shah Muzaffar al-Din (r. 1898–1907), the Alliance Israélite Universelle was permitted to establish schools in Teheran, Hamadan, Isfahan, Shiraz, Senna, and Kermanshah, and played an important role in the struggle of Persian Jews for religious survival in the face of the double threat of Christian and Bahai missionary activities. This and other incipient contact in the late nineteenth century with the external world, and especially with the West, motivated an increasing number of Persian Jews to emigrate. Simultaneously, the Zionist idea began to spread among them and resulted in settling in Palestine of a certain number of them from practically all the major Iranian cities.

The Jews of Meshhed, because of their specific situation as Jadīd al-Islām, as a community officially Muslim, were unable to participate in this movement of Jewish national awakening. The only external sign of a resurgence of Jewish consciousness among them was a growing dissatisfaction they felt at having to live under the mask of Islam, which translated into an increased impetus to emigrate. But they moved not only to Jerusalem but also to Teheran, to neighboring Sunnī Muslim countries, as well as to Bombay and London. By the early twentieth century, there was a veritable Meshhedi Diaspora in Asia, Europe, and America, numbering several hundreds of families.

The most vital issue that preoccupied the Jadīdīm of Meshhed for decades after their forced converson was how to adhere to Judaism while at the same time keeping their Jewishness secret from the prying eyes of their Muslim neighbors. The issue was quite literally a vital one, for the Muslim law that ruled supreme in Meshhed prescribed the death penalty for persons who, whether born Muslims or converts to Islam, were found following another religion. As shown by the stories told by Farajullah Nasrullayoff and presented in this book, as well as by historical sources, following the Allahdād it happened several times that certain fervently religious Muslim elements in Meshhed tried to demonstrate to the authorities that the Jadīdhā (the Persian plural of Jadīd) had remained Jews in secret, and that therefore they were guilty of the capital crime of apostasy from Islam.

Following the Allahdād, the Jadīdīm had to be extremely careful to observe the Jewish rituals, ceremonies, and feasts in the greatest secrecy and not to act or behave in any manner that could have aroused even the slightest suspicion among their Muslim neighbors that they had remained faithful to their ancestral religion. They performed conscientiously the rites of Islam, went to the mosque to pray, married among themselves but performed the Muslim wedding ceremony, buried their dead in accordance with the Muslim ritual, and made the required pilgrimage to Mecca and Medina, and/or to Karbala, and thereafter attached to their names the honorific titles of Hājj (Hājjī) or Karbalā'ī. Nothing, however, could prevent them from reciting the Jewish prayers in the privacy of their homes and maintaining the consciousness of being Jews and not Muslims.

Some twenty years after the Allahdād, the enmity surrounding the Jadīdīm abated to some extent, and they had the courage to conduct themselves in private more and more as Jews, and to observe more and more of their religious commandments and traditions. Several factors facilitated this development. One was the concentration of the Jews in their own quarter, the 'Ēdgāh, which was visited by Muslims but rarely. Another was the manner in which dwellings, both those of the Muslims and those of the Jews, were built: because of the Islamic insistence on the strict segregation of women, the houses were built in such a manner that each constituted a closed unit, with an inner courtyard, which no one could look into from the outside. A third was the absence in the traditional Muslim world of socializing among families. The places for men to meet were the mosque, the bazaar, and the café, while women's social life was confined to occasionally visiting one another in their homes. The social worlds of men and of women were more strictly segregated in the fervently religious sanctuary city of

Meshhed than in many other Muslim cities. This meant, among other things, that a man could not enter the home of another man without being especially invited by the family head, who would make sure that at the time of the visit the womenfolk were not visible to the visitor. The Jews of Meshhed adhered to these customs even before their conversion, and after it, the Muslims took it for granted that in this respect, too, the Jadīdīm would behave as the Muslims. The result was that outsiders could have no direct knowledge of what was happening inside the home of a Jadīdī family.

Nevertheless, it was inevitable that as time passed and the Jadīdīm were less apprehensive, and hence less secretive, in observing their Jewish customs, the Muslims suspected more and more that they adhered to Judaism. Before long, a situation developed in which the Muslims were quite sure that the Jadīdīm were not at all true Muslims but secret Jews. But the problem remained of how to prove it. If the Jadīdīm could be caught in observing Jewish rites, such as preparing their dead for burial in the Jewish manner, or eating no bread but only *maṣṣot* on Passover, that could serve as a basis for legally (that is, according to Muslim traditional laws) inflicting on them the death penalty for apostasy. Unsuccessful attempts to do precisely that form the subjects of several stories, told as true accounts of what really did happen and circulated among the Jadīdīm of Meshhed. Several of them are presented in this book.

For several decades after the Allahdād, the Jews of Meshhed could never for a moment forget that they were living a life that, according to Muslim traditional law, was a life of mortal sin, punishable by death. But they also knew that as long as they managed to keep their Judaism secret, the Muslim authorities of the city would not proceed against them, and would protect them, even if only halfheartedly and reluctantly, against mob attacks. It is not easy to imagine what living in such conditions must do to the mentality, character, and personality of a community. That the Jadīdīm nevertheless managed to preserve their mental health, their vitality, and their positive, optimistic outlook on life, as they evidently did, is no small miracle.

The city of Meshhed was, for more than two centuries, the home of the Jewish community discussed in this book.

Meshhed (in its literary form Mashhad), the second largest city in Iran and capital of its northeastern provnce of Khorasan (Khurāsān), had by the mid-1990s close to two million inhabitants. In it is located the most important Iranian shrine of Shī'ī Islam, built around the tomb of the Eighth Imām, 'Alī al-Riḍa (ca. 768–818), popularly known as Imām Reza or Riza, who is buried in Meshhed. This fact made Meshhed the Iranian holy city of Shī'ī Islam.

Imām Reza, although eighteen years older than the Caliph and Seventh Imām al-Ma'mūn (786–833), was his son-in-law and was appointed by him in

817, while the Caliph resided in his capital, Merv (Marw), heir to the Caliphate. Al-Ma'mūn considered 'Alī al-Riḍa "the best of the descendants of 'Alī and of al-'Abbās," and gave him the honorific title al-Ridā Min ā Muḥammad (satifaction from the kinsfolk of Muhammad). This move, however, aroused considerable opposition among the 'Abbāsid princes in Baghdad, and in 818, al-Ma'mūn set out from Merv for Baghdad to assert his supremacy. He was accompanied by 'Alī al-Riḍā, who, however, died on the way in Tus and was buried in the nearby village of Sanabad. According to Shī'ī historians, he was poisoned—some hold that it was al-Ma'mūn himself who handed him the poisoned drink. He was fifty when he died, he became venerated as a martyr, and soon the locality where he was buried was renamed in his honor Meshhed, that is, "sanctuary," or "sepulchral shrine," or "place of martyrdom."

The veneration of Imām Reza attracted many pilgrims to the shrine, and many pious men of religion settled in Meshhed, which rapidly grew to a city of considerable proportions. Tus itself was invested and destroyed by the Mongols in 1389, and those who survived the massacre settled in the shelter of the sanctuary. When the first Safawid ruler, Shah Ismā'īl (r. 1501–1524), established Shī'ism as the state religion, he paid much attention to the Meshhed sanctuary, whose veneration and visitation increased considerably. In the sixteenth century, the city was several times besieged and taken by Uzbeks, each time with terrible bloodbaths, and in the early eighteenth, it was for a short time under Afghan rule. The Persians retook the city in 1726, and a few years later, Nadir Shah Afshār (r. 1736–1747), of whom we shall hear more in this book, built himself a mausoleum in it. Following Nadir Shah's death, Meshhed came again under Afghan suzerainty, and all of Khorasan remained separated from Persia until 1795. The Afghans succeeded in taking, and permanently detaching, the eastern part of Khorasan, thus reducing Persian Khorasan to barely half its former size.

Throughout the nineteenth century, Meshhed (and Khorasan as a whole) was at times independent, at times under central Persian rule, and intermittently the scene of bloody rebellions. The people also suffered from periodic famines and Turkoman and other tribal incursions. In 1911, an Afghan leader, Yūsuf Khān of Herat, took Meshhed and, under the name of Muḥammad 'Alī Shah, declared himself independent. This gave the Russians a pretext for armed intervention, and in March 1912, they bombarded Meshhed, causing severe damage.

Like most premodern Persian cities, Meshhed, too, was surrounded by a city wall and moat and defended by a big citadel. The city was comprised of six big and ten smaller quarters (*maḥallah*). Across its middle, it was divided by the broad Khiyābān promenade, along which ran the canal that was its main water supply. By far the most impressive structure in the city consisted of the buildings of the sanctuary, the Ḥaram-i Sharīf, often called the Bast, literally "place of refuge, asylum," straddling the lower part of the Khiyābān and containing some of the finest examples of Shī'ī religious architecture.

Until modern times, much of the existence of the city depended on the sanctuary and the thousands of pilgrims it attracted year after year. The presence of the sanctuary gave life in the city as a whole a religious coloration and rendered more of its inhabitants fervently religious and religiously intolerant than was the case in other places lacking such an overpowering physical presence of a religious institution. This has remained the situation through the mid-1990s, even though the city has grown into a metropolis of close to two million inhabitants.[10]

In the first twelve chapters that follow, an attempt is made to sketch the most important events in the history of the Jews of Meshhed by combining what could be elicited from two very disparate types of sources: the few available documents left behind in writing by contemporary observers (mostly foreign visitors) and the oral traditions preserved among the Meshhed Jews themselves. The combination of such greatly differing types of sources may be a rather unusual procedure in historiography, but, in view of the scarcity of the historical documentation, I felt that the utilization of folk traditions to supplement it was warranted. My approach was justified by one additional circumstance: the brevity of history of the Jews in Meshhed. In fact, the presence of Jews in Meshhed was very short compared to the documented past of the Jews in other parts of Iran and in the neighboring countries: it extended over a mere two centuries, which is not long enough to allow folk memory to unduly distort, embellish, or transform historical events. It therefore seemed likely that what the Meshhed Jews retained in their memory as significant events of their past could not have been too far from the actual historical occurrences that gave rise, to begin with, to those folk traditions.

In gathering information in Jerusalem in the mid-1940s about the life of the Jews of Meshhed, I was fortunate in finding an informant of broad knowledge and excellent memory in the person of Farajullah Nasrullayoff, the head of the community of Meshhedi Jews in Jerusalem, who, up to his immigration from Meshhed to Jerusalem in 1929, had been closely involved with the life of the Jews in his native city and was himself greatly interested in their past. Āqā Farajullah ("Āqā" is the Persian equivalent of "Mr." but has a more honorific connotation) was in his seventies at the time and was the well-to-do owner of an Oriental carpet store in the Geulah quarter of Jerusalem. He was assisted by his three sons, so that he had sufficient free time to listen to my questions and to answer them in detail. Most importantly, he instantly grasped the significance of the study I was undertaking from the point of view of preserving the heritage of the past of Meshhed Jewry for its future generations, and therefore did not begrudge to spend as much time with me as I was able to devote to interviewing him. Since his speaking knowledge of Hebrew was limited, we made use of the good services of his son Yoḥanan, who translated my Hebrew questions into Persian for his father and then translated his father's Persian answers into

Hebrew for me. This procedure had an added advantage for me: not having shorthand at my disposal (recording machines were unknown in those days in Jerusalem), the added time it took for Yoḥanan to make the translation sentence by sentence enabled me to write down then and there in Hebrew both my questions and his father's answers almost verbatim, and also to ask for elucidations whenever any detail in the answer was not completely clear to me.

All that is by now at a distance of fifty years in the past, but I still remember most vividly the many hours I spent day after day in the Nasrullayoff store, in the midst of the hundreds of Persian rugs heaped up all along the walls, giving off their faint but distinctive odor. Facing me sat the serious, dignified, and friendly old man behind his small desk, who answered patiently the seemingly never-ending questions with which I was trying to elicit from him all the details I could think of. I asked, Yoḥanan translated, Āqā Farajullah answered, and I wrote and wrote until my right hand did not "forget her cunning" but hurt so that I had to stop.

I also remember the pride I felt when, having published the first article based largely on my interviews with Āqā Farajullah in the fourth issue of the quarterly *Edoth*, which I started to edit and publish shortly before in Jerusalem (it dealt with the Hebrew education of the Meshhed Jadīd al-Islām), I presented him with an inscribed copy, which he received with visible gratification. A footnote appended to that article reminds me that, in addition to Farajullah Nasrullayoff, who served as my chief informant, I also obtained details from his three sons—Daniel, Ḥananiah, and Yoḥanan—and several more Meshhedi Jews—Farajullah Ya'quboff, Yiṣḥaq Ya'qubi and his wife, Eliyahu Ben-Moshe, Reuben Siman-Tov, and Nissim Ben-Efrayim. No mention is made in that footnote of Yiṣḥaq Gōhari, whom, it seems, I interviewed at a somewhat later date. Let me express here again my indebtedness to these kind, knowledgeable, and patient people, who unsparingly gave of their time to the inquisitive and ignorant young man I must have appeared to their eyes in those days.

In addition to these Meshhedi informants, who are actually coauthors of this book, I am indebted, as in my earlier books, to the New York Public Library, and especially to Leonard Gold, head of its Jewish Division, and the staff of that division, as well as to John M. Lundquist, head of the Oriental Division; Todd Thompson, head of the Middle Eastern Section; Gamil Yousef, Arabic specialist; and Massoud Pourfarrokh, Persian specialist, for their expert help with both linguistic and bibliographic problems. I also wish to express my sincere appreciation to Wayne State University Press, which has to date published ten of my books.

I

HISTORY AND TRADITIONS

I
Early Times

The question of when the first Jews arrived in Meshhed has preoccupied both Jewish historians and transmitters of Jewish folk traditions. In a Hebrew study titled "Qorot Anusē Meshhed l'fi Ya'aqov Dilmanian" (The History of the Forced Converts of Meshhed according to Jacob Dilmanian),[1] Amnon Netzer presented an overview of the relevant material and came to the conclusion that "the beginning of the settlement of Jews in Meshhed is a subject that still requires investigation."[2] However, the majority of scholarly opinion, in agreement with the unanimous folk tradition, holds that it was Nadir Shah (r. 1736–1747) who brought the first Jews to Meshhed. One of the measures Nadir Shah instituted with his wonted cruelty was to transfer sizable populations from various parts of Iran to Meshhed and to other cities and districts.[3] The transfer of Jews from Qazwin, Gilan, and other parts of Iran to Meshhed was part of this general policy. When precisely during the rule of Nadir did the transfer of the Jews to Meshhed take place is an issue on which opinions vary. Ḥabīb Lēvī, an Iranian Jewish historian, wrote in 1960 that Nadir ordered many Jews to be transferred from Dilman and Qazwin to Meshhed in 1730—six years before he ascended the throne!—in order to develop the city. According to the same author, more Jews moved to Meshhed in 1734.[4] Other authors consider 1734, 1743, or 1747 as the year of the arrival of the first Jews in Meshhed.[5]

My own perusal of the sources and studies, added to the oral traditions that survived among the Jews of Meshhed, leads me to the conclusion that the arrival of the first Jews in Meshhed took place in 1747, the year of Nadir Shah's assassination. Before Nadir's rule, because Meshhed was a city of powerful sanctity, the holiest city of Shī'ī Islam in Persia, no Jews were allowed to settle there. The two seventeenth- and eighteenth-century Persian Jewish poet-chroniclers, Babai ibn Luṭf and his grandson Babai ibn Farḥad, do not mention Meshhed among the places where Jews lived in their days. Even Nadir Shah himself did not intend to settle Jews in Meshhed, and it was only because of a special concatenation of circumstances that, as a result of his ordering several Jewish families from Qazwin to Kalat, the first Jewish families arrived in Meshhed. According to the available, admittedly very scanty, historical sources, supplemented by the practically unanimous folk tradition as recounted to me by Farajullah Nasrullayoff, Yiṣḥaq Gōhari, and other Meshhedi informants, the following is what happened.

Returning from his victorious Indian campaign in 1740, Nadir Shah brought with him an enormous loot of precious stones and other treasures, and decided to fortify the old mountain fortress of Kalat (Qal'at, ca. fifty miles to the north of Meshhed) and make it into his treasure house. Thereafter, the fort became known as Qal'at-i Nādiri, Nadir's Fort. He had the construction executed by Indian craftsmen. When it came to manning the fortress with guards, since he did not trust the Shī'ī Persians, who hated him because of his pro-Sunnī policies, he instructed the city of Qazwin to send forty Jewish families, chosen from among the leaders of the community, to Kalat and its environs. He did so because he considered the Jews more loyal and reliable than the Shī'ī Persians. The Jewish families did not all start out at once; several of them went ahead, while others lagged behind. Thus it happened that when Nadir Shah was assassinated in 1747, only seventeen of them had arrived in Kalat, while sixteen had got only as far as Meshhed, and the remaining seven had only reached Sabzawar (one hundred and ten miles west of Meshhed). Once Nadir was dead, his decrees lapsed, and the Jewish families stayed on in Meshhed and were subsequently joined by those who had reached Kalat and by those who were still in Qazwin. This is how the Jewish community came to be established in Meshhed in the year 1747.[6]

Some vague memories of Kalat were retained in the folk tradition of the Meshhed Jews. Farajullah Nasrullayoff, for example, knew that the fortress was surrounded by forbidding mountains and that wheeled vehicles could reach it only by two narrow roads. There were also nine footpaths, which could be negotiated only by people good at mountaineering. The work done for Nadir's fortress in Kalat involved the hauling and assembling of enormous blocks of hewn stones and reinforcing the natural caves in the mountains, which Nadir wanted to use as his treasury.

As for the presence of Jews in Qazwin (located some ninety miles northwest of Teheran), we do not have to rely on folk tradition alone, since it is attested by historical sources. Apart from the writings of the two Babais, referred to above, an old cemetery in Qazwin also testified to the existence of an ancient Jewish community in the city. In addition, I was told by Yiṣḥaq Gōhari that once he saw in the home of a Jewish acquaintance in Meshhed a manuscript book that contained the Persian translation of the Koran and a brief history of Persia until the rule of Reza Shah (r. 1925–1941). In it were several derogatory remarks about the Jews of Persia, and, incidentally, the author stated that the Jews had settled in Qazwin in the year that was the Muslim equivalent of the Christian year 1483.

According to Āqā Nasrullayoff, the Jews had lived in Qazwin for about one hundred years prior to the move of the forty families to Kalat, which would date their settlement in Qazwin at about 1650. He also knew that the Jews in Qazwin spoke the so-called Gilak dialect, named after the Gilan district located to the southwest of the Caspian Sea. Gilak is still spoken in Gilan as well as farther to the east, in the Mazenderan province which forms a narrow strip along the southern shores of the Caspian Sea. There was a tradition to the effect that the Jews had come from Mazenderan to Qazwin.

The historical memories about the Jews in Qazwin belong among the few examples of a folk tradition that attributes a shorter span to the life of a community than do actual historical documents. According to the famous Arab geographer and cosmographer Zakariyya al-Qazwini (1203–1283), in his days there existed in Qazwin a ruined old Jewish cemetery, which shows that at that time the Jewish settlement in Qazwin must have been at least several generations old. The poet-chroniclers Babai ibn Luṭf and Babai ibn Farḥad report that the Jews of Qazwin suffered under the persecutions of Shahs 'Abbās I and 'Abbās II, that is, beginning with the late sixteenth century.

After the removal of the forty families from Qazwin, the Jewish community in that city experienced a rapid decline. Even though sixty Jewish families remained, they suffered persecution and a generally harsh attitude from the Qazwinis, and consequently they, too, gradually drifted away from the city. By the end of the eighteenth century, no Jews were left in Qazwin (according to Āqā Nasrullayoff).

The Jewish houses of Qazwin fell into ruin; the synagogue remained unused and decayed. The Muslims did not touch the Jewish houses and plots of land, because they considered them unclean. Finally, in the early 1900s, the mufti of the city, Sayyid Ḥusayn by name, found a way for the Muslims to take possession of the abandoned real estate. He declared that the power of uncleanness of the buildings and the lands lapsed after three generations. And since the plots were ownerless property, the mufti himself took possession of them under the rule of finders keepers and sold them for good money. It was on this formerly Jewish property that the new quarter of Qazwin was built in the last generation, as Āqā Nasrullayoff himself had an opportunity to see before his emigration to Jerusalem.

As for the Jews who went to Meshhed, once Nadir Shah was dead, the people of the city did not allow them to settle inside the city but confined them to houses hugging the city walls—something they would never have dared to do while Nadir was still alive. Three years later, the seven families who had stopped at Sabzawar also reached Meshhed, and, within another few years, several Jewish families from Kalat moved to the city as well. Thirteen or fourteen years after the first Jews arrived in Meshhed, they were able to purchase parts of the gardens just inside the city wall, and they built themselves houses on those lands. This is how the Jews settled in Meshhed, and how their quarter, the *'Ēdgāh* ("Feast Place"), came into being.

Because of the Allahdād (see below), extremely few historical documents survived among the Jews of Meshhed. That scarcity is matched by the equally few details transmitted by their folk traditions about their life prior to the forced conversion. However, it would appear that despite the strictly Shī'ī environment, never friendly to the Jews, the community thrived, for its numbers grew rapidly, as indicated by the fact that the first Jewish cemetery filled up within two generations after their first arrival in Meshhed, and they purchased a large tract of land some three miles from the city and began to use it for the burial of their dead.

In 1830, a cholera epidemic struck Persia, and many Jews in Meshhed fell victim to it. In those days, the spiritual head of the community was Mullah Siman-Tov, a disciple of Mullah Abraham, about whose work and writings we shall hear below. And then, in 1839, came the Allahdād, the most traumatic event in the history of the Meshhed Jews, which must be discussed in some detail.

2

Before the Allahdād

The situation in which the Jews of Meshhed found themselves after the forced conversion of 1839 has been repeatedly described, so that quite a bit is known about it. Much less is known about the life of the Jews in Meshhed prior to the Allahdād, to which subject we now turn.

The first thing we have to keep in mind when trying to visualize the life of the Jews in Meshhed is that in Shī'ī Persia in general, the Muslim attitude toward the Jews was more inimical and contemptuous than in the Sunnī Muslim world. Shī'ī Islam, whose major stronghold Iran has remained to this day, has always been much more intolerant of other faiths than Sunnī Islam, and "other faiths" in its view quite emphatically included also the "people of the book," Jews, Christians, and Zoroastrians, who were regarded with lively aversion, whose persons were considered unclean, and whose touch was avoided because it was defiling. One outcome of this attitude was that in Shī'ī Persia, in the course of the three centuries preceding the Meshhed Allahdād, Jews were repeatedly forced, in various localities, to convert to Islam. Another outcome was that it was considered right and proper to make the Jews feel that they were unwanted, barely tolerated, inferior creatures. In this respect, the Shī'ī Muslim attitude resembled that of Medieval Christianity toward the Jews.

A dismal picture of the severe limitations imposed upon the Jews of Iran with the avowed purpose of humiliating them is conveyed by two surviving lists of prohibitions, one issued before the Allahdād and the second some three decades after it, by Muslim religious authorities. The first, recorded by an anonymous chronicler who calls himself "One of the children of the ghetto," is as follows:

1. The Jews who pay no taxes have no claim to safety.
2. A convert who returns to his Judaism is to be punished by death.
3. If Jews and Muslims have a quarrel, woe to the Jew who comes to the help of his brethren: his punishment is death.
4. A Jew who calls upon Allah or his Prophet to help him against a Muslim will be put to death.

5. The Jews are forbidden to build prayer houses in cities where Muslims live.
6. The house of a Jew must not be higher than that of a Muslim.
7. A Jew must wear a badge on his coat, and his garb must be different from that of a Muslim.
8. When riding a donkey, a Jew must keep his two legs hanging down on one side of the animal.
9. A Jew is forbidden to purchase a horse for himself.
10. A Jew is forbidden to carry arms.
11. A Jew must walk at the very side of the street.
12. A Jewish woman must not dress like a Muslim woman: she is not allowed to wear a veil over her head.
13. The blood-price of a Jew is forty *toman*.
14. If a Jew converts [to Islam], all the property of his family passes to him.

A few points in this list need elucidation. Point 4 meant that Jews, who, when speaking Persian, referred to God as Allah, as did the Muslims, were not allowed to invoke the help of God when quarreling with a Muslim. On the other hand, this point can also be interpreted as showing that occasionally Jews did get involved in quarrels with Muslims, and could do so with impunity. Point 5 means that the Jews were forbidden to build new synagogues; however, they were allowed to maintain and use their old synagogues, built prior to this decree. Point 11 is a humiliating decree: the side of the street was usually full of refuse and also served as a sewer. In point 12, for a woman to appear with uncovered head (or face) was a humiliation. Point 13 sets the blood-price (the compensation to be paid by a murderer to the kin of his victim) much lower than that payable for the killing of a Muslim—another humiliation. Point 14 is intended to serve as an inducement to conversion: a Jew, by converting, could appropriate everything his relatives owned.

In 1870, a Muslim religious authority by the name of Mullah ʻAbdallah issued a decree containing further restrictions:

1. On a rainy day a Jew must not go out into the street.
2. The veil of a Jewish woman must be of two colors.
3. The Jews must wear coats of blue color.
4. A Jew must step aside to let a Muslim pass.
5. A Jew must not raise his voice when speaking to a Muslim.
6. A Jew must ask in a tremulous and submissive voice the payment of a debt by a Muslim.
7. He must not wear a matching pair of shoes.
8. He must listen to insults by a Muslim with a lowered head and without opening his mouth.

9. A Jew must wrap up thoroughly the meat he buys, lest a Muslim eye see the impurity.
10. A Jew must not dwell in a beautiful house.
11. He must not clean the furniture of his house.
12. The door of his house must be low.
13. A Jew must not take off his coat and carry it in his hands.
14. A Jew must not comb his beard.
15. He must not take walks outside the city.
16. A Jewish physician is not allowed to ride a horse.
17. If a Jew is found drunk in the street, his punishment is death.
18. A Jewish wedding must be arranged in secret and without any noise.
19. A Jew must not eat fruits, except rotten ones.[1]

The purpose in all these prohibitions was clearly to humiliate the Jews. Similar restrictions, with the same purpose in mind, were imposed also upon the Jews of Yemen, another Shīʿī Muslim country. The basis of point 1 in Mullah ʿAbdallah's restrictions is the Shīʿī Muslim view that a Jew is impure, and that impurity is transferred by wetness more than by contact between dry bodies or objects. Hence, when it rains, and the Jew's body or clothes become wet, his impurity could be transferred to a Muslim who happens to touch him or his clothes. The intention in points 2 and 3 is to make Jewish men and women recognizable from afar. While point 6 intends to keep the Jew low, at the same time we learn that some Jews were sufficiently well-to-do to engage in the money business and make loans to Muslims. Point 14 bars a Jew from taking care of his beard, which was an important part of the Iranian male Muslim toilet. Point 15 keeps Jews from enjoying a walk outside the city—a favorite pastime and recreation in a Muslim city. Point 16 is interesting: since all Jews were forbidden to ride horses, the special mention of a Jewish physician as having to obey this prohibition shows that a Jewish physician, sought after also by Muslim patients, even though he occupied a privileged position, nevertheless had to obey this rule. Point 17 is related to the general Muslim prohibition of drinking alcoholic beverages: a Jew was not forbidden to take drinks, but woe to him if he offended Muslim sensibility by appearing in the streets in an inebriated condition. From point 18, one can conclude that of all Jewish celebrations, that of a wedding was the most pompous, most public, and most noisy; hence, it was felt necessary to single it out for stringent restrictions. Point 19 is a restriction made purely for the purpose of humiliation.

Several points in these two lists merely repeat the restrictions contained in the *Jāmiʿ-i ʿAbbāsī* (The ʿAbbāsian Collector), Muḥammad al-ʿĀmilī's (1547–1621) popular repertory of Shīʿī law, as it had developed by the time of Shah ʿAbbās I (1571–1629), under which the Jews of Persia had to live for close to three centuries.[2] These malicious restrictions indicate their life was one of humiliation and degradation. Actually, however, that was not entirely the case. There is no question that to be a Jew in an Iranian city meant to live a life of mortification and abasement. A Jew had to be subservient and self-effacing. Still, the specific limitations contained in the various decrees were frequently not insisted upon by the Muslims, or their transgressions were overlooked. The rich Jews of Meshhed, for instance, did build for themselves luxurious houses, one of which, quite a palatial residence, is shown in a photograph in Y'hoshu'a-Raz's book *MiNidḥē Yisraēl* (quoted above in note 1), between pages 126 and 127. Others simply could not be enforced, such as the prohibition of cleaning the furniture in the home or of eating fruits other than rotten; it was, of course, impossible to check whether the Jews kept their furnishings clean or whether in the privacy of their homes they ate fruit that was not rotten. The Jews, for their part, were able to make adjustments, and they conducted their lives largely within the Jewish quarter, where Muslims rarely entered and where they could comport themselves more or less as they wished.

That this, indeed, was the case in Meshhed we learn from the few eyewitness accounts given by early-nineteenth-century travelers, from whose writings one can glean some information about the life of the Jews in Meshhed in the decades preceding the Allahdād. The earliest reference by a European visitor (as far as I was able to ascertain) is that of the French traveler M. Truilhier, who visited Meshhed in 1807. He states that there were about a hundred Jewish families in Meshhed and that he was told by them that Nadir Shah had brought their forefathers to Meshhed in order to increase the commercial activities in the city. After the death of Nadir Shah, "they lost all protection, and were now living in utter opprobrium. Their condition under the Persian government is generally much more deplorable than among the Afghans and the other Sunnī Muslims."[3] Truilhier's observation about the worse treatment of the Jews by the Persian, that is Shī'ī, Muslims than by the Sunnīs is borne out by numerous reports and accounts, and by the fact that during and after the days of the Allahdād, many Jews fled from Shī'ī Meshhed to Sunnī Herat in Afghanistan.

In 1820, the Russian traveler Baron Yegor Fiodorovich de Meiendorf visited Bukhara, and the Jews there told him that three hundred Jewish families were living in Meshhed.[4] Since natural increase cannot account for a trebling of the number of Jews in Meshhed in thirteen years, unless there was a sizable Jewish immigration between 1807 and 1820, one must assume that either Truilhier underestimated their numbers, or the Jews of Bukhara exaggerated it, or both.

A year after Meiendorf, the British traveler James Baillie Fraser visited Meshhed and reported, "There are in Mushed [sic] many merchants, with a due proportion of shopkeepers and tradesmen, to supply the wants of the population; and one quarter of the city is appropriated to the Jews, of whom there is a considerable number, who exercise their customary professions of scrap sellers, in the miserable way common to this oppressed and ill-used class of men."[5]

A valuable and detailed account of the life of the Jews of Meshhed is contained in the travelogue of Lieutenant (late Captain) Arthur Conolly, who sojourned in the city in 1830. He reported that in that year, there were about a hundred Jewish families in Meshhed, which was a city of forty-five thousand inhabitants. He also observed the oppression the Jews suffered and reported that shortly before his arrival, a Jew was stoned to death "for intrusion into the sanctuary of Imām Riza."[6]

Conolly was introduced to the son of the Jewish *ketkhoda* ("chief," who was none other than Mullah Mahdī), who in turn enabled him to use the Jewish bath, which was heated twice a week. The Jews of Meshhed, he wrote:

> are chiefly engaged in petty traffic, and, though not rich, their situation is respectable compared with that of their brethren in the cities of Tehraun [Teheran] and Isphahan, who go about, as in European countries, selling and exchanging old garments; but they are not without a share of the indignities that are entailed to their race. They may not pass the pale of the sanctuary, neither may they put foot within the college-squares in which good men are buried; on their clothes, however new, they must wear a patch at the breast; their caps must not be of the same form as those worn by true believers, and they dare not return abuse, much less a blow given by a Mohummudan; children throw stones and dirt at them in the street unchecked by their parents, who think it a very meritorious act to worry the soul of an unbeliever; and I one morning saw a fakeer [faqir, poor man, beggar] take an old Jew by the beard, as if he would have pulled it from his face, and accuse him of having been party to selling him some years before to the Toorkmuns [Turkomans]; nor did he release the terrified old man till he promised to pay a few reals, the crowd looking on as Englishmen do at badger-baiting, and thinking it capital sport.
>
> We attended the Jewish synagogue one Saturday, and the Rabbis were so captivated by the Syud's [Sayyid's] unprecedentedly liberal opinions, that they made a point of showing all that they thought would interest us. The synagogue was a square room on two sides of which was a gallery, with a lattice skreen [sic] work for the women to sit behind. From the centre of the chamber, from the floor to the ceiling, rose four posts, and on steps within them there was the altar. Their chanting was in the Persian style, and very discordant; parts of the Old Testament were read in Hebrew, and a homily was delivered in the Persian language. When praying they turned to Jerusalem, and covered their heads in white mantles [talliths], and, at one part of the service, the priests standing on the altar-steps held up the Pentateuch, written on large rolls of parchment, and the congregation crowded eagerly round to look at it. It was an affecting sight, this "fragment of Israel," in Oriental garb, adhering

religiously to the ordinances of their forefathers, amid the persecutions of the most bigoted of a bigoted race. Not a man, they said, had gone out from them.

After the service we were shown into a small room, where were preserved with great care more than fifty copies of the scripture, written on rolls of parchment by devout individuals who had presented them to the synagogue. Each roll was kept in a case like a drum, on which was a plate telling the name of the donor and the date of the gift, and one copy, we were told, was used in turn every Sabbath.

From the synagogue we repaired to the Ketkhoda's house, consisting of a range of double-storied rooms on one side of a neat garden, round which vines were carried on a treillage. We sat on the walk, under the shade of a fine tree, and the Jew, though he would not drink with us, by reason of its being the Sabbath-day, produced some bottles of strong arrack and thin bad wine of his own manufacture, and, seeing that we would only taste it, lest some keen-nosed Mohummudan should scent us, he begged us to take the liquor home to comfort our hearts with at leisure. There was such an air of comfort about this man's house, that he thought it necessary to apologise for it, saying, that we saw all his wealth, that formerly the Jews had money, but now, God help them, they had ceased to hoard it, since some extortionate ruler or other was sure to take it from them.

We became very intimate with these people, and in many of their houses I observed much to contradict their outward appearance of poverty. On one occasion I was invited to a wedding in their quarter. At evening I was introduced to a company, who were seated in a square, on a broad terrace, having before them trays containing burnt almonds, pistachio nuts, and confectionary, and flasks of arrack, which they drank from small cups in such immoderate quantities that I expected them to lose their senses; but it merely appeared to have the effect of exciting them. The seat of honor was kept for the bridegroom, a most uninteresting youth, who, looking very much ashamed of himself, entered with a boy on either hand singing a discordant epithalamium, and when he had taken his place next to his father at the head, the company severally complimented him. Meat and broth was then brought in, and when it had been partaken of, health was wished to the bridegroom and to his father, the host, bumpers of arrack were tossed down, and some of the company got up one after another, and danced a ridiculous sort of *pas seul.* It was next proposed to sing, and some of the best performers being called upon, sang from the Psalms of David very sweetly. The audience were frequently moved to tears, and once, when a young man sang a psalm which by Mehdee [Mehdi] Beg's translation I knew to be that (even in our language) most beautiful one, "By the rivers of Babylon there we sat down, yea, we wept when we remembered Zion," they sobbed aloud. They were all somewhat under the influence of their potations, but men in their situation must ever be affected by the beautiful words of the Psalmist, and it was easy to believe their grief sincere. In the height of the entertainment, came a loud knocking at the door. In the early part of the eve-

> ning the *darogha* [footnote by Conolly; "Police-master. Such of the faithful as require spirituous liquor for medicine must make their wants known to the *darogha* who will procure it for them. All jolly fellows in a city are consequently on very good terms with that officer"] had sent for some arrack, for medicine, but as he required a large dose, it was refused to him. He therefore now sent his myrmidons to put a stop to what he called the disturbance in their quarter, as it was the night of the Mohummudan festival. A little money sent the officers away, and, shortly after, the bride being brought to the house with music and torches, and a large attendance of female friends, the party broke up.[7]

These pages of Conolly afford a most valuable and, as he would put it, "affecting" insight into the life of the Jews of Meshhed in the years prior to the Allahdād. They were well-to-do, had comfortable houses with gardens, but had to wear distinguishing caps and patches on their chests. They were exposed to the harassment of the Muslims, even of Muslim beggars, and the Muslim children were encouraged by their parents to throw stones and dirt at them in the streets. They had to supply the *darogha* with arrack, which the Muslims were allowed by the rules of their religion to drink as medicine, and it seems that they got no payment for providing the *darogha* with this medicinal beverage. When a contingent of Muslim soldiers knocked at their door, they had to give them a bribe to make them go away.

Most "affecting" is the scene Conolly describes at the Jewish wedding he attended. When a young male singer sang Psalm 137, "By the rivers of Babylon," which expresses the age-old yearning of exiled Jews for Zion, the celebrants "sobbed aloud." Evidently, the love of Zion was embedded deeply in the hearts of the Meshhed Jews and was a part of their religious sentiments. We also learn from Conolly that at the time of his visit, no Meshhed Jews had converted to another faith, that the sermon ("homily") on the Sabbath was delivered in Persian, that the well-to-do donated Torah scrolls to the synagogue, and that they loved to drink arrack. In another part of his travelogue, Conolly mentions that he had received loans from the Jews, which indicates that some Jews were engaged in the money business.

In the year following Conolly's arrival in Meshhed, another visitor from England came to Meshhed and reported on his experiences with, and impressions of, the Jews of the city in a book titled *Researches and Missionary Labours among the Jews, Mohammedans, and Other Sects.*[8] Its author was Joseph Wolff (1795–1862), a converted Jew of German origin, the son of a rabbi in Württemberg, who served as a Church of England missionary and undertook several journeys to the Levant, Abyssinia, Yemen, and central Asia, each of which resulted in at least one book. He was an intrepid traveler, who shrank from no hardship or danger. While in Khorasan, he was captured and made a slave. After being liberated, he walked on foot and naked six hundred miles through central Asia to Kabul, Afghanistan. In 1843, he made another journey to Bukhara in behalf of a British committee to ascertain the fate of Lieutenant Colonel Charles Stoddart and Captain Conolly, who had been captured in that country and (as it subsequently transpired) had been executed. In his *Researches,* Wolff makes brief and rather one-sided references to the Jews of Meshhed, where he had arrived on December 5, 1831. He revisited Meshhed in 1844 and gave more detailed accounts of the life of the Jews, who by that time lived as Jadīdīm, crypto-Jews.

Wolff was rather secretive when it came to identifying himself during his visit to central Asia. Among the Muslims, he presented himself as a British Christian, but in his contacts with Jews, he said he was a Jew who believed in Jesus, and it was this kind of faith to which he tried to convert them. One can imagine the confusion this must have caused among the Jews of central Asia, who may have imagined that to believe in Jesus was part of Judaism as practiced in that fabulous faraway land called *Englestan.* On the other hand, in order to show his British Christian sponsors that his missionary work stood a good chance of leading the Jews of the central Asian countries he visited to a belief in Jesus, Wolff painted them (or at least some of them) in his book as being interested in, and even receptive to, other religions. Hence, whatever he writes on this subject is, to say the least, open to doubt and is in all probability slanted and exaggerated.

In any case, when Wolff arrived in Meshhed, he sought lodging among the Jews without telling them, at least not to begin with, that he was a Christian missionary, but pretending to be a Jewish scholar in search of his brethren. This was not difficult to do, since, after all, he was the son of a German rabbi and not only knew Hebrew and the Bible but also had a good knowledge of the post-biblical Jewish religious literature.

A few days after his arrival in Meshhed, he entered into his diary:

> His Royal Highness 'Abbās Mīrzā desired the Jews of Meshhed to discuss the subject of religion with me in his presence. The Jews here are now in great trouble, being obliged to lodge a few officers in their houses; but I think it is foolish of them [to complain], for if the officers were not with them the common soldiers would commit mischief among them. . . . I sometimes go with them to their synagogue, wearing the tallis, i.e. veil, and tefillin, i.e. frontlets, and read aloud in the Law of Moses, and then preach to them.[9]

Wolff does not state whether his preaching was Christological, but his wearing of the prayer shawl and the phylacteries shows that his visits to the synagogue took place on weekdays and that he tried to appear an observant Jew.

Although Wolff's subsequent tendentious presentation of the Jews' interest in his Christological preaching diminishes the truth value of the picture he paints of the Jews of Meshhed, his report still retains considerable interest because he was an acute observer and, more importantly, because there is no other eyewitness account of the life of the Jews of Meshhed in the pre-Allahdād years.

When Wolff arrived in Meshhed, he first went to pay his respect to "His Royal Highness Aḥmed 'Alī Mīrzā, who is one of the King's sons by a Jewess." The young prince sent him on to the head of the Jewish community, whom Wolff calls *nasī* (Hebrew for "chief" or "prince") of the Jews and whose name was Mashiaḥ Ajun. (Wolff writes "Meshiakh Ajoon," but here and in the following I substitute the modern accurate transliteration of foreign names for Wolff's haphazard one.) The Muslims called this man by the Persian version of his name, Mullah Mahdī, Mahdī being the equivalent in Muslim religious tradition of the Jewish Messiah. Since it was the prince who sent the foreigner to him, Chief Mashiaḥ had, of course, to put him up, so that during his stay in Meshhed, Wolff was Chief Mashiaḥ's houseguest. The chief told him that he, Mashiaḥ, was a descendant of the biblical Bezalel of the tribe of Judah and that he had in his possession a copy of the New Testament in Hebrew that had been brought to him by "the Jew Nissan Azariah Kohen, when he returned from Vilna." This book was but part of the interfaith library owned by Chief Mashiaḥ. Another was a defense of the Koran, written by an ex-Jew named Ḥājjī Amīn, formerly Mullah Benjamin, who had converted to Islam and had prepared a translation of the entire Bible into Persian, written in Hebrew characters, with explanatory notes, "in order to convince the Jews that Moses and the Prophets have predicted that both Jesus and Muhammad should be sent by God with prophetic power." As the title "Ḥājjī" preceding his name shows, the author of this work had performed the pilgrimage to Mecca.

It can no longer be established whether Ḥajjī Amīn's Judeo-Persian Bible translation which Wolff saw in the possession of Chief Mashiaḥ was a copy of one of those translations of which other copies are known. The earliest of the known Judeo-Persian Pentateuch translations is the one dated 1319 in the British Library. Also from the early fourteenth century date the biblical commentaries written by the Jewish poet Shahin of Shiraz in the form of poetic paraphrases, in Persian, in Hebrew characters, titled *Sēfer Sharḥ Shāhin 'al haTorah* (The Book of Shahin's Commentary on the Torah). From 1546 dates the Pentateuch translation into Judeo-Persian, written in Hebrew characters, of Jacob ben Joseph Tavus, of whom otherwise nothing is known. The sixteenth- and seventeenth-century copies of these manuscripts were often beautifully illustrated in the well-known manner of Persian miniature art. The book Wolff saw in the possession of Chief Mashiaḥ may have been a copy of one of these manuscripts. It would seem that Chief Mashiaḥ had an interest in Christianity and Islam and, moreover, as we learn from Wolff, was an adherent of what seems to have been a Jewish variety of Islamic Ṣūfī mysticism.

Before continuing the story of the years that led to the 1839 Allahdād in Meshhed, a few words are in order about the role British agents played in Khorasan in the early nineteenth century in trying to tilt the balance between Russian and British political influence in favor of the latter. British travelers who planned to visit the area were frequently asked by the British government to supply information about the attitude of the local leadership toward Russia and toward Britain, and to give suggestions about what should be done to increase British influence. In this political game, leaders of the Jewish community of Meshhed, with whom the British visitors could more easily establish contact than with Muslim potentates, played a definite, albeit rather limited, role. When the three British travelers James B. Fraser, Arthur Conolly, and Joseph Wolff, who visited Meshhed in 1821, 1830, and 1831, respectively, state that Mullah Mahdī Āqājān (Chief Mashiaḥ), head of the Meshhed Jewish community, served as chief British agent in the area, one must not read more into this statement than the fact that Mullah Mahdī was willing to talk to the Britishers and tell them about the impressions he had of the attitude of their acquaintances toward the Russians and the British, and to tide them over with temporary loans, which the British consul was supposed to repay.[10] This financing of British visitors was subject to considerable risk, since it happened more than once that adventurers posed as British officials, managed to obtain sizable loans from Meshhed Jews, and then disappeared. These experiences made the Meshhed Jews think twice before giving loans to foreigners who claimed to be British agents. Mullah Mahdī himself gave a loan of 900 *tomans* (the equivalent of 675 pounds sterling), quite a fortune at the time, to such a European adventurer by the name of Diskin, of which he was able to recover only two-thirds from the British envoy in Teheran.[11] Still, Mullah Mahdī went on helping the British and even undertook trips out of the country in their service. On one occasion, the governor of Herat, Afghanistan, in order to harm the British agents, ordered the people of his city not to accept English money from them, and as a result the value of the British currency plummeted in the Afghan markets. Thereupon, Mullah Mahdī, in the company of two other Jews of Meshhed, went to Herat, took the British money, and exchanged it in Yezd at its full usual value, with the help, it would seem, of local Jewish merchants.[12]

This episode shows not only that Mullah Mahdī was an international merchant and dealer in currency but also that he was a very wealthy man, able to engage in large-scale financial transactions. It so happened that on the day of the Allahdād (March 27, 1839), Mullah Mahdī was likewise away, sojourning in Kandahar in southern Afghanistan, in charge of a British contingent that was purchasing supplies for the British army.[13]

Apart from the meager data contained in these travelers' accounts, very little is known of the life of the Jews of Meshhed prior to the Allahdād. This is the case even with regard to their religious leaders. The most important among them was Mullah Siman-Tov Melamed, who was a prolific author but of whose life so little is known that not even the date of his death has been firmly established. According to Walter J. Fischel's note in the *Encyclopaedia Judaica* (11:1276), he died about 1780. According to an interview conducted in 1939 with Samad Āqā ben Yosef Dilmānī (preserved in the Central Zionist Archives, Jerusalem, no. S25/5291), he died 112 years prior to that date, that is, in 1827. However, according to one of the three folktales told me by Āqā Farajullah Nasrullayoff in Jerusalem in 1945, Mullah Siman-Tov died in the days of a great cholera epidemic in Meshhed, and that epidemic is known to have taken place in 1830 (see below, chapter 14). From the same tale, we also gather that Mullah Siman-Tov was a pupil of Mullah Abraham, whom he venerated as a saintly person but about whom otherwise nothing is known. The first of the three folktales about Mullah Siman-Tov presented below in chapter 14 tells of his role in disputations into which the Jews were forced by the Muslim religious authorities of Meshhed, and in which his opponents were Muslim scholars and converted Jews—this, too, seems to be historical.

Of the writings of Mullah Siman-Tov Melamed, two books have been published. One is a multilingual volume titled (in Hebrew) *Azharot in the Holy Tongue and in the Persian Tongue*, published with additions by Rabbi Mattityahu Garji in Jerusalem in 1896. *Azharot* ("warnings") is the generic term for liturgical poems for the feast of Shavu'ot which discuss the 613 commandments. Mullah Siman-Tov's *Azharot* are in Hebrew, Aramaic, and Judeo-Persian. A manuscript copy of this book, prepared in 1791 by a certain Samuel ben Reuben, is in the library of the Hebrew Union College, Cincinnati. His other published book, written in Judeo-Persian, is the *Sefer Ḥayāt al-Rūḥ*, (Book of the Life of the Spirit), which was printed by the brothers Israel Nethanel and Benjamin Shauloff in Jerusalem in 1898. This is a religio-philosophical treatise, containing a commentary on Maimonides' teachings on the Thirteen Articles of Faith, a disquisition on Israel's existence in the Diaspora and its ultimate salvation, and a *piyyuṭ* (liturgical poem) in Hebrew and Persian. It evinces strong influences of Baḥya ibn Paquda, whose *Duties of the Heart* Mullah Siman-Tov evidently greatly admired, and of other medieval Jewish and Muslim thinkers.

Of Mullah Siman-Tov's unpublished work, manuscripts of the following have survived and are in the library of the Hebrew Union College, Cincinnati: a commentary on *Pirqe Avoth* (The Chapters of the Fathers) (no. 2092); a poem in Judeo-Persian beginning "*Dāre dalki čun muhabbi, bā namaki, bā namaki* . . ." contained in a compendium of hymns and poetry (no. 2136); a Judeo-Persian translation of a poem by Efrayim ben Yitzḥaq Mibuna titled "*Tafsīr am afs l'Siman Tov Melamed: gar az vaṭan gashteh īm* . . . ," contained in a compendium of poems and *piyyutim* from Hamadan, dated 1860 (no. 2137); a translation of

a poem, "*Shirah neḥmad. Ba tafsīr: 'et dodim kallah bo'i l'gani: parḥah hagefen heneṣ rimmoni* . . ." by Ḥayyim Naḥman Bialik, contained in a compendium of poems and hymns dated 1897 (no. 2167); a Judeo-Persian translation from the Hebrew titled
"*Tafsīr am afs az jafteh haRav M[ullah] Siman Tov Melamed,*" in a compendium for the High Holidays (no. 2175).[14]

This is all one can tell at this stage of research about the history of the Jews of Meshhed prior to the Allahdād.

3
The Ṣūfī Lure

In the years preceding the Allahdād catastrophe, the Ṣūfī movement exerted considerable attraction upon the Jewish community of Meshhed. This is not the place to tell the story of the origin, spread, and influence of the Muslim mystical movement of Ṣūfism, but it may be mentioned in brief that it arose in the eighth century, reached a high development in the ninth, and won especially many adherents in Persia, where one of its greatest exponents, Ḥusayn ibn Manṣūr al-Ḥallāj, was born in 857. One of the most influential Ṣūfī masters of a later age, Abū Ḥamīd Muḥammad ibn Muḥammad al-Ghazālī, was born in 1058 at Tus near Meshhed, and died in the same place, in a Ṣūfī convent, in 1111. The essence of Ṣūfī teachings was the search for unity between the individual and the godhead, often by way of an ecstatic experience. Hence Ḥallāj's famous outcry, "*Anā 'l-ḥaqq*," "I am the [divine] truth!" which the non-Ṣūfī Muslims considered blasphemous and which led to his execution as a heretic in 922.

Jewish influence on Ṣūfism is a fascinating subject but does not belong in the present context. Influences in the opposite direction can also be touched upon only briefly. Baḥya ibn Paqūda was exceedingly familiar with Ṣūfī literature, and the very title of his famous work *Duties of the Hearts* (written ca. 1080) betrays Ṣūfī influence. Both Maimonides (1135–1204) and Joseph ibn Aknin (1150–1220) were acquainted with stories of Ṣūfī mystics. Maimonides' son Abraham (1186–1237) quoted with approval the Ṣūfīs in his *Kiyāfat al-'Ābidīn* (Directions for the Servants [of God]) and even tried to introduce certain Ṣūfī practices into the synagogue. In 1349, Ibn Tufayl's *Risālat Ḥayy ibn Yaqẓān* (Treatise of the Living, Son of the Wakeful One; Ḥayy ibn Yaqẓān is the symbolic proper name of the Active Intellect), one of the most remarkable books of the Middle Ages, was translated into Hebrew by an unknown translator with a Hebrew commentary by Moses of Narbonne.

The positive reaction of Jewish thinkers to Ṣūfism was partly because of the attractive features contained in the Ṣūfī doctrines and partly because of the universal element in it, which is expressed clearly, for instance, in the verses of

Muḥyi 'l-Dīn Ibn al-'Arabī (1165–1240), one of the greatest Ṣūfīs of Islam, who wrote:

> My heart is capable of every form,
> It is a pasture for gazelles and a convent for monks,
> A temple for idols, and the pilgrim's Ka'ba,
> The tables of the Torah, and the book of the Koran.
> I follow the religion of Love,
> Whichever way its camels take,
> My religion and faith is the true religion.

Little wonder that a doctrine that explicitly included the Torah in the "true religion" was attractive to the Jews who were acquainted with it. This was the case especially in Iran. A letter preserved in the Cairo *Genizah* testifies to the attraction Ṣūfism had for the Jewish lower classes in the fourteenth century.[1]

To judge from the information furnished by Joseph Wolff, in the years prior to the Allahdād, the Jews of Meshhed, and in particular the leading element among them, were not only attracted to Ṣūfism but formed Ṣūfī circles under the guidance of a Muslim Ṣūfī *murshid* (spiritual guide). Wolff himself was fascinated by what Chief Mashiaḥ told him about the interest in Ṣūfism among the Jews of his community. According to Mashiaḥ, there was a group of Ṣūfīs among the Meshhed Jews who were the disciples of the *murshid* Muḥammad 'Alī, whose very name shows that he was a Muslim. The Jewish Ṣūfīs, Wolff reports, acknowledged Moses, Jesus, Muhammad, and 124,000 prophets but did not "feel themselves bound to act under the control of any one of these prophets." What is even more interesting is that, according to Mashiaḥ as quoted by Wolff, "those crimes considered as crimes in a revealed book, are not crimes with the Ṣūfīs: as drunkenness, adultery, and other worse crimes; they think that to one that is perfect none of these things can do any harm." Wolff goes on to quote Chief Mashiaḥ to the effect that the Jewish Ṣūfīs, like the Ṣūfīs among the Muslims and the dervishes, "smoke a kind of intoxicating plant in order to withdraw their mind from the world; each sings a song of his beloved object, and strives to become absorbed in the contemplation of the universe, which is, as they say, God."

According to Mashiaḥ as reported by Wolff, the Jewish Ṣūfīs of Meshhed had in their possession a Judeo-Persian version, written in Hebrew characters, of the famous medieval Persian poem "Joseph and Zulaika," describing the love of Zulaika, the wife of Potiphar, for Joseph. Under this title, several versions of a romantic *mathnawī* (poem written in rhyming couplets), based on the twelfth Sura of the Koran, were current in Persia. It used to be attributed to Firdawsi, but recent research has ascribed it to a certain Amani, who wrote it after 1083.[2]

According to Wolff, the Judeo-Persian version was written by a Jewish poet whom he calls Shakem Mawlane, which name seems to be a distortion of Mawlana Shāhin, that is, "our master Shāhin," as the well-known fourteenth-century Persian Jewish poet of Shiraz was most frequently referred to. Shāhin's commentary on the Torah and other works were popular among the Persian Jews, but I found no other reference to a "Joseph and Zulaika" written by him.[3]

The Jews of Meshhed (still according to Wolff) owned copies, transcribed in Hebrew characters, of the poems of Ḥāfiẓ (ca. 1320–1390), the great Shirazi lyricist, commonly considered in Iran the preeminent master of the *ghazāl* form, whose *Dīwān* secured him lasting fame, unequaled popularity, and even reverence. Chief Mashiaḥ explained to Wolff that the wine of which Ḥāfiẓ sang was the mystical wine of truth.

In addition to Christianity and Ṣūfism, Chief Mashiaḥ also had interest in the Koran and kept in his house a Hebrew translation of that holy book of Islam, whose title page Wolff translates into English as "The Law of the Ishmaelites, called Koran, translated from the Arabic into French by Durier, and from the French into Dutch by Glosenmacher, and I, Immanuel Jacob Medart, have now translated it into the holy language, written here at Kogen, by David, the son of Isaac Cohen of Berlin."

Wolff's transliteration of non-English European names is not more precise than his rendering of Oriental names. His Durier is André du Ryer, who translated the Koran into French in the seventeenth century, and whose translation served as the basis for the Dutch translation of Ian Hendrik Glazemaker (Wolff's Glosenmacher), published in Leiden in the eighteenth century in several editions. It was this Dutch text that was used for the preparation of the Hebrew version by Immanuel Jacob Medart, a manuscript copy of which is in the Library of Congress in Washington, D.C.

As for Medart and Cohen, thanks to a piece of extraordinary literary detective work by Myron M. Weinstein, retired head of the Hebraic section of the Library of Congress, their identity is known.[4] Weinstein has shown that Medart or Medort (as his name is given in Wolff's *Journal*) is none other than Immanuel Jacob van Dort, who also used the variant forms of the name "von Dort" and "de Dort," which in its Hebrew form would be "mi-Dort" ("of Dort"), transliterated by Wolff as Medort. This man was a Jew from the Duchy of Juliers, who converted to Christianity and was a professor of theology in Colombo, Ceylon, where he arrived in 1754–1755. While there, he prepared the Hebrew translation of the Koran, probably in the 1750s or '60s.

The copyist David Cohen of Berlin was, as shown by Weinstein, a Jew who arrived in Malabar sometime before 1757, lived in Cochin (transliterated by Wolff as Kogen), where he is known to have been engaged in copying Hebrew texts, and died probably in 1772–1773. His Hebrew Koran manuscript,

Weinstein assumes, reached Meshhed most probably by overland route, sometime prior to 1830.

That those of the Meshhed Jews who were interested in and influenced by Ṣūfism read the Koran is known from a reference made by Wolff. He does not mention whether they read it in van Dort's Hebrew translation, but since Chief Mashiaḥ owned a copy of this Hebrew version, it is most likely that they read it in that language. On the other hand, since the average Meshhed Jew was more fluent in Persian than in Hebrew, it is also possible that they read the Persian translation of the Koran, in which language several translations were available from the tenth century on. The Meshhed Jews did not know Arabic, and they could not read the Koran in the original.

Wolff mentions the Meshhed Jews' reading of the Koran in connection with his reference to their studies under the guidance of a *murshid.* Wolff has little sympathy for these Ṣūfī endeavors. He writes: "They read, with their *murshid,* the Koran and other religious books, to find a confirmation of the truth of their systems, for, like infidels in Germany, France and England, they inconsistently try to prove the truth of their tenets from books, the authority of which they are studying to undermine." Its critical-satirical vein apart, this statement means that the Jewish Ṣūfīs, under the guidance of their Muslim Ṣūfī *murshid,* studied non-Ṣūfī religious books in order to find in them proofs that the Ṣūfī doctrines were true. Since one cannot assume that the Persian Muslim *murshid* knew Hebrew, and since also the Hebrew knowledge of many Meshhed Jews was not very strong, one must assume that the religious books they read were in Persian. If so, we have here an eyewitness account of Meshhed Jews studying Persian Muslim religious literature.

At this point, we must return to the question of Wolff's reliability in reporting on the Jews of Meshhed. As mentioned in chapter 2, Wolff tried to make it appear that his missionary work among the Jews was successful, presented the attitude of the Jews toward Christianity as a rather positive and receptive one, and consequently whatever he says about the interest of the Jews in Christianity must be taken with a grain of salt. This, however, is not the case when Wolff speaks of what he found among the Jews apart from the issue of Christianity. He was unquestionably a keen observer, and when he had no Christian missionary axe to grind, he gave accurate accounts of his observations. What he says about the interest of the Meshhed Jews in Ṣūfism can be taken at face value.

According to Wolff, the interest of Meshhedi Jews in Ṣūfism went so far that they themselves felt a certain dualism in their religious life: "I frequently heard the Jewish Ṣūfīs at Meshhed say that they had two religions: the *ẓāhir* [Wolff misspells the word *bahir*], i.e. the Exterior, and the *bāṭin* [misspelled *datin*], i.e. the Interior; or, the religion of the people, and the religion observed in their lodges."

This dualism led to some confusion in the religious concepts of the Meshhedi Jewish Ṣūfīs: "They tell me that they never saw with their natural eye Mīrzā Abu 'l-Q̱āsim of Shiraz; but they had seen him with their spiritual eye. They believe the Prophet Obadiah to have been a Ṣūfī, and they relate of him that he had been an Edomite, and tuned externally to the Jewish religion. In spite of their own philosophy, if it may be so called, they believe the legends of the Jews, whilst they decline belief in the revelation."[5]

It is difficult to establish the identity of Mīrzā Abu 'l-Q̱āsim of Shiraz, who appeared to the "spiritual eye" of the Jewish Ṣūfīs of Meshhed. However, considering the inaccuracy with which Wolff quotes personal names, he might well have been Abu 'l-Q̱āsim 'Abd al-Karīm b. Hawāzin al-Qushayrī (986–1072), the famous theologian and mystic who spent most of his life in Khorasan and whose works were very popular and highly venerated among the Persian Ṣūfīs. If so, Chief Mashiaḥ's reference to Abu 'l-Q̱āsim is yet another indication of the influence Persian Muslim mystics had on the Jewish Ṣūfīs in Meshhed.

As for the attribution of Edomite descent to the Prophet Obadiah, it echoes the Midrash according to which Obadiah was a descendant of Eliphaz, first-born son of Esau, that is Edom.[6] This statement is found in various Midrashim,[7] at least one of which must therefore have been familiar to the Meshhed Jews. Wolff's remark that the Meshhed Jews "believe in the legends of the Jews" is significant, since if they "believed" in the legends, they must have been acquainted with them, which shows a considerable familiarity with Rabbinic literature. That they "decline belief in the revelation," on the other hand, shows that they were unwilling to accept the teachings of Wolff about the miracles attributed by the Gospels to Jesus.

The Meshhedi Jews' familiarity with Midrashic material is shown also by the comments of Wolff that Chief Mashiaḥ told him in accurate detail the legend of the childhood of Moses: Pharaoh placed a precious stone and a coal of fire before the infant Moses, and Moses grasped the coal, which convinced Pharaoh that he was but an innocent child who represented no danger to him, and consequently he spared his life. This legend is contained in its full form in the *Sēfer haYashar*, which therefore seems to have been familiar to Mashiaḥ and probably also to other Meshhed Jews but was not known to Wolff. Thus, these chance remarks of Wolff afford an insight into the not inconsiderable Jewish and Muslim *Bildung* of the Meshhed Jews, or at least the leading element among them, just prior to their forced conversion to Islam.

According to Wolff, the Jewish Ṣūfīs of Meshhed disbelieved the tradition about the Sambation River which is supposed to block the approach to the ten lost tribes of Israel by its sand and stones which, on the six working days, tumble over one another with such vehemence that it is impossible to ford it, but on the Sabbath, when Jewish religion forbids the crossing of a river, subsides into quiet.[8] If they disbelieved it, they must at least have been familiar with the legend. About the Meshhed Jews' familiarity with traditional Jewish literature in general, Wolff remarks that "the Talmud is scarce at Meshhed and Torbad [Turbat], and is not to be found at all among the Jews of Sarakhs, Mowr, Maimona, and Ankhoy," and that "they do not know the Apocryphal Books of the Maccabees, Tobit, etc. . . . but are acquainted with their history, by their rabbinical writings."

Wolff deals very summarily with the actual religious life of the Meshhed Jews, which interests him only inasmuch as it manifests Ṣūfī influences or shows receptivity to Christian teachings. Nevertheless, he mentions that "they have very fine synagogues at Meshhed, from the time of Nadir Shah," and that

> their hierarchy consists of כהנים Priests, לויים Levites, רבנים Rabbis, דינים Vice Rabbis, נשיאים Princes, מלמדים Teachers. Only their Rabbis speak pure Hebrew. They keep themselves entirely secluded from their neighbors, and never intermarry with them; the Jews of Meshhed do not even intermarry with those of Yazd, on account of the bad character of the latter. The Jews of Meshhed, Turkestan, and Khorasan have no intercourse with those of Europe. They have no hatred toward Jesus Christ [the missionary speaking!], which makes me suspect of their being of the ten tribes who had no share in the crucifixion of our Lord.

The statement that the Jews of Meshhed "keep themselves entirely secluded from their neighbors" is, of course, invalidated by the detailed account Wolff himself gives of the contact between the Jewish Ṣūfīs and the Muslim Ṣūfīs, their mutual visitations, their common studies and discussions. Since Chief Mashiaḥ, the head of the Meshhed Jews, seems to have been a key figure in this contact, and Mullah Pinḥas, the *dayyan* (one of Wolff's "vice rabbis"), another, one must conclude that under their leadership, a certain element of the Meshhed Jews participated in the Ṣūfī brotherhood of the city, which involved considerable Jewish-Muslim contact. Such religious-spiritual contact is something entirely different from intermarriage. The Jews of Meshhed, like all the other communities in Persia (and in the Middle East in general), practiced strict endogamy, with the preferred marriages being between children of two brothers.[9] To marry outside one's own community was frowned upon and was the greatest exception in every community. It was this generally followed custom that made it possible for the Meshhed Jews after the Allahdād, when they were officially Muslims, to avoid intermarriage with the Muslim Persians of the city.

On the interest Meshhed Jews took in Ṣūfism, Wolff has a lot more to say. On December 11, five days after his arrival in Meshhed, he received a visit from the Muslim Ṣūfī *murshid,* who was the spiritual guide of the Meshhed Jewish

Ṣūfīs. Wolff was not at all impressed by this man. He writes: "The teacher of the Jewish Ṣūfīs called on me; there was nothing in him which could engage me to like him; he sometimes expressed devotions, which he spoiled again by evident lies."

Nevertheless, Wolff learned from the *murshid* the Ṣūfī principles that, evidently, both the Jewish and the Muslim Ṣūfīs embraced:

> 1. That there is no evil in the world.
> 2. That to a man whose mind is absorbed in God, adultery can do no harm, or any other vice.
> 3. The world stands from eternity.
> 4. The world and God is one and the same thing.

These doctrines are not precisely identical with the tenets that are basic to Ṣūfism in general but are close enough to be recognizable as variants of Ṣūfī ideas. On the other hand, each of the four principles constitutes an explicit contradiction to the teachings of Judaism. If, therefore, the Jewish disciples of the *murshid* actually did subscribe to them, they were, from the Jewish point of view, *posh'ē* Yisraēl, apostates. In any case, we learn from a statement of Wolff that there was in Meshhed in the early 1800s a circle of Jews who were definitely open to the teachings of Ṣūfism, and this intelligence throws a new light on the willingness of some of the Meshhed Jews to opt for conversion to Islam rather than emigration in the fearsome days of the 1839 Allahdād.

The house of Chief Mashiaḥ was, according to Wolff, a kind of study and discussion center, in which Muslim and Jewish Ṣūfīs met and threshed out the differences between their views. Wolff writes: "It was amusing this evening to hear those Jewish and Mohammedan Ṣūfīs discussing with great gravity, and with eye lifted up with devotion, the propriety of eating pork, drinking wine, and eating without first washing their hands." One of the Muslim Ṣūfīs who was a habitué of Mashiaḥ's house was a certain Dervish Mushtāq-Fars, who, "though a Mohammedan [was] connected with the Jewish Ṣūfīs."

Interesting and instructive are the details Wolff learned from Mashiaḥ about the duties of a *murshid.* They show that this head of the Meshhed Jewish community was thoroughly acquainted with the role a *murshid* played in the life of a Muslim Ṣūfī community:

> I spoke with Mullah Mashiaḥ about the duties of a *murshid.* He tells me that a *murshid* does not give lectures, but speaks the language of the heart. Mullah Mashiaḥ became very thoughtful and gloomy. I asked him the reason of it; he replied that something had happened to his Jewish friend, a Ṣūfī, which he could not reveal to me; that friend was endowed with prophetic power, and therefore he must console himself by singing, in a mournful tone, the sorrows

> of the Loving, and his sympathy with the Beloved, which is more sweet than the voice of the nightingale, and therewith, as the Dervishes had done before, he began to sing.

Again, inadvertently, Wolff here tells us something quite remarkable about the Jews of Meshhed: their *Nasi* Mullah Mashiaḥ, himself a Ṣūfī, has a Jewish Ṣūfī friend, who he believes possesses "prophetic powers." Moreover, we learn that the Jewish Ṣūfīs were in the habit of giving expression to their innermost feelings by singing Ṣūfī songs about the Lover and the Beloved, a favorite theme of Ṣūfī mystical expression. The Lover, of course, is the soul, and the Beloved is God.

Several entries in Wolff's book add details to the portraiture of the Meshhed Jews prior to the Allahdād and, in particular, to their relationship with Muslim Ṣūfīs. On December 14, he writes, a high-ranking Muslim Ṣūfī, 'Abbās Kulī Mīrzā, paid a visit to Mullah Mashiaḥ. On December 28, "His Royal Highness 'Abbās Mīrzā desired the Jews of Meshhed to discuss the subject of religion with me in his presence." On January 18, 1831, Mīrzā Hadāyat Ullah, *mujtahid* of Meshhed, invited Wolff to his house, and on that occasion, "the room was crowded, even Jews were present."[10] On January 22, "Several Jewish Mullahs and Mussulman Sayyids and Mullahs assembled in the house of Mullah Muḥammad 'Ali [the *murshid* of the Jewish Ṣūfīs]. Mullah Pinḥas, the Dayyan or assistant to the Chief Rabbi, who is a Ṣūfī, was present; here I saw him, to my great surprise, eating with Mullah Muḥammad 'Alī." At that gathering, Wolff read passages from the New Testament in Hebrew, and Mullah Pinḥas translated them into Persian. All these meetings definitely give the impression that the Ṣūfis in Meshhed constituted a brotherhood to which both Jews and Muslims belonged.

If Mullah Pinḥas the *dayyan* was a Ṣūfī and ate nonkosher food in the house of a Muslim fellow Ṣūfī, we shall not be surprised to learn that several members of the Meshhed Jewish community vacillated between Judaism and Islam. Wolff reports having met at least two such persons: "One day an odd and singular character entered my room: Mullah Levi ben Mashiaḥ, a Mohammedan at Meshhed and a Jew whenever he goes to Sarakhs; his wife and children still professing the Jewish religion. He came to see me and asked me whether I would not go to his house to bathe; as he keeps a bath for Jewish travellers who come here; for the Mussulmans here do not admit a Christian or a Jew to their bath. I promised to go the next day."[11]

Another such marginal character was Nissim: "Nissim is a complete infidel in sentiments: at Meshhed he is a Mussulman, and a Jew at Sarakhs, Khiva, and on his journeys to Europe." This Nissim, despite his own infidelity, had a very low opinion of the Jews of Khiva: "He gives a very bad account of the Jews of

Khiva; which account I heard confirmed all over Turkestan: they are traitors, despisers of the Law, have Mussulman concubines, and rob foreign Jews who go among them. The Jews of Khiva are called *Mamzerim,* i.e. bastards, even by those of Bokhara, as Nissim assures me; for all of them left Bokhara on account of their ill conduct." Among the Jews of Bokhara also, the Meshhed Jews had a bad reputation, "on account of their spending their time in reading Ḥāfiẓ," while the Bukharan Jews "are prohibited by their rabbis to learn either Persian or Arabic."[12]

In Meshhed itself, it was the Jews from Yazd who had the worst reputation. Around 1770, there was a severe famine in Yazd, which prompted its Jews to move to Meshhed. "They are unclean, dishonest, and despised by the rest of the Children of Israel at Meshhed, and are considered by them as ערב רב, i.e. Mixed Multitude, mentioned in Exodus 12:38."[13]

As far as sexual morality was concerned, Wolff heard the worst reports about the wives of the Muslim religious functionaries. He writes, "It is generally reported that from the wives of the Mujtahid down to those of the lowest Mullahs, all are prostitutes; but crimes much worse are committed at Meshhed," and goes on to mention organized attacks on caravans and the like.[14]

A number of concrete details about the Jews of Meshhed can be learned from Wolff. He lists by name the heads of the Meshhed Jewish community: Mullah Daud, the rabbi of Meshhed; Mullah Jonathan; Aga [Āqā] Benjamin Ḥakīm, the "*G'vir,* i.e., Principal man"; Mullah Pinḥas, "*Dayyan,* i.e., Assistant Rabbi, a Ṣūfī in secret"; Mullah Eliahu Dayyan; Aga Abraham Serkar; Aga Raḥmūn (Raḥmān); Mullah Yūsuf.

Next, Wolff supplies several details about the history and the life of the Meshhed Jews. Since these details must have been based on information supplied by his Jewish friends, what he says allows us a glimpse of the attitudes and historical traditions as they existed among the Jews of Meshhed in the early nineteenth century. Thus, he states that the Meshhed Jews disliked being called "Jews"; they wanted to be called בני ישראל, Children of Israel. The folk history he recapitulates contains several items of interest:

> When Nadir Shah arrived in Qazwin [Wolff writes], he took the Jews from there together with the Armenians from old Julfa, and brought them to Meshhed, where he gave to all of them the privilege of erecting synagogues; several Jews from Sabzawar joined them. Nadir Shah, anxious to know the religion of the Jews and Christians, and having had the design of establishing one religion accommodated to all religions, ordered both the Jews and Christians to translate their books of Moses and the Psalms of David into the Persian tongue, first written in characters of their own, and then copied in Persian characters by one of the Persian Khosh-Newees [*khōsh nawīs*], or fine-writers. The Armenians translated the New Testament into the Persian tongue.[15]

Wolff refers to a Meshhedi Jewish tradition according to which Nadir Shah encouraged also among the Jews the study of science and poetry. Somewhat later, Wolff adds that "Nadir Shah took several of them [the Jews] with him to Kabul, and since then many Jews from Meshhed have gone to Kabul; and just now [ca. 1832] the Jews from Kabul begin to return to Meshhed. So great is the hatred between the Sunnī and the Shī'ah that Jews who have turned Mohammedan at Meshhed, among the Shī'ah, again openly profess Judaism among the Sunnī as soon as they are going to Sarakhs or to any other part of Turkestan."[16]

The Jews of Meshhed, according to Wolff, were in possession of historical traditions also concerning the Afghans: "Aga Levi and the rest of the Jews of Meshhed believe the Afghans to be descendants from the Jews. . . . Aga Levi tells me that the tribes of Benjamin, Simeon, and Joseph were carried to Kandahar, where they lost their books, and then turned Mohammedans." Another Meshhed Jew told Wolff that "there is a mountain there [where?], called *Takht Sulayman,* Solomon's Throne, and that Asaph is buried there."[17]

4
ALLAHDĀD!

The Allahdād (literally, "God gave" or "God's gift"), as the Muslim attack on the Jews of Meshhed, the massacre of thirty-six of them, and the forced conversion of the rest were called by the fanatic mob, was the most traumatic event that befell the Jews of Meshhed. It has remained etched into their consciousness to this day, whether they stayed on in Meshhed, where in the 1990s a few dozen Jews still were found, or lived in their widespread Diaspora in Asia, Europe, and America, where by the 1990s they numbered several thousand. It took place in the spring of 1839, and its memory was preserved in several versions that show certain discrepancies among them in minor detail but agree in the essentials of what happened.

The first to write about the Meshhed Allahdād was the same missionary Joseph Wolff who first visited Meshhed in 1831, and whose references to the Meshhed Jews were analyzed above. In 1844, Wolff returned to Meshhed, was told about what had happened just five years earlier, and wrote about it briefly in his book titled *Narrative of a Mission to Bokhara in the Years 1843–1845*, which was published in 1845 in Edinburgh and within seven years reached no less than seven editions. In the book, we meet again several persons with whom Wolff had established contact in 1831 and whom he found alive and well in 1844. The most prominent among them was Mullah Mashiaḥ, whom Wolff now calls by the Persian equivalent of his name, Mullah Mahdī the Jew, in whose house he stayed again as during his first visit, and who again proved very helpful.[1] We are now told that Mullah Mahdī not only was friendly to Wolff but was a friend of "all the English nation; and this kind Jew was, during the invasion of the English in Afghanistan, employed by Major Rawlinson at Qandahar, and Major Todd at Herat, and suffered reportedly for his attachment to our people. In proof of it I record the following fact. A German from Hamburg, named Dieskau, came from India to Meshhed, pretending to be the English ambassador. Mullah Mahdī lent him twelve hundred ducats, with which the rascal escaped."[2]

The "English invasion" of Afghanistan took place in February 1839, when an Anglo-Indian army advanced through Sind and the Bolan Pass on Qandahar and, after taking the city, marched on Kabul. The incident with the loan to the German Dieskau shows that Mullah Mahdī must have been a very rich man. This little item illustrates the general statement made by Wolff about the wealth of the Meshhed Jews on the eve of the Allahdād.

As for the Allahdād itself, this is what Wolff found out about it five years after the event:

> All the Jews of Meshhed, a hundred and fifty families, were compelled seven years ago to turn Mussulmans. The occasion was as follows: A poor woman had a sore hand: a Mussulman physician advised her to kill a dog, and put her hand in the blood of it: she did so; when suddenly the whole population rose, and said that they had done it in derision of their Prophet. Thirty-five Jews were killed in a few minutes; the rest, struck with terror, became Muhammedans, and the *fanatic* and *covetous* [italics in the original] Muhammedans shouted, "Light of Muhammed has fallen upon them!" They are now more zealous Jews *in secret* than ever; but call themselves like the Jews in Spain, *Anusim*—"the compelled ones." Their children cannot suppress their feelings when their parents call them by their Muhammedan names. But Mullah Mahdī and Mullah Moshe believe in Christ, and Mullah Mahdī asked me to baptize him. He has been of the greatest use to the English in Herat and Qandahar, as his testimonials from Rawlinson and others amply indicate.[3]

This passage contains one inaccuracy and what seems to be a purposeful misstatement. It was written in 1843 or 1844; hence, the forced conversion of the Meshhed Jews took place not seven years earlier but four or five years earlier, in 1839. In his 1835 book, as well as in later entries in this book, Wolff speaks repeatedly of Mullah Mahdī but never mentions that he "believed in Christ" or that he asked him "to baptize him." (On this issue, see below, chapter 5.) Nor does he mention again that Mullah Moshe believed in Christ. One suspects that these throwaway statements were not based on facts but served the purpose of demonstrating the effectiveness of the Christological influence Wolff the missionary claimed to have had on the Jews of Meshhed. On the other hand, there is no reason to doubt the accuracy of Wolff's observation that the Jews of Meshhed were, after the forced conversion, "more zealous Jews *in secret* than ever." That they did not hide this from Wolff shows that they fully trusted him, and this trust was not misplaced. After a brief absence, Wolff returned to Meshhed and recorded more details:

> On my second arrival I heard more fully the history of the massacre of the Jews. The Jews for centuries had settled there [in Meshhed] from the cities of Qazwin, Rasht, and Yazd. They were distinguished advantageously by their

> cleanliness, industry and taste for Persian poetry. Many of them had actually imbibed the system of the Persian Ṣūfīs. We heard them, instead of singing the hymns of Zion, reciting in plaintive strains the poetry of Ḥāfiẓ and Firdawsi, and the writings of Mathnawi. They had accumulated great riches, and did not busy themselves in propitiating the authorities of Meshhed by occasional presents. Their wealth had long excited the cupidity of the people of Meshhed, who only sought an opportunity to seize on their possessions. The following occasion presented itself, which enabled them to realize this object.
>
> In the year 1838 [*sic*] the Mohammedans celebrated the feast of Bairam. On that very day a Jewess slaughtered a dog, at the advice of a Mohammedan physician, for the purpose of washing with the blood of the dog her own hands. One of the Mussulman Sayyids, who heard it, and to whom the Jews previously had refused a present, called together all the Mussulmans in the mosque of Imām Riza, and addressed them in the following manner: "People of Muḥammad and 'Alī, the Jews have derided our feast of Bairam, by sacrificing on the very day of our feast a dog. I shall now tell you in two words what must be done—*Allah-Dād,* which means, "God has given." They took the allusion and whilst the Assaff-ood-Dowla [Asaf al-Dawla], the Mirza Askeree ['Askarī], the Imaum Jumaa [Imām Jum'ah], and the rest of the authorities, were sleeping, the whole populace shouted "*Allah-Dād,*" and with this shout of *Allah-Dād* they rushed into the houses of the Jews, slew thirty-five of them, robbed and plundered their property, and the rest of them saved their lives, but not their property, by reciting the Mohammedan creed. Only a few of them preferred death to apostasy. Mullah Daoud Cohen, the Chief Rabbi and High priest of the Jewish nation of Meshhed, gave the first example of apostasy. The year in which this happened still goes by the name of Allah-Dād among both Jews and Mohammedans. In secret they observe the Jewish religion, and tell their children not to forget the event of Allah-Dād.[4]

The date 1838 (instead of 1839 given by practically all the other sources) must be a simple mistake. The attraction of Ṣūfism and classical Persian poetry for the Jews of Meshhed conforms to what Wolff said about them twelve years earlier. The motivation of simple robbery ("cupidity"), making use of a religious excuse, seems likely. So is the mob action, upon incitement by a Sayyid and without the knowledge of the leading religious authorities of the city. Mullah Daoud Cohen, "Chief Rabbi and High Priest," who was the first to accept Islam, is mentioned in the earlier book of Wolff as "Mullah Daud, Rabbi of Meshhed."

Wolff (and, as we shall see, Ferrier as well) gives the Feast of Bairam as the date on which the Allahdād took place. That feast is called in Arabic 'Īd al-Aḍḥā, 'Īd al-Qurbān, or 'Īd al-Nahr ("Sacrificial Feast"), or al-'Īd al-Kabīr ("the Great Feast"), while in Turkish it is called Buyuk Bayram or Kurban Bayram. It is celebrated on the tenth of the month Dhu 'l-Ḥijja, and is considered one of the most important Muslim festivals.

Most interesting is that a mere five years after the forced conversion, the continued secret (actually not so secret) adherence of the Meshhed Jews to Judaism became known to Wolff, who evidently did not feel that it was necessary to hide the fact from the chief Imām of Meshhed, Mīrzā 'Askarī. Wolff was staying in the house of Mullah Mahdī, and, as he writes:

> Mīrzā 'Askarī, the Imām Jum'ah, or chief of the mosque, called on me in the night time, for I was exceedingly unwell. He made me a present of a turquoise ring. . . . I besought him to protect the Jews and not to allow the Mohammedans to carry on against them a regular system of inquisition. Mīrzā 'Askarī is very fond of money, and after receiving a few *tomans* from a Jewish family, he allowed a considerable number of them to emigrate to Herat, Yazd, and Teheran, where they live again as Jews. How affecting it is to look at the Jews of Meshhed![5]

Some of the Meshhed Jews were so shaken by the attack that they became deranged. Wolff saw several "poor old women go about, continually exclaiming, '*Allah-Dād! Allah-Dād!* God has given! God has given!' the exclamation used by the Sayyids to excite the populace to murder the Jews of Meshhed." An educated Jew, Raḥamīm, whom Wolff had known "in former times," also lost his mind as a result of the trauma of the massacre:

> He was not only learned in Jewish learning, but also in Persian literature, and rather given to the system of the Ṣūfīs. When he saw the Jews massacred, and the shout of Allah-Dād became universal, he turned Mohammedan with the rest, but soon after was struck with madness. The word of "Allah-Dād" struck him with consternation: he tears his clothes, and runs about in the streets, and the only word he utters is "Allah-Dād!" I asked him, "Raḥamīm, if I give you a suit of clothes, will you wear them?" "Yes." I gave him a suit of clothes; the next day he tore them into pieces, exclaiming, "Allah-Dād! When my mosque shall be built I will wear clothing. Now, Allah-Dād! Allah-Dād!"[6]

From Wolff we also learn that five years after the Allahdād, the Muslim authorities of Meshhed did know that the Jadīd al-Islām observed Judaism in secret and yet did nothing to punish them for what in their eyes was the mortal sin of falling off the Muslim faith. Wolff writes:

> Whilst I was with the Jews of Meshhed the time came that the Jews commemorate their Day of Atonement. The poor women and the old Jews fasted in secret. The Mussulmans were informed by those Jews who had been real apostates to the Mohammedan faith, and who voluntarily embraced that faith for the sake of convenience, previous to the event of Allah-Dād, that the Jews converted in the year of Allah-Dād were Jews in secret. Whilst I was with them the servant of Mīrzā Sayyid 'Askarī, the Imām Jum'ah, entered the house of a

> Jew in the evening time, in order to find out whether they celebrate the Atonement. I was informed of the fact, and sent him word to leave immediately the house of the Jew, which he did. The next morning I wrote to the Imām Jum'ah a serious letter, and gave him to understand that most of the European powers take an interest in the condition of the Jews, and told him that he would make himself an immortal name if he would protect the Jews; which he promised to do.[7]

What is noteworthy in this account is that, in trying to protect the Jews, Wolff did not argue that since they had converted to Islam they are Muslims who must not be harmed. Evidently, such an argument would have been futile in view of patent facts. Instead, he based his appeal to the Imām Jum'ah on the argument that the European powers were interested in the fate of the Jews, and that the Imām Jum'ah would acquire great fame by extending his protection to the Jews.

Wolff closes his report on the Jews of Meshhed by printing the text of a long missionary letter he wrote to them. In it, in the style of the biblical prophets of old, he reproaches them for their lack of true religious feelings, because of which the calamity of the Allahdād overtook them, and exhorts them to turn to Jesus. On a more practical note, he advises them to write to Sir Moses Montefiore, who will be able to help them. The much tried Jews of Meshhed, whatever their feelings were about Wolff the missionary, did not break off relations with him, and when a few days later he left Meshhed, he was accompanied "by the Jews of Meshhed and many Mohammedans."[8]

Here we must take leave of Joseph Wolff, this son of a German rabbi, who in his youth converted to Christianity and became a missionary. He was an intrepid traveler and explorer of untamed central Asian Muslim lands hostile to Christians and hazardous to all outsiders, who, while pretending among the Jews of those countries to be Jewish, tried unsuccessfully to convert them to Christianity but retained all the time an atavistic sympathy for the Jews and an almost instinctual readiness to help them in their plight. For us, what he observed in Meshhed and reported about its Jews is of prime historical value, for his is a rare eyewitness account of the status of that unique Jewish community in the most crucial years of its existence a few years before and a few years after the Allahdād.

In 1845, just a year after Wolff, a French traveler, J. P. Ferrier, visited Meshhed and obtained information about the Allahdād that differed in several points from that given by Wolff. He writes:

> There are also in the town about 600 persons of Jewish origin, who, since 1839, as I have already remarked, are Mussulmans in form but not in heart: life is dear, and to save theirs they adopted the faith of Mahomet. The story of this forced conversion is as follows: A Jewish woman having consulted a Mussulman

> doctor for an abscess she had on her hand, this empiric ordered her to open a dog recently born, and to keep her hand for one hour in the bowels. The good old lady did as she was bid; unfortunately, however, this was done on the day of the *Koorban Beiram,* the festival of the victim, the most remarkable of Mahomedan holidays: a sheep is killed in every Mussulman family on that day, and eaten with great rejoicings. This act of the Jewess having come to the ears of some fanatical Mussulmans, they propagated all kinds of lies in connection with the circumstance; they asserted that the unfortunate dog had been killed in the presence of an assembly of Jews, and that in doing this they intended to cast ridicule upon the Mahomedan religion. These statements lost nothing in the telling; and at length the town was in a state of ferment and agitation, the soldiers of the garrison hurried to the Jews' quarter, pillaged it, and killed several of the wretched inhabitants. Their remainder were pursued like wild beasts, and, receiving no protection from the officers of the local government, they, to save their lives, embraced a faith which they abhorred. During the time they were paralysed by these scenes the Imaum Jumeh and other mollahs, as well as some noblemen of Meshhed, seized the prettiest Jewesses and married them.
>
> Assaf Doulet, usually reputed so just, did not take the measures he should have done to repress these disorders, nor affect even to inquire into them until it was too late; and some persons went so far as to say that he secretly promoted this disgraceful and brutal piece of tyranny. This was not proved; but it is well known that his hatred of the Armenians and the Jews was intense; which gave a certain credibility to the report. Fanaticism, however, was not the only motive which roused the Mussulman population to the commission of these crimes. They were jealous of the Jews, and vexed to see them wealthy, and the most profitable commercial operations in their hands; they also imagined that their houses were full of treasure; these they pillaged and carried off everything, even to the doors and the windows. From the period at which this took place the Jews of Meshhed have never set their foot within the walls of their synagogues; on the contrary, they make a point of going every day to the mosque of Imaum Reza, in order that their conversion may not appear hypocritical, which would, without doubt, subject them to fresh persecutions. They have also pledged themselves to send their children to the mollahs to study the Koran, and never to teach them the Hebrew language. Those who emigrated to Herat have openly returned to their ancestral faith, for which they would certainly suffer if they were to revisit Meshhed. The Jews of this town appeared in every way superior to those generally met with in Asia. They have not, perhaps, the same astuteness, but they have not the same servile air. They are ready to be of service, polite, and certainly more loyal than what one generally expects, or, indeed, sometimes finds in persons of that nation.[9]

Ferrier's account agrees with that of Wolff in reporting that the Allahdād took place on the Muslim feast day of Kurban Bȧyram, that is, on the tenth of the month Dhu 'l-Ḥijja, which therefore can be considered as the actual time of the event. (Later Jewish tradition postponed the event by one month and considered it as having taken place in the month of Muḥarram.) On the other hand, Ferrier's account differs in two important points from that of Wolff. He puts greater emphasis on the Muslims' envy of Jewish wealth as a motivation that led to the outbreak of the attack, stating that the most profitable commercial operations were in the hands of the Jews, which can only mean that the Jews were the richest, or among the richest, people in Meshhed; and he knows nothing of the secret adherence of the Jews to Judaism, which Wolff reports. The first can be explained by the lesser interest Wolff as a missionary may have had in the material aspects of the Jews' lives; the second, by the greater openness of the Jews in their contact with Wolff, who pretended to be a Jew, than with the Christian Ferrier. Apart from this, the two accounts complement and dovetail with each other.

The Allahdād of Meshhed was the subject of quite a number of later reports and accounts found in the writings of Jewish authors and published in various Hebrew books and periodicals. Most of them are mere repetitions of earlier accounts, with the addition of a few details and embellishments. Several of them, however, are of sufficient interest to be presented and briefly analyzed.

The most detailed account was given in 1839 by the Jadīdī Samad Āqā ben Yosef Dilmānī, and was recorded in 1945 by Āqā Mullah Yosef ben Āqā 'Abdul-Samad Dilmānī. It is preserved in the Central Zionist Archives in Jerusalem.[10] It states that after their forced conversion, the Jadīdīm, afraid lest any document found in their possession and indicative of their Jewishness provide a new excuse for the Muslims to attack them, destroyed all receipts and other papers. For the same reason, they refrained from writing *gittim* (letters of divorce), which also would have testified to their continued adherence to Judaism. Also, they sent all the Torah scrolls and other Jewish books to other cities (Yezd, Kirman) for safekeeping, so that even in 1939, only a very few Jewish books were in the possession of the community.

After these preliminaries, Āqā Dilmānī states that the catastrophic event took place on "the Great Sabbath" preceding Passover, on the twelfth of Nissan 699 (i.e., 1839), which was the tenth day (*'Ashūrah*) of the month of Muḥarram 1255, of the Muslim calendar, a day of mourning and self-laceration for the Shī'īs in commemoration of the death of the Imām Ḥusayn.

This date not only differs from that given by the quasi-contemporary observers Wolff and Ferrier but is also inaccurate in identifying the Jewish date twelfth of Nissan with the Muslim date tenth of Muḥarram. Since the months in both the Jewish and the Muslim calendar are lunar—that is, the first day of each month in both is that on which the new moon appears—the twelfth of Nissan cannot correspond to the tenth of Muḥarram. This inaccuracy apart, what happened according to Āqā Dīlmānī on that fateful day was as follows:

> A [Jewish] woman, whose hand was leprous, was told by somebody that if she wanted to be healed of the leprosy she should take a dog, cut open its belly, and

stick her hand into its intestines. The woman did as she was told, and on Friday the 11th of Nissan she slaughtered the dog. The Muslims hated the Jews in those days, and were looking for excuses to attack them. The thing the woman did with the dog became known to a Muslim man, and he hurried to tell about it to others. The rumor spread in the city that the Jews slaughtered the dog on that very day out of hatred of the Muslims and in order to mock their feelings by representing ['Alī al-Riza, the holy Imām of the Muslims] as if he had been a dog. The man who spread these news, together with many other Muslims, went to the Imām Jum'ah, the chief Imām of the city, and told him about the event. While they were still consulting with the Imām Jum'ah, a crowd of Muslims who had come from the villages to celebrate the day of mourning [of the tenth of Muḥarram], was incited by the rumor, and in its rage attacked the Jewish quarter, broke into the Jewish houses, and robbed and looted everything they could lay their hands on. They beat the Jews cruelly, killed 36 Jewish men, and abducted many beautiful Jewish maidens taking them into the houses of Muslims. Two of the girls were taken to the house of the Imām Jum'ah himself, and became his wives. After his death they returned to the houses of the Jews.

Evil days followed for the Jews. They went to the house of the Imām Jum'ah to ask his protection against the wrath of the mob. But the Imām answered that as long as they adhered to the religion of their fathers he could not help them. They must convert to Islam, and then he will protect them and their property, their freedom will be restored to them as of old, and the mob will no longer persecute them. Since the Jews had no other choice, for they could not turn to the central government whose seat was already in Teheran, they were forced to accept the demand of the Imām—to proclaim, *La Ilāha ill'Allāh waMuḥammad Rasūl Ullāh* [There is no god but Allah, and Muhammad is the Messenger of Allah], and thereby become Muslims.

The Imām Jum'ah announced to the mob that the Jews had converted to Islam, that from then on it was forbidden for the Muslims to harm them and their property, and that everybody who looted anything from the Jews in the days of the attack must return it to them. The Muslims returned to the Jews those pieces of the loot which they did not need. One Muslim, obeying the order of the Imām, returned seven or eight *man* [21 to 24 kilos] of silk that he looted during the attack, but since the owner of the silk could not be located (perhaps he was one of those who were killed), the Jews kept the silk for a year, and then, since the owner did not reappear, they were forced to sell the silk. For the money, which amounted to about 80 *tomans,* they purchased the plot of land for the cemetery which the Jews use to this day for burying their dead. [The Jadīdīm were forbidden to bury their dead in the old Jewish cemetery, and they did not want to bury them in the Muslim cemetery. The solution found was to bury their dead in a new cemetery special for the Jadīdīm.]

During their attack on the Jewish quarter the Muslims destroyed the synagogues and forced the Jews to sell the furnishings. The building materials were used by the Muslims to build a mosque, known as the Ḥusayniyya Mosque, which has remained in use to this day. Every year in the month of Muḥarram

> the Muslims set up a tent in the courtyard of that mosque, and gather there, crying and mourning over the death of Ḥusayn, and distribute meals to the Muslim poor. [This custom is known as *Taqiyya.*]
>
> The courtyards of the destroyed synagogues remained desolate for several years. Then the Jews used them to build homes for the poor Jadīdhā. In 1933 the municipality took possession of the plot, demolished the houses, and built in their place a Persian school. All the expenses of building this school, amounting to about 300,000 *tomans,* were defrayed by the Jadīdīm in Meshhed, London, and India. [Most of the pupils attending this school were children of the Jadīdīm, who attended this *madrasah* (school) in the morning, and the Jewish *midrash* in the afternoon.] The number of the Jews in Meshhed at that time was about two hundred families, or 1,000 souls.
>
> After the forced conversion several of the Jews who did not want to convert fled, together with their families, to Afghanistan and Turkestan, and they are still living there. Others of the Jews, who hoped that God would help, stayed on in Meshhed, and were forced outwardly to be Muslims, but in secret remained faithful Jews, who observed the religion, and believed that the day would come when God would save them and redeem them. There was also a part of the Jews who were forced to adapt to the spirit of the times and to the religious piety that was customary [among the Muslims], and outwardly pretended to be pious Muslims. They made the pilgrimage to Mecca and Karbala, prostrated themselves in the mosques, prayed and fasted, and ate *t'refa* meat of Muslim slaughtering. But the wives of the Jews never cooked the meat that was bought in the marketplace, and obeyed with great piety all the laws of the Torah: they destroyed the *t'refa* meat that their husbands brought, and in its place cooked kosher meat that was bought in secret from Jews.

About the event of the Allahdād itself, a contemporary reference, written two months after the event, is found in a note written on the inside of the binding of the prayer book of Hoshea Rabbah Kohana, printed in Amsterdam in 1727, of which, evidently, a copy found its way to Meshhed. It is in Persian, and reads:

> A memorial. In the year 5599 [1839] evildoers calumniated the Jews. On the 12th of Nissan they broke into the camp [quarter] of the Jews and killed about 32 of them. The others they forced to convert—had they not converted, they would have killed all of them, Israelites, judges, Kohens and Levites. Having no choice, all of them said *La Ilāha ill'Allāh* . . . [There is no God but Allah . . .]. Now we have no other hope, unless, first, God has mercy upon us; second, King Messiah comes; and third, the English come and save us. May the Holy One, blessed be He, protect us, and in His mercy let His face shine upon us and redeem us from this exile of Ishmael. Let this writing remain as a memorial. Written by Samuel, in the year 5599 [1839], month of Siwan.[11]

This inscription says nothing about the reason (or excuse) for the Muslim attack on the Jews and is incomplete in this respect. On the other hand, its mention of the hope that the English would come and redeem the suffering Jews is interesting, because it shows that in 1839, the Persian Jews knew about the British penetration to India, and perhaps also of Britain's interest in establishing its influence in Iran.[12]

Another version, written by Yiṣḥaq Kleinbaum, an emissary of the Jewish Agency, is based on what he learned in the course of his visit to Meshhed on May 15–19, 1946. It is preserved in the Central Zionist Archives in Jerusalem (no. 25/5291). According to it, a Jewish woman, who had a wound on the hand, was advised by her physician to slaughter her dog and put its blood on the wound. When the Muslims noticed the blood spots in her courtyard, they began to spread the rumor that the Jews had slaughtered a Muslim child and used its blood for the baking of *maṣṣot.* This led to the attack on the Jewish quarter.

Ya'aqov Dilmanian, a Meshhed Jew who in 1960 wrote a history of the Jews of Meshhed, has yet another version of the Allahdād story. Dilmanian's treatise is still unpublished, but a hectographed copy of it was available to Amnon Netzer, who summarized its contents in an article in the Jerusalem periodical *Pe'amim.* According to Dilmanian, Abraham, a Jew of Hamadan, who settled in Meshhed several years after the foundation of the community in 1747, was advised by a Muslim physician to treat the afflicted hand of his wife with the warm blood of a freshly slaughtered dog. (Netzer remarks that such treatments to heal malignant wounds were well known in Iran.) As Abraham was throwing the body of the dog out of his house, a Muslim religious procession, which, it seems, started out on the eighth or ninth of the month of Muḥarram, was approaching. It was headed by a Sayyid who had a tobacconist's store in the Jewish quarter and was used to getting payments from the Jews to protect them from the Muslims. However, that year, the Jews refused to pay the Sayyid protection money, because the Muslims had increased year by year their persecution of the Jews. Now, leading the procession, the Sayyid noticed the body of the dog, saw an opportunity to avenge himself on the Jews, and claimed that the Jews desecrated the memory of the saintly Imām Ḥusayn by slaughtering a dog and throwing its body in the way of the procession. The participants in the procession administered a cruel beating to Abraham, and then hurried to the *mujtahid* of the city, Ḥājjī Sayyid 'Askarī, and demanded that he issue a religious decision against the Jews. The *mujtahid* postponed the issuance of the decision until after the 'Ashūrah, the day of mourning in memory of Imām Ḥusayn. The Jews did not know what was about to happen, but they sensed danger and locked themselves into their houses. On the Sabbath, the thirteenth of the month of Muḥarram, in the morning, the Muslims penetrated the Jewish quarter and began to kill and loot. The Jews hid in cellars and wells, on the roofs of houses, and in the cemetery. After the massacre, which lasted several hours and brought death to tens of Jews, five or six Jews of the Ḥakīmī family and one of the Raḥmānī family gathered in the house of one of them and decided to convert to Islam. They went up to the roof and in loud voices proclaimed their wish to convert. They were immediately taken to the Imām Jum'ah, the head Imām of the city, and recited the Shahāda (testimony), the formula of conversion. They were given Muslim names and undertook to bring, within one day, the Jews of Meshhed to the *mujtahid* for conversion. It was the *mujtahid* who called the day of the conversion Allahdād, that is, "God's gift," meaning that the conversion of the Jews was an event that God wanted and that God gave as a gift to the Muslims and the Jews who converted. The converts were called Jadīd al-Islām or, briefly, Jadīdīm. The Jews, too, called the event Allahdād but did not know the precise meaning of the expression. Subsequently, they interpreted it as meaning that the event was God's punishment, meted out to them for their sins.

A particularly sensitive blow for the families who survived the Allahdād was that the Muslims captured several young Jewish women and took them into their harems or sold them to others as servants, that is to say, concubines. That this indeed did happen was reported a few months after the event by Mullah Harun (Aharon), one of the Meshhed Jadīdīm, to the British traveler J. Abbott, who recorded it in his 1842 book, *Narrative of a Journey from Herat to Khiva.*[13] Dilmanian himself reports that two young Jewish girls, Hannah and Mikhal, were taken by the *mujtahid* of Meshhed as his share in the Allahdād, Allah's gift.

A painful development that disturbed the inner peace of the Jadīdī community for many years after the Allahdād was remembered by successive generations and reported by Dilmanian: the Jadīdīm felt strong resentment toward that handful of Jews who, inadvertently or purposefully, played a role in triggering the Allahdād and initiating the mass conversion to Islam. They could not forgive Abraham his carelessness in throwing the carcass of a dog in the way of the Muslim religious procession and thereby giving the excuse or the impetus to the rioters to attack the Jews. As the years passed, Abraham's position in Meshhed became untenable, and twenty years later, he and his family felt forced to leave the city. The Jadīdīm were also resentful toward the Ḥakīmī and Raḥmānī families, whose members had been the first to save their lives by announcing that they were ready to accept Islam, and had given in to the demand of the Muslims to see to it that the rest of the Meshhed Jews also converted. The guilt ascribed to these families rankled for several generations, and as recently as 1966, a descendant of the Ḥakīmīs, himself a fervent Zionist and a teacher in a Tel Aviv school, felt motivated to reexamine what had happened and wrote a pamphlet in which he tried to explain the events of the Allahdād.[14]

A different version, based on other contemporary sources, was given in an article by Y. Ben-'Ami.[15] It states that in the year 5599 (1839), the year of the pogrom, the Jewish community of Meshhed consisted of some four hundred families, most of whom were well-to-do. On the day of the 'Ashūrah, the tenth of the month of Muḥarram, a young Meshhedi Jew by the name of Nadir slaughtered a dog after his friends advised him to immerse his hand in the warm blood of the dog. When Nadir slaughtered the dog, its yelps were heard outside the house, and a Muslim who happened to pass by alerted his Muslim brothers and told them, "The Jews killed a dog on our national day of mourning—intending to indicate that this dog symbolized the holy Riza 'Alī!"

Hundreds of fanatic Muslims broke into the Jewish quarter, murdered thirty-seven Jews, wounded many others, and destroyed much property with fire. Of the dozens of stores owned by Jews, only four remained undamaged. Thirty Jews were arrested and taken before the local mufti, the Imām Jum'ah, who told them that they would be spared only if they accepted Islam. The captives accepted Islam outwardly, and at the demand of their captors promised them that they would influence the other Jews of Meshhed to convert likewise.

Yet another version differs in several details from the others. It states that the attack took place not in Nissan 1839 but in the summer of 1840, and it gives the number of Jews killed not as thirty-six or thirty-seven but as fifty-two:

> Meshhed, Great Persia. There the Jews were libelled with an evil libel that they took the little son of a Persian woman from his mother, and killed him and threw him into the courtyard of the synagogue from the roof. Then, right away, they [the libelers] went and complained against them to the Persian ruler of the city, and said that in that night the Jews had stolen a Persian infant. They went to the houses and courtyards quickly that same night, to search for him, but did not find him. Then they went to the synagogue and found the infant, whom they themselves threw into the courtyard, and took the murdered infant to the ruler, and he gave permission to the men of the troops, and they left not even one child, and they killed the heads of the families, about 52, in two days, and only twelve handsome young men of beautiful stature were spared, for pederasty, and they had to convert in order to save themselves.
>
> This event took place between the months of Tammuz-Av. And in that year the men of the troops were changed, and went to Urmi, the land of Af-shar in Little Persia, and some of those young men fled to Teheran, the place of the royal throne. When the troops returned to Urmi in the course of forty days, [the youths] told King [Shah] Muḥammad (r. 1834–1848) everything that had passed in Meshhed, and asked the permission of the king to return to the faith of Moses and Judaism, and should he want to kill [them], let him kill [them], for they wanted only Judaism, and converted [to Islam only] to be able to tell him [this].
>
> And the wrath of the king was kindled because of the evil that the enemy did, and he gave them [the youths] permission to return to their faith, with good gifts for having told [him], and the king sent a *sarhang* [officer] with troops, and they apprehended all the chiefs who were guilty of treason, about thirty or forty, and killed them in painful ways, and despoiled them and their

> houses. And the young men, who did not want to go to any country, said that they were afraid, and stayed in Teheran. The oldest was Zekhariah, master of the community. And all of them came to Teheran by way of the garden of Shah Bagi.[16]

This version differs greatly from the others. It does not speak of the killing of the dog at all, but instead tells of the murder of a Muslim child by Muslims, who threw its body into the synagogue courtyard and then accused the Jews of having killed the child. Once the murdered child was found in the synagogue courtyard, the attack and mass murder of the Jews followed inevitably. This version contains several other items not found in the others: twelve handsome Jewish youths are not killed so as to be used for pederasty; these youths escape from their captors and manage to complain to the Shah, who thereupon metes out severe punishment to the culprits.

Before leaving the Allahdād, which was to remain in the memory of the Meshhedi Jadīdīm as the most traumatic event of their history, let us try to reconstruct what truly seems to have happened. What actually caused the outbreak is probably lost forever. But once it started, it seems that some thirty or more men were killed by the mob, and the rest, under the threat of death, converted to Islam. Conversion was a rather simple procedure: it consisted of reciting the Muslim confession of faith, the Tawḥīd. Thereafter, each family had to make its own individual choice: to stay in Meshhed and live as Jadīd al-Islām, "new Muslims," while adhering to Judaism in secret, or to leave the city and seek safety in a Sunnī Muslim country, where the attitude toward the Jews was less inimical. It is not known how many of the Jadīdīm chose the first and how many the second alternative. But it is clear that for many years after the Allahdād, considerable numbers of them did emigrate, and consequently the size of the Jadīdī community went on shrinking. Those who stayed behind were such devoted Jews that after the forced conversion, it was most exceptional that a Jadīdī should actually abandon Judaism.

When the news of the Allahdād reached the capital, Teheran, it created considerable consternation in the court of Muḥammad Shah (r. 1834–1848). The Persian minister of foreign affairs, Mīrzā Mas'ūd, was dispatched to Meshhed to inquire into what actually had happened to the Jews of the city and to try to effect the return to them of the property looted from them. According to one source, Muḥammad Shah even received a delegation of Meshhed Jews, who gave him an account of the attacks, and the Shah gave them presents.[17] Dilmanian reports that after the Jews of Meshhed converted to Islam, the Imām Jum'ah agreed to return their looted property to them, and that a quantity of silk merchandise, whose owner had been killed in the Allahdād, was handed back to the Jewish community. The Jadīdīm sold the silk and used the money to purchase a plot of land for their cemetery.[18]

This last detail is characteristic of the position the Jadīdīm occupied in Meshhed after their conversion. Officially, they were Muslims, and it was mandatory for them to observe the laws and customs of Islam. But, at the same time, it was not expected of them that they would merge into the Muslim population; on the contrary, it was taken for granted that they would retain their ethnic individuality, marry among themselves, bury their dead in a separate cemetery, and gather for prayers in a mosque of their own. Such ethnic separatism under the canopy of a common religion was typical of the situation in Meshhed, not only among the Muslims but even among the Jews. Both before and after the Allahdād, groups of Jews who had moved to Meshhed from various places retained their separate identities and remained known as the Yezdis, Heratis, Qazwinis, and so on.

5
After the Allahdād

After the Allahdād, despite the basic change that it introduced into the life of the Meshhed Jews, now known as Jadīd al-Islām, they continued to pursue the occupations that had provided them with a living before. The merchants continued to sell their wares in the bazaar, those who had been engaged in trading across the Russian or Afghan border went on with their travels, those interested in Ṣūfī doctrines maintained friendly relations with the local Muslim Ṣūfī leaders, while a few continued to serve British interests in central Asia.

The tragic fate of the Jadīdī Efrayim Raḥman illustrates the dangers that had to be faced by those who engaged in diplomatic activity in central Asia in those days. In December 1841, British Foreign Secretary Lord Palmerston and the British Ambassador to Teheran, John MacNeil, entrusted Efrayim Raḥman with the mission of delivering by hand letters they wrote to the emir of Bukhara. Once Efrayim arrived in Bukhara, the letters, written in English, had to be translated into Bukharan, which was done by the Jew Yosef Shalem, a native of India, who had settled in Meshhed. He seems to have known not only Bukharan and English but also Italian and was involved in the fruitless efforts to liberate Stoddart and Conolly from Bukharan captivity.[1]

The emir of Bukhara was dissatisfied with the letters—he may have expected a response from Queen Victoria herself to letters he had written to her—and imprisoned the Jewish emissary. Efrayim was tortured, and it was demanded of him that he convert to Islam. It seems that Efrayim refused, arguing that he had already converted in Meshhed, as had all its Jewish inhabitants. This did not satisfy his captors, who continued to torture him until his ability to resist was broken, and he pronounced the conversion formula. Thereupon, instead of releasing Efrayim, the next day they beheaded him, in order, as they said, to prevent him from returning to Judaism.

Efrayim Raḥman, as well as his two brothers, Mullah Safi and Mullah Raḥman, served the British in the capacity of messengers, as we learn from a letter to the British envoy in Teheran written in April 1842 by Āqā Muḥammad 'Alī Yishqaft, who was a leader of the Ṣūfīs in Meshhed and in control of the work of the Raḥman brothers:

> A letter came from Bukhara in the affair of Efrayim, who was certainly executed. The reason was that the letter he brought did not contain a reply to the letters of the Emir of Bukhara. . . . Efrayim had no other purpose but to serve the British faithfully, and in doing so he lost his life. . . . Efrayim's brother, Mullah Safi, carried letters to Kandahar to Mayjud Tod . . . and the third brother, Mullah Raḥman, was sent by me to Khiva. . . . In short, these brothers were, and are, faithful servants of the British government. Because of me one of them fell victim to the gentlemen in Bukhara, and lost his life on a mission for the government of Britain.[2]

Ambassador MacNeil mentions in his letter of April 29, 1842, to the British foreign secretary the same incident and the other two Raḥman brothers:

> I enclose herewith the translation of a letter received from the agent in Meshhed. Your Excellency will learn from it with regret that Efrayim, a messenger who was employed by our mission through that agent, was executed in Bukhara. Nurullah Khan confirmed this information. . . . Efrayim's brothers, too, undertook missions in behalf of our public service, and gave proof of their unusual loyalty. Two of them were sent with large amounts of money to Conolly in Khiva, and continued to Kokand. . . .
>
> I was informed that Efrayim left behind a wife and children. It seems to me that it will be proper to give them something for their livelihood. I assume that the amount of one hundred pounds sterling will be sufficient. I request permission to recommend that such an amount should be given to the family of Efrayim, in addition to the fee for his last mission that was promised him when he went to Bukhara, and I shall pay it instantly from the account of the mission.[3]

A few months later, MacNeil obtained more information about the death of Efrayim from Ragheb Bey, the servant of the British emissary Stoddart (also killed in Bukhara): "The Jew Efrayim was with us. . . . He was imprisoned in the fortress. . . . Efrayim was repeatedly beaten in order to force him to recite the *kalām* [conversion formula] and to convert to Islam. Finally Efrayim was broken, and recited the *kalāmeh*. . . . Next day he was brought out of the pit, and we thought that he would be freed, but they cut off his head; this was done in order to prevent him from repenting and returning [to Judaism]."[4]

We know of two other Meshhed Jews who undertook to serve the British. They were Ibrāhīm and Mūsā Nathan.[5] Even after the execution of Efrayim in

Bukhara the new British ambassador in Teheran, Justin Sheil, was of the opinion that a Meshhed Jew stood a better chance of obtaining information in Bukhara about the fate of Conolly and Stoddart than a Persian Muslim. He therefore suggested to Foreign Secretary Lord Aberdeen that a Meshhed Jew should be found to undertake the trip to Bukhara and to institute inquiries about the fates of Stoddart and Conolly. In the same letter, he informed Aberdeen that he had sent a messenger to Meshhed with instructions to the former secret agent of Stoddart to locate and engage a Jew to go to Bukhara for this purpose. He also told Aberdeen that according to a Jewish informant, it was known in Kabul, Merv, and Meshhed that the two officers had been executed.[6]

Mullah Mahdī, with whom we are by now well acquainted, continued to play an important role in the service of British diplomacy after the Allahdād. In a letter Joseph Wolff addressed to the British Foreign Office on November 30, 1844, he writes:

> Mullah Mahdī, the Jew of Meshhed, who served the British in Kandahar in the role of *kazad bashi* [chief emissary], wrote to Yar Muhammad Khan [the ruler] in Herat, that if he wished to improve his relations with the British and to create ties of friendship with them, now is the right time for it. Therefore, Mullah Mahdī advised Yar Muhammad Khan to write to the king of Bukhara that he should receive Joseph Wolff with honors, and should send with him the officers Stoddart and Conolly, if they are still alive; and if they died, let him send Wolff back in honor, and with him the bodies of the two officers. . . . Yar Muhammad is a good friend of the Emir.[7]

The very fact that Mullah Mahdī could write such a letter to the ruler of Herat shows that he was a man of considerable influence, that he had personal connections with the ruler of Herat and was in a position to address suggestions to him.

While Wolff gives full credit to Mullah Mahdī for the services this head of the Meshhed Jews rendered him, he seems to have been less than truthful in stating that Mullah Mahdī asked him to baptize him.[8] This claim was "furiously" denied by Mullah Mahdī, as we know from Ferrier's report. Ferrier returned to Meshhed on December 5, 1845, a short time after Wolff had left the city, and reported:

> When I returned to Meshhed I again saw my old acquaintances Mirza Mohamed, the Tajar Bashi [chief of the merchants], and the English agent Mollah Mahdī. The latter was furious against Dr. Wolff, who had published a letter in an eastern paper, saying that he had converted the Mollah to Christianity. "How," he said, "could I, a Hebrew by birth, and by force a Mohamedan, how

could I be converted by the mediation of that crazy man? It would be to expose myself to the resentment of the fanatical population of this town. May the head of Wolff be covered with cinders, *khākister be ser-esh,* may he go blind, *kūr sheved,* for having told such a falsehood!" I could only console him by promising to send a letter from him to Dr. Wolff, in which he would desire him to retract his statement. By the intervention of this worthy man I made the acquaintance of the learned Kazi [*qāḍī*] of Herat, Mohamed Hasan.[9]

Apart from Mullah Mahdī's denial that he had converted to Christianity, which, considering the circumstances, seems to be the truth, we learn from this passage that Mullah Mahdī did not hide from a foreign visitor that he was "a Hebrew by birth, and by force a Mohamedan," and that he was a personal acquaintance of Muhammad Hasan, the *qāḍī* (chief religious judge) of the Afghan city of Herat. Thus, we get yet another detail about the influential position Mullah Mahdī occupied in Meshhed and in Afghanistan in the years immediately following the Allahdād.

In 1848, the Jewish traveler Israel Joseph Benjamin, who called himself Benjamin the Second (the first having been Benjamin of Tudela), visited Persia, but all he had to say in his travelogue of Meshhed was a very brief reference to the Allahdād.[10]

Armin Vámbéry, too, visited Meshhed in 1863–64, but the brief comment he makes about meeting a Jew there contributes nothing to our knowledge of the Jadīdī situation.

It was not until 1887 that a European Jewish traveler visited Meshhed and gave an account of the condition of the Jews and the trauma they underwent in 1839. Ephraim Neumark was born in Eastern Europe but taken by his parents to Eretz Israel and grew up there. At the age of twenty-three, he left Tiberias and set out on a three-year journey that took him to the Jewish communities of the eastern Mediterranean and central Asia. His travelogue was brief but informative. Neumark's Hebrew is typical of that of the Haskala, the Jewish Enlightenment, but he was a good observer and looked with a critical, almost scholarly, eye at the scenes he encountered. Of Meshhed, he writes (my literal translation from the Hebrew):

There can still be found in Meshhed old people who remember their religion and observe it in secret. But the children, who are recent arrivals, never saw Judaism in their days, and are total *goyim* [gentiles]. This thing is a well-hidden secret in Persia. . . . And after these refugees settle, each one where he finds [a place], he calls them S'domi [Sodomite], so that nobody of the people of the land [i.e., the non-Jews] should know that they are from Meshed. . . . I saw people with this designation in Kermanshah and Hamadan. . . . There is a

> street in Meshhed which is called "Maḥallah 'Edgar" [*sic*], a street of the Jews, and there are those who call it today "Maḥallah Jadīd," street of the converts. There did the Jews dwell formerly; however, today, if a Jew goes to that street, they will not let him cross the threshold of their house, lest he render unclean everything that is in the house, and, perhaps, lest they be accused of loving in the secret of their heart the sons of their fathers' religion.

Following a brief description of the Allahdād, which contains nothing new compared to the other accounts presented above, Neumark dwells at greater length on what had happened afterward:

> Slowly, slowly they forgot the religion of their fathers, except for a few, who separated themselves from the ways of the world, and remained secluded in their houses, and did what their heart desired. . . . The community remained without an arouser and without a reminder, except for two *s'gullot* [precious things], which had remained in their hands, and which they, both the righteous and the evil, guarded like the apple of their eyes: they were the Fast of the Tenth [Yom Kippur] and the Feast of Matzoth [Passover], as prescribed by law. The inhabitants of the city, far as they were from a place of [other] Jews, did not know when precisely was the time of these feasts of Israel. However, they would not transgress these two, but observed them in the secret of their tent. These two pearls were for them like two faithful witnesses that they were of the seed of the Jews. Nor were mixed marriages entered into during these years among the approximately four hundred families who were found there, with only about five or six exceptions. Also, every male child born to them they circumcised according to the law, since also the Persians do likewise, and to the *p'ri'ah* [uncovering the corona in circumcision] the simple people did not know how to pay attention.
>
> Some fifteen years passed over them in this condition, when God awakened the spirit of the young people among their notables, and they followed after God. Also, there was found among them one man of pure thought, who succeeded on his own in the study of the Torah, and became knowledgeable in the 'En Ya'aqov [Source of Jacob, a collection of legends from the Talmud, by Jacob ben Shlomoh ibn Ḥabīb, ca. 1445–ca. 1515], in research, homily and ethics, and all his days he studied the Torah of God. The whole community loved him very much, and he did not derive any benefit from them, but supported himself with difficulty from the work of his hands. . . .
>
> From that time on they would slaughter lambs for themselves according to the law [of the Torah], and the *t'rēfot* [unclean ones] they would sell through middlemen who were astute in their work and knew how to keep a secret. On every Sabbath day they would open their stores and would leave there somebody to watch over it, and they would gather in a secret place to pray in [a group of] ten. At midday they would again gather in the secret of the stairway,

> and bend their ear to hear studies from the mouth of their dear teacher, who is about thirty-five years old. They also arrange marriages in secret, and then go to the mosque to do according to the [religious] law of the inhabitants of the land. They visit diligently, day after day, the doors of the mosque that is over the tomb of Imām Riza, as do the strictest among the Persians. They also travel to visit the tomb of Muhammad in Mecca, and come back through Jerusalem, and see there the face of the rabbi, the Rishon l'Tziyon ["The First of Zion," title of the chief rabbi of Erez Israel], and take sweet counsel together. . . . However, there are among them also those who behave arbitrarily, with nobody protesting. But where are such people not found? Many fathers removed from their houses unclean soup vessels, and brought new ones in their stead, upon the endeavor of their children. . . .
>
> They are good-hearted, and each time there was a looting in the city of Herat they collected for the oppressed money and clothes and bread, and sent it to them through an occasional man. And if they recognize that a Jew came from afar, they seek counsel to speak to him in secret and to ask about the peace of their brethren, and to seek Torah from his mouth, if he has an answer.

Following these details, Neumark observes that Meshhed Jews are wont to visit the markets of Nizhnii Novgorod and Merv every year, from which we learn that in those days, the Meshhed Jews engaged in international commerce. Neumark continues:

> These Jadīdīm are honored in the eyes of the government and in the eyes of the other inhabitants, and are reputed to be of a faithful spirit. If an inhabitant comes to buy something in the evening and pays its price, or if he steps in to change a silver *kran* [q'rān] for copper coins, the storekeeper will scrutinize the *kran* with seven eyes to make sure that it is not a counterfeit; but if one of the Jadīdīm comes, and a silver *kran* is in his hands, the merchant will take it even at night with a mere glance. After three hours of the night have passed, the policemen who make the rounds of the city arrest everyone they find [outside], except the Jadīdīm. Also many of the public affairs are given into the hands of the faithful Jadīdīm. Even though in the secret of their hearts the inhabitants know that the Jadīdīm are not faithful to the ruling religion, that which answers everything [i.e., the silver] blinds the eyes of the *mujtahid*s at all opportune times, and the merchants keep their mouth closed, lest their business be harmed, and in general the inhabitants do not wish to reveal their shame, for their lives depend on the guests who visit the tomb of their saint, and therefore they cannot desecrate his honor, for if it should become known that Jews [too] enter that house, and there are among them even those who are appointed to be in charge of the affairs of the house and its income, the house will become defiled, and all its pomp will depart from it, and the people of Meshhed, where will they be? And where should they go with their shame? Hence there is nobody who opens his mouth and whistles. . . .

> In Meshhed the Jadīdīm do not buy bread from a bakery, but each one of them bakes bread in his house, and if their vessels run out of bread, and there is no place from where they could borrow, only then do they buy bread in the marketplace, very unwillingly. This custom seems to have been retained among them from ancient times.[11]

In addition to the lively, and unquestionably reliable, picture of the life of the Jadīdīm given by Neumark, we learn from him three important new details. One is that the Jadīdīm were considered honest and were trusted by the Muslim merchants, allowed to walk about at night when others would be arrested by the police; the second is that some of them were in charge of the financial affairs of the great mosque of Imām Reza; and the third is that their adherence to Judaism was known to the people and their religious leaders, but because of the financial advantage they derived from the Jadīdīm, and the damage the pilgrimage business would have suffered had the admission of secret Jews to the mosque become known, they kept silent about it.

Neumark did not spend enough time in Meshhed to become cognizant of the internal divisions that had developed by the time of his visit. What had taken place was that while the Jadīdīm sought to adjust to the new life that was imposed upon them by the Allahdād and their forced acceptance of Islam, marked differences developed within the community between those who remained as committed and as faithful to Judaism as was possible under the circumstances and those who inclined more to Islam and felt that the Jadīdīm should conduct themselves according to the laws and rules of Islam and thus avoid further clashes with the Muslim majority of the city. It was not until the middle of the twentieth century that an Iranian Jewish student of the history of the Jews in Iran paid attention to this issue and discussed it in a study that has not been published in full. The scholar is Ya'aqov Dilmanian, whose treatise, written in Persian and titled "Tārīkh-ī Isrā'īlhā-ī Meshhed az vorūd bi Meshhed dar zamān-ī Nādir Shāh-i Afshār ilā muhājirat az Meshhed" (History of the Israelites in Meshhed from Their Arrival in Meshhed in the Days of Nadir Shah Afshar Until Their Emigration from Meshhed), which he completed after 1960, was distributed in a few typewritten copies and was summarized in Hebrew by Amnon Netzer in a 1990 article. From Dilmanian's account, as well as from other sources, it appears that most of the Jadīdīm belonged to the first group, those of the faithful. They tried to justify their act of apostasy by arguing that unless they were willing to sacrifice their lives and the lives of their families, they had no choice, and for the sake of their safety, they were forced to assume the guise of Muslim observance, at the same time doing everything possible to maintain the knowledge and practice of Judaism in secret within the community. They objected to any close contact with the Muslims, including, in the first place, intermarriage with them. The details presented in chapters below on the life of the Jadīdīm will be a description of the thinking, feeling, and acting of this group. This faction was headed by the Kūlī, Nasīmī, and Aqlarī families and several immigrant families from Yezd.

Many members of this faction chose emigration over living as Jadīdīm in Meshhed. It was not easy to leave Meshhed, for the religious authorities kept a tight watch over comings and goings in the city. However, against payments of bribes, departures could be arranged. Most of those who left went to other cities in Khorasan, neighboring Herat in Afghanistan, others to Bukhara. Some seventy families settled in Deregez, a similar number in Turbat. In these two cities, they established Talmud Torah schools and *miqvehs,* ritual baths. (In Meshhed itself, more than a generation had to pass after the Allahdād before the Jadīdīm felt safe enough to reestablish schools and baths.) In the places of their settlement, they maintained their separate identity as Meshhedis, continued to speak the Gilaki dialect of Persian, and kept up correspondence and familial and commercial contact with their brethren who remained in Meshhed. The fact that the language of the letters was Judeo-Persian, written in Hebrew characters, contributed to the survival of familiarity with Hebrew among the Jews of Meshhed.[12]

Some information about the life and fate of those Meshhed Jews who chose to move to Herat rather than submit to forced conversion to Islam is available in a treatise written by R. Mattityahu Garji, who was the rabbi of Herat about the turn of the century.[13] He writes:

> Those who feared the word of God travelled from the city of Meshhed and came to Herat. From the year 5600 [1840] they lived in quiet and safety for seventeen years. . . . In the year 5617 [1857], because of our many sins, there came the army of Naṣr al-Dīn Shah, the Kajar king, upon the city of Herat and the city was under siege for nine months. At the end of the month of Tishri, 5617 [1856], the city was captured by tricks and wile, in peace [i.e., without fighting]. And day after day they abused the Jews with false accusations, and threatened us saying, "This and this is what you did; this and this is what we shall do to you." And they denounced us with calumnies, in order to decree exile for us, to make us go from this city and to exile us to Meshhed. And on the 15th day of Shevat, in the year 5617 [1857], oppressors attacked us, beating us with blows of death and destruction, saying: "Get out of your houses, for this is what the king decreed." And they drove out everybody, men, women and children, from their places, and did not respect either old or young, and none had mercy or pity. And the whole city resounded with the cry of the poor and the orphans, and they had no time to gather their money or to prepare provisions. And within three days they drove all of us out of the city, to a place called Mosallah. And on the 19th of Shevat they removed us from there. And close to thirty days we were on the way, and all around us were troops of *goyim,* and from Heaven, too, there came snow and hail and cold, and many souls perished

> on the way from the great cold and lack of bread, and other sufferings that cannot be described. And in the month of Adar, close to Purim, we reached the city of Meshhed, and they did not let us enter the city, but put us in animals' corrals, in a fortress called Bab Qudrat, a tight place and a prison, and we were subject to abuse and contempt.
>
> And several people abandoned their religion on the way because of the great suffering, and because of our sins the verse "Without shall the sword bereave, and in the chambers terror . . ." [Deut. 32:25], for the oppressors administered every day cruel punishment they inflicted upon us. And as for the renting of the camels that brought us from Herat, the camels were the property of the king, and most of those who rode them were poor and miserable, and they [the soldiers] imposed the rental fee on the rest of the people. And on the other hand, there was, God forbid, sickness and epidemics, and many souls died, and also other sufferings that are too many to tell, and as our masters had said, "captivity is harder than the sword." . . . And we were there two years, and at the end of the two years our sins were atoned, and our cry rose to God, and He put it into the heart of the king to allow us to return to our place. And in the month of Kislev, in the year 5619 [1859], we left Meshhed, and on Monday, the 13th of Teveth, we entered Herat, each man to his place, and blessed be He who has mercy on the creatures.[14]

This account given by Rabbi Garji of the two-year captivity of the Herat Jews in Meshhed, although detailed and accurate with dates, reveals nothing about the help the Jadīd al-Islām extended to their captive brethren. Below, in chapter 16, is a fuller version of the story of this captivity and release, as it was known to Āqā Farajullah and told by him to me in Jerusalem in 1946. The details contained in Āqā Farajullah's account, about the amount of ransom the Meshhed Jews paid to the governor of Meshhed and the manner in which they raised the very large sum, lend it a definite verisimilitude. The dates given in the two accounts differ, but the discrepancies between them are minor and insignificant.

One of the most important religious leaders of the Meshhed Jews in the late nineteenth century was Mullah Murād (Mordechai) Aqlar. Born in 1850, he was taught Torah by his father, then went on to studying Mishna and Gemara on his own, and later even translated much of these sacred texts into Judeo-Persian. He became a successful merchant, had commercial relations with Russian Turkmenistan, but while still young fulfilled the role of spiritual leader in his community. He became known as a great teacher, and on Sabbath afternoons, prior to the traditional Third Meal, people would gather to listen to his expositions. One of the community's synagogues was in the cellar of his house, and it was in the secrecy of that hidden place that he taught the youngsters Torah and the observance of the commandments. He functioned as circumciser and ritual slaughterer and issued decisions in religious ritual questions. All this he did without receiving any remuneration. He was also active in charity, gathering alms to support the poor and to provide poor girls with dowries, arranging weddings in accordance with the Jewish religious law. In times of trial, he was a veritable pillar of strength for his community. His son, Rafi Aqlar, assisted him in all his activities.

Since many members of the community had insufficient knowledge of Hebrew, Mullah Murād prepared Persian translations of the daily prayers, as well as the prayers for the Sabbath and the holidays, the Passover Haggadah, the *s'liḥot* (penitential poems) and other *piyyuṭim* (liturgical poems). His two prayer books—one for weekdays, titled *'Avodat haTamid* (The Perpetual Service), the other for the Sabbath, titled *'Olam Shabbat* (Sabbath World)—were published in 1908 with an approbation by Rabbi Eliyahu M. Panizhel and reprinted in 1970. His Persian translations of *piyyuṭim* for the High Holy Days were reprinted in Jerusalem and B'ne B'raq in 1975. His Persian commentaries to several books of the Bible have remained in manuscript.

Just prior to the Russian Revolution, Mullah Murād spent some time in Russia taking care of business affairs. At the outbreak of the revolution, he returned to Meshhed and stayed there until 1927, when he made his *'aliya* to Jerusalem. Settling in the Bukharian quarter, he continued to serve as religious leader of his community. He died in 1936 and was buried on the Mount of Olives.[15]

While Mullah Murād did his best to keep Jewish tradition alive in his community, some leaders of the "assimilant" faction, in particular the Ḥakīmī and Raḥmanī families and some of the Dilmanīs and Namdarīs, had shown an inclination toward Islam even prior to the Allahdād, and a few of them actually converted. It was a few Ḥakīmīs and Raḥmanīs who initiated the movement toward conversion during the Allahdād itself. Even though they took this step under the threat of death during the violent outburst of Muslim Allahdād frenzy, the majority of the community disliked them, and to some extent even ostracized them. After the Allahdād, members of this faction tried to behave in every respect as true Muslims, fulfilled the Muslim commandment of pilgrimage to the holy places, assumed typical Muslim names (such as Ḥājjī Muḥammad Ḥusayn, Ḥājjī Muḥammad 'Alī, Shaykh Abu'l-Qāsem), visited the mosque diligently, observed the mourning for the saintly Imāms, and invited Muslims to meals in their homes on festive occasions. Some of them even intermarried with Muslims, while others found employment in the Muslim religious institutions of the city. One Jadīdī, Mīrzā Āqājān Kurd, worked as guard of the public buildings of the great mosque complex. Another, Ḥājjī Nizār 'Alī Baṣṣālī, was in charge of the treasury of the mosque whose income was derived mostly from contributions by the many pilgrims, and in this capacity had to go frequently to Teheran. There, he tried to free himself of his Meshhed obligations, and after some difficulties, including a period of imprisonment, he succeeded in around 1866 in remaining in Teheran.[16]

Travels to other countries, especially to Afghanistan, Bukhara, India, Iraq, and later also to Turkey and England, and contact with the Jews in those places resulted in strengthening the Jewish consciousness of the Jadīdīm. About a generation after the Allahdād, Ḥājjī Mullah Amīn Kurdvānī, a leader of the community, traveled frequently to Hamadan and Teheran, and upon his return to Meshhed, he would bring with him copies of the Persian translation of the Bible, which he gave as gifts to young couples and students who excelled in their studies in the secret Jewish school maintained by the community.[17]

According to Dilmanian, the first copies of a Persian Bible translation, prepared by a Christian Bible society in London, reached Meshhed in 1856, and "prior to that time the Jews of Meshhed had no complete knowledge of the content of the Torah." The copies of the Persian Bible were so much sought after that parents included them among the bridal outfit they supplied to their daughters. Dilmanian adds, "In my opinion, one of the factors that made for the survival of the religion of our fathers was the distribution of this Persian translation of the Torah."[18]

6

Conversions to the Bahai Faith

What Āqā Nasrullayoff had to say about the danger posed by the Bahai faith to the Jews of Meshhed is most interesting. The Bahai faith was founded by Mīrzā Ḥusayn 'Alī (1817–1892), known as Bahā' Ullah ("The Splendor of God"), who built on the teachings of his predecessor Sayyid 'Alī Muḥammad (known as al-Bāb, i.e., "The Gate"). It began to spread in Persia in the middle of the nineteenth century and, despite energetic and often cruel measures taken to suppress it, won many followers, whose numbers were variously estimated to have reached between half a million and one million in Iran by the end of the century. The Bahai faith upholds the oneness of God, enjoins its followers to search after the truth, teaches the unity of the human race and the essential unity of all religions, requires science and religion to be in harmony, insists on equal rights and duties of men and women, opposes all kinds of prejudice (national, religious, political, economic, etc.), demands universal education, has world peace as its ultimate goal, and espouses several more such lofty ideals. No wonder that, as against the intolerance and narrow-mindedness of Shī'ī Islam in whose shadow the Jadīdīm were forced to live, Bahaism appeared to some of them a noble and ideal religion of considerable attractiveness. This is what Āqā Nasrullayoff had to say about the encounter of the Meshhed Jews with Bahaism:

> There were a few instances of conversion of Meshhedi Jews to the Bahai faith. The events that led up to it were as follows. Prior to the conquest of Turkmenistan by the Russian army, the Turkomans of Merv [Marw], Tajan, Yamut, and Gurgan[1] would frequently attack and loot the defenseless inhabitants of the land. Especially the Iranian province of Khorasan suffered much from their incursions, which made the roads so insecure as to render them practically impassable. But since the Meshhedi Jews needed to trade in order to subsist, they began traveling to the nearby city of Turbat,[2] to conduct their business dealings there and provide their families with a livelihood. Turbat was a populous city, and since the Meshhedi Jews had adopted Muslim names, they were able to set

up shops there. At one point in time, the Meshhedi Jews, who posed as Jadīd al-Islām, owned as many as seventy shops in Turbat. They continued to reside in Meshhed and commuted back and forth. The changing times led to transformations in the lives of the Jews of Meshhed.

This period coincided with the advent of the Bahai movement. The Bahai leaders managed to mislead a large segment of the population of Birjand,[3] and with their intensive propaganda induced them to convert to Bahaism. Their propaganda efforts reached Turbat, with the result that many of its inhabitants also converted. Since the Jews suffered much from Islam, they allowed themselves to be deceived by the Bahai movement. Of the seventy Jewish shopowners in Turbat, sixty-three converted to the Bahai faith.

The Bahai movement was very active. Several times a year, the Bahais would receive additional religious instruction [from the movement's founder and self-proclaimed prophet, Sayyid Muḥammad Bāb].[4] Religious instruction for the Bahais was given by Gabriel the Messenger.[5] Suddenly, a new religious law was issued; it prohibited the consumption or use of alcoholic beverages, intoxicating substances, and tobacco products. Any substances that could cause inebrity to any extent, such as salt, pepper, onions, cinnamon, garlic, cloves, and similar spices, were considered intoxicating substances. In fact, no less than some seventy kinds of spices were specified as contributing to inebrity according to these new Bahai laws. The prohibition banned the use of salt, pepper, and other spices in dough or other food, as well as the consumption of onions and garlic. The ban included tobacco, opium, hemp juice, as well as smoking pipes, hookahs, and narghilehs.[6] As a result of these new laws, a large majority of the new Bahai converts found their lives too restrictive, and most of them eventually abandoned the Bahai faith as too demanding and burdensome.

A year after the mass desertions from the Bahai faith, new religious decrees were handed down. They contained revised articles of the faith and cited the hardships imposed upon the Bahais by the previous prohibitions as the basis of a complete reversal. The seventy substances originally prohibited, such as alcohol, tobacco, and spices, were now declared lawful and ritually permitted. As soon as these new decrees were issued, the seven Jewish shopowners who had not previously converted to Bahaism saw an opportunity to expose the Bahai faith. They explained to the Jews who had accepted Bahaism that divine laws were permanent and irrevocable and could not simply be modified or annulled in order to satisfy human desires. The Bahai laws were obviously man-made and not of divine origin. After all, did the god, who only a year previously gave commandments banning alcohol, tobacco, and spices, not realize in advance that these restrictions would impose great hardships upon the Bahai people, and that they would not be able to subsist without salt, pepper, and spices in their food? Can a god act in error that he should declare lawful that which previously he himself had prohibited, and do so only after their prophet was informed of the people's hardships? This god therefore was not a god, and neither was the prophet a true prophet. Realizing their grave error, the Jews who had joined the Bahai faith returned to Judaism.

However, seven individuals remained committed to Bahaism until the very end. They were Āqā Shavardī Zargar, Āqā Shavardī Zuqālī, 'Azīzullah Namdar (the brother of Mullah Khudādād Kohen), Ḥājjī, the son of Mullah Nāṣir, Āqāi Beth Āqā Raḥmanī, and Āqā Ṣādiq, the son of Mullah Yehudah Nissim. As to this last one, although he outwardly professed his commitment to Judaism, it was clear to all that at heart he remained a Bahai. The others did not hide their strong commitment to Bahaism. Mysteriously, each and every one of them suffered the punishment of divine wrath. None of them, nor the children they had at the time, had surviving offspring. Their seed became totally cut off. The only exceptions were two of their children who later repented and reaffirmed their faith in Judaism.

Let me mention here that there were also a few individuals of the Ḥakīmī family who had become Muslims at heart. None had surviving children, and their seed was also cut off. All the other Jews remained committed to Judaism despite all the hardships. Their families have survived to this day.

This brief account of Meshhedi Jews who converted to the Bahai faith and of members of the Ḥakīmī family who truly and fully adopted Islam is, as far as is known to me, the only existing reference to individuals who became guilty of apostasy among the Meshhedi Jews.

7

A Decade of Blood Libels and Other Incidents, 1892–1902

Even after the Allahdād and the forced conversion of many of the Jews of Meshhed, the Muslims again and again accused them of criminal wrongdoing, with the intention of creating a situation in which the Jadīdīm would come to grievous harm. However, as Āqā Farajullah never tired of repeating in the course of his stories, with the help of God, their wicked plots were foiled, and the Jews remained unharmed. One such case took place in 1892:

> In the year 5652 [1892], Ḥājj Shaykh Muḥammad Tāghī Bijnāwardī was the foremost religious leader in Meshhed. Among the other religious leaders were Ḥājj Mīrzā Ḥabībullah, Ḥājj Muḥammad Bāgher Shefātī, Āqā Mīrzā Muḥammad, and Ḥājj Mīrzā Ibrāhīm. In those days, religious scholars and clerics were very influential in Meshhed. It was common knowledge that Shaykh Bijnāwardī hated the Jews with a passion.
>
> It was in those days that seven Sayyids [religious functionaries who claimed descent from the Prophet Muhammad], who resided in the vicinity of the ʻĒdgāh (the Jewish quarter), plotted against the Jews: they hid an eight-year-old Muslim boy and then appeared before Ḥājj Muḥammad and the other clergymen with a false testimony. Mullah Ibrāhīm, the rabbi of the Jews, they asserted, had kidnapped the boy, slaughtered him in his home, and disposed of his body in the latrine. They claimed to have located the child's body after a thorough search, to have administered the ritual "sixty immersions," and then buried him as required by Islamic law.
>
> The accusation created great uproar in the city, and the mob went into action against the Jews. At noontime and in the evening, they assembled in the Gōharshad mosque[1] and gathered up the prayer mats, preventing thereby the clergymen from praying. They clamored for justice and demanded that all the Jews of the city be killed.
>
> The Muslim clergymen and scholars knew that the blood libel was but a conspiracy against the Jews, nor did it remain hidden before them that Ḥājj Muḥammad was its prime instigator. The situation deteriorated to the point where it was dangerous for a Jew to appear in public or to go to the marketplace.

The Jews felt unsafe even in their own homes, and many sought refuge in the houses of the Muslim clergymen and religious authorities. Some went to the residence of Ḥājj Mīrzā Ḥabībullah, others gathered at the homes of Āqā Mīrzā Muḥammad and Ḥājj Mīrzā Ibrāhīm. There was even a group of some seventy to eighty Jewish men who sought refuge in the home of Ḥājj Muḥammad Bijnāwardī. However, unlike the others, Ḥājj Muḥammad did not allow the Jews to enter his house, so that they crowded in his entrance hall and occupied his corridors, sitting about on the floor. They had to face constant mockery and annoyance, and Muslim scholars and scribes repeatedly approached them and dinned into their ears the principles of Muslim law and doctrine, trying to provoke them to a quarrel. By contrast, other clerics treated the Jews courteously and gave them places to sit.

Reports of the disturbances reached the provincial governor general. He summoned Nāyeb Muḥammad, the Muslim head of the ʿĒdgāh quarter,[2] and questioned him about the veracity of the reports and accusations about the kidnapping of a Muslim boy by the Jews and the details of the alleged murder. Nāyeb Muḥammad gave no credence to the reports and said that had such an occurrence taken place, the governor would have been notified immediately. He stated that he was convinced that the accusations were totally false and fabricated. The governor on his part promised Nāyeb Muḥammad a generous reward if he succeeded in locating the missing boy.

The Nāyeb had considerable experience in locating missing children. However, by sheer coincidence, as he was passing the Pey Bareh street on official business, he spotted a young boy playing in the street and recognized him as the boy whom the Jews were supposed to have killed. He immediately grabbed the child's hand and quizzed him about what he was doing in that place. The child's answer was: "Three days ago, my father brought me here to my aunt's house. He told me not to leave the courtyard under any circumstance. Today, when my aunt went to the bathhouse, she again warned me not to go outside. But I was so bored and homesick that I went out to play in the street." Nāyeb Muḥammad brought the child before the governor and identified him as the boy the Jews had been accused of having killed. The governor instructed the Nāyeb to take the boy to the homes of the clergymen where the Jews had taken refuge, so that all should be witness that the boy was alive and well. He also commanded the Nāyeb to inform the clergymen that it was the boy's father who had hidden his son in the house of an aunt, as part of the conspiracy to wreak havoc upon the Jews of Meshhed.

I myself [writes Farajullah Nasrullayoff] was among the group that had sought refuge in the home of Ḥājj Shaykh Muḥammad Tāghī Bijnāwardī. [He was nineteen years old at the time.] Half an hour before sunset, the seven Sayyids appeared, accompanied by a mob of some two hundred men. They repeated their allegation that the Jews had brutally slaughtered a Muslim boy and disposed of his body in the latrine of their rabbi, Mullah Ibrāhīm. They testified that they personally had seen twenty-seven slashes on the body of the innocent child. The seven Sayyids threw their turbans to the ground, demanding justice. They importuned Ḥājj Muḥammad to sign a decree permitting the massacre and—*ḥas v'shalom* [God forbid!]—extermination of the Jewish community of Meshhed.

In the midst of all this commotion, Nāyeb Muḥammad entered the room, holding on firmly to the boy's hand. Because of the dense crowd that filled the room, only those near the entrance realized that the Nāyeb had found the boy. The seven Sayyids and the other instigators continued to rage and demand "justice." Suddenly, the news spread [like wildfire] that the boy had been found and was right there in the room. The seven Sayyids realized that their deception had been exposed, and they quickly fled the scene. Also, the other instigators made themselves scarce. Ḥājj Muḥammad, who was believed to have been the chief architect of the conspiracy, grew pale and grim-faced. But—instead of thanking God that the boy had been found sound and safe—he arrogantly instructed the Nāyeb to take the boy to the governor. Nāyeb Muḥammad replied that the governor had seen the boy, and that it was he who instructed him to take the boy and show him to all the religious leaders before returning him to his parents.

Ḥājj Muḥammad's servants informed us that we were excused and could return to our homes. However, the elders of our community replied, "We shall not budge until we are given a signed document stating that the entire incident was a conspiracy, and that two hundred Muslim men were willing to give false testimony in order to bring harm upon us merely out of contempt for the Jews." Ḥājj Muḥammad refused to issue such a document. Thereupon the Jews themselves drafted a letter, describing in detail all the events, and had it signed and certified by all the other clergymen involved. Then they presented it to Ḥājj Muḥammad and told him that they would not leave his house until he signed the document. Seeing that all the other clergymen had signed it, the Ḥājj had no choice but to append his signature as well, otherwise his own evil intentions would have been exposed.

That night, we reached our homes about midnight. Following this incident, the Jewish community of Meshhed enjoyed a long period of peace.

This incident was described also by Mullah Yosef ben Āqā 'Abdul-Samad Dilmānī of Meshhed in 1939.[3] Yosef Dilmānī was a teacher of the Jewish school in Meshhed who by 1939 could look back upon many years of service in the community. Incidentally, among his pupils in the 1920s was Yoḥanan (Nematollah) Livian, the son of Āqā Farajullah Nasrullayoff, who in 1944–45 in Jerusalem, and again in 1993–94 in New York, rendered me invaluable help in writing this book. Dilmānī places the incident not in 1892, as does Nasrullayoff, but in 1890. The villain of the piece, according to Dilmānī, was called Shaykh Muḥammad Tāqī (according to Nasrullayoff, Shaykh Muḥammad Tāghī Bijnāwardī), and the one who protected the Jews was Ḥājjī Mīrzā Ḥabīb (in Nasrullayoff's account, Ḥājj Mīrzā Ḥabībullah), who gave them refuge in his house. These minor discrepancies apart, Nasrullayoff's version is much fuller and more detailed than the one given by Dilmānī.

A third version of the same incident found its way into the memoirs of Ya'aqov Dilmanian, according to whom it took place in 1891. Dilmanian also reports on two more attacks that occurred in 1902, about two years later. The instigator of these two attacks was a certain Shaykh Ibrāhīm, and both were stopped by the intervention of soldiers.[4] According to Mullah Yosef Dilmānī, who reports on them in some detail, these incidents took place in 1900 and 1902. He writes that 1900

> was a year of famine in Meshhed, and the price of commodities was very high. The Muslims gathered in the courtyard of the mosque, and accused the Jews of having hoarded and hidden in their cellars all the wheat and other foodstuffs, "and we are starving to death. Come, let us break into their houses, seize the wheat and loot what we can." When they left the mosque on the way they first attacked the bakeries which belonged to Muslims, and then they moved on the houses of the Jews. On their way there they attacked the house of one of the respected Muslims, by the name of Naqib, and looted it. Then they went on, but before they could reach the Jewish houses they were stopped by soldiers who had been sent by the authorities, so that they could not carry out their intentions.

Two years later, in 1902, the Muslims again went into action against the Jews. Dilmānī relates:

> They gathered in the mosque, and planned to attack the Jews, saying, "They all are *zhīds* [sic], they do not intermarry with us, the real Muslims, the meat we eat they do not eat, and on the Sabbath they do not work." Among them was Shaykh Ibrāhīm. When they fell upon the houses of the Jews they broke into the house of Yaḥya Baṣṣāl, and began to destroy it and to loot it. May God remember Ḥājjī Mu'ban, who was one of the respected Muslims, and have mercy on him! At the time of the attack he was in his house, having his midday meal, and since he was a man who loved his fellow-men and a well-wisher of the Jews, when he heard of the attack he rose up from his table, bare-footed and dressed only in his undergarments (for he had no time to put on his clothes), and hurried to help the Jews. This event took place in the month of Tammuz [July–August]. When he got to the house of . . . Mr. Yaḥya, he pulled Shaykh Ibrāhīm from the house, put him on the donkey, and took him from there. And the crowd dispersed.[5]

These libelous accusations leveled against the Jadīdīm in 1890 (or 1892) and again in 1902 indicate that by the end of the nineteenth century, the pretense that they had become Muslims was largely abandoned, and their continued adherence to Judaism was public knowledge. However, for various economic and administrative reasons, and most probably also because the Jadīdīm knew how to buy the authorities' goodwill with lavish gifts, no official proceedings were instituted against them, even though, according to Muslim law, any Muslim, whether of old Muslim stock or newly converted, who abandoned Islam became guilty of a capital crime. It was in this situation that some fanatically religious Muslim clergymen (such as the Sayyids who figure in the accounts) resorted to blood libel in order to incite the mob against the Jews, who, they felt, deserved death.

The accounts of the 1890 (1892) incident also afford a certain insight into the power structure in the intensely religious city of Meshhed. The mob was suffused with strong anti-Jewish feelings, nourished by the Shī'ī doctrine according to which Shī'ī Islam was the only correct religion, and all other religions, including those followed by the "People of the Book," that is, Jews, Christians, and Zoroastrians, and even Sunnī Islam, were sinful aberrations from the truth. The religious fervor became intensified especially around the tenth of the month of Muḥarram, the 'Ashūrah, when Shī'ī Islam commemorates the martyr death of its greatest religious figure, Ḥusayn, the son of 'Alī and grandson of Muhammad, with public mourning that included (and in many places still includes) self-laceration with swords and chains. The religious frenzy of the mob triggered by the sight of the bleeding mourners was easily transformed into rage against all those who were not followers of 'Alī and Ḥusayn, and it took not more than a word from a Sayyid, one of the venerated descendants of that sacred family of prophets and Imāms, for the pent-up emotions to overflow into bloody attacks against the only visible unbelievers in Meshhed, the Jadīd al-Islām, that is, the Jews.

This was the background of the Allahdād of 1839, and the fact that no such attack took place in 1890 (or 1892) indicates that in the fifty or so years that had passed since the Allahdād, the power of the authorities in the city had increased, and the Sayyids felt that no longer could they with impunity incite the mob to action. Instead, as the reports show, they tried to obtain legitimization of killing the Jadīdīm by having the supreme religious authorities in the city issue a decree that the Jews were guilty of having killed a Muslim child and therefore were to be punished by death.

Characteristic of the situation is the role of the unnamed governor of the city. He did not try to prevent the planned mass murder of the Jadīdīm by insisting on a proper legal procedure to establish who, if any, among them was guilty of killing the child. It seems that he did not feel strong enough to oppose the crowd clamoring for Jewish blood and the religious leaders who incited them. The power of the religious authorities in the shrine city of Meshhed seems to have been supreme. Even when the innocence of the Jadīdīm was proven by the reappearance of the missing child safe and sound, the governor did nothing more than have the child shown to the Sayyids and the mob, to make them desist from their murderous plan. We hear not a word about any punishment meted out to the conspirators, who plotted the murder of hundreds of innocent Jadīdīm. Had they been punished in any way, it would undoubtedly have been preserved in the Jewish folk tradition.

The picture we get of the ambiguous position of the Jews in Meshhed in the late nineteenth century is that it was generally known that they adhered to the Jewish faith, and this was tacitly albeit grudgingly tolerated by the Muslim civil and religious leadership. But the mood of the crowd remained strongly anti-Jewish throughout, and the slightest provocation or excuse was sufficient to bring its feelings to the point of outbreak. What made the position of the Jadīdīm especially precarious was the fact that, in those days, the city's authorities had no effective police or any other armed forces at their disposal, so that the mob, once aroused, could attack the small Jewish minority practically unhindered.

In conclusion of this sorry chapter in the history of the Jadīdīm, a few words are in order about blood libel in Islam. While in the Medieval Christian world the libel that Jews used Christian blood for ritual and other purposes was first leveled in Norwich, England, in 1144 and was repeated thereafter frequently all over Europe, in the Muslim realm such accusations were rare. Still, they were of sufficient import to induce Sultan Mehmed II ("the Conqueror," r. 1451–1481) to issue a decree removing such cases from the jurisdiction of local governors and judges and ordering them to be brought before the Imperial Divan in Istanbul, where, as Bernard Lewis put it, "presumably, the high officers of state would be less subject to bigotry and superstition and less open to local pressures."[6] The same decree was renewed by Suleyman the Magnificent (r. 1520–1566) and repeated by subsequent rulers in the sixteenth and seventeenth centuries. It was, however, not until the nineteenth century that such libels became common and began to constitute serious problems for Jews in the Muslim world. To quote Lewis again, "by this time, the European and Christian origin of these charges is beyond doubt."[7]

Most famous (or rather infamous) of these libels was the one that became known as the Damascus Affair of 1840, in which Jews were accused of having killed for ritual purposes a Capuchine monk and his servant. A large number of Jews were arrested, many of them tortured, and it took the energetic intervention of the most influential Jewish statesmen of England and France to obtain the release of the surviving Jewish prisoners, and the issuance of a *ferman* by the Sultan denouncing the ritual murder accusation as baseless libel and reaffirming the intention of the Ottoman authorities to give full protection to the Jews.[8]

Despite this offical position, the blood libel reappeared within the boundaries of the Ottoman Empire dozens of times between 1840 and 1902.[9] In contrast, in Iran, which remained longer unaffected by European influence, the blood libel appeared later and was relatively rarer. In the early 1850s, a Jew of Urmia was accused of having murdered a Muslim child and was killed and burned by the mob, but there is no indication that the accusation had a ritual character.[10]

Next in chronological order comes the Meshhed blood libel of 1890 or 1892. It is followed by a case in Shiraz in 1910, which seems to have originated in the libel of a vengeful Jewish prostitute who had been punished by the Jewish community for her misconduct.[11] Again, in 1942 and 1946, about Passover, as detailed below in chapter 9, rumors that the Jews killed or planned to kill Muslim children in order to use their blood for their holiday were sufficient to trigger bloody attacks on the Jewish quarter of Meshhed. The saddest aspect of these occurrences is that the blood libel, which was imported into the Muslim world as recently as the late nineteenth century, became soon thereafter part of the Muslim stereotype of the Jews and the basis of repeated mob attacks on them.

8

ZIONISM AND EARLY *'ALIYA*

Observant Jews recite three times daily the 'amidah prayer, part of which is voicing the hope that God will return to Zion and the request that he rebuild Jerusalem. This was the basis of the religious Zionism that for centuries has been an integral part of Jewish consciousness in all parts of the Diaspora. Iranian Jewry was no exception in this respect. Despite the existence of only the most tenuous contacts between it and the rest of the Jewish world, and hence a general ignorance of what was going on in the faraway Palestinian provinces of the Ottoman Empire, the desire to settle in Jerusalem burned in their hearts and motivated some of them to undertake the hazardous journey.

The first group of Persian Jews to go to the land of Israel set out in 1815 from Shiraz in a caravan, trekked to the port of Bushehr (usually a two-week trip), and waited there for a ship to take them to Basra in southern Iraq, from where they went overland to Baghdad and then on to Damascus, where they arrived half-dead from thirst and starvation. Some of them remained in Damascus, and the rest went on to Safed and Jerusalem,[1] establishing the nucleus of an Iranian Jewish community in those two holy cities.

Another route taken by the early Persian Jewish immigrants to the Holy Land was by ship from Bushehr to Port Said, Egypt, and from there by caravan across the northern Sinai Desert to Jerusalem. Both journeys took months and abounded in dangers. Still, the number of Persian immigrants increased in the course of the nineteenth century, and by 1892, the number of Shirazi Jews in Jerusalem had reached one thousand.[2] In the three decades from 1919 to 1948, 3,536 Iranian Jews settled in Palestine, which number was dwarfed by the large-scale *'aliya* that followed the establishment of Israel: in the first twenty-five years of the Jewish state's existence, no fewer than fifty thousand Jews went from Iran to Israel, of them nine thousand to fourteen thousand from the city of Shiraz.[3]

The share of the Meshhedi Jews in this movement from Iran to Palestine-Israel was initially slight. Because of their special status as Jadīd al-Islām, the establishment of contact between them and the outside Jewish world was more difficult than it was for Jews in the other Iranian cities. In the other major Iranian cities, the Alliance Israélite Universelle established Jewish schools beginning in the late nineteenth century; in Meshhed, the first openly Jewish school was established only after 1945 by the Ozar Hatorah.

At the same time, the crypto-Jewish status of the Meshhed community enabled some of its male members to visit Jerusalem. They were able to do this while ostensibly fulfilling the Muslim religious commandment of making the pilgrimage to Mecca and Medina. Some of the Muslim pilgrims visited not only those two most holy places of Islam but also its third most holy place, Jerusalem, with its famous el-Aqsa mosque and Dome of the Rock. The Jadīd al-Islām pilgrims did the same, and thus had a chance to become acquainted with the Jewish community in the Holy City, which, as a result of the early Zionist immigration from the West, experienced some expansion around the turn of the century. Returning to Meshhed, these pilgrims spread the good news about Jewish life in Jerusalem and in the "colonies," and thus contributed to an increasing interest among the Jadīdīm in what was going on in the Holy Land.

In any case, in 1903, 1906, and 1908, groups of dozens of Meshhedi Jews made their way to Zion. A scion of Meshhedi Jews, Mullah Binjamin Shauloff, himself born in Herat, Afghanistan, made use of his close contacts with the Ottoman government to help the Meshhedi immigrants in Jerusalem and built dwelling units for them. Other Meshhedi Jews purchased plots of land in the Bukharan Quarter in Jerusalem. Among them was Muḥammad Ismā'īl, known by his Jewish name as Ḥājjī Y'ḥezq'el ben Ya'aqov Halevi, who in 1906 built a unit of twenty-one rooms for the poor Meshhedi immigrants, as well as a beautiful synagogue, known as the Ḥājjī Y'ḥezq'el Synagogue, which is a center of religious life of the Meshhed Jews in Jerusalem to this day. Another synagogue was built by the eldest of the five sons of Mullah Aharon Kohen, Ḥājjī Adoniyah Hakohen.[4]

Following World War I, several hundred Meshhedi Jews made their 'aliya to Jerusalem. Among these were well-to-do merchants with international commercial connections in Asia, Europe, and America, including the Azizullayoff, Aminoff, and Nasrullayoff families. With them came the spiritual leader of the Meshhedi Jews, Mullah Murad (Mordecai) Aqlar, the author of several religious books in Judeo-Persian, which were printed in Jerusalem and distributed also among the Jews in Meshhed.[5]

Back in Iran, Zionism gradually spread in the Jewish communities despite internal and external difficulties. The Iranian Zionists elected two representatives to attend the Twelfth Zionist Congress (1921), but they encountered difficulties on the way to Europe and were unable to attend. In the early 1920s, the Iranian Zionist movement split into two competing factions, and the leader of one, Shemuel Haim, was accused of conspiracy against the government, arrested, and executed in 1931. Under the rule of Reza Shah (1925–1941), all contact between Iranian political groups and foreign organizations was outlawed, and Zionism became officially prohibited. The political and civic conditions of the Iranian Jews improved only with the Allied conquest of Iran in August 1941, following which contact was established between Iranian Jews and world Jewry, the Jewish Agency set up an office in Teheran, and emissaries from the *yishuv* began to pay visits to the major Iranian Jewish centers. In 1950, Iran extended de facto recognition to Israel.[6]

As for the history of the Jadīdīm in the half-century between 1892 and 1942, much too little is known about it. Some spotty information is contained in the memoirs of Āqā Farajullah Nasrullayoff (see below, chapter 12), who, however, concentrates on the affairs of his family and does not say much about the situation of the community as a whole. Moreover, he left Meshhed for Jerusalem in 1929; after that date, he was no longer an eyewitness to the situation and events in Meshhed.

What Āqā Farajullah emphasized in telling me about the life of the Jadīdī community of Meshhed prior to 1929 was the manner in which communal charity was practiced. It was considered the duty of the well-to-do members of the community to see to it that the poor among them did not suffer undue want. However, since the poor were ashamed of their poverty and would not ask for charity, it was up to the leaders of the community to make discreet inquiries and find out who was in need. The main seasons for the distribution of food and clothes among the poor were the days prior to Rosh haShana in the fall and Passover in the spring. Special care was taken to make the food and clothing available to the poor without offending their sensibilities. The heads of the community would get up before dawn and, under cover of darkness, deposit bundles containing food and clothing at the doorsteps of the poor. In this manner, nobody knew who received donations, and the recipients did not know who were the donors.

A little more about the life of the community can be gathered from the interview conducted in 1936 with Mullah Yosef ben Āqā 'Abdul Samad Dīlmānī in Meshhed, which was quoted in chapter 7.[7] Ten years later (in 1946), its transcript (typed, in Hebrew) was forwarded by Yitzḥaq Kleinbaum, an official of the Jewish Agency in Teheran, to the head office of the Agency in Jerusalem, in whose archives it is preserved.

From it, we learn that after 1928, when military duty was introduced in Iran, some three hundred Jadīdīm were conscripted into the army and served two years. None of them was an officer, but several became noncommissioned officers, such as sergeants, and others were put in charge of supplies. In 1936, according to Dīlmānī, there were twelve synagogues in Meshhed, and they had among them some thirty-five Torah scrolls, all of which had been brought from Jerusalem. Four Hebrew schools had a total of one hundred and forty pupils, who were taught the Bible with Hebrew commentaries, writing, Persian, and arithmetic. The total number of the Jews in Meshhed was about three thousand, constituting about five hundred and fifty families. By that time, there was already a sizable Meshhedi Diaspora in other cities. In other parts of Iran, there were eighty families or three hundred persons in Deregez; fifteen families or one hundred persons in Teheran; and ten families or fifty persons in Sarakhs and elsewhere. There were also one hundred and fifty families or eight hundred persons in Erez Israel; fifty families or three hundred persons in London; fifteen families or fifty persons in India. About half of the Jews in Meshhed were merchants of rugs, karakul and other skins, textiles, and other merchandise. The other half consisted of middlemen, shopkeepers, and peddlers. The big merchants also owned houses and plots of land in the city.

Characteristic of the attitude of the Jews of Meshhed to the government of Reza Shah Pahlavi is what Dīlmānī has to say about their position at the time of the interview: "The attitude of the present government, may its honor be exalted, [and of] Reza Shah Pahlavi, may his reign be firm forever, to the Jews is very good. He does not tolerate that they should be oppressed. But because of the crisis in the world, here too the economic conditions have somewhat worsened, and there is no [sic] buying and selling. The position of shopkeepers, peddlers and small merchants is bad, and they eke out a living with difficulty."

Dīlmānī also reports that there was an influx of Jewish refugees from Russia into Meshhed in the early 1930s, and concludes the interview with these comments about them:

> About three years ago [ca. 1933] about two thousand Jewish refugees fled from Bukhara, Samarkand, Tashkent, and other cities of Russian Turkestan, to Meshhed. Most of them were arrested at the border, and their money and property were taken away, so that they arrived in Meshhed, in whatever manner they could, without a penny in their pocket. Some of them were arrested at the border and only their wives succeeded in escaping; while among others it was the wives who were arrested and the men escaped; yet others lost their children on the way. When they arrived in Meshhed, it was necessary to help them in everything. The [Meshhed Jewish] community spent about 10,000 *tomans* on helping the refugees, to provide them clothes, lodging, and the like. Some of them obtained visas to Palestine; about 1,000 of them went on to Palestine with [immigration] certificates, and the rest, about another 1,000, are still in Hamadan, Kermanshah, Shiraz and other places. All of them are waiting for immigration certificates, and their situation is very bad.

A few details about the internal life of the Meshhed Jewish community in the early decades of the twentieth century can be gathered, or rather concluded, from the picture material presented by Ben-Zion Y'hoshu'a-Raz in his book *MiNidḥē Yisraēl b'Afganistan l'Anusē Meshhed b'Iran.* A picture taken in 1920 shows six Meshhed Jews "in Russia," probably in Russian Turkmenistan, three of them members of the Ḥakīmian family (Tāber Ḥakīmian, Gulmani Ḥakīmian, and Lutfullah Ḥakīmian) and three others (Qāsem Ḥajijit, Abraham Tavudoff, and Ismā'īl Rajabzadeh), all neatly dressed in traditional Persian robes, unmistakably well-to-do people, who undoubtedly sojourned in "Russia" in connection with business affairs. Another picture, evidently taken several years later, shows one of these six men, Tāber Ḥakīmian, in a European-cut long jacket, with his eight- or ten-year-old son and the four- or five-year-old girl who was the son's promised bride. Yet another picture, taken in Meshhed in 1925, shows Fatḥullah Livian, a youth of about twenty, with his ten- to twelve-year-old fiancée. These two pictures illustrate better than any verbal description the custom of childhood betrothal practiced by the Jews of Meshhed (see below, chapter 24). The emigration of Meshhed Jews to, and commercial activity in, India is illustrated by the picture showing three Meshhed Jews (Ya'aqov Dilmanian, 'Abdul-Raḥīm Idanian, and Abraham Raḥmanian) in Peshavar, India, in 1930, in typical Indian garb. The person in the middle holds what seems to be a ledger, and all three are evidently well-to-do merchants. Yet another picture shows thirty-one pupils of Rabbi Yosef Dīlmānī's Hebrew school in Meshhed in 1925. They are all neatly dressed, with small caps on their heads—clearly a group of boys from middle-class families. Another, undated picture shows a group of eighty-three boys and thirteen adults, the pupils and teachers of the Ozar haTorah school in Meshhed, all in European clothing. Since Ozar Hatorah, a society for religious education of Jewish youth in the Middle East and North Africa, was founded in 1945, this picture cannot be of an earlier date than that. By 1970, Ozar Hatorah was running forty-one schools and a summer camp in Iran. These two pictures are eloquent testimony to the adhesion of the Jadīdīm to Judaism: they wanted to make sure that their sons learned Hebrew and grew up to be Jews. A picture taken in 1936 shows eight girl pupils in European-style school uniform, with their teacher Ḥabab Gafuri, in an embroidery class in the Arz Agdaz school in Meshhed. Two pictures, taken in 1925 and 1935, respectively, illustrate the transition from traditional to modern (European) garb among the Meshhed Jews. The one taken in 1925 shows the Ḥakīmian (Mortazaoff) family. The older members wear traditional Persian garb; one young man and a child wear European clothes. The 1935 picture shows members of the Kordovani family on the occasion of a wedding; the three older men wear traditional Persian, and the two younger ones are in European clothes. An undated picture shows two young women in traditional Persian clothes, with kerchiefs over their heads, one of them smoking a *qalyun* (*narghīleh*). Characteristic of the manifold cultural influences to which the Meshhed Jews were exposed is a picture taken in 1930, showing a group of twelve; five of them wear traditional Persian robes, four wear colorful Bukharian garb, and three are dressed in modern European clothes. Most interesting is a picture taken in 1935 showing ten members of the soccer team of the Tajadod youth club of Meshhed in their striped uniform and nine other youths in a variety of European-style clothes, short-sleeved shirts, pullovers, and so on.[8]

The pictures show that despite the constant pressure to which they were exposed and the need to keep their Jewishness under cover, the Meshhed Jews were able to lead what they undoubtedly considered satisfactory lives. They had commercial contact with other countries, maintained schools and classes for their boys and girls, conducted communal and social activities, and even engaged in group sports such as soccer. Their life was colorful and challenging, and Jewishness was at its core. At the same time, they knew how to combine modernism with tradition or, rather, how to walk the narrow path between the two.

As for the Zionist movement in Meshhed, it encountered greater obstacles than those that impeded its development in Iran as a whole. In Iran, the problem was similar to that of Zionism in the Arab countries: Muslim sympathies lay with the Arabs of Palestine and with their efforts to thwart the Jewish endeavor to build a national home for the Jews in Palestine. In Meshhed, these country-wide difficulties of the Zionist movement were aggravated by the local problem of the crypto-Jewish status of the Jadīdīm. Even when their adherence to Judaism was no longer a secret, they still felt that at least the appearance of their adherence to Islam had to be maintained, and this made them apprehensive when it came to engaging in any Zionist activity. Thus, the love of Zion, which was in no way less powerful in the bosom of the Meshhed Jadīdīm than among the other Jews of Iran, had to remain a private, personal affair and could not be given any overt organizational manifestation. Still, quite a number of Meshhedi Jews managed to leave the city and to make their *'aliya* to Palestine and later to Israel. By the 1990s, practically no Jews were left in Meshhed and only a very few in Iran as a whole.

9
Disturbances in the 1940s

In the 1940s, Meshhed was the scene of two bloody disturbances of which accounts survived and a third one to which reference was made in a brief document issued by the Muslim religious authorities of the city.

The first incident took place in 1942 and was reported by a Meshhedi Jew, Tziyon (Ṣiyon) Zabīḥī (b. Meshhed, 1924; original name Raḥmatullah Zabīḥīoff), in an interview conducted in 1966 in Jerusalem by Nāṣer Kamil Humayūn. A transcript of the interview, which dealt mainly with the experiences of the Iranian Jews in Israel, is preserved as document 813 in the archives of the Avraham Harman Institute of Contemporary Jewry of the Hebrew University of Jerusalem.[1] The following is my literal translation of the part of the interview that pertains to the 1942 Meshhed disturbances:

> It was the time [Zabīḥī stated in response to a question by Humayūn] of World War II, when the Allies were in Persia. Meshhed was in the Russian-controlled area, because it was close to the Russian border, and was practically the only place through which the British were able to transfer arms and other aid to Russia. The supplies came from Pakistan, from Karachi, through Zāhedān,[2] and from Meshhed and Darra Gaz,[3] Bajnurd [Bujnurd],[4] they crossed over into Russia. So there were Russians in Meshhed. On the eve of Passover—it happened to be also the eve of Muḥarram—we were in the synagogue. When we returned home, we felt stirrings of unrest in the quarter and in the alley but did not know what was the reason. While we were reciting the Haggadah, we heard whistling from the roof of the neighbor—somebody on the roof was blowing a whistle. We knew that it was a signal of calling the police. We the boys quickly rushed out and went to the neighbor. We asked him what had happened, and he told us that at a distance of two alleys three Jews had been given a terrible beating, and they were still at the police station. Several people went there to set them free and take them home on the eve of the feast. The reason—of course—had been the one known for decades: a blood libel. They said that a Muslim boy was missing from his home. Where could he be? Undoubtedly the Jews slaughtered him and used his blood for the *matzoth*. To

this day, I don't know whether this was manipulated by somebody or was spontaneous—but this is what happened. There were attacks on houses, on people, beatings, and slowly a crowd gathered, there may have been some ten thousand people, and they began to pour gasoline on several doors of houses and set them on fire. But they did not enter the houses, even though attempts to do so were made here and there. Of course, not a single Jew was outside his house. The men who went to the police to liberate the three arrested Jews were beaten bloody, some of them were severely wounded, but they managed to return home with the three.

The shouting and yelling continued until after midnight. In the meantime, the police arrived. But next morning the attacks were renewed. This went on three days. The situation was very serious, very dangerous. The police either did not succeed to disperse the mob, or did not want to, I don't know why. On the third day, they even brought the army. Everywhere in the Jewish quarter there were soldiers with guns and bayonets. But still it was extremely dangerous for a Jew to venture out of the house. The matter reached Teheran, from where strict orders were issued that the matter must be ended instantly. I don't remember well, I was young, and I was busy with small missions, to go from house to house, to ask, to tell something, to hear. The house of the uncle that was next to our house was the headquarters. Officers of the police and simple policemen came and went, ate and drank. We begged them that they should do something. On the third day of Passover, it was the eve of 'Ashūrah, the tenth day of the month of Muḥarram [see comments below], they went and got in touch with the Mujtahid Ayatollah Nihāwandī—may he rest in peace!—an old and God-fearing man, and when he heard was was happening (I remember well, for I lived in a three-story house and from its roof I could see the whole street and observe everything), he came riding on a small donkey, three men were accompanying him, two walking before him and one after him, he came, went up to an elevated place, and called upon all the thousands who were there, and explained to them that the Jewish people, or the Jews who were here, they too have their book and are God-fearing, and they too are under our flag. And, as it is written in the Koran, we are forbidden to harm them. And he asked and ordered that all the men should disperse and should cease forthwith to harm the Jews. Then he pronounced a ban upon all those who would remain on the spot, and said that their property and their wives would be banned for them. This had a great effect. The Ayatollah gave them permission to go out in groups into the street, to sing and to shout, provided they went away from that place and did not harm the Jews of Meshhed.

The people dispersed. Some 90 percent of them went and busied themselves with their religious duties. Only some 10 percent of the mob remained, but soon, partly due to the action of the police and partly due to the money we gave their leaders, they too dispersed. However, this tension continued for several more days, almost to the end of Passover. We received beatings. We were unable to appear in many places. To walk alone was dangerous, for the Muslim children of our age, those ten, twelve, or fifteen years old or older, were

> convinced that a Jew has to get beatings. We got beatings. Some of them were eighteen years old. If their parents saw what they were doing, none of them told them to desist, "This is not good, don't do it, don't hit, why are you doing this?" Until a man passed by who, because of religious or human feelings, saved the Jewish child and enabled him to get away.

In trying to recall the date of the event twenty-four years later, Zabīḥī contradicts himself and gives two different identifications according to the Muslim calendar, both wrong. At first he says that the eve of Passover "happened to be also the the eve of Muḥarram." Since both the Jewish and the Muslim calendars date the first day of each month from the appearance of the new moon, the eve of Passover, the fourth of the month of Nissan, cannot be "the eve of Muḥarram," that is, the last day of the month Dhu 'l-Ḥijja, which precedes the month of Muḥarram. The second time he says that the third day of Passover (seventeenth of Nissan) was the eve of 'Ashūra' (ninth of Muḥarram), which again is wrong. However, these discrepancies are but insignificant lapses, understandable in the course of an interview given so long after the event described and mentioning in passing Muslim calendar dates with which the interviewee could not have been too familiar to begin with.

Four years after the 1942 incident, a more serious anti-Jewish outbreak took place in Meshhed, again in the spring, when Muslim religious sentiments ran high and when, coincidentally, the Jews celebrated their Passover holiday. News of these disturbances reached me in Jerusalem a few weeks later, in the form of a detailed letter from Meshhed written by Soliman Muradi, a Meshhed Jew with whom I had had some correspondence previously. I published Muradi's account in the original Hebrew in the October 1946–January 1947 double issue of *Edoth* (vol. 2, no. 1–2), the journal of the Palestine Institute of Folklore and Ethnology, of which I was editor. What follows is my literal translation of that letter:

> The first days of Passover 5706 [1946] were days of mourning for the Muslims, for it was in those days that the prophetess Fātima al-Zahrā'[5] died. On the Sabbath preceding the Passover, the heads of the Jewish community warned the entire community in the synagogues that they should be especially careful during the holiday not to have any contact with the Muslims, to refrain from holiday visits, from putting on new clothes, and the like. But it seems those who instigated the disturbances had definite plans to begin the disturbances during our holiday.
>
> Several days prior to Passover, some of the Muslim youth began to loiter in the Jewish street. They played ball, and when a Jewish woman approached, they threw the ball at her, and as she passed them, they pulled off the *chādor* [veil][6] from her head. The Jewish men who saw this reproached them and recovered the *chādor* from their hands. A few days later, these Jews were taken to the

police station. In these incidents, we saw as yet nothing exceptional, for such events used to take place quite often.

On the first night of Passover, as we came out of the synagogue and went homeward in the Jewish quarter,[7] we again saw those boys playing ball. They approached a [Jewish] girl, tore the veil from her head, and ran away. It seems that these youngsters were sent by those who planned the disturbances. Next day, the first day of Passover, the brother of that girl met the youngsters and asked them to return the veil, and even offered them a reward for it. Meanwhile, several Muslim women appeared, and burst into cries of "Where are those men who reproached our sons and wanted to drag them off and use their blood for their holiday?" (One has to know that also Muslims live in the Jewish quarter.) The Jews answered: "For tens of year we have lived together, and we did nothing bad to you; why are you now shouting and accusing us falsely?"

In the meantime, some dozens of Muslims gathered from all over, but after being repeatedly requested, they dispersed. However, some of them did not pass in silence over the event and reported it to the police. On the second night of Passover, policemen and soldiers came, arrested several Jews and took them to the police station, for the police were told that they wanted to catch a Muslim boy and use his blood for the holiday. On the way to the police station, many Muslims joined them, and also several Jews accompanied their brothers to the police. The crowd grew, and the police tried to disperse it but could not. The people started to cry, "Death to the Jews!" and shout curses, and before long fell upon the Jews and started beating them. Nobody helped us; in whatever direction we turned, we found our way blocked. The number of those participating in the disturbance grew to hundreds, and wherever they met a Jew, they beat him bloody. Some of them entered the Jewish quarter, and we hurried to withdraw to our houses, and locked the gates and the doors. The crowd shouted *Yā 'Alī!* (O, 'Alī!), broke the doors and the window panes and whatever they could lay their hands on. Some of us ran to the police station to notify them of what was happening but were intercepted by the rioters and beaten up cruelly. Some were even stabbed with knives, so that they fell down bleeding in the streets. These wounded were robbed by the rioters of whatever they had on them.

That evening, the second evening of Passover, was for us a very bad and difficult time. The wounded were taken to the hospital or carried home. Those who were taken to the police were interrogated by the officer in charge. At the end, he told them: "I know that this libel is a lie, but I cannot set you free tonight, for the rioters will not remain silent about it. It is better that you remain here until tomorrow, until things quiet down." The Jews who had accompanied their brothers to the police requested that policemen should escort them home, but this was not done. They had to risk their lives and go by themselves. They were attacked on the way, beaten up, and arrived home wounded.

Several young men decided, despite the danger, to go out and inform of the danger the new Jewish quarter that is located on the other side of the city and is called Janāt. They succeeded in reaching the place. The inhabitants of

Janāt got in touch with the governor, the police commander, and others. On the second day of the holiday, all the Jews remained in their homes. Beginning with the morning, masses of rioters began to enter the Jewish quarter. They threw stones, broke windows, burnt gates, poured gasoline on the doors, and set them on fire. In some cases, they broke into the houses and wounded men and women, old and young. In these attacks also Muslim women took part. We kept quiet, suffered the blows, and there was nobody to help or save us. Some people heaped up rows of bricks behind the gates so that the attackers should not be able to enter. Women cried and fainted, and did not know how to save their children. The policemen who guarded the quarter could not overcome the rioters. Also, soldiers of the army came to help them, they got orders to shoot into the air—but had to be given "presents" in order to fire any shot. In the afternoon, the crowd attacked the synagogue and broke its windows. The neighbors cried [for help], whereupon a policeman came, and after receiving respectable presents, he began to shoot into the air. The attackers disappeared.

During the night, several of our young men stood guard, together with the policemen, and in some cases were beaten up badly. In the evening, a high police officer came to the quarter and addressed the rioters, saying: "The Russian army left arms in the hands of the Jews, and if you enter their houses they will kill you." This lie and strategy had a great effect, and thereafter they were afraid to enter the houses, and satisfied themselves with breaking the gates. We were able to go up to the roofs and inform one another of the situation. Among the Muslims, there were volunteers who received gifts and informed the Janāt quarter of our situation. Several of those who came to our help from Janāt in carriages were caught by the rioters and beaten up or stoned.

The Jews also turned to the British and Russian consulates, and two days later, an emissary from the Russians came to visit the quarter and also photographed the sites of the attacks and the destruction, and sent the pictures to the Russian press. It seems that also the Russian radio made a broadcast about the situation. After the officers too were honored with gifts, they approached the leader of the Muslims and demanded that the disturbances be terminated. The old and honored leader, whose name is Nihāwandī,[8] gave an address in the big mosque, and it was he who, in effect, saved the situation. He even troubled himself and came personally to the Jewish quarter, and spoke there too to the rioters and said:

"These Jews are Jadīd al-Islām (new Muslims),[9] and for many years have lived among us, and we saw nothing bad from them. Stop these acts and accusations. Every Muslim who touches them is a traitor to his people and religion!"

The words of this old man made a great impression, and the crowd dispersed. They also printed circulars for our benefit, and threw them down from government planes over the quarter and the whole city.

Also in the other [Jewish] quarter, the Janāt, there were attacks, as in the 'Ēdgāh (the old Jewish quarter). In the evening, finally there was quiet, but the

> Jews were afraid to go out, and they recited the holiday prayers in their houses. At the Seder nights, there were those who could not celebrate the Seder until midnight. People could not eat and observe the holiday. Many went around and gathered from all the Jews gifts and food for the policemen and the guards of the quarter. For several days thereafter, the Muslims still looked at us angrily and wrathfully, and toward evening we all withdrew to our houses. There were still several cases of attacks on passersby in the streets. We think that the hands of strangers were involved in them. We also sent information to the sons of our community who live in Teheran,[10] and they had a meeting with the heads of the government and gave them details about our situation. Several weeks later, representatives of the Jewish Agency, Mr. Kleinbaum[11] and Mr. Landstein,[12] came to our city. They met with the British and Russian consulates and wanted to meet also the governor of the district, but the heads of the [Jewish] community advised them against it.
>
> I wrote these things in accordance with the request of Mr. Raphael Patai. May God give that we all should soon go up to our land and get out from the yoke of exile.

This eyewitness account shows the difference between the attitude of the mob, the common people, on the one hand, and the religious and civil officials of Meshhed on the other, toward the Jews, that is, the Jadīd al-Islām of the city. The people considered them suspect and were ready to go along with the age-old blood libel alleging that the Jews used Muslim blood (in Christian countries, Christian blood) for their Passover ritual. The vaguest statement to the effect that the Jews *wanted* to kill a Muslim boy for that purpose sufficed to inflame the mob to brutal action against them. As is only too well known, events such as this frequently occurred in the Christian world until the end of the nineteenth century, and from this account of Solimān Murādī, we learn that they took place in the world of Shī'ī Islam as recently as after World War II.

As for the authorities, as represented by the police, they protected the Jews only reluctantly and had to be bribed to stop the attacks. Still, both the police chief and the religious leader, Mullah Nihāwandī, knew that the blood libel was a lie and were ready to protect the Jews. It was in this inimical atmosphere that the Jews of Meshhed (and of Iran as a whole) had to live.

A few weeks after the events described by Murādī, an official of the Jewish Agency for Palestine stationed in Teheran, Yitzḥaq Kleinbaum by name, visited Meshhed, and on May 26, 1946, he sent a report of his visit from Teheran to the executive of the Jewish Agency in Jerusalem, with the request that the executive "discuss urgently ways of rescuing the Meshhed community, and let me know your resolutions." Kleinbaum's report is preserved in the Central Zionist Archives in Jerusalem, and a major part of it is devoted to a description of the incident that took place during the days of Passover 1946. The following is my literal translation from Kleinbaum's Hebrew report:

Even though—as stated—the crypto-Jews of Meshhed lived all the time in a certain fear and lack of security, until the last few days there were in Meshhed no pogroms that would have endangered the lives of the Jews in this city.

In the days of the recent Passover, a short time after the Red Army left the city (Meshhed is located in the eastern part of Persia, which since 1941 had been under Russian occupation), a crisis occurred in the history of the Meshhed community.

As it had happened 107 years ago, again there was in Meshhed a blood libel. The tense political situation, and with it the fanaticism of the Muslims, found expression in disturbances against the Jews. There are several versions of the direct cause that triggered the blood libel and the disturbances. One of them—and it seems that it is the correct one—tells that while Jewish and Muslim children were playing ball, a quarrel broke out between them, and one of the Muslim boys, who was hit by a Jewish boy, ran away, and for a while his whereabouts remained unknown. Thereupon, the Muslims spread the rumor that the boy was killed by the Jews in order to use his blood for the baking of *matzoth*. According to another version, a Jewish merchant seriously insulted a Muslim, who was spreading the rumor that the Jew had mocked Islam—and hence came the blood libel. It is difficult to determine what really was the immediate reason for the libel. But one thing is certain: one must look for it in the political situation that developed in those parts of Persia which for six years had been under Russian occupation. The Jews, who were more able than the Muslims, could speak Russian and knew how to make use of commercial contacts, established relations with the Russians both as contractors for the [Russian] army and as officials, translators, etc. This was the situation also in Meshhed. Some Jews even became rich during the occupation, thanks to their relations with the Russians. Even though also many Muslims did the same thing, the contact of the Meshhed Jews with the Russians was more conspicuous, and the Muslims accused the Jews of being Russian agents. If we add to this the fanaticism of the people of Meshhed and their traditional hatred of the Jews, we shall understand that after the departure of the Red Army from the city, the relationship between the two communities became more tense, and in these circumstances it is not difficult to explain the blood libel.

There are those who explain the events as follows: it does not represent an episode in the present political situation in Persia. The reactionary elements that supported the totalitarian regime of the cabinet of Gavam al-Sultaneh [prime minister of Iran] were interested in proving to the world that the only regime that was suitable for Persia was a totalitarian one, and therefore they tried to bring about unrest in the country. In opposition to them, the leftist and democratic elements were interested in peace and order in the country. The regime of Gavam al-Sultaneh has not yet been able to free itself of these elements, which still continue to occupy important positions in the administration. It is these circles that were behind the events in Meshhed. It is too early to form a judgment about whether this concept is correct, but one has to admit that it seems logical enough.

What is said above about the relationship of the Jews of Meshhed with the Russian authorities during the occupation pertains only to the "middle class" of the Meshhed Jews. The rich ones among them are more inclined toward the British, and they maintain good relations with the British consulate in Meshhed.

On the basis of information supplied by the Jews of Meshhed, this is what happened. After the news spread in the city that a Muslim boy was killed (which happened on the eve of the second day of Passover), a crowd of several thousand Muslims gathered in the Teheran Street that leads to the ghetto and tried to break into the Jewish quarter. The Jews locked the gates and hid in the houses. A part of the crowd succeeded in breaking down one of the gates and penetrated the ghetto. Several Jewish houses were damaged, doors and windows were broken, and the rioters even tried to set fire to some houses. Those Jews who were caught by the crowd were beaten severely, and some fifteen of them sustained serious injuries. One of the most cruel acts was committed against a Jewish youth who fell into the hands of the crowd; he was doused with gasoline, and an attempt was made to set him on fire. It was a miracle that he escaped with his life. The Muslim Mullahs and the authorities intervened. It is said that a Mullah called upon the crowd to disperse and argued that these events can only serve as an excuse for a foreign power to intervene. Also, the governor of Khorasan province, in which Meshhed is located, intervened to protect the Jews. A proclamation was issued in the original with a translation. The leaders of the Tudeh party [the Persian left wing] advised the Jews to send a delegation to the Russian consul. The Jewish elite, whose pro-British position was mentioned above, did not follow this advice, arguing that such a step could anger the Persian authorities. It seems, however, that nevertheless unofficially the Jews applied to the Russian consul. In any case, there is no certainty whatsoever that either the British or the Russian consul intervened with the Persian authorities. The Jews of Meshhed even relate that a Muslim official of the British consulate was among those who threw stones at a Jewish house outside the ghetto, near the consulate.

According to what the Jews relate, the policemen who were sent to the streets where the attacks took place did not manifest any will to act energetically. But the calls of the Mullahs and of some of the Muslim notables had the effect of quieting down the crowd to some extent, and it began to disperse. However, some two hours later, there was another attempt to break into the ghetto. Next morning, the situation was much more quiet, but most of the Jews stayed in their houses and did not go to the synagogue. Throughout the remaining days of the Passover, the Jews lived in fear and apprehension.

The events shook the Jews, and they no longer feel safe in the city, surrounded as they are by an inimical fanatic crowd. They are afraid of the repetition of the events, and worry about what will happen to them.

Immediately after the events, the Jews of Meshhed reported of them to the Teheran office of the Jewish Agency, and requested that the information be forwarded to Erez Israel, to the Jews of America and England, and to the

> Meshhedi Jews in Palestine and in the Diaspora. They also requested the Teheran office of the Jewish Agency and the institutions of the *yishuv* to enable them to make their *'aliya* to Erez Israel.

The Murādī and Kleinbaum accounts are identical in most of their details, so that one can take it for granted that they present a true picture of what actually happened.

The 1946 disturbances were not the last outbreak of Shī'ī antipathy to the Jadīdīm. A rather enigmatic brief document, also preserved in the Central Zionist Archives in Jerusalem, indicates that on April 13, 1949, renewed accusations were directed at the Jadīdīm, and in their wake yet another attempt was made at attacking them. The document in question is a brief memorandum in Persian issued by the Muslim religious authorities of the city. It reads as follows in a literal English translation:

> In behalf of Āqāyān Ḥajaj-Islām Kathrullah and others, in order to quieten down the spirits of all the people of Meshhed, and to reassure the city, we proclaim that the rumors that have been spread since yesterday in the city and caused worry among many were disseminated by ignorant persons. It is desirable that all the Muslims should not be misled by the rumors, and that everyone should keep the peace and the quiet.
>
> And peace will be for him who followeth the right guidance.
>
> The insignificant Aḥmad al-Khorāsānī, 'Alī Akbar al-Nihāwandī, Ḥusayn Faqiye Sabwzārī.

The sentence preceding the three signatures is a quote from the Koran 20:49, but it contains two spelling errors: the Koranic text reads:

والسلام على من اتبع الهدى

(*was-salāmu 'alā mani 'ttaba'a 'l-hudā*), while the memorandum quotes the last two words as

التبع الهدا

(*'l-tab'a 'al-hudā'*). These minor inaccuracies apart, the memorandum is interesting for its purposely vague phrasing. It speaks of "rumors" which it pronounced to be false and admonishes the Muslims to preserve peace and quiet, but it does not say anything about what those rumors were and who were the people who suffered from the absence of peace and quiet. Only the record of anti-Jewish outbreaks in Meshhed that preceded the date of this memorandum lets us suspect that its purpose was to deter the people from attacking the Jews because of some libelous accusation against them.

10

A Picture of Jewish Life

The Kleinbaum document quoted above in chapter 9 also presents some data about the Jews of Meshhed that give us some idea of the community ten years after the Dīlmānī interview. He writes:[1]

> In view of the situation, on May 13 of this year [1946], a delegation consisting of the undersigned [Yitzḥaq Kleinbaum] in the name of the Jewish Agency, his wife, and Mr. A. Landstein representing the head office of the Keren Kayemeth l'Yisrael [Jewish National Fund] left Teheran for Meshhed. Because of the great distance between Teheran and Meshhed, the difficulties of transportation in Persia in general and to Meshhed in particular, and also in order to reach the place as soon as possible, the delegation flew in a plane of the regular Russian service between Teheran and Meshhed. The delegation spent five days in Meshhed. It investigated the situation, gathered information about the events, and held consultations with representatives of the Meshhed Jews about the possibilities of saving the community of the *anusim* [crypto-Jews], who continue to live in insecurity. The following are the impressions the delegation got in its visit to Meshhed.
>
> Because of lack of statistical data, it is difficult to establish the exact number of the Jews in Meshhed. It is estimated at 3,000 to 4,000 persons, but it seems that actually the number does not exceed 3,000. Of this number, several hundred move back and forth between Teheran and Meshhed, in search of work or in business activities. In addition, several dozens of Meshhedi families live permanently in Teheran. As mentioned above, there are colonies of Meshhedi Jews in Erez Israel, in London, New York, and India. Not more than 2,000 to 3,000 Meshhedi Jews live outside their native city. The contact between the Meshhedi Jews in the world and their brethren in Persia is a very close one.
>
> Meshhed can be called the Jerusalem of Persia. The Jews of Meshhed are the best Jews among all the Jews of Iran. This community, which for several decades was forced to maintain its Judaism in secret, remained faithful to the religion and the people, and has a special character. The deep and convinced Judaism of the Meshhedi Jews does not at all resemble the religiosity of the

Jews of other Eastern countries, let alone that of the Jews of Eastern Europe. It is pure in both its inner and outer form, is free of all fanaticism, of superstitions, and is combined with a strong Jewish national feeling. The ties between the Jews of Meshhed and Zion are strong. When one find oneself among these Jews, talks to them, prays with them in the synagogue, one forgets that this is a community of *anusim* in a remote corner, at a great distance from other Jewish communities, let alone from Erez Israel (ca. 3,000 kilometers). Hebrew is spoken by most of the Jews of Meshhed, and almost all of them understand it. The synagogue is the center of their communal life. They not only pray in the synagogue and study the Torah but read the newspaper of Erez Israel and all the publications sent to them from the institutions of the *yishuv*. In the synagogue, they hold conversations about the situation of the Jews in the world and about the events that take place in the *yishuv*. In the synagogue are held all the public meetings in which communal affairs are discussed. The Jews of Meshhed, moreover, like simply to sit in the synagogue. This is fully understandable if one takes into account that the synagogue has been for them for generations the only place of assembly.

Most of the Jews of Meshhed are concentrated in the ghetto (*maḥalleh*). In it are found most of the synagogues, of which there are in Meshhed several, and one can say that the ghetto is the center of their religious and communal life. Those who had become rich moved to the center of the city.

In the ghetto are found the Persian schools for the Jews, under the supervision of the government, one for boys and one for girls. Since the Jews of Meshhed are officially Muslims, it has thus far not been possible for the Alliance Israélite Universelle to open schools in Meshhed or to take under its wings the existing schools. By the way, the boys' school is in a building that belongs to Jews. Of course, in these two governmental schools, there is no instruction at all of Jewish religion or of Hebrew. But the Jews of Meshhed were not satisfied with the schools established for them by the government, and established on their own a Jewish school called *Midrash*, in which the children get a Jewish religious and national education. In addition, there are evening classes in Hebrew for the youth. All this has been established by the Jews of Meshhed by their own efforts. The religious and national education in this place is nothing short of astounding. One can say with absolute certainty that it is highly worthwhile to send to Meshhed educational materials from Erez Israel, schoolbooks, copybooks, songbooks, etc. Not a shred of this material is going to waste in Meshhed but is utilized to the maximum. Everything that comes from Erez Israel is sacred for the Jews of Meshhed: be it a Y'sodot textbook, or 'Aleh, a pamphlet about the history of Zionism, about our parachutists, a newspaper, a flyer about the Keren Kayemeth or the Keren Hayesod—everything is carefully kept, everything passes from hand to hand, everything is studied diligently. The Jews of Meshhed bind the books that come from Erez Israel so that they should not get torn, they paste the flyers and posters on cardboard, carefully collect all the pictures from Erez Israel, etc. One feels no difference between the holy books and the new Hebrew publications. "We got this from Erez Israel," say the Jews of Meshhed with pride and respect.

The *Midrash,* the Hebrew school, is quite a special institution. Because of lack of experienced teachers from Erez Israel, the headmaster and the teachers themselves try to imitate the Hebrew educational methods as practiced in Erez Israel, as far as they can learn about them from the materials sent them by the *yishuv.* Even gymnastics, with clothing similar to that used in Erez Israel, has been introduced in the *Midrash.*

The children persevere in learning Hebrew and know by heart all the books and songs that were sent to them. It was a truly captivating and encouraging sight that our delegation witnessed when we visited the school: little children aged six or seven made speeches in pure Hebrew about the history of the settlement of Erez Israel, the Biluim, Pinsker's *Autoemancipation,* and the like. All this they learned by heart from the Y'sodot or 'Aleh textbooks. The Meshhed children also know the songs most popular in Erez Israel. Likewise, they can tell jokes about the Jecke, about the new immigrant, who comes to register to evening classes, or who complains to the municipality that his landlord demands of him rent for thirteen months, when in Europe a year consisted of twelve months only, about a phone conversation between Ḥayyim in Tel Aviv and Sarah in Haifa on buying *totzeret ha'aretz* (the product of the country), etc. Palestinian life, so different from life in the Meshhed ghetto, is throbbing in the small *Midrash* school of the Jewish community!

Kleinbaum did not overlook one serious problem that he found troubled the relationship of the Meshhed Jews to the *yishuv:* the phenomenon of reemigration from Erez Israel. He writes:

There is in Meshhed one phenomenon that fundamentally contrasts with the Jewish national life of the community. There is a goodly number of Jews, especially young men, who had been in Erez Israel and returned to Meshhed. There are among them even such as returned after having spent several years in Erez Israel. At first glance, this phenomenon seems to negate the feelings of the community as a whole. However, once one looks into the causes and circumstances that brought about this phenomenon, a totally different picture emerges. The reasons for their return given by the men involved are not important in themselves. They claim that they came back because the Persian authorities put pressure on their families to call them back so that they can fulfill their duty of service in the army. They even add that the authorities threatened their families with imprisonment if the young men did not return. There are among them those who proffer other causes, but all these excuses cannot be taken seriously or accepted as the real reasons for their return. After thorough investigation, one is led to the conclusion that the young men returned to Meshhed for more serious reasons, and that the guilt is not actually theirs. The *'aliya* of young men from Meshhed had been unorganized and undirected. Because of their yearning for Zion, many young men left their families and went to Erez Israel. Many of them left behind also their wives and fiancées (the Persian Jewish custom is for a boy and girl to become engaged in their childhood). Due to the character of the Meshhed community, which constitutes a united and closed group in its relationship to other Jewish communities (in general, the Jewish men of Meshhed do not intermarry with women from other Jewish communities, even when they live outside Meshhed), the young men in Ereẓ Israel missed their families they left behind in Meshhed and did not feel happy living far away from their native city. In these circumstances, their power of resistance in case of personal failure or of a general crisis in Erez Israel was very weak, and one single one of these reasons was sufficient to induce them to return. But one can say that right after their return, the young men regretted this step, and today all of them again yearn for *'aliya*. One gets the impression that after the terrible years of the war, and especially after the disturbances that took place in Meshhed, the phenomenon of return from Erez Israel will not recur.

As stated, the Meshhed community lives today in conditions of insecurity and apprehension of what the future will bring. Many of the Jews want to go to Erez Israel and see in *'aliya* the only way out of their present predicament. It should, therefore, not be surprising that our delegation was received by the Jews of Meshhed with exceptionally great warmth and love, and that they saw in its arrival a manifestation of the close ties between the *yishuv* and the Jews of the Diaspora. It is difficult to imagine a heartier reception than the one they accorded to the delegation. The meetings in the synagogue, in which members of the delegation spoke of the conditions in Erez Israel and in the Jewish world, were attended by masses of Jews who came to hear about Erez Israel and Zionism, and to present their requests to the delegation.

After the members of the delegation paid official visits to the British and Russian consuls in Meshhed, they began to take care of the tasks that had brought them to Meshhed. They informed the Jews of the conditions in Erez Israel from the point of view of both politics and the chances of immigration available in various categories, established a branch of the Ḥalutz movement, and initiated a Shegel campaign, which, according to the latest information, has been developing most satisfactorily. The members of the delegation also held several consultations with the representatives of the various sectors of the Meshhed Jewish community and youth concerning the steps of rescue that could be taken.

In a conference with the wealthy people of Meshhed, who already had considerable capital in Erez Israel and who, according to information received by the delegation, were able to make additional investments, it was suggested to the leaders of the community to establish, jointly with their rich brethren in London, America, and Erez Israel, an agricultural, industrial, or mixed settlement in Erez Israel, in which Meshhed Jews who had no means of their own could find employment after a way was found to enable them to make their *'aliya.* It was explained to the notables that such a project would be of advantage to the *yishuv* as well as to the Meshhed Jews. The members of the delegation also added—of course, in a noncommittal manner—that if the rich people of Meshhed were to raise the money for the establishment of such a settlement, the institutions of the *yishuv,* and especially the national funds, would participate in its financing. The rich people were made to understand that such a project would constitute a promise for their own future, because one could never know what could happen to their possessions in the Diaspora. They were warned not to follow the ways of the rich Jews in Europe, who too thought that their position was secure, and whose tragic fate is known to all. Even though the rich people promised to think about the project, the delegation got the impression that, as is the case with the rich Jews everywhere in the world, they were not ready to establish on their own, or with but minimal help, a constructive project for their poor brethren. On the other hand, the impression was gained that if the institutions, and especially the Keren Kayemeth and the Keren Hayesod, were to support it effectively (with financial participation and with securing credit for investments), the rich Jews of Meshhed would be willing to participate in such a project. In fact, we discussed with the notables the establishment of a *moshav* or of a *moshav shitufi* [two forms of cooperative settlement] of Meshhed Jews in Erez Israel, and possibly also of an industrial plant in it. This was the reaction of the well-to-do layer of the Meshhed Jews.

Very different was the reaction of the representatives of the ghetto, of the poor people. They did not believe that with the help of the rich people of Meshhed or of other places it would be possible to establish a *moshav* of Meshhed Jews in Erez Israel. On the other hand, they suggested that the two national funds should set up such a *moshav,* and then all the Jews of the ghetto—the rich (there are such), those of modest means, and the poor—will be ready to invest everything they have into participation in the project. Already the representatives of the ghetto have begun to compile a list of the Meshhed Jews, indicating the amounts they are ready to contribute to the project. This list will be sent to you [the Jewish Agency in Jerusalem] as soon as it is received in the Agency's Teheran office.

After having investigated the situation on the spot, it is the opinion of the delegation that about a thousand Jews, among them many young men and women, are really ready to go to Erez Israel right away, in whatever way or manner available to them, and to invest all their savings into the establishment of a settlement for Meshhed Jews. The delegation is further of the opinion that by suitable pressure exercised upon the rich Meshhed Jews in Meshhed itself, in Erez Israel, and in other places, it will be possible to move them to considerable participation in initiating such a project.

As for the *'aliya* itself, it should be noted that the ways of immigration suitable for the young people would be unsuitable for the adults and for families.

As is the case in Persia in general, the young people of Meshhed require preparation for their *'aliya.* The most suitable form, taking the local conditions

> into consideration, is training in trades. In Teheran, the building of a Ḥalutz-house has been started; it will serve as a center for the training of youth. It is planned to establish at this center a trade school, jointly with the Alliance. There can be no doubt that the establishment of branches of such a project in other cities will be most useful. If a trade school were established in association with the Ḥalutz movement in Meshhed, it would greatly contribute to solving the problem of training the youth of Meshhed.
>
> The institutions to which this report is being submitted are herewith requested to consider urgently the ways of saving the Meshhed community, along the lines and data given above. It should be unnecessary to note that the *anusim* of Meshhed, in their present extremely difficult situation, are awaiting with deep longing word and help from the *yishuv*. Evidently, other burning problems occupy at present the attention of our institutions. But it would be wrong, even in the present circumstances, to abandon a Jewish community in a remote corner of the world, which for more than a hundred years had preserved its Jewishness in the underground, and which today faces the danger of annihilation.
>
> The office of the Jewish Agency in Teheran, which maintains constant contact with the Jews of Meshhed, and follows closely the developments in this community since the disturbances of this past Passover, awaits your immediate answer to the cry of the Meshhed Jews for rescue and *'aliya*.

At the very time Yitzḥaq Kleinbaum wrote his alarming report warning the Jewish Agency of the danger of annihilation facing the Jewish community of Meshhed, unbeknownst to him, effective help was on the way. The Ozar Hatorah, an international organization established in 1944 for religious Jewish education in the Middle East and North Africa, and recognized by the United States government in 1946 and by the American Jewish Joint Distribution Committee in 1947, was busy making plans to establish schools in Iran. It appointed Rabbi Isaac Lewi head of its Iranian operations and actually opened its first school in Iran in 1948, a school in Shiraz. This was followed in quick succession by schools in Teheran and other places, and in Meshhed in 1954. Subsequently, Ozar Hatorah continued to expand its activities, and by the 1960s, it had established a network of forty schools in Iran, with an enrollment of 8,600 students, providing them with religious and secular education, as well as free lunches and medical care. In addition, Ozar Hatorah made an arrangement with the Alliance Israélite Universelle, to provide ten hours weekly of Jewish education in all Alliance primary schools.[2]

The opening of a Jewish school (even though under foreign auspices) in Meshhed speaks volumes about the changes that had taken place in the lives of the Meshhed Jews by 1954. For Jadīdī families to send their children to a Jewish school meant that they openly admitted that they adhered to the Jewish religion their ancestors had given up during the 1839 Allahdād. That they dared to do this indicates that by 1954, the authorities and the people of Meshhed had tacitly accepted that the Jadīd al-Islām were not Muslims at all but had remained Jews or had returned to Judaism, and no longer considered this an apostasy punishable by death. Also, the very fact that the authorities in Meshhed gave permission to Ozar Hatorah, a foreign Jewish religious organization, to open a school testifies to a diminishing of the influence of the religious bodies in the official leadership and public life. Whatever the enabling circumstances, the opening of the Ozar Hatorah school represented a most significant contribution to the preservation of Jewish life in Meshhed.

II
EMIGRATION, *'ALIYA*, DISPERSION

From the documents available in the Central Zionist Archives in Jerusalem, it appears that the impassioned plea with which Yitzḥaq Kleinbaum closed his memorandum resulted in no action on the part of any of the six offices to which he addressed it, nor was any communal action taken for the emigration of Meshhed Jews to Palestine-Israel following the 1946 visit of the delegation. Kleinbaum continued to urge the political department of the Jewish Agency in Jerusalem to take action for the Meshhed Jews, but without results. Typical of the department's attitude was the letter A. Eshel sent to Kleinbaum in Teheran on June 11, 1946:[1]

> It fell to me to acknowledge your letter to the political department. This time, I must thank you for the report on the visit to Meshhed. Since our people are overburdened, and their time does not permit them much reading, I concentrated your words and passed on the essence of your words to the director of the department and to several other people. However, I don't know whether their reading will be accompanied by results. There are no immigration certificates, and I doubt whether the 100,000 (if and when they will be given) will be able to serve Jews outside those uprooted in Europe.

Even after the independence of Israel, the Jews of Meshhed had to wait patiently until their turn came for *'aliya*. The very news that the Jewish state was established created great enthusiasm among them and intensified their desire "to go up." According to Zion Zabīḥī (original name Raḥmatullah ben Mahdī Zabīḥīoff), a member of the Jewish community who himself lived in Meshhed in those years and subsequently (in May 1951) made his *'aliya* to Israel, the eight thousand Jews who at that time lived in Meshhed started to liquidate their possessions and to make preparations for moving to Israel. They sold their stores and houses, even though they were able to realize only a fraction of their value, since the Muslims figured "if we don't buy it today, we shall get it tomorrow as ownerless property." However, arrangements for the transportation of Meshhed

Jews to Israel were made in an extremely leisurely manner, and even by June 1950—more than two years after the establishment of the Jewish state—only two hundred of them were able to make their *'aliya*. On June 23, 1950, the committee of Meshhed Jews that had been organized in London wrote a despondent letter to Eliyahu Elyashar, president of the Council of Sephardi Jews in Jerusalem:

> We are the Jews of Meshhed, one of the cities of Iran. In our ill fortune we have always been victims of pogroms and massacres, and our forefathers in consequence of these pogroms and massacres were forced 111 years ago to convert from Judaism to Islam, despite which we remained a hundred percent Jews to this very day, and even though it had to be done in secret, have always prayed for redemption. Thank God, the yearned-for day of the redemption of our brethren and the ingathering of their dispersion has arrived. News and facts about the efforts of the Government of Israel to help us to return to Erez Israel having come to us day after day, we too submitted about twelve months ago our demands and requests to the competent authorities, to the Jewish Agency, through the intermediacy of Dr. Levenberg, to the consul of Israel in London, and to the ambassador of Israel in the United States. As a result, 200 of our unfortunate people were transported from Meshhed through Teheran to Israel without any expenses—an operation for which we are greatly indebted.
>
> When the joyous news about the arrival of these brethren in Israel reached the other poor people of our community, most of them left their work, sold their houses and personal effects, and moved from Meshhed to Teheran, where they waited for their transportation to Israel, which, in their naïveté, they thought would be done right away.
>
> Unfortunately, no help at all came from the authorities in Israel, and these poor people—homeless and without any financial means—were abandoned in Teheran, where, in addition to deprivation, hunger, and lack of a roof over their heads, their very lives are also threatened.
>
> Today there are in Teheran about 1,000 such miserable people who wait and yearn for your help. All they want is help to go to Israel, where they will work and earn their livelihood.
>
> We the undersigned beg, yea, entreat, the authorities to pay heed to this request of ours and to save our unfortunate brethren one way or the other, so that they too should be able to live in a free atmosphere and to return to a life of work.
>
> We hope and pray that this request, which is submitted in the name of our brethren, should merit your immediate attention, and that you will do as best you can to induce all the institutions to take action for the rescue of our brethren from their desperate situation.

I was not able to ascertain what action, if any, Eliyahu Elyashar undertook in response to this desperate cry for help.

At about the same time, the Meshhed Jews in the United States also tried to help their brethren who were stuck in Iran waiting for *'aliya* to Israel. Their committee applied to President Chaim Weizmann of Israel and also the American Jewish organizations, requesting their help in enabling the Meshhed Jews to go to Israel. In response to their intervention, Yitzḥaq Raphael, head of the Jewish Agency's Department of Immigration and himself a religious Jew (he was a leading member of the Mizraḥi Party), turned to the two chief rabbis of Israel for their authoritative opinion on the religious status of the Jews of Meshhed. The reason for this step was that in certain religious circles, doubts were entertained about the Jewishness of the Meshhed Jews, similar to the doubt that attached to the status of the Ethiopian Falashas. The significance of the issue lay in the fact that Israeli law accorded the right of immigration to Israel to all Jews, but only to Jews; the Israeli institutions were supposed to bring to Israel only Jews who had the legal right to immigrate; non-Jews could come to the country only if their individual applications for immigration were approved. Yitzḥaq Raphael felt that before he could mobilize institutional help for the Meshhed Jews, he first had to ascertain whether rabbinically they were considered Jews who had the right to come to Israel. The opinions of the two chief rabbis differed substantially. The Ashkenazi chief rabbi, R. Yitzḥaq Halevi Herzog, wrote (my literal translation from the Hebrew):

> 1. The Gates of Repentance are not closed even to a voluntary apostate, God forbid, much less so to those who are the children of the children of forced converts, and whose souls yearn to return to the source of their origin, to our holy land, may it be rebuilt and firmly established.
>
> 2. What has to be considered in connection with them is the following: perhaps there are among them offspring of mixed marriages, that is, of a forced convert who married a non-Jewish woman, and the children born of such a union require conversion before a religious law court according to the Torah and the commandments. Likewise there is the apprehension that perhaps *mamzerim* [bastards, illegitimate children] were born among them, or such as are suspected *mamzerim*, that is, children of a couple that was married according to the laws of Moses and Israel (of course, in secret), but since there were no rabbis among them to arrange divorce, their divorce was arranged by a *qadi* [a Muslim religious judge], which, according to the law of our Holy Torah, is invalid, and then the woman married a Jew, on the basis of that divorce. It is, of course, possible that no such event ever occurred, since they are the minority.
>
> 3. My opinion is that one should send a rabbi to them who should clarify all the particulars. If there are among them offspring of mixed marriages of the kind explained above, they require conversion—if they can be converted individually, so much the better; if not, he [the rabbinical emissary] should take from them a promise with an oath on their faith in God that they would convert immediately upon their arrival in Israel. If it should be found that there

> are among them those concerning whom there is a suspicion of illegitimacy, let him [the rabbi] provide us with an accurate list, detailing all the facts, and concerning them we shall make a decision later.

The Sephardi chief rabbi, R. Ben-Zion Meir Ḥay Ouziel, wrote:

> According to reliable information, these *anusim* [forced converts] of Meshhed preserved their Jewishness in their homes, veritably at the risk of their lives, and especially in matters of the family: they celebrated marriages only by "canopy and sanctification" [the Jewish ritual], according to the Torah of Moses and Israel, and if they needed a *get* [letter of divorce], they went to the Jewish communities, and there arranged for the letter of divorce according to the law and the Halakhah. Therefore they are pure Jews in everything they say.[2]

Ben-Zion Y'hoshu'a, after reprinting these two rabbinical opinions, remarks caustically in a footnote that neither of the two learned rabbis was aware of the fact that among the Jews of Meshhed there were simply no divorces. In any case, the conclusion the Israeli authorities reached was that the Jews of Meshhed were *kosher* Jews in every respect, and they were given institutional help to come to Israel.

After the Khomeini revolution in Iran (1979) and the establishment of the fundamentalist Muslim government in the country, most of the Meshhed Jews who still lived in Meshhed, Teheran, or other cities of Iran left and immigrated to Israel and to other parts of the free world. By 1995, no more than a dozen or so Jewish families still remained in Meshhed, but the communities of Meshhed Jews in Israel and the Diaspora, and especially in New York, continued to preserve their traditions; maintain their own congregations, synagogues, schools, and cultural activities; and perpetuate the memory of that unique form of Jewish life that was developed by their ancestors as Jadīd al-Islām in Meshhed.

12

A Meshhed Jewish Family: Āqā Farajullah's Memoirs

This story of a leading merchant family among the Jadīd al-Islām of Meshhed was written in Judeo-Persian in Jerusalem in 1944 by Farajullah Nasrullayoff Livian (1874–1951), a member of that family who in 1929 moved to Jerusalem and became the head of the Meshhedi Jewish community there. In 1944–46, when I studied the Meshhedi Jews in Jerusalem, Nasrullayoff was my main informant, and since his knowledge of conversational Hebrew was limited, his son, Yoḥanan Livian, interpreted for me.

Almost fifty years after our original collaboration, I was fortunate to meet again Yoḥanan Livian—it turned out that he was a neighbor of mine in Forest Hills, N.Y. He informed me that he had in his possession a manuscript by his late father, describing briefly the origin of the Jews of Meshhed and dwelling in greater detail on the history of his own family and his own life. At my urging, Livian undertook to translate the text from his father's Judeo-Persian into Hebrew, and after he prepared the translation, I used his Hebrew version as the basis for my own translation into English. Together, we went over my English translation carefully and compared it with his father's Judeo-Persian text, to make sure that it was faithful to the original. Livian also helped me in identifying several of the place names mentioned in the text and explaining many of the references to matters that were not sufficiently clear.

In my translation, I tried to follow the original as closely as possible, even when this required a nonidiomatic use of English. Nor did I try to improve the style or give it a more literary cast. In my judgment, Āqā Farajullah's writing, with his style and manner of telling his story, is in itself a cultural document that should not be tampered with.

What emerges, first of all, from this story is the personality of Farajullah Nasrullayoff as a youth, and later a young man, of surprising self-assurance, able to take control of the family's big export-import business at a very early age, and daring to oppose and to overrule the business decisions of his uncles who had brought him up from the age of seven (when his own father had died). He also appears as a man of considerable resourcefulness, able to cope with repeated emergencies and dangers that threatened to annihilate him and his family and to wipe out the enterprise that he had built up. What is lacking in his personal reminiscences is any reference to his wife (he mentions only briefly that he got married) and his children. His autobiography breaks off when he was about forty-five years old, but all we learn about his children is that he had five sons, two of whom died in infancy (he lists their names). He does not mention at all whether he (or, for that matter, his brothers) had any daughters and what was the relationship among him, his wife, and his children. Evidently, when it came to matters of sentiment, of feelings that tied him to wife and children, he was not able to overcome his deeply ingrained, culturally determined inhibitions. Yet, despite his silence on these matters, the very context of his narrative testifies to his devotion to his immediate family and, beyond it, to his unswerving loyalty to the large Nasrullayoff clan consisting of the numerous progeny of Farajullah's grandfather, Karb Āqājān.

While Farajullah was an astute businessman, he was also a deeply religious Jew. When, as a young boy, he arrived in Deregez (Darre Gaz, a town in Iran, also known as Mohammadabad, on the U.S.S.R. border, about 130 kilometers north-northwest of Meshhed), he was scandalized to learn that the Meshhedi Jewish men who lived there without their families (they had left their families behind in Meshhed) ate non-kosher meat, did not observe the Sabbath, and had no synagogue. The manner in which young Farajullah induced his fellow Jadīdīm in Deregez to observe the Jewish precepts is one of the most interesting parts of his account. Incidentally, we learn that for several years there was a sizable Jewish community in Deregez, as well as in Merv (Marw, Mevy, full name Marw al-Shāhijān, the major city of Turkmenistan), recruited from Meshhedi Jews who sojourned there in connection with their business enterprises. Nothing of this has been known until now.

In addition to all this, we learn much about the conduct of the family's export-import business, which had branches in several cities in Persia, as well as in Russian Turkmenistan. Especially noteworthy in this connection is not the manner in which the business was conducted or the disagreements between Farajullah and his uncles and brothers who were his partners, but the participation of the leading members of the Meshhedi Jewish community in settling differences among the partners. The heads of the community seem to have functioned as a forum of arbitrators, in whose presence the partners discussed their differences, and who appended their signatures to, and thereby validated, the agreements reached by the partners. This was a remarkable institution, and it was a poignant manifestation of the cohesion within the community.

The same cohesion was expressed also in the support the family and the community provided when one of their members fell ill. When young Farajullah became sick in Merv, there was a whole group of men, both relatives and unrelated Jadīdīm, who took care of him, drove the semiconscious boy to a distant healer, assisted at the painful treatment he had to undergo, and stayed with him until he recovered. Marriage and death in a family were likewise community affairs.

From these reminiscences, we also learn about the relationship between the Meshhed Jews and the non-Jewish population of the places in which they lived. Quite remarkable are the incidents that show how close and friendly was the relationship between the Jews and the Turkomans. Not only did Turkoman healers save young Farajullah's life, but, some years later, it was Turkoman guides who smuggled him and his friends, disguised as Turkomans, out of Russian territory, saving them at the risk of their own lives. The Meshhedi Jewish merchants entrusted their merchandise to Turkoman caravans, which faithfully delivered the consignments to their destinations despite the ever-present danger of highway robbery. Jadīdīm from Meshhed who sojourned in Merv would buy up the cotton crop from Turkoman cultivators and advance them the money at the time of sowing, with the understanding that after harvest the crop would be delivered to them. The Jadīdī financiers then would ship the cotton by train to Moscow to sell it there.

The relationship between the Meshhedi Jews and the local governors, whether Persian or Russian, was also friendly. The Merv oasis was occupied by the Russians in 1884. In the 1890s, when a cholera epidemic broke out in the area, the Russian governor, whose name Farajullah spells Gropatkin but who must have been a member of the well-known Russian princely family Kropotkin (and a relative of the well-known scientist, sociologist, revolutionary, and theorist of anarchism, Prince Peter Alekseyevich Kropotkin), permitted two groups of Meshhedi Jews, numbering more than a hundred men, to leave Merv by train for Persia. Another decade or so later, after Farajullah had become a wealthy man, he gave large loans to several governors of the Persian town of Deregez.

All in all, this autobiographical writing affords a rare insight into the life and tribulations of a practically unknown Jewish community on the Persian-Russian border in the late nineteenth century. It is an extremely valuable document.

Farajullah Nasrullayoff's Account of the History of the Jews of Meshhed, of His Family, and of His Own Early Life (Date: Thursday, eighth of Tammuz 5704 [1944])

I, Farajullah[1] (Yonathan), son of Nasrullah (Nissan), son of Karb[2] Āqājān[3] (Nethanel), son of Simḥa, son of Khudādād (Nethanel), son of Abraham Levi of Meshhed, inhabitant of Jerusalem, feel it is my duty to write down the chain [of descent] of the family, as far as possible, for our family and our children, and to tell them about it, as far as is known to me, so that they should know their chain [of descent], and also to tell them about the Jews of Meshhed, the elders of our old generation, from where they came and what was the reason of their move to Meshhed.

At the date of 5502 [1742], when Nadir Shah Afshar[4] ruled in Iran, he returned from a victory in India, brought with him very many precious stones and all the treasure of India, and wanted to transport them to Kalat which is in the district of Khorasan, and to hide it there. And since he did not trust its Muslims,[5] he wanted to appoint Jews over all the treasure, for he trusted them. He therefore ordered that of the men of name from among the Jews of Qazwin[6] they should select forty families and transfer them to Meshhed, and from Meshhed they should send them on to Kalat.

In accordance with Nadir Shah's order, they sent forty families from among the Jews of Qazwin to Meshhed. Seventeen families, who were sent to begin with and had reached Meshhed, were already sent on to Kalat, sixteen families reached Meshhed, and seven families of Levites got as far as Sabzawar,[7] when Nadir Shah was killed in Tas Tepe,[8] between Rādkān[9] and Qazwin. After he was killed, the Jews who had reached Kalat remained in Kalat, and the Jews who had reached Meshhed remained in Meshhed, and those who reached Sabzawar remained there. After the assassination of Nadir Shah, there was widespread revolution in Iran: every district governor and every army commander became independent, and great disturbances took place in the country, so that it was not possible to go from one city to another or from one village to another. This situation continued three or four years, until it became somewhat more quiet in Iran, and the roads were opened up for travel from city to city. The seven families of Levites who had remained in Sabzawar went on from there to Meshhed and joined the families that already were there, and since the Muslims in Meshhed were all of the Shī'a sect and the Jews were considered by them unclean, therefore all the Jews who had remained in Meshhed were living close to the walls in the 'Ēd-Gāh [lit. Feast Place] area, where there were woods and gardens all over.

For several years, the Jews were living between these walls, and since the Jews were considered unclean, there were no commercial connections between them [and the Muslims]. Those were difficult years for the Jews until gradually they purchased plots of land in the area in which they lived and which was called 'Ēdgāh, and began to build houses for themselves. In the course of time, they moved out from the walls and lived in their houses, and their life began to be better also in economy and commerce, and the community began to grow, as we shall tell in these reminiscences.

As far as is known to me, the name of our great-grandfather, whose children, the Levites, were by the order of Nadir Shah brought from Qazwin to Meshhed, was Abraham Levi. The name of his son in Persian was Khudādād (in Hebrew,

Nethanel). The name of Khudādād's son was Simḥa, and since the name of Khudādād's wife was Bemōnī, who was the daughter of Simḥa Na'mat, when a son was born to her, she called him by the name of her father, so that the son was called after his mother Simḥa Bemōnī. At the end of his life, he became well known by this name.

To Simḥa Bemōnī, six sons were born in Meshhed, as follows: the first was Barham [Abraham], the second Mullah Ya'qov, the third Karb Āqājān (Nethanel), the fourth Yiṣḥaq, the fifth Moshe, the sixth Eliyahu.

(1) Abraham, who later was called Abraham Khadkhuda because he was the head of the [Jewish] community, had one son, Āqāi. Āqāi had two sons, the first Yosef Khadkhuda, and the younger one Ḥājjī, who died at a young age. Yosef Khadkhuda had a son called Āqāi, who is still alive and lives in Meshhed. Abraham Khadkhuda, their father, was sent by the English through Afghanistan to India, and he got lost there. It is not known what happened to him. Rumor has it that he died on board a ship and that he was cast into the sea.

(2) The second son, Mullah Ya'qov, was a *mullah* [teacher] and also a ritual slaughterer, and he had four sons in Meshhed, as follows: Ḥājjī Ismā'īl Levi (Ḥājjī Y'ḥezq'el), Mullah Yaḥya (Y'hudah), Ḥājjī Mahdī (Mattityah), Āq Rafi' (R'fa'el) Levi. Ḥājjī Ismā'īl had no children. Of the children of the others, we shall tell later.

(3) Karb Āqājān, who in Hebrew was called Nethanel, had four sons, as follows: from his first wife, he had a son called Nasrullah and two daughters, one Mikhal and the other Sarah. His [first] wife was the daughter of Ḥājjī 'Alī Ḥakīm, and she was deaf. After her death, Karb Āqājān married again, and from his second wife he had three sons, 'Azizullah ('Azaryah), Ḥabibullah (Ḥanukah), Raḥmatullah (Yirm'ya).

(a) Nasrullah, who was our father, and his wife the daughter of Moshe Ḥakīm, had six sons as follows: the first, Qajin (Nethanel), the second 'Abdullah (Mord'khay), the third Mahdī (Mashiaḥ), the fourth Nūrullah (Sh'ma'yah), the fifth Farajullah (Jonathan), the sixth Fayzullah (Sh'mu'el).

(b) 'Azīzullah ('Azaryah) had in Meshhed six sons, the first Shukrullah (Simḥa), the second Yosef, the third Amīn (Binyamin), the fourth Ramazān (Moshe), the fifth 'Abdulraḥīm (Aharon), the sixth Ḥājjī (Efrayim).

(c) Ḥabībullah (Ḥanukah) had two sons as follows: 'Abdulraḥmān and Hādī.

(d) Raḥmatullah had six sons as follows: Ibrāhīm (Avraham), Yiṣḥaq, Ya'aqov, 'Abdulkarīm (Levi), Nabīullah (Shlomoh), Y'hudah.

If I shall have time, I shall perhaps write down later the names of their sons.

(4) The children of 'Amo[10] Yiṣḥaq, the fourth son of Simḥa Bemōnī, were four, as follows: Ramazān (Mishael), Ḥājjī Naurūz, Amīn, Ḥājjī Suleymān. If I shall have time, I shall write down later the names of their children.

(5) 'Amo Moshe, the fifth child of Simḥa Bemōnī, had one son named Ḥājjī Mahdī, who went with his father to Bejenurd [Bujnurd] and died there in his youth.

(6) The children of 'Amo Eliyahu, the sixth son of Simḥa Bemōnī, were four sons as follows: 'Abdulkarīm, 'Abdulraḥīm, Ṣadīq, and Elisha'.

(a) 'Abdulkarīm, whose wife was my elder sister Shifrah, had one son who died at the age of two, and then his father died, and six months later his wife, too, died.

(b) 'Abdulraḥīm had one son who was called Elias. Elias had no children, and died.

(c) Ṣadīq had one son named 'Abdulkarīm, and he is still alive.

(d) Elisha' had four children as follows: Moshe, Ya'qov, Yiṣḥaq, and Eliyahu.

Some fifteen to seventeen years ago, I drew a [family] tree, intending to establish the [genealogical] chain of Simḥa Bemōnī in the shape of a tree whose base would start with Abraham Khudādād, and the tree would [start] from Simḥa Bemōnī and its big branches from the children of Simḥa Bemōnī, and the branches of its branches from their seed and the seed of their seed, the names according to the order, each branch with its descendants, and the *mappah* [map] of the three is now in our house, but thereafter the names of the newborn children were no longer entered.

Earlier, I enumerated the names of the children who were born to my father. He had six children.

(a) The first was Āqājān, who at the age of nineteen went to Deregez, and when he was twenty he fell ill with a serious throat illness [and died], and his body was transported to Meshhed, and [he was laid to rest] in the Tah 'Ēdgāh [bottom of the 'Ēdgah] cemetery. He was buried behind the courtyard of the Meshhed synagogue. He died on the sixteenth of Tammuz 5641 [1881] in Deregez, and was buried in Meshhed on the twenty-sixth of Tammuz 5641.

(b) The second son, 'Abdullah (Mord'khay), had four children as follows: Nasrullah (Nissan), Luṭfullah (Mord'khay), David, Suleymān (Shlomoh). My brother 'Abdullah died in Deregez on Iyyar 28, 5667 (1907), and his body was taken to Meshhed and he was buried in the courtyard of the cemetery (under the bazaar) of Zir Bazarcheh 'Ēdgāh.

(c) The children of my brother Mahdī are: two sons, Moshe and Babajān (Y'hoshu'a). My brother Mahdī died on the New Moon of Kislev 5669 [1909] in Merv,[11] and was buried there in the cemetery of the Meshhedis.

(d) The children of my brother Nūrullah were two, as follows: Ḥājjī Āqā (Nethanel) and Elias (Eliyahu). My brother Nūrullah died in Meshhed on the ninth of Elul 5679 [1909], and was buried in the cemetery outside the gate of the 'Ēdgāh.

(e) I, Farajullah (Yonathan) Levi (Livian), had five children, as follows: the first Qudratullah (Daniel), the second Naṣratallah (Ḥananel), the third ʻUzzatallah (Ḥananyah), the fourth Nematollah (Yoḥanan), the fifth Najatullah (Mattityah). Naṣratullah and Najatullah died in their childhood in Deregez and were buried in the cemetery of the Meshhedis.

(f) My brother Fayzullah had four children, as follows: Fatḥullah (Y'hudah), Khudabakhsh, ʻAbdulraḥmān (Raḥamīn), Āq Buzurg (R'fa'el). Thank God, all the family is still alive.

It seems that our great-grandfather Khudādād and his wife Bemōnī and their son Simḥa went to Bukhara, and great-grandfather Khudādād died there and was buried there. His wife Bemōnī and the child Simḥa returned with Turkoman caravans to Meshhed, and it seems that instead of the *khajāwa* or *falqi,* which at that time was a kind of conveyance (*makhshir*) like a saddle in which they traveled, they arranged for them two *kavārehs* (big baskets) and put into them hay so that it should be comfortable for them, and put them on a camel on its two sides. In one sat the mother, and in the other the son Simḥa. They were on the way six months until they reached Meshhed, and because of this her grandsons called her Sabta Kavare (Grandma Basket).

After they reached Meshhed, they saw that the Jews had no place for [ritual] immersion. There was a network of cisterns under several houses of the Jews, called *khārīz* (cistern). Several owners of those houses arranged for themselves *fayub,* like a *miqveh,* not deep, and the women used to immerse themselves there.

In those days, the Gebers[12] (the Persians who prayed to fire) suffered very much from the Muslims who caused them great sufferings, so that many of them fled abroad from Meshhed, and only a few families remained in the streets of the ʻĒdgāh. They had a bathhouse which they wanted to sell before they left. For the Muslims, the bathhouse of the Gebers was unclean, and they did not want to buy it, and they [the Gebers] wanted to get rid of the bathhouse and wanted to sell it very cheap. At the end, they wanted to sell the bathhouse and the land around it (*gov ambār andbul ḥand*) (places where they heated the bathhouse) and the lands around it, about 5,000 *zar* (meters), for a hundred *tomans* (Persian money), which was 1,000 *q'rān.* At that time, Bemōnī, the mother of Simḥa, gathered the whole congregation of the Jews and told them that "The bathhouse is needed for the Jews. If we buy it, there will be a place for the whole community to bathe, both women and men, and also a place for submersion for the women." Then the congregation said, "We have no strength to pay one hundred *tomans* and to buy it. And even if we should buy the bathhouse, the Muslims will not work for us, and we have nobody who would take care of it and would gather *gūd* (cattle dung) and would light for us the *gulḥand,* the place where the water is heated. And also it is necessary to draw water from the cisterns for the pool of the bath and to collect water, therefore the bathhouse is out of the question for us." Bemōnī, the mother of Simḥa, said to the community that "one half of the money for this—let the community pay it, and the second half I myself shall pay. As for drawing water for the bath, my son Simḥa will draw the water and collect water from the cisterns [and gather] *āmbār* (cow dung), and as for lighting the fire, all that my son Simḥa will do. During the time that the bath will be [open] for men, my son will sit in the bathhouse and take care of it, and during the time of the women, I myself shall sit in the bathhouse and shall take care of all the things of the bathers."

When the community heard her words, they agreed to buy the bathhouse for the Jews from the Gebers for a hundred *tomans* cash money, half of which Bemōnī, the mother of Simḥa, paid, and the other half the community. For several years after the community thus obtained the bathhouse, Simḥa Bemōnī worked in the bathhouse, and all the time he was drawing water from the cisterns which were underground, and was filling the cisterns of the bathhouse, and always he himself was going to the caravansary, where there were horses and donkeys, and under the houses he was gathering the *āmbār* (the dung of the animals), drying it, and collecting it for the winter that it should be ready for lighting. Every week, twice or three times, he heated the bath. In the mornings the men, and during the day the women, would bathe. For the submersion of the women, the *miqveh* was open every day, as Bemōnī, the mother of Simḥa, promised it to the community. She fulfilled her promise, and as long as the bathhouse was under her management, Bemōnī would bring *āmbār* and put it on the roof of the bathhouse and arrange it to dry it, and then she would arrange it in heaps for the winter and also for the summer, and therefore their children called her *āmbār pāzan* (dung preparer; one who prepares the dung of the animals by treading it with the feet), and the descendants of Bemōnī were proud of the name by which they were called, for Simḥa Bemōnī worked voluntarily for the community without getting any payment. Now, as I am writing these reminiscences, I [too] am proud that I am one of the descendants of such benefactors of the Meshhed community.[13]

When I was six years old, my brother Āqājān went to Deregez. I remember exactly the faces of my brother and father. A year later, my brother fell ill in Deregez of a throat disease and died there. His body was sent to Meshhed, and on the twenty-first of Tammuz 5641 [1881], his body arrived in Meshhed. At that time, my father was very sick, he was not allowed to get out of bed, and the man who brought the body demanded stubbornly that my father should go to the gate of the house, and when they took my father to the gate, he felt (understood) that they had brought the body of his son Āqājān. As they were taking down the body from the horse, my father fainted and collapsed. The relatives took him instantly back into the room and put him to bed, and in the meantime they took Āqājān and buried him. On the eve of the seventh day of mourning, as they were sewing up the cut [on the coat][14] of my father, two hours later my father died, on the twenty-ninth of Tammuz 5641 [1881], and the whole community gathered, and they buried him next to his son in the 'Ēdgāh cemetery, behind the synagogue of the community. My father was fifty when he died; I was seven years old.

After the death of my brother and father, my mother could not be comforted. Her economic situation became bad, and she lived amidst great difficulties, even though, as was the custom, they prepared food for her for a whole year, such as wheat flour, oil, wood for lighting the hearth, and the like.[15] For her expenses, they [the family] gave her only five *q'rān* per month, even though she had five children. My mother had five children [*sic*] and three daughters, and she had to bring up the children, and life was very difficult for her, she was crying day and night. All the children had to go to school, and there were expenses. I myself was seven when they put me into the *maktab* [school] of *ākhūnd* [teacher] Muḥammad Ḥasan. It is from him that I learned all my Persian, also the Jadīdī (Rashi)[16] writing, which I use. That teacher taught me *abgad*[17] [the aleph-beth]. And since I knew Persian, right away the same day, I learned the Jadīdī (Rashi) script. The same day, I wrote a letter in the Jadīdī script to my big brother 'Abdullah, and in the evening, I took the letter and went to his house and gave it to him, and he gave me a gift, half a *pūl,* that is, half a penny. For that half *pūl,* next day, I bought dry ink and went to the *maktab* and sold it for a *pūl,* and for that money I bought and sold, so that on the day I left the *maktab,* I already had several *q'rān*s, and for that I went and bought a complete prayer book and several other Hebrew books. Three *q'rān*s were left over, and my mother asked me to buy for her for that money *ṭās badiyah,* a brass plate and pot. I bought them and gave them to her. After I left the *maktab,* for two or three days, I worked in our store. During the days, I was writing and learning more Persian so that my handwriting should be better. Our store was in the Shahvardikhan caravansary, one of the first stores, on the first floor.

At that time, the late David 'Azizullah was in Meshhed and managed the business. Guests and relatives, acquaintances who had something to do, used to sit and talk, and the first thing one had to offer them was *qalyūn* (*narghīleh*), and the water of the *qalyūn* had to be renewed, and fire had to be put on the tobacco at the top of the *qalyūn,* and one had to pull in the air so that it should be *dūdī* (smoky), and then to hand it to them. And I, since I was not used to smoking, did not inhale the air, but put fire on the tobacco and blew on it with my mouth so that the fire should turn red, and then passed it to them. Then the late David 'Azīzullah said to me that the *qalyūn* must be made *dūdī,* that it should smoke, "and then give it to the guests." At least five or six times a day, I had to prepare the *qalyūn* and draw in the smoke and place it before the guests; therefore, when I reached the age of eleven or twelve, I was already poisoned by the smoke of the *narghīleh.*

In those days, the late Ḥājjī Ismā'īl Levi, who was the husband of my aunt Mikhal, had a commercial store in the Seray Nasriyyah,[18] and he wanted me to work for him, and also my uncles ordered me to go to work for him without any salary. I agreed and went to work for Ḥājjī Ismā'īl, who at that time was bringing from Istanbul all kinds of Chinaware and glassware and pocket watches and *mahūt* (a velvet-like textile). The pocket watches were sold one by one in the store, and for each piece they sold he gave me half a penny (*niss pūl*). During the month that I was with Ḥājjī Ismā'īl, I accumulated fifteen *pūl.*

Then I again became desirous to go to Mullah Abba to learn Hebrew. When I got home, I told my mother that I had the idea of learning Hebrew, but the monthly tuition fee was one *q'rān,* and I don't have it, and if I go half a day, until noontime, to study, and half a day to work, by the end of the month I shall lack the money. "Are you willing to pay for me to go to learn Hebrew?" My mother embraced me and kissed me and said, "Go, my son, go to learn Hebrew, and every month if you will lack money, I shall pay for you." I was very glad, and next day I went to the store of Ḥājjī Y'ḥezq'el [Ismā'īl] and told him that I had the desire to learn Hebrew. "Will you permit me that half a day, until noontime, I should go and study with Mullah Abba, and after noon I should come to work for you?" He too accepted the idea gladly, and thereafter I began to study half a day and work half a day. And since I had a command of Persian, I quickly learned to read and write [Hebrew]; in brief, in six months, I read and learned the Persian translation of the Book of B'reshit [Genesis] from Mullah Abba.

In those days, it was very difficult to learn Hebrew, for one had to study in secret. In the courtyard of Mullah Abba, there was a cellar, and in it he taught ten to twelve children Hebrew, and all the time the door of his courtyard was closed, and the children who wanted to study went into the Ḥājjihā[19] street, and from the courtyard of Mahdī Kal,[20] [they went] to the house of Āqāī Shafī', and from the house of Āqāī Shafī', they crossed over on the roof of the house to the roof of Mullah Abba's house, and went down into his courtyard, and studied in the cellar of his house.

After having studied six months with Mullah Abba, my uncles told me that I had to go to Deregez to work for Uncle Ḥabībullah and Uncle 'Abdullah. Incidentally, during the six months of my study, I never had to ask my mother for money—it was all covered by the half *pūl* gifts I got for selling watches in the store of Ḥājjī Ismā'īl.

In the last month in which I worked for Ḥājjī Ismā'īl, one day my Aunt Mikhal (my father's sister) came to my mother and brought a *plastiq*[21] coat of brown color, its price was possibly five *q'rāns*, as a present for me for having worked in their store, and said to my mother that since Ḥājjī Ismā'īl had no children, he wanted to take me to him as a son, and all his richness he would transfer to my name. In the evening, when I returned to the house of my mother, she brought out the *plastiq* coat and put it before me, and said in great joy that

"Aunt Mikhal brought this as a present for you and said that 'I want to take Farajullah to me as a son, so that he should be my heir after my death.'" When I heard these words from my mother, I began to cry and said to my mother that I do not agree, and do not accept her present, and shall return to her the coat. My mother wanted to explain to me that Ḥājjī Ismā'īl was rich, and "all his richness will be yours." I told my mother that as long as I shall live, it would be a shameful thing for me to become rich from the property of others. If I shall be a man, God will give me according to His will what He thinks was coming to me, and if I shall not be a man, then all the richness that Ḥājjī Ismā'īl would give me would be lost within a few years, but this shame would follow in my footsteps all my life, and I shall not accept the gift. The same day, I returned to her the coat and told my mother that she should tell her that if they should again speak of this thing, I would no longer come to their store. The day after that, my aunt brought coats and gave them to my mother and went away.

Sometime later, they sent me to Deregez with horses and men who worked for us in the transport of merchandise. At that time, Uncle Ḥabībullah and my brother 'Abdullah were in Deregez and managed the business. In Deregez, there were seventeen stores owned by Jews (Jadīdīm), all of whom were used to eating meat from the marketplace and did not observe the Sabbath. When I arrived in Deregez, all the Jadīdīm were sleeping in their stores, and they had in the same stores *ojāq* (ovens), and they were preparing and cooking the food, and preparing water for tea, for in those days there were no stores in which tea was prepared and distributed, so that everyone was forced to prepare tea for himself in the morning and in the evening. There was no difference at all between the weekdays and the Sabbath, and since every evening they put out the lights, they were forced to put out the lights also on the eve of the Sabbath.

When I arrived in Deregez, they told me from which butcher to buy meat and taught me how to prepare soup. The first evening, when I prepared soup, since the meat was not kosher, I myself did not eat of it. The second night, when I made soup and presented it to the grown-ups, I myself did not want to eat of it. My big brother 'Abdullah shouted at me angrily and said, "This is not the house of Mother, and you must eat." They forced me, and I had to participate with them in the food, and from that day on, I did eat together with them. For the Sabbath, I had to prepare *pilaw*, Sabbath rice, whose oil was of butter and the meat was meat from the marketplace.[22] I wanted to prepare the food for the Sabbath on Friday, but Uncle Ḥabībullah told me not to do that, so that the *goyim* [the Muslims] should not notice any difference, that this was the Sabbath. I wanted to prepare the rice and to cover it with blankets so that it should become cooked and I should not have to touch the fire a second time, but the uncle said it will not be good to cover the pot, one had to put fire also on top of the lid of the pot so that the rice should be cooked well. On that occasion, since I was like a worker working for them, I was forced to obey their instructions. What I did was to tell [the owners of] three stores on one side of our store and three stores on the other side, who were also Jews from Meshhed, and ask them that they should observe the Sabbath and should not touch the fire; since I desecrated the Sabbath anyway, I would take their teapots and prepare them in our place, and return them when they were ready to drink. And every Friday night, before going to sleep, I went and put out their lights, and I said to myself, I must in any case desecrate the Sabbath and touch fire. So I did not let them touch fire and desecrate the Sabbath. At that time, I was thirteen years old.

All the work in the store was on my shoulders, such as cutting up wood, drawing water from the cisterns which were far from the store, and taking it to the store. Every day, I had to draw water five or six times and bring it to the store. And, in addition, since all the cooking was done with wood, and the wood was brought by the Kurds on camels from the gardens of Kakistar,[23] when they arrived outside the gate of the city, I went there and bought several bundles from the cameleers and stored them for a while. And every day or every other day, I had to chop up the wood and prepare it, all alone, for I was like a worker in the store. And in the winter season, or always, early in the morning, before the grown-ups woke up, I had to get up and prepare hot water and set the table for breakfast, so that when the grown-ups got up, everything should be ready. Even in the evening, I had to prepare the sleeping places of the grown-ups (in those days, they slept on the floor), and in the morning I had to gather them.[24] All day long, I had to prepare, according to their instructions, all kinds of food. I also had to clean the store. All this was too much for a child of twelve or thirteen, so that I never slept enough.

Since our store was located in the central street, our sales were *angro* [*en gros*], that is, wholesale. The small stores that sold to individuals were buying from us merchandise, textiles, black tea, blocks of sugar, *nīl* (a kind of stone to whiten the washing), and the like. Occasionally, during the day, when I had a chance and I had the time, I went into the storeroom where was stored the sugar (*kale qand*), whole big Russian pieces, weighing a hundred to two hundred *man* (Persian weight, about three kilos), weighed them and put them aside, and sold them to individuals, and put the money aside, and when the grown-ups needed money, I gave it to them, and when they asked from where did I have the money, I told them that I had bought from the storehouse a hundred or two hundred *man* of sugar at five *q'rāns* less than for what the grown-ups sold it wholesale, and that was my profit. They were glad to hear this, and said nothing [against it]. And at the time of the sales, I also sold at the market price, and all the profit was mine, for they gave me nothing in any other way, nor a salary for being a worker, since we were partners in the business. I stayed fourteen months in Deregez, and then returned to Meshhed together with Uncle Ḥabībullah.

In connection with our partnership with the family and the uncles, I must mention what happened to me. When our grandfather Karb Āqājān was at the end of his life, he contracted the illness *shevāvil* (a kind of wasting disease) in his feet, and was confined to bed for about three years. In those days, the Jews in Meshhed were called Jadīd al-Islām, and they had commercial relations among themselves. At that time, the Muslim merchants were importing Kirmanian merchandise from Kirman, such as *shawls* and other things that were in demand in the Russian market in Bukhara. The Jews of Meshhed imported much merchandise and bought it on credit, with payment due after fifteen to twenty months, and were dispatching it with Turkoman caravans to Bukhara. There the merchandise would be sold at good prices, and there they purchased merchandise that was in demand in Persia and sent it to Meshhed with the same caravans. When this merchandise arrived in Meshhed, it was sold at good prices, with much profit, at three times the price they had paid for it. What happened was that a caravan that left Meshhed arrived in Bukhara six months later, and the trip back from Bukhara also took six months; the same caravan went in both directions. Each caravan had to be big, some three to four hundred camels. The man who was in charge of such a caravan had to be of the Turkomans, known and reliable and accepted by the merchants. The *kāravān-bāshī* (leader of the caravan) took along a hundred armed men to protect the caravan on its way from Meshhed to Bukhara or back, for the roads were not safe, and there were many highwaymen on the roads, and the consignments had to be protected so that they should arrive safely at their destination.

In those days, the profession of the Turkomans from Merv, Tajānī, Akhālī, Kobehī (Turkoman tribes) was to rob. Those robbers attacked the caravans on their way and robbed them, so that the whole caravan was robbed. However, a caravan that was [accompanied] by armed guards would succeed in fighting off the robbers and would reach its destination unharmed. All merchandise that arrived undamaged was sold at a threefold price, and likewise also the merchandise that arrived from Bukhara was sold at a price no less than threefold. For this reason, the Jewish merchants who sent merchandise by caravans divided it into three consignments and sent it with three caravans, so that if two caravans were robbed, the [merchandise sent by] the third caravan could be sold with a profit. Likewise, the carpets they brought from Bukhara they would divide into three consignments, and send them with three separate caravans. And since the Jews were honest people and worked faithfully, they had credit with the Muslims, and every merchandise that arrived in Meshhed they sold on long-term credit, for the Jews were trustworthy.

In those days, my grandfather Karb Āqājān was in this business, and since at the end of his life he contracted the *shevāvil* in his leg and was unable to leave the house, my father, Nasrullah, who was the oldest of the sons and had a wife and children, undertook to manage the business. It so happened that while my grandfather was sick and bedridden, several of the caravans, which transported also our merchandise, were attacked and robbed by highwaymen. When my grandfather heard what had happened, he died in Meshhed.

At his death, he left behind three small children by his second wife: the oldest was 'Azīzullah, seven years old, the second Ḥabībullah, five years old, and the youngest Raḥmatullah, six months old. After the death of Karb Āqājān, Ḥājjī Ismā'īl Levi, who was a cousin and also a son-in-law of Karb Āqājān, came to my father, Nasrullah, and said to him, "Render accounts, and let me know what are your assets, so that when the children grow up, there should be no problems within the family." My father, since our caravans were just at that time robbed by highwaymen so that our merchandise was lost, had nothing to declare, and, in addition, had debts in the amount of five hundred *tomans*. He did not want people to learn that we had lost everything, for if it had become known, all our credit in the marketplace would have ceased, people would not have made business with us, and would not have given us merchandise on credit, so that we could not have conducted our business as usual. Therefore, my father thought that it was better that nobody should know what was going on in the family business, and said to Ḥājjī Ismā'īl that he did not want to render accounts. However much Ḥājjī Ismā'īl pressed him to reveal the accounts, my father refused, saying that he did not want the family to know how much there was, for if we have richness, they will not want to go to work, and if there is a lack and we have lost, then, again, they will be discouraged and will have no will to work. Therefore, this is not the time to render accounts.

As a matter of fact, the accounts, in all detail, were entered into the books, but my father did not want even the brother of his wife to know them. He was apprehensive that the information could go from mouth to mouth, and if it would become revealed that there was a loss, this would cause damage to the conduct of the business that was working with credit.

At the end of his life, my father contracted tuberculosis. He knew that he would not recover and wrote out a will in his own hand, in which he specified all accounts from beginning to end, and also told about how he had brought up these children [his young brothers] in all kinds of difficult conditions, and did not let them feel any poverty. And now, of what there is, with the help of God, he and his three brothers are equal partners, and "since of all the property that we now have one quarter is coming to me, and since I have a wife and a big family, five children[25] [*sic*] and four small daughters, let them consider and let them allocate to my children one half, and let them take one half. But if they don't want it, and want to take also my share, since they are my brothers, I agree willingly. God who had given life to my sons and daughters, will also give them a livelihood in honor."

Six months after he had written this will, he died.

After the death of my father, the uncles Ḥabībullah and Raḥmatullah went to Deregez, to manage the business, and Uncle 'Azīzullah went for a week to Kochan, after which he returned to Meshhed. At the time my father died, 'Amo 'Azīzullah was newly married, he married the daughter of David Baṣṣāl. Also, Uncle Ḥabībullah got engaged to the second daughter of David Baṣṣāl. Four or five months after the death of my father, Uncle 'Azīzullah went to Deregez to take the place of Uncle Raḥmatullah and Uncle Ḥabībullah, who returned to Meshhed to manage the business there. These uncles were good to us, the children of their big brother, and treated us kindly. After they arrived in Meshhed, they opened our father's will, and once they understood the accounts, and saw how our father behaved toward them when they had nothing, and he was in debt, and carried on the business with loans and credits, until he achieved the good situation in which they now were, they felt grateful and wanted to do the will of their deceased brother, my father, and to fulfill his last will properly. One day, they called together some twenty from among the leaders of the community, and also all the uncles and cousins, and in that assembly they announced [the will of] their big brother and the benefits he in the past let his little brothers have, and produced the will that he had written, and said that "We want to fulfill the will of our brother with regard to the property that was left, to give the children of our brother one half of the amount we have, and the three brothers shall accept the other half, and, moreover, for ten years, until these orphans grow up, whatever God, blessed be He, will give us, one half of it will belong to us and one half to the children of our deceased brother."

After they announced their decision and will to the leaders of the community who were present, Āq David Baṣṣāl objected and said that since their elder brother 'Azīzullah was not present, "you, without obtaining his opinion, should not do this." Uncle Ḥabībullah explained in front of everybody that their deceased brother revealed more than what he wrote in his will, "and we want to fulfill his command." But David Baṣṣāl made more and more efforts not to let it happen until their brother 'Azīzullah came, "and he would do what he wanted." Except for David Baṣṣāl, all the leaders of the community and its elders and others praised the act and words of Uncle Ḥabībullah. Finally, Uncle Ḥabībullah saw that David Baṣṣāl objected strenuously, without shame and embarrassment, and he said to David Baṣṣāl, "Even though my brother 'Azīzullah has married your daughter, and I am engaged to your second daughter, and even though it appears that you oppose the whole matter in the interest of your daughters, nevertheless we shall carry out the will, and shall give one part of the three parts that are coming to us to the orphans of our brother, and we shall make it half and half. And should our brother 'Azīzullah not agree and not accept it, he will get his part in full, and I and my brother Raḥmatullah will take a quarter, that is, one quarter of the other half, and the other quarter we shall give to the orphans. True, our brother 'Azīzullah married [your daughter], and you oppose this because of your daughter and take the side of our brother 'Azīzullah, but I, too, am your son-in-law, even though I have not yet married your daughter in your house, and if this is the reason, then your daughter will remain with you. In this place, we want to fulfill the will of our brother, and in this manner to appease [satisfy] our brother who brought us up in his most difficult days and worked hard and paid the debts of our father, and instructed us in the right way, and did not withhold from us anything, so that we are indebted to him, and shall fulfill his will. My brother Raḥmatullah is here, the community can ask him whether he is satisfied in his heart with this, and let then the leaders of the community sign it [the will]."

The leaders of the community asked my brother [Raḥmatullah], and as an answer he said that "I am satisfied with this division. Compared to all the benefits our brother let us have, it can be considered a small thing that we should fulfill his will."

Thereafter, David Baṣṣāl said nothing and did not object any longer, and the partnership agreement which we drew up for another ten years was signed by the whole community present on that occasion. At that time, I, Farajullah, was seven years and six months old.

This meeting took place in the cellar of the old courtyard that we inherited, and I was there and heard everything and saw their behavior. Therefore also, we the brothers, after we entered into the business and worked another ten years in partnership with the uncles, we let them rest in the family, and be with their children, and what God, blessed be He, gave us in His grace, we got our half part, and the other half we gave to them, and we did not change the partnership contract, for until the end of the [ten] years, we did not want for the sake of money to arouse unpleasant things before the uncles.

Earlier, I mentioned that after fourteen months, I returned from Deregez to Meshhed and stayed there for fourteen months. Then the uncles sent me to Merv, where a store was opened. After the opening of the store there, we were selling to the Turkomans green tea and other things. I stayed there and managed the business for about ten months and then returned to Meshhed, stayed for a while there. Then I returned to Merv with my brother Mahdī, and we worked together, and Vali 'Akas and David the son of Uncle Murād Kohen were working for us.

At that time, an unpleasant event occurred: in Meshhed, a strong epidemic of cholera spread about, and because of it, all the roads between the cities were closed. It was not possible to travel from one city to another, and for two months no news or letters came from Meshhed. Finally, the cholera also reached Merv, and several of the inhabitants of Merv died of the disease. Almost all the Meshhed Jews in Merv were there without their families, which stayed behind in Meshhed. They all were in a great anxiety; they did not know what happened to their families and what they had to endure. The Russians closed the borders and did not allow anybody to enter or to leave. Then, greatly worried, all the Jews gathered, trying to find a way to return to Meshhed. At that time, the General Gropatkin[26] was the governor of those districts. They sent a telegram to General Gropatkin stating that all their relatives were in Meshhed, and asked him that he should permit fifty men to travel by train to Dushakh.[27] The same day they got a telegram in response that the train will sell them tickets for the trip. The same evening fifty-three men took the train to Dushakh, and from there they traveled on to Meshhed.

Thereafter, no more patience was left, and they [those Meshhed Jews who had stayed on in Merv] sent another telegram to the general and again requested of him permission for the departure of another fifty men. Their request was approved, and the second evening, I and my brother Mahdī, with Vali ʻAkas and David Kohen and another forty-nine men, traveled by train to Dushakh. After we arrived in Dushakh, we saw that there was no connection from there to Meshhed. But it so happened that there was there a caravan of camels from Afghanistan, which had a hundred camels loaded with barrels of *nafṭ* to be transported to Meshhed. We spoke to them, and it was agreed that for a payment of fifty *tomans,* they would load our luggage and all our things on the camels. In addition, there were five sick people among us, whom too they would take upon the camels and transport them to Chashme Bilan,[28] and the rest of us would go on foot [with the caravan]. As agreed, the owners of the caravan loaded up all our things and the five sick men on the camels, on top of the barrels of *nafṭ*. The same evening, we started out[29] on foot with the caravan, and next noon we reached Chashme Bilan. Also, several other caravans from Meshhed had arrived there with merchandise, and stayed there, and they unloaded the merchandise, and collected it in one place and watched over it, for because of the cholera they were not allowed to proceed. Among them, there was one called Mashdī Muḥammad Turk, the owner of a *fayton,*[30] whom the Russians had expelled from Russia, and he was waiting there hoping that perhaps he could return to Russia.

Since we were walking all night from Dushakh, and since the air was very warm, several men fainted because of the heat and the thirst, and collapsed on the road before we reached Chashme Bilan. I was the first to enter Chashme Bilan, and the moment I reached a spring of water, I threw myself on the ground and began to drink the water of the spring with my mouth, but before I could swallow a few mouthfuls, the same Mashdī Muḥammad Turk pulled me up from the ground, saying that one must not drink much water at once, one has to drink it little by little, until one felt better. He gave me a little water every few minutes, until I felt well. Then I took a pitcher from the guards, filled it with water, and ran back to the road from where we came and gave everyone a little water to drink, until they felt better. Thus, all of them reached the spring of Chashme Bilan, and the camel caravan, too, arrived. But here, too, there was no transport, and we again paid fifty *tomans* to the cameleers for taking the sick and our belongings to the city of Qara Tuqan.[31] Early in the evening, the cameleers again loaded up our belongings and our sick, and set out on the road, and the rest of us, again as on the previous night, went on foot together with the caravan, and next day at noon we reached Qara Tuqan. By that time, already four hundred *bals* [bales] of merchandise owned by Jews had arrived there, sent that month from Meshhed. They unloaded the *bals* in a garden, and five to six men were set to watch over them. They also had with them three hundred to four hundred letters for the Jews who were in Merv and had come from there. Each one went and got his letter and read it. There they read about the death of their relatives, and made *qrī'ah* for their relatives who died of cholera.

We stayed one night in Qara Tuqan, and next day we rented horses and donkeys. Those with donkeys formed one group, and those with horses another. We set out for Meshhed. The group on the horses arrived in Meshhed three days later, and the group on donkeys after five days. Thank God, by the time we arrived in Meshhed, the cholera was over.

A few days after our arrival in Meshhed, the uncles asked that we give them an account of the sales and of what was left behind [in Merv]. Since at the time we left [Merv] there was no time to make an inventory, we brought along the books, and from them we copied and gave them an account of the sales and of what was left in the store there.

Sometime later, after all the dangers and illnesses had passed, I alone went back to Merv, and saw that all the merchandise had remained intact, and that only one package of *'alije* was missing. On that trip, apart from the sales, I bought from the Turkomans merchandise for the cities of Sarakhs, Qahqeh, and Qazal Arwad,[32] and sent it to the agents whom we had in those cities. All the purchases and sales were done twice a week, on the market days, in the Bazār Také.[33] On those days, the Turkomans and the other people would bring all they had to the market, and would buy and sell there. I, too, bought on the market days everything I wanted. From among the relatives and cousins of mine, there was nobody with me except Valī 'Akas, who was working for me. I had many friends and acquaintances among the Turkomans.

One day in the evening, when I returned from making purchases in the bazaar, I felt that my left cheek was swollen and was itching.[34] Ḥasan 'Awwaz, one of the Turkomans from among our acquaintances, came to the store and saw my face and said, "Farajullah Āqā, your cheek is afflicted by the *ōt bāsh* disease. You must take care of it right away, and if not, it will be dangerous." I was a young boy and did not know what *ōt bāsh* was. (Sometime later, I heard that in Persian it was called *dagi.*) I did not pay attention to what he said. He urged me, but I paid no attention to his words and pleadings. He insisted and said, "Give something for the Evil Eye." I took out of my pocket one *q'rān* and gave it to him—perhaps he would cease pestering me. He took the money, wrapped it in a piece of linen, and stuck it into one of the holes in the wall. When he saw that I did not listen to him, he got up and went to Mullah Yaḥya and Ḥājjī Naurūz, my father's cousins, and gave them an account of my illness and told them that this was *ōt bāsh* which had fallen upon the cheek of Farajullah, that I would be in danger, and that this was a bad malady which must be treated right away. "He does not understand it. You go to him, and take care of him as quickly as possible so that the illness should not spread. If twenty-four hours pass [without treatment], it will become dangerous." I had scratches on the face, and I wanted to sleep all the time. In those days, I was living in my store in the building of Shafī'off. I went to the back of the store and slept. In the evening, Mullah Yaḥya, Ḥājjī Naurūz, and Ṣadoq Levi, cousins of my father, and Mullah Āqā Baṣṣāl, who is known by the name of Yishai Hindī, brought him [Ḥasan 'Awwaz] to the store and woke me up. He saw my face and he stuck a *nishtar,* a big and thick needle, into the place where there was a black spot on the cheek, and then he said that they should bring dates and the tail fat of a lamb and should crush them together and put it on the cheek on the black spot. They did as he told them, and bandaged the place [the cheek] with the crushed tail fat and dates, and went away. I went to sleep. Some two hours passed, and they came again and awakened me and said that for this illness I must be taken to the camp of the Turkomans, and there they will heal me. "The village of that physician is far, and we have no time, we now came to take you in a *fayton* to the village of the Turkomans." They quickly put me into a carriage together with two men, and the others sat in a second carriage, and we began to drive. When I sat in the carriage, I opened my eyes and saw that on both sides of the street were standing all the Meshhed Jews looking at me. The carriages drove fast and reached the villages of the Turkomans. Before dawn, we reached one village, and in front of the house of one of the Turkomans, they took me down. That house was the house of the physician famous for [the treatment of] this disease. After the people of the house understood why we had come there, to have the disease cured, they said that just half an hour earlier, the physician had left the house and went to visit his flock. Instantly, they sent one of his sons to call him back. The sun was already shining when they returned. When the physician came, he said that there was here in the village another old physician, it is worthwhile to call him. They sent somebody to fetch him, and they consulted together, and said that it was necessary to cut the place of the wound and to burn the place. By that time, my left cheek was very swollen, and the black spot into which Ḥasan 'Awwaz had stuck a needle at the beginning of the night had grown to the size of a nut. They brought a razor and cut the black spot and removed it. It did not hurt me at all. When they cut the spot, black blood came out, as if it were congealed old blood. After he cut out the black spot which was the size of a nut, the second old Turkoman said that the spot must be burnt with iron heated in fire in order to be sure that it was successful, for if as much as a smell of it remains in the place, the illness will return again, and then there will be no remedy. But the physician to whose house we had come, it seems he had a merciful heart, for he said that perhaps they are *Mūsā'ī*s (the Turkomans called the Jews sons of the religion of Moses), and the Jews have soft flesh.[35] And he cut the wound all the time with the razor in his hand, and cut it until he reached live flesh, and that already hurt. Then he brought a bottle of *tīzāb* (a kind of chemical material), and stuck a piece of wood into it and instantly removed it, and at that moment a drop of the material fell on the floor and made in it a hole the size of a finger, and the piece of wood which he had stuck into the bottle turned into coal as far as it had entered the material (the *tīzāb*). And he said that that material was like iron in fire, and of that material he poured on my cheek on the place where he had cut with the razor. And then he brought a piece of *zumeh* (another hard chemical material) and stirred it like flour, and put it into that hole, and filled the hole and closed the wound, and said that it will be all right. And he said that I could drink green tea without sugar, with bread, but that I was forbidden to eat sweets and meat and oil. It seems that the medicine of tail fat with dates which Mullah Āqā used at first was not healthful and suitable for this illness. After the treatment, we returned with the carriages and arrived in town at noontime. They took me to my store, and the others returned to their places and their work. After I returned to the store, I again went to sleep.

It seems that after we left the village, the second old man said to the physician, "You killed the Jew by treating him mercifully. After you cut the place of the wound, you should have burnt it with fiery iron." It seems that these words influenced the physician, and he instantly mounted his horse and rode to us to the city, and went to Āqā Ṣadoq Levi and said to him that he wanted to see the patient. Āqā Ṣadoq Levi came to my store and woke me and took me to the store of Mullah Yaḥya, and there the physician opened the bandage from my face and took out all the chemical material from the hole, and with the razor shaved the inside of the hole and saw that at the bottom of the hole there was a liquid like white water and said that this was good. He said that they should bring salt, and he filled the hole with salt and bandaged it and went away. I returned to my store and slept. I felt that every moment my face swelled [more and more], and I had a very strong desire to sleep. When I slept, if somebody came to wake me, I was ready to give him the whole store that he should not wake me. In those days, Mullah Āqāī Mungi had a store in our *seray,* the Seray Shafīʿoff. He came and watched over me and took care of me. Since the air was warm in the evening, I asked Mullah Āqāī to take my bed and place it in the courtyard. In the courtyard, there was a board like a bed, and he took the mattress and blankets to the courtyard and arranged on the board a place for me to sleep, and he, too, lay down next to me. I slept and dreamt suddenly that my hands and feet were tied upon my belly, and straps of iron were over my head and closed me in as one closes big packages with iron [straps], and pressed upon me strongly. Because of the pain, I awoke and saw that Mullah Āqāī, who up to that time was awake and stood above my head, was already asleep. I said nothing, and did not awaken him, and fell asleep again. I felt that every minute the swelling of my cheek grew, until it covered my whole face and entered under my jaw and into my throat. I fell asleep again, and this time I dreamt that they brought a piece of square iron and put me into the iron and squeezed me, and because of the great pain of the squeezing, I awoke. I felt that my condition was not good and that weakness overwhelmed me, and the swelling reached the throat, and I was not able to speak well as usual. I knew that I was going to die. I awakened Mullah Āqāī and told him, "Take me into the store, to the back part, spread a sheet on the floor and put two bricks under my head, put a sheet over me." When he heard my words, he began to weep and to cry. I said to him again, "Take me to the back of the store." So he carried me to the back of the store and placed me on my bed. But what I told him, that he should put sheets under me and over me, he did not do. Instead, crying, he ran to Mullah Yaḥya and Āqā Ṣadoq Levi and Ḥājjī Naurūz, woke them up, and told them what had happened. Āqā Rajab Baṣṣāl, who was known as Rajab Armānī, he, too, joined them, and they took *fayton* carriages. Āqā Ṣadoq Levi traveled to another village to find another Turkoman physician. Ḥājjī Naurūz and Rajab Baṣṣāl drove to the village of the Turkoman physicians who had treated me. Three hours after sunrise, the two physicians who had treated me arrived. At that time, the swelling already covered my whole face and throat, all my teeth were closed because of the swelling, I could not speak, my eyes were covered because of the swelling so that I could not see at all, only with the ears I was able to hear. The physicians spoke, I heard them. Meanwhile, all the Jews gathered around. The Turkomans who saw me in this condition said to Mullah Yaḥya and Āqā Naurūz and Āqā Ṣadoq and Āqā Rajab Baṣṣāl and the whole community which gathered there: "There is only one way to cure him: only with iron heated in fire. Either he will recover due to that cure, or he will die under the cure of the iron heated in fire. If he is not treated in that manner, he will die within two hours."

Mullah Yaḥya and Mullah Naurūz heard these words, and said: "If he must die without the cure in two hours, it is worthwhile to treat him with iron heated in fire; perhaps there is hope that he will be cured, and if not, he will die two hours before the time." Then the physicians agreed that they would treat me in the manner they suggested. Then the Turkoman physicians arose and went out into the courtyard to confer, and then they returned and said that "We think that only hot iron is his cure. But perhaps he will die under the treatment, and then we shall be murderers before the government, and they will accuse us. Therefore, we do not want to treat him." Then Mullah Yaḥya and Ḥājjī Naurūz swore before the physicians and took upon themselves that in case this man should die under the treatment with hot iron and if the government should accuse them, then they would go to the government and tell them that this was done at their request and that the physicians applied the cure of the hot iron according to their will. Then the Turkoman physicians agreed, and sent to bring eight or nine big and thick iron nails whose length was about a quarter of an *alchin.* And they also brought five or six *man* of charcoal, and lighted it in the courtyard, and from the willow trees in the street they cut a branch and made handles for the nails, and the other ends of the nails they put into the fire, until they were all red from the fire. And me they took out into the courtyard, and laid me on my back, one man sat on my legs and two men sat on my two arms, and one held my head very firmly, and then the treatment began. They took the nails which were red from the fire, one by one, and put them on the place of the wound. This brought me an easing. After they used three nails, I felt that my teeth opened, and my eyes began to open a little. From the hole into which they put the nails, I heard a swishing sound of air coming out from the wound, and from my eyebrows and face something murmured and came out, I felt and heard the sound of air coming out, and the teeth and the eyes opened more and more. Until seven hot nails which they used in my face, it was pleasant for me and I felt well, my eyes and teeth opened completely, and I saw the people and also could speak. The Turkoman physicians were very glad and said that I was saved from death, and hoped that I would recover completely. When they applied the eighth and ninth nails, it already hurt me and I cried, until the twelfth hot iron which they used, I hurt very much and my cries reached high heaven, and I screamed, "Enough!" Then they released me and said that this was enough and it was finished. But the second old physician who came together with the first physician said that "This disease has to be combatted powerfully. There in the village, I said that he has to be cured with hot iron, and you did not do it; had you applied the fiery iron then, the matter would have been settled. Now, too, I am telling you that the face has to be burnt with three more hot nails, so that not even the smell of the disease should remain in the living flesh. True, if you will do it, the wound will be deeper and bigger, and after it heals there will remain a scar in the face, but the fear of death will be removed. And if you don't burn more of the living flesh and the disease returns, then no hope will remain."

Then all of them together said, "Let the place of the wound be burnt another three times so that we should be sure." So they again laid me down as at the first time, somebody sat on my legs, and two men on my two arms, and one on my head, and they began to burn with three more big nails the living flesh of my face, and my cries shook the heavens. And while I was crying, Ḥājjī Naurūz said, "Better that you should cry than that we should cry."[36] Then they released me and said that there was no more danger at all. And they said that now it is necessary to put a medicine upon him, and they asked for a big *chudan,* a kind of metal pot, and wheat flour and salt. They brought the pot, and poured about half a kilo of wheat flour and salt into it, and put it on the fire, and said that instead of water each one should urinate into the pot. The men who stood around were all ashamed at first. The first who started to urinate was Rajab Baṣṣāl, who said that since it was needed for a medical treatment, one should not be ashamed, and then several others followed him and urinated into the pot, until there was enough. The physicians boiled up the pot and made a kind of dough. Once it was ready, they put the dough on a piece of linen and with it covered the place of the wound and my face and neck, and placed me on my bed, and gave instructions that my food for several days should be only green tea without sugar, and bread. For three days, twice a day, they changed the bandage. The swelling of my face and head went down, and they warmed salt and filled the place of the wound. The physician who treated me stayed there for a week, and every day he examined me. After two or three days, I asked that they should permit me to drink chicken soup, to soak bread in it and eat it, and finally they allowed me to drink soup, and also soup made of the meat of a three-day-old goat kid. They gave me only the liquid of the soup without the meat and without fat. The day thereafter, which was the day of the market (called Bazār Také), they went and bought a three-day-old goat kid and slaughtered it and made a soup for me. On that day, some twenty men came and made a feast and prepared the table, and put enough water into the pot for each of the twenty guests to get a plateful of soup, and they sat and ate together with me the soup with bread, and all were joyful that I remained alive.

After seven days, they opened the bandage from my face and put other bandages for forty days, until the place of the wound healed, but the wound itself remained for six months, until it healed and was like the rest of my face, but the place of scar remained. . . .

When I contracted the disease, there was nobody in Merv of the family of Karb Āqājān, that is, of the family of my father. With the help of God, and then with the help of my father's cousins, Mullah Yaḥya, Ḥājjī Naurūz, Āq Ṣadoq Levi, and other men of the community, who helped me to live, I returned to new life. They took care of me during my illness, and they sent word to Meshhed about my illness. Forty days from the onset of the illness passed, and then they sent Uncle Raḥmatullah, who arrived in Merv. I was sixteen years old at the time, and about to reach the age of seventeen.

For six or seven months, I remained in Merv with Uncle Raḥmatullah, until the wound in my face healed well, then I went to Meshhed. I stayed in Meshhed for a year and then returned to Merv, and received the store after an inventory, and then Uncle Raḥmatullah returned to Meshhed. For six or seven months, I was alone in Merv, until Uncle Ḥabībullah came to Merv in order to get the accounts of the store. I collected the moneys they owed me, and prepared to go to Meshhed. Prior to my departure for Meshhed, I sent ten bales of green tea to Mullah Āqājān Nissim, and I also had accounts of tea with Āq Naurūz Kashi, who was our agent in Qahqeh. Two days after the arrival of Uncle Ḥabībullah in Merv, I put before him all the accounts so that he should see that I collected and concluded all the work and did not sell merchandise to people on credit. Without even looking at the accounts, he said to me, "Farajullah, you want to go to Meshhed to become engaged, without collecting the money for the sales that you made on credit?" I did not expect from him such words, and answered him that "I had no merchandise that I sold on credit, there are only ten bales of green tea that I sent to Bukhara to Mullah Āqājān Nissim," and I asked him that instead of paying me, he should buy for me *nabāt* (sugar), "and I shall go tonight to Bukhara to get from him the *nabāt* that he bought for me, and shall send it to you."

The same evening, I set out for Bukhara. Mullah Āqājān had sold the green tea and instead of it bought *nabāt* and sent it by train to Merv. I took along the consignment papers and gave them to Uncle Ḥabībullah. Next night, I traveled to Qahqeh and finished the accounts with our agent 2,-30,0-Aq Naurūz, and bought sixteen wagons of wheat from Āq Naurūz, that he should deliver them by train to Bukhara. I returned to Merv, and delivered the completed accounts to Uncle Ḥabībullah, and the account that was due to us from Āq Naurūz Kashī, which I passed on to the account of Meshhed. All this I delivered to Uncle Ḥabībullah, and told him that "We had no more accounts with people and nobody owed us anything, and I am not going to Meshhed, and I don't want any help from the partnership." But I did not tell him of the purchase of the sixteen carloads of wheat. Next night, I went to Bukhara, took a little money on loan from Āq Veli Ḥakīm and bought two hundred sacks and sent them to Qahqeh, and wrote to them that they should fill the sacks with wheat and send them to Bukhara. Seven carloads of the wheat arrived in Bukhara, and the rest, since the price of wheat went up and Uncle Ḥabībullah learned about the wheat deal, he instantly wrote to Āq Naurūz that we don't want wheat, and Āq Naurūz, since the price of wheat went up, did not give us the wheat. I sold the seven carloads of wheat that reached me, and sent the money of the debt to Qahqeh, and with the profit from this I made a fund, and began to work [to deal].

I stayed in Bukhara six months, and after all the expenses, I earned 1,672 *tomans* net, with which God graced me. After I returned to Merv, Uncle Ḥabībullah had a loss of almost the same amount from buying and selling in that period. Thereafter, he urged me to go to Meshhed. In those days, the business in Deregez began to flourish. Until then, my brother Mahdī and my brother Nūrallah managed the business there. Everybody who went to Deregez had to eat *t'rēf* [non-kosher] meat. The uncles again sent me to Deregez to take over the store there from my brother Nūrallah. After I took over the store, I stayed on in Deregez for a year and a half, and I, too, like the others, ate *t'rēf* meat. Six or seven months later, I returned to Meshhed and got married, and in the year of my marriage, I went to Mullah Yosef and studied the laws of ritual slaughtering, and he took me along to each place where he went to slaughter, and he let me slaughter and make the investigation [of whether the animal was kosher or not]. After I learned everything and got a certificate from him, I returned to Deregez, and again took over the store from my brother Nūrallah, and began to work in commerce. In the meantime, I wanted to prepare the Jews [for religious observance] and to find a butcher so that we should be able to slaughter the animals for ourselves and eat kosher meat. Some of the Jews were afraid of the Muslims, that perhaps they will object and will say that "these are Jews, and don't want to eat the meat that is slaughtered by us."[37] At the end, it was agreed that we shall slaughter lambs, and those who want to eat kosher will buy kosher meat and will buy also from the *goy* butcher but will not eat it but throw it to the dogs and cats. In this manner, we began to eat kosher meat. Those who did not buy kosher but bought from the *goy* butcher, we did not force them to buy kosher, and those who bought kosher meat exchanged all their utensils in the house, and made also in the house everything kosher. In the morning and in the evening, we arranged a place for a synagogue, and we were praying. And to those who ate kosher meat, we said that if they go to the houses of people who do not eat kosher meat, they should not only not eat there, but should not even drink water or tea, and should tell them that since their dishes are not kosher, "we cannot drink." In this manner, it took six months until all the Jews in Deregez ate kosher, in every respect, had kosher utensils, and were praying morning and evening. Thereafter, the men began to bring their wives and children to Deregez. I was the first to bring my family to Deregez, and thereafter also others brought their families to Deregez. Within three years, fifty Jewish families lived in Deregez. Until that time, if somebody died, they either buried him in the Muslim cemetery or sent his body to Meshhed. I then decided to find a plot of land to serve as cemetery for the Jews. Two or three of the Jews objected strongly, but still we purchased a piece of land next to the Muslim cemetery and set it up as the Jewish cemetery. Eventually, we brought two Torah scrolls, and set up two synagogues, and morning and evening all of us went to pray in the synagogues.

Above, general view of Meshhed with the sanctuary of Imām Reza in the background.

Left, Meshhed: street in the ʿĒdgāh, the Jewish quarter.

Top, Meshhed: street with stores in the ʿĒdgāh, the Jewish quarter.

Street in the ʿĒdgāh, the Jewish quarter.

Top, a room in the ʿĒdgāh serving as synagogue, with the Torah shrine behind the curtain.

Wall in the Jewish cemetery with inscription in Persian and Judeo-Persian, reading "In memory of Elijah ben Yishai Baṣṣal, 5692 (1932)."

Right, tombstone in Persian and Hebrew, reading "This is the burial monument of Sarah daughter of David, Adar 22, 5709 (1949)."

Below, members of the Ḥakimian family in Russia, ca. 1900.

Āgā Farajullah Nasrullayoff and his wife, Meshhed, ca. 1905.

Karbalā'ī Nauruz with two men and children of the Kalati family, Meshhed, 1905.

Above, pupils of the Muslim boys' school in the Ēdgāh, ca. 1920. About 90 percent of them were *Jadīdī* children.

Left, a young *Jadīdī* couple in traditional garb, ca. 1920.

Above, Pupils of the Talmud Torah school, ca. 1920. To the right the teacher Yosef Dil (Dilmānī).

Right, Karbalā'ī Āghājān Raḥmani with his wife and son, ca. 1921.

The *Jadīdī* midwife M'shateh, ca. 1922–25.

The Ibrahimoff family, ca. 1925.

Above, Āgā Jabar Ḥakimian with his son and the son's fiancée, 1925.

Opposite page top, Āgā Aharonoff with his wife, two daughters and a grandchild, ca. 1925.

Opposite page bottom, Male members and children of the Ḥakimian (Mortezaoff) family, 1925.

Above, Passover gathering in the home of Āgā Yusef Levi, 1927. Note that the only females present are small girls. In the background *Jadīdī* musicians.

Right, three nephews of Āgā Farajullah Nasrullayoff in India, where they worked as rug merchants.

The wife of Āgā Farajullah, with her son Daniel on her right, and her son-in-law Yiṣḥaq Rishtahari on her left, ca. 1930.

Āgā Ibrahim, head of the Ibrahimoff family, with his wife, ca. 1930.

Above, opening of the three-story gallery of stores built by the ʿAzizullayoff family just outside the ʿĒdgāh. The stores were individually rented to Jewish and Muslim merchants. Ca. 1935.

Right, Āgā Yusef Aminoff and family in front of their residence in the ʿĒdgāh. To the right a veiled Muslim woman servant, to the left a Muslim man servant. Ca. 1935.

Top, girl students of the *Jadīdī Arz Agdaz* (Persian for "Holy Land") girls' school in Meshhed, 1936.

Boy students and teachers of the *Otzar haTorah* school in Meshhed, 1940. The sign in the front reads, in Hebrew, "Hebrew, speak Hebrew," and "Study in evening classes."

Top, at the wedding of Yoḥanan Livian, Jerusalem, 1942. Standing in the back row on the right is Āgā Farajullah Nasrullayoff, Yoḥanan's father.

Group of *Jadīdī* amateur actors performing the popular "Yusef and Zulayka" play in Meshhed, 1943.

At the end, with the help of God, Jewishness in Deregez became complete. Another man or two learned how to slaughter, for by that time all of them ate kosher and prayed openly, so much so that if the Muslims invited the Jews to a meal, the Jews either did not go, or, if they did go, they somehow said that they did not feel well, and [thus] they did not eat *t'rēf* meat. I hope and pray to God that He should forgive me those days in which I ate *t'rēf* meat against my will, at the order of my uncle.

After *kashrut* was fully observed in Deregez, and without exception all ate kosher, several years later, Bolshevism began in Russia, but the Bolsheviks had not yet reached Merv and Ashkhabad,[38] and these cities were in the hands of the Mensheviks. I went to Merv, and several months conducted business there, but my family stayed in Deregez. At that time, we were taking and sending textiles, and that was good business. After I had been in Merv six months without my family, and also Āq 'Alī Muḥammad Baṣṣāl and Āq Amīn Kabūlī were in Merv, the Bolsheviks prevailed over the Mensheviks and took Merv. They imposed a tax on Merv, about half a million *manāt* [rubles], half of which the Jews had to pay. They gave us a week's time to collect the money and to pay it. When they went to collect the money among the Meshhed Jews, there was one, the younger son of David Shams, who said, "If you want to take money from me, I shall go and inform the Bolsheviks that Farajullah Levi is rich, let them go and get from him whatever they want, why should they want to take from us poor men?" People came to me and told me that the son of David Shams, wherever he sat in the midst of the community, said these things. I felt that this did not give off a good odor, and could even result in a bad situation, so I called two Turkomans whom I knew, and told them that "I want you to take me to Deregez without anybody knowing about it." They agreed, I paid money, and they bought three horses and saddles for the horses, and I transferred everything that was in the store to the storage of the house in which Uncle Raḥmatullah lived, and without telling anybody, Āq 'Ālī Muḥammad with his son 'Abdulraḥīm, Āq Amīn Kabūlī, and I, early at night, as if we were going to take a walk, went out of the city two by two, some distance on the road leading to Yultun.[39] I had arranged with the Turkomans that they should send somebody to take us from there.

Āq 'Alī Muḥammad and the son of his sister, Āq 'Abdulwahhāb, who had long wanted to go to Qahqeh, and could not go because the road was closed, told me that he, too, wanted to join us, and he prepared his horse, and put his things on the horse and went to the appointed place. When all of us reached the appointed place, one of the Turkomans who was waiting for us there on the road gave us the signs upon which we had agreed in advance, so that we knew that he was waiting for us. And he took us on foot close to the village, to a garden, where they had prepared for us clothes like those of the Turkomans, with two horses which they had brought to that garden. We all put on the Turkoman clothes over our own clothes, and we threw away our hats, and put on hats like those of the Turkomans. Two of us mounted one horse, each of the two horses, and set out on a tortuous road, and about midnight we reached a village, where Āq Murād was. All the people of the village were asleep, only Āq Murād and his wife were awake, and they prepared green tea, and prepared also the horses, and put saddles on them, and they put the things on the backs of the horses, and we all rode on the horses, and left the village, and reached a distance of about eleven kilometers, and reached a small brook.

The Turkomans said that here one must rest a little, and also the horses had to rest while we put the dry water-skins into the river so that they should expand, and then we would fill them with water, for on the way farther on there was no water.

We rested there about an hour, on the ground, and lay down until the skins expanded, and we filled them with water, and mounted again the horses and continued hastily in the *ṣaḥarā*, in sand, for the Bolsheviks had issued an order that if somebody was caught trying to escape, his punishment was death, and also his family was to be killed. Fearing this, we hurried on. The Turkomans, who were our friends, because of their great love took upon themselves this danger, and smuggled us out, and this was truly the greatest devotion. Two hours passed after sunrise, and we reached a cistern in the sands. This cistern was prepared by the shepherds for themselves, their sheep and their cattle. We stayed about two hours at the cistern and rested. We let the horses go free, without being hobbled. The horses ate the dry thistles, but did not go far from us, neither did they fight among themselves. The water of this cistern had a foul smell and was very heavy. The Turkomans threw into it the skins which were tied with ropes, and two men pulled up the skins full of very heavy water. They urged us to drink the dirty water, and also gave it to the horses to drink. I could not drink it, but they by force drew water, and I closed my nose with my hand, and with great difficulty drank half a skin of water.

Then we continued to ride the horses and went on. At midnight, we rested in some place, and then again continued to ride. Next day, at noon, we reached another cistern. We always rode far from the villages of the Turkomans and in the sands, so that every three or four hours, we reached another cistern of water, and every night and day, we rested twice, each time an hour and a half to two hours. We were on the way five days, and on the fifth day, in the evening, we reached the border, and passed through customs in Luṭfabād,[40] and from there we rode on to Deregez, still wearing the same Turkoman clothes. An hour after sunrise, we reached our houses, the women and the children.

At that time, the Bolsheviks had already reached Dushakh, and the Mensheviks reached Qahqeh, and they were fighting, and sometime later also, the English army was fighting together with the Mensheviks. They defeated the Bolsheviks (as far as Chahār Ju),[41] and Merv was again captured by the Mensheviks. After its recapture by the Mensheviks, I went back again to Merv. All the merchandise that I had hidden in the cellar I found, thank God, preserved in its totality. I brought out the merchandise for sale, and it was sold at very good prices. And the money I received for all the merchandise I instantly sent with Turkomans to my brother Nūrallah in Meshhed, and I ordered all kinds of textiles for the local market, and also my brother Nūrullah bought much and sent it to me through Deregez and Artoq.[42] The work was fruitful and successful; on the average, I sold five to six thousand *manāt.* We brought all kinds of textiles of silk that the Turkomans used. My dear Mūsā, son of my brother, helped me.

Meanwhile, I fell ill with a serious disease. Against my will, I had to go to the house of Nasrullah, and forty days I lay in bed there. At the end, my two legs were so weak that two men had to take me to the lavatory. I already thought that I would not survive, when, by chance, on the fortieth night, I perspired profusely, and continued to perspire until noon on the following day, so much that all the blankets and the two mattresses on which I slept were full of water. After this, I recovered, and could stand up, and God gave me new health. I started to work again, and every day I increased the business.

After a while, the Bolsheviks became stronger again, and in the meantime, I sold all the merchandise for more or less money, and as for the merchandise that reached the border, I informed them that they should not send it, since the conditions were very bad. I informed the family of Uncle Raḥmatullah that the situation was bad, and that the place had to be abandoned. Within a day or two, they, too, packed up their belongings together with our belongings, and we delivered his merchandise to the train and sent it to Artoq. We ourselves and the family of Uncle Raḥmatullah traveled by night train to Iran, and we shipped to Iran to the customs all the merchandise and belongings that we had earlier sent to the frontier. And we brought the whole family of Uncle Raḥmatullah to Deregez to our family.

Within a few days, the Bolsheviks became stronger and conquered the places until they reached the city of Bayram 'Alī.[43] The Mensheviks in Merv announced that all those who wanted to escape from Merv should come to the railway station. All the Jewish families from Meshhed who were there, about one hundred and fifty families, with another ten to twelve Afghan and Bukharan families, left Merv on that train in time before the Bolsheviks came there. They reached the Persian border at Artoq. They informed me, and I instantly went to the border, and prepared some forty carriages from Luṭfabād and sent them to the border that they should bring the travelers to the Persian customs border. Then I liberated about 40,000 *tomans* of merchandise that had been left at the Russian border, and sent it to the Persian border. Part of this merchandise was already in the train, and part of it in the Russian customs, and I returned everything to the Persian customs. There were also some seven or eight bales of textile merchandise of the Agayoff family in the Russian customs, and those, too, I returned to the Persian customs. Then, with those carriages, in two days we liberated the merchandise from the customs and sent it to Deregez. In Deregez, in two or three days, I did my best to find vacant houses for them, and transported them to those houses. About fifty families remained with me in the houses, and they arranged themselves on the floor for about three days, until I found houses for them, too, and they moved to those houses. As much as it was in my power, I helped them with money and everything. They remained in Deregez for about a month and a half, and then the Afghans and the Bukharans returned to Merv and to Bukhara, and all the Meshhedis went on to Meshhed. Those who remained in Deregez began to work, they bought textiles in Deregez and sold them in Ashkhabad. We had much merchandise that was suitable for the Russian market, and we had already once brought all of it back from Artoq. We had in Meshhed debts of about 27,000 *tomans,* so we were forced to make money one way or another from the merchandise and send the money to Meshhed to cover the debts.

Meanwhile, a telegram came from Meshhed that my brother Nūrullah did not feel well, and I had to go instantly to Meshhed. Uncle Raḥmatullah with his family joined me, and we traveled to Meshhed. Ever since Uncle Raḥmatullah returned from Russia with his family, since they had nothing, they were taking money from me as a loan for their livelihood, and when they reached Meshhed, there, too, they did not go to their brothers but stayed with us.

Sixteen days after I arrived in Meshhed, my brother Nūrullah died. On the very day of his death, Ḥājjī Yūsef ʻAzaryah celebrated the marriages of his son and the son of his brother, both of whom had their weddings on the same day. Between our house and the house of Ḥājjī Yūsef there was the house of Fatḥallah Āq Rajeb Nissim. Two houses farther, their guests were already finishing the meal, and they arose to go and fetch the brides, the orchestra was playing, when suddenly Ḥājjī Rajeb [Nissim] heard the sound of weeping and the crying of the mourners, and he felt that something had happened in our family next door. He instantly ordered the orchestra to stop playing, and sent them home, and asked of all the guests to forgive him and go home, for such and such an event had occurred. And he told the relatives of the family, several men and women, to go without the orchestra to fetch the brides, even though they were no relations of ours. (In those days in Meshhed in our community, it was customary that the guests went on the night of the wedding after the meal to the house of the bride with an orchestra and they brought the bride with joy and dancing in the street with the orchestra.)[44] And thus, he paid respect and gave honor, may God have mercy on him.

I suffered great anguish at the death of my brother Nūrullah. Until the seventh day [of mourning], tears were streaming from my eyes, so much so that I felt weakness in seeing. Throughout the week, all the community came and visited to comfort us. On one occasion during the week, we were visited by one of the leaders of the community, Ismā'īl Dasfarūsh by name, who was a neighbor of our uncles, and he asked, "Are they the sons of your Uncle 'Azīzullah? What kind of people are they? Such a close relative of theirs, a cousin, died, and they, all day and night, play the *patefon* [phonograph] in their house and make merry." when I heard these things, I felt more and more sad, my heart hurt me. I thought in my heart that Ḥājjī Yūsef 'Azīz, who was no relative of ours at all, when he heard of the loss in our family on the night of the wedding of his son and nephew, stopped the orchestra in the rejoicing of his family, and sent home the guests, and did not perform, as was customary, the *'arūs kashan,*[45] and stopped his rejoicing and sent several of the relatives of his family to fetch the brides—and these, who were our cousins, during the days of the *shiv'ah,*[46] they played the patefon day and night, and made merry. This thing angered me and saddened me, so much that the tears were flowing from my eyes without stopping.

On the seventh day, when the *shiv'ah* was finished, they brought me the telegrams and the letters [of condolance], so that I should read them. I was unable to see the writing, everything was blurred. I felt I needed glasses, went to the market, bought myself glasses, and then returned and read the letters. And since we had debts in Meshhed, I stayed on in Meshhed for eight months, until finally moneys came from Deregez, I paid the debts, and then I went to join my wife and family in Deregez.

The work and the business were good, and from day to day there was more blessing. The Jadīdīm, who had escaped from Russia and were in Deregez, had gone on to Meshhed, and the family of my brother Mahdī and the family of my brother Fayzullah also went to Meshhed. I with my family stayed in Deregez.

One Sabbath afternoon, when I was sleeping in the house, I woke up and went to the lavatory. There I felt pain under my left knee, as if somebody had stuck a knife into me, and I felt that from the leg of my trousers something came out, the size of a bird, and it ran and fell into the lavatory. From the middle of Sabbath night, I did not feel well in my body, I was hot like fire, and could no way endure the heat and the pains. Several people came to visit me, and offered their opinion that a little animal called *gāl* or *shter zanak*[47] stung me, and that the poison of that animal was very dangerous. By the morning, it seemed that the poison of the sting spread over all my body. They gave me milk to drink, and it returned in vomit in something like cheese. Finally, they said that this did not help, one had to prepare a rope and arrange a kind of swing, and put me into it and spin me around and around. In the meantime, they gave me much milk to drink, and they spun me around with the rope and let the rope spin back by itself. This spinning caused nausea, and a vomiting of the milk together with the poison. They instantly sent five or six men to the houses that had cows, and they milked the cows, so that there should be fresh milk, and they brought much milk, and gave it to me to drink, and they spun the ropes and then let them go to spin back. I vomited all the milk like cheese. They did this two or three times, after which the milk returned as milk, and they said that there was no longer any poison in the body. And they took me and lay me down in the bed. On the second day, they fetched a surgeon, and he cut the place of the sting and used home remedies. For seven days, my left leg could not be used, it was as if it were asleep and could not be moved. After a while, gradually, it seemed as if blood had begun again to flow in it, and forty days later, I was able to walk, and went to work.[48]

Thirty-one years ago [i.e., in 1913], I sent my family, my wife and the children, to Meshhed, and I remained alone in Deregez.

In those days, we had, in partnership with Siman Maretoff and Mashdi Rustam,[49] a factory for manufacturing cotton. We ordered the machines from Germany, and they arrived packed in crates. The crates were too heavy, and at that time there were no utensils for unloading heavy things from the carriages. All the machines arrived in carriages to the customs in the city of Artoq, at the border of Russia, and they put them on carriages and took them to the factory. In order to take them down from the carriages, they put one end of a wide and thick plank on the carriage and its other end on the ground, and so that the plank should not break, they put a bale of cotton under it in the middle. I was standing below and was holding the plank with my foot so that it should not move. In this manner, they unloaded two or three carriages, and when they wanted to unload the fourth carriage, suddenly the horse which was hitched to the carriage moved ahead, so that the top end of the plank that was on the carriage slipped off its place, and the heavy crate that was on the plank pushed the plank down, and since the sack of cotton was under the middle of the plank, the plank became like a see-saw, and the other end, where I stood on the plank so that it should not move, rose up suddenly and threw me up in the air some eight or nine meters. As I fell back down, I held my right arm in front of me as a protection, and when I hit the ground, I felt that the bone in my arm escaped from its place and entered the upper part of my arm. I went home and sent for the bone setter,[50] who was known at that time, and with great difficulty he put the arm back in its place. This, too, took some forty days [to heal], after which I was able to use the hand for writing and other activities.

In those days, we the brothers were working and the uncles did not work. We were satisfied with this, for the ten years during which they worked and we were small and did not work [passed], and now we wanted to return to them the work, that they should not work for ten years and we should work. My late brother Mahdī was at that time in Merv, and I and my brother Nūrullah were in Deregez. Every fifteen or sixteen months, we changed places.

Several years passed in this manner, until one year an event took place. As always, my brother Mahdī gave an advance to Turkoman agriculturists to sow cotton. (It was the custom to give money every year to the agriculturists so that they should work the land, and at the end of the harvest they returned the money.) It so happened that in that year, the cold ruined the crop in Merv, and all the cotton was smitten by the cold and was damaged. The agriculturists brought the ruined cotton and gave it to us instead of money, and my brother Mahdī was forced to accept it, and thus he accumulated much damaged cotton. On the other hand, the cotton market also was weak. After they cleaned the cotton, they sent some ten wagons of it to Moscow, which did not yield even half of the investment. That year, we had great losses in the business, so that we were forced to enter into business debts with interest. In this manner, we conducted the business for several years, until once when I was in Meshhed, an epidemic of cholera reached Deregez. My brother the late Nūrullah, together with the other Meshhedis, returned to Meshhed.

I thought all the time about how to get out of the game of promissory notes, for I was afraid that it might cause us great losses. I figured out what was our capital in cash, and [decided] to pay out of that capital to each man 500 *tomans*, and each of the men who went to work outside the city of Meshhed should get an additional share. Each one who worked better should get a bigger share, and each one who took less for his expenses would get his capital increased, and he would have a greater share in the profits. And as for the children, from the day that they started to work, they would get a special share. Perhaps in this manner, they all would start to work and would work better. And those who took less for living expenses would get a greater share in the profits.

With the uncles we had already spoken about this. My brother Nūrullah, too, had arrived in Meshhed, and with him, too, we spoke and consulted, and he, too, liked the plan. At the end, we decided one night that we would bring in also the late Ḥājjī Y'ḥezq'el (Ḥājjī Ismā'īl) Levi, and in this manner we would write the work contract before him.

That night, on which we agreed and on which we invited the late Ḥājjī Ismā'īl, the sons of 'Amo 'Azīzullah came and took my brother Nūrullah to their home, and plied him with alcoholic drinks. That night, the uncles came, and also the late Ḥājjī Y'ḥezq'el, and we were waiting for my brother Nūrullah. After part of the evening passed, my brother Nūrullah arrived with the children of Uncle 'Azīzullah. My brother Nūrullah was totally drunk. We wanted to begin the talk, when suddenly my brother Nūrullah, because of the great heat of head and drunkenness, began to speak harshly. He turned to me and said, "Farajullah, what do you want to do? We don't want to change the order of work." I answered him that the present way of work will have no good end, one must proceed in a manner that each one should begin to work. Everyone who works more and works better, we shall give him a bigger share, so that everyone should try to work more energetically and to advance, and should not put obstacles and excuses to traveling to work. Perhaps God, too, will help us and give blessing to our business. "And if you want to continue as it has been until now, the business will go into bankruptcy."

Nūrullah was angry, and he again said harshly that "We don't want to change anything." Until the afternoon of that same day, he had agreed with all of us, and justified my words, and agreed with my plan. Now it was clear that the sons of Uncle 'Azīzullah had taken him to their house and given him to drink much alcoholic drink, and spoken to him in opposition to the plan that I proposed, and pressed him to object to the entire plan (for, it seems, they did not like to work), and not to agree to sign the work contract. Therefore, I told them that "If you don't agree to my proposal, I shall resign from the business." He said, "It does not matter, resign!" When they saw that there was no agreement, they all rose and left the place and returned to their houses. As for me, from that day on, I did not go to the office and to work.

I stayed on in Meshhed for about six months, and then I decided to go to Bukhara and work there alone. Once or twice, I met with the uncles, and we sat over the accounts, and I told them that "Since, as far as I feel, the business will not succeed, and you did not agree to change your ways, in order to try to stop the way it is going toward freezing, therefore I give you my entire share in the partnership. The main thing for me is to be able to leave freely, without any money that I would have to get from you. I want to start working alone, and God is He who gives the livelihood of mankind."

After several months passed, one day I went to Mashdī Karīm, who had horses. I rented from him a horse, to ride through Qahqeh to Bukhara, and took from him also a *gōyecheh* (a container in which one puts belongings and clothes), and prepared all my things, and was ready to leave. That morning, just as I wanted to start out, suddenly the late Uncle Ḥabībullah and the late Ḥājjī Ismā'īl Levi and the late Mullah Yūsef Baṣṣāl came to my house. They asked me not to go, and Uncle Ḥabībullah swore that in the business works they would do everything as I wanted or suggested, and they would follow in my footsteps, and according to my suggestions. I accepted their request, canceled my trip, and returned to the office and started to work.

A few days later, I went to Deregez to our office, and took over the work from the hands of my brother Nūrullah, and began to work. The work made progress, but the debts and the exchange of promissory notes remained in their place, for without it, it was impossible for us to continue the work. Thereafter, the uncles, too, entered the work, went to Merv, and gave a share of the money to the children of Uncle 'Azīzullah, so that they should be able to begin to work for the office, and they went to Qahqeh and opened a store there, and began to work.

Thus passed years. My brother Nūrullah remained in Meshhed all the time, and I, Farajullah, with wife and children, stayed in Deregez. In those days, the governor of Deregez was from among the sons of Suleyman Khan, and the children of the governor were in disagreement with one another, and all the time they changed around. One of them became the governor, the second resigned. Each one of the brothers got loan moneys from me, and told me that when his turn came to govern, he would repay me. Sometimes, even before they finished their debts, they were dismissed, and I was forced to accept from them a piece of land. In this manner, once I received for their debt Kalatéh and Khonjeh,[51] for 1,000 *tomans* of their debts, once I received half of Kalachah[52] for 1,000 *tomans* of debt, and once, in place of ready cash, I took Kurchashméh[53] for 600 *tomans*. Each of these lands was a big agricultural land. In the meantime, I took agriculturists and began to work the lands, and I settled on each of them several families and turned them into settlements. I grew trees and turned the lands into flowering gardens. The business was successful and also blessed.

Yoḥanan Livian's Memoirs

At my request, Yoḥanan Livian wrote up a brief account of the last phase of his father's life, continuing the life story at the point where his father's own account stopped. He prepared this brief document in New York in 1994, in Hebrew, and the following is my literal translation of it.

> I, Yoḥanan (Nematollah) ben Yonathan (Farajullah) Livian Nasrullayoff, wish to add a few lines to the life story of my late father, until his last days in the Land of Israel.
>
> Late in 1917, when I was two years old, my family fled from Merv to escape the frenzy of the Russian Communists. We passed through Ashkhabad, the border city on the Russian side, and Luṭfabād, the border city on the Persian side, and reached Deregez, where we remained about eight years. My father had business affairs in that city already before that time, and was well known there. He had entered the family business at the age of seven, and worked in it fifty years. Brothers and cousins had a share in the business, as mentioned in his reminiscences. After fifty years, he decided to stop working (you could say he went into retirement). When I was ten [in 1925], the whole family left Deregez and went to Meshhed. We stayed in Meshhed three years, while my father delivered [to the other family members] all the accounts, and closed all the accounts in our office. During those three years, I studied Hebrew in the

Talmud Torah of Meshhed, where I was a pupil of Rabbi Yosef Dīlmānī of blessed memory. I did not study in the Persian school to which all the children went, but had a private teacher, who had come from India. His name was Mulavi, and he taught me English. At the age of thirteen, I celebrated my bar mitzvah in Meshhed, and after it my father decided to go to Eretz Israel, and to stay to the end of his life in Jerusalem.

In those days, the relationship between Iran and Iraq was very tense, and the Iranian government did not issue passports for travel through Iraq. Therefore, all those who wanted to go to Eretz Israel had to travel through India, and from there by ship to Aden (Yemen) and Alexandria (Egypt), and thus to Eretz Israel. This meant a voyage of almost six months. For those who were able to travel through Iraq, the trip was easier: they could reach Eretz Israel in three to four weeks, including the delays in the various countries and cities.

My father had at the time a good friend in Teheran, who was the head of the textile merchants in the Teheran bazaar, and he was also elected by the merchants to the Iranian parliament. He had good connections with the people of the government, and my father asked him to obtain passports that would enable us to go to Eretz Israel through Iraq. His friend promised he would obtain the passports, and we went to Teheran, and, indeed, within a month my father's friend got us the passports. Our own office had business connections with Iraq, and we stayed there some two or three weeks, while my father settled all the accounts. From there, we went to Damascus, where our office also had business connections.

We got the entrance visas to Eretz Israel from the British consulate in Damascus, for at the time of the British Mandate, there was a law that anyone showing that he had 1,000 Palestinian pounds was given an immigrant's visa. Thus, we got our visas and entered Eretz Israel late in the month of Teveth [January] 1929. All this because my father desired to live in Eretz Israel. (Perhaps he could be described as a Zionist.) Two weeks after our arrival was the feast of the fifteenth of Shevat, and we celebrated for the first time the feast of planting trees, together with the children of the schools. It was for us a great experience. The month after that was the month of Adar, and we went to Tel Aviv, which was a new city all of whose inhabitants were Jews, and on Purim they all made merry and were playing about in masks and dancing in the streets all night until daybreak. This was another great experience for us, for until then, we knew no such Jewish freedom, and we enjoyed ourselves tremendously.

However, all the merrymaking came to an end, and we reached the days of the Arab disturbances in Hebron and all the other cities, also in Jerusalem. In Hebron, many Jews were killed, including students of the *yeshiva,* and the rest fled to Jerusalem and other places. I shall not say more about this, since this cruel thing has entered in the history of the state.

Let us go on with the family history as it continued in the midst of these events. Our first home was in the Bukharan quarter in Jerusalem, where several Arab families were also living at the time. When the riots broke out, some of them fled, while others did not have the time to flee. I remember especially one family that lived close to our house; my father brought them to our house and guarded them until the British police were notified and came and took them to safety. This was a veritable Qiddush haShem [sanctification of the Name of God], performed by my father within the first few months after he arrived in Jerusalem. That same year, my father bought a building plot in the Geulah quarter, and began to build a house on it. After it was completed, we moved into it. It stands today at the corner of Geulah Street (at the Sabbath Square).

During the days of the Mandate, my father helped many hundreds of immigrants who came from Meshhed in various ways to Eretz Israel, so that those who helped them pass through Syria and Lebanon, when they heard somebody say that he was going to Mr. Nasrullayoff, instantly and without any discussion helped them across. Most of them crossed into Eretz Israel through Metullah. Before long, the Jews in Metullah wanted to know who was that Nasrullayoff to whom hundreds of people were going? One day, one of the organizers of this transit in Metullah (perhaps he was an official of the Jewish Agency) came to Jerusalem to make the acquaintance of my father. He was greatly surprised to learn that the Arabs who helped in smuggling these illegal immigrants into Palestine, and got paid for it, trusted that ultimately they would get their fee from him. Apart from that, every person who reached Jerusalem was given by my father right away three pounds, which in those days was much money. He sent them on to Tel Aviv so that they should not fall into the hands of the British police. There were those who nevertheless were caught by the police while crossing the Lebanese-Palestinian border, and put in jail; in that case, people from Metullah notified us, and my father somehow managed to have them released from prison. I myself went several times to Beirut and Damascus, where groups of would-be immigrants got stuck because they had no money. I went and spoke to them and helped them to go on to Beirut, where I made arrangements to have them sent on to Jerusalem.

In the meantime, my father was elected president of the Meshhed community of Jerusalem, and all the affairs of the community were managed by him. Especially before the Passover, they distributed kosher food for Passover, sugar, oil, *matzoth*, rice, and all kinds of other foodstuff, which they had bought in behalf of the community. A month before the holiday, they prepared a list of the needy families from Meshhed and other Persian towns, and each one of them was given food according to his need and the size of his family. This is being done to this day prior to Passover.

My mother passed away on the twenty-sixth of Iyyar (May 13), 1942, and my father on the twenty-fourth of Ḥeshvan (October 11), 1951, in Jerusalem. Until the end of his life, he remained the president of the community. When the news of my father's death reached Deregez, the Muslim leaders and the people of that town publicly mourned him for seven days.

II

TALES AND LEGENDS

INTRODUCTORY NOTE

It was inevitable that in a community that was determined to preserve the values of its past, at considerable risk to its safety and even to its very life, tales of past events should survive and be passed on from mouth to mouth from one generation to another. It is characteristic that the central themes in the tales I was able to record from the mouths of the last heirs of the secret and yet heroic life of the Meshhedi Jadīd al-Islām are stories of trials and tribulations to which their ancestors were exposed and which they survived because of their decency and honesty, their ability and cunning, and also their faith and unwavering trust in God. The stories relate how when they were faced with the danger of utter destruction, when everything else had failed, their pious leaders threw themselves upon the mercy of God, even sacrificed themselves, and, lo and behold, events turned around so that, often at the very last minute, they were saved.

This characteristic of the Meshhedi Jewish tales and memories is accompanied by another common feature: the stories tell about events that either actually did happen or the narrators believed had happened in the manner described in the tales. Because of this characteristic, the stories are not what one usually finds in folktales. They are devoid of all fantastic elements, and are not legends in the sense of telling miraculous or wonderful details about the lives of saints and other heroes. There is, to be sure, a wonderful element in them, but it is characteristically not explicit, but hidden and merely implied, evident only to those who know that behind every overt event is the secretly working hand of God.

I have arranged the six chapters constituting part II of this book chronologically, according to the time in which the protagonists of the stories lived. The hero of the first story (chapter 13) is not a Jew at all but the great Persian ruler Nadir Shah, famous equally for his conquests and for his cruelty, who was responsible for the settling of the first Jews in Meshhed, the holy city of the Shīʿīs of Iran, where formerly Jews were forbidden to set foot. An interesting aspect of this story is that because Nadir Shah was "good to the Jews," it dwells with undisguised admiration on his heroic exploits and has very little to tell about his cruelty, which was unusual even for an age in which ferocity was the order of the day. In this sense, the story of Nadir Shah as it survived among the Jews of

Meshhed and came down to Farajullah Nasrullayoff, who told it to me in 1946 in Jerusalem, is an unusual *Jewish* popular "Life of Nadir."

Chapter 14 presents three stories about Mullah Siman-Tov Melamed, who lived in the late eighteenth and early nineteenth centuries and came closest among Iranian Jews to the *Tzaddiq*, the saintly wise man, of the Hasidic Jews of East Europe. The stories do not tell that Mullah Siman-Tov performed miracles but describe his wisdom, his sense of justice (even if the culprit exposed by justice is a Jew), and his ultimate self-sacrifice to bring about the cessation of the plague that threatened to destroy the Jewish community of Meshhed.

Chapter 15 presents two stories about the Jews of Kalat: one telling about a conflict between a Jew and his thieving Muslim neighbor, in which the Jew is vindicated by pure chance, behind which, however, the hand of Providence is felt; the other about the divine response to the desperate cry of the Jews for rain—a typical story of rainmaking competition, the earliest of which is contained in the Bible, in 1 Kings 18.

The story of how the Jews of Herat were saved (chapter 16) has a historical basis, inasmuch as the Persians actually did conquer Herat in 1856 and were forced to evacuate it the next year as a result of a peace treaty concluded in Paris between Great Britain and Persia. After the 1839 Allahdād, most of the Jews who lived in Herat were emigrants from Meshhed, and in 1856–57 many of them were expelled from Herat and forced to settle in the vicinity of Baba Qudrat (popularly Baba Ghodrat). This is the historical background of our story, in which, however, the emphasis is on unstinting help the Meshhedi Jadīdīm gave their unfortunate brothers in their dire need.

Chapter 17 tells the story of a providential rescue of the Jadīdīm of Meshhed on the very verge of being unmasked as false Muslims. Evidently, the act performed by the woman Gohar (who in one of the versions of the story is identified with rather unusual frankness as a prostitute) made a deep impression on the contemporaries who witnessed it, to the extent that several versions of what happened did survive and were transmitted, and that not a word of opprobrium about her immoral comportment is contained in any one of them.

The story about the death of Ḥājj Hasan Eshaq (chapter 18) comes closest to containing a miraculous element, inasmuch as the death of the Ḥājj the night before he was about to carry out his evil scheme against the Jadīdīm is told as nothing short of miraculous. Yet even here, the details of his death—his inability to obtain medical help because of the curfew, and so on—are painted in simple, realistic colors.

All in all, these few examples out of what must have been a much richer storehouse of Jadīdī folktales show the Jews of Meshhed as a hardheaded, realistic group of people, who knew how to make the best of a bad situation, who were always ready to help one another, who knew exactly how far to go between the two contrary demands put to them, on the one hand by the Muslim majority of the city which required them to live as Muslims, and on the other by their ancestral faith that did not allow them to abandon their Jewish traditions. Their folklore—again, to judge by the meager available material—did not indulge in describing a never-never world of supernatural beings and events but kept alive, in a moderately embellished form, the memory of the actual happenings that marked their lives during and after the Allahdād.

13
A Popular "Life of Nadir"

The history of Nadir Shah (1688–1747), king of Persia, whom Armin Vámbéry justly called "the last great Asiatic conqueror," is well known thanks to a number of contemporary biographies and accounts written by both Oriental and European authorities. The Persian authors either stood directly in Nadir's service or at least were eyewitnesses of much of what they recorded. Some of the Western sources, too, are either eyewitness accounts or are based on information derived from persons who witnessed many phases of Nadir's career. In the two hundred and fifty years that have passed since Nadir's death, hundreds of authors have studied his life and published books or articles concerning his history. Laurence Lockhart published in 1938 a careful and detailed critical study of Nadir's life based mainly on contemporary sources.[1] Nadir's career is thus as fully documented as could be wished.

This circumstance gives additional interest to the study of the folk traditions about Nadir that still live in that district of Khorasan that witnessed his birth, childhood, and early career. When viewed against the background of historical fact, the particulars handed down in the popular "Life of Nadir" throw a sharp light on the working of folk tradition. We see events that in reality took place at a distance of many years from each other thrown into one by the legend; we find that different persons are fused into one and geographical features confused; we note that great and important happenings left no trace at all in the folk story, while, on the other hand, we find recounted incidents that lack any historical foundation. Stories already told of Cyrus in Herodotus's time become attached to Nadir. The emphasis, too, is quite different in the folktale from that in the historical narrative. A gigantic military operation such as Nadir's invasion of India is remembered only in the form of two anecdotes telling what happened on the way there and back. An insignificant accident, on the other hand, such as the jokingly made promise of Nadir's former master that he would conquer Baghdad for him, becomes a weighty event, pregnant with "historical" consequences, for owing to it Nadir finally succeeds—according to the folk story—in taking Baghdad. Nothing is remembered in folk tradition of the misery, famine, illness, and death Nadir's constant wars brought upon the great masses of Persia's peoples, almost no word of the enormous loss in life suffered and caused by his armies, but it is meticulously recorded that he took seven *rotl* (about forty-six pounds) of eyes from his own army and that he wished to make a tower out of a million skulls. Of the later phases of Nadir's life, well documented in history, the folktale has comparatively little to tell. But his early life, of which history knows practically nothing, is described in great detail. It is thus the humble birth, the simple childhood—which could have been that of any one of those who loved to tell this tale or hear it—the early steps that gradually led him to the throne, on which the popular tale dwells with special interest everywhere when it comes to tell of a hero. In Nadir's later life, it is the colorful or the terrible, the picturesque or the extraordinary happenings, that remain alive in folk memory or, rather, which folk fantasy attaches to the figure of its hero.

In the following pages, I give an almost verbatim translation of the popular "Life of Nadir" as it was told to me by Farajullah Nasrullayoff in Jerusalem. The notes point to some of the main discrepancies between his story and the historical data of the life of Nadir. The lower-case letters *a* through *m* refer to the notes written by Dr. Lockhart, who was good enough to go over the manuscript when I first prepared it for publication in *Edoth*. Nasrullayoff told the story in the course of several meetings in the early summer of 1946. In March 1947, I asked him to repeat parts of the story in order to check the precision of his memory and narration, and I can state that the repetitions corresponded to the first version down to the minutest details. Nasrullayoff himself lived from 1895 to 1920 in the town of Muḥammadābād, the chief town of the district of Deregez (Darra Gaz)[2] in northern Khorasan, northwest of Meshhed. This town is generally referred to as Deregez—that is, it is called by the name of the district of which it is the capital. It was in this district that Nadir was born and spent his early youth. Thus, the first part of the story, which in fact is the richest, falls into the category of local tradition. Nasrullayoff heard the story from the elders of Muḥammadābād,[3] among them the "governor" of the town and a certain Muḥammad Ḥusayn Beg, a member of the Turkish Afshar tribe, to which Nadir also belonged.

The little town of Kona Gale (Kohnah Qal'ah, i.e., Old Fort) in which Nadir was born, Nasrullayoff told me, was situated about half a *farsang* (i.e., about two miles) from Muḥammadābād. At the time of Nadir's birth, Kona Gale was the chief town of the district of Deregez. It was surrounded by a city wall with three gates, corresponding to the three roads that led through the mountains into the city. Round about Kona Gale and very near to it were high mountains. Outside the city wall were wells, the water of which was conducted around the city and used to irrigate the gardens. The water was, however, not allowed to run into the town, for the town was situated in a depression, lower than the surrounding countryside. The stream was bordered by numerous watermills; some houses also stood there. This outer part of Kona Gale was called Dastgird, "hand-girdle." Kona Gale suffered much from the attacks of robbers who could easily direct their shots into the city from the surrounding mountains. About 1817, when Nasrullayoff's great-great-grandfather died, he was buried in the Jewish cemetery of Kona Gale. At about the same time, all the inhabitants of the town decided to leave it and to settle at a new point in the midst of open country, where they would not be exposed to the attacks of robbers. This new town is Muḥammadābād, the new capital of the district. Kona Gale is today a ruin; only the city walls can be seen.

It was in Kona Gale that Nadir was born. His father was a poor man, the shepherd and cowherd of the town. Each inhabitant had a few sheep and a few cows. He would gather these in the morning, take them into the pastures, and bring them home in the evening.[4] In the early days of her pregnancy, Nadir's mother dreamed a dream: she saw herself standing on a high mountain. She began to urinate, and the urine turned into a flood that rose and engulfed the whole land. The flood rose and covered the mountain on which she stood, until it reached her own feet, and yet it continued to rise. Then she awoke with terror. She was much frightened by her dream and went to ask its meaning from a *mullah*.[5] The *mullah* listened to the woman's story and then, although as yet no signs of her pregnancy were visible, he asked her, "Are you pregnant?" She answered, "Yes." Thereupon, the *mullah* said, "Know you then, that if you give birth to a son, he will become a king and will conquer all the lands; and if it be a girl that you give birth to, she will become a queen, the wife of the greatest king on the earth."[6]

Despite this prediction, no unusual attention was paid to the child when he was born. He was brought up in the Turk mother tongue. When Nadir was seven years old, he was attacked by an illness that left him bald.[a] It was about this time that his parents began to send him with the other boys of his age to gather brushwood and grass for heating. Every day, the children would set out together, carrying their food with them. Before long, Nadir had become the leader of his band. When six months had gone by in this manner,[7] Nadir said to the boys, "Let us not eat until we have gathered the brushwood and thorns for heating. When we have done our work, let us sit down together and share the food we have received from home. If there is in our midst a boy who is poor and has no food, we shall give him from ours." All the boys agreed, and thenceforth they did as he had said. One day it happened that one of the boys sat down to eat his food alone, before the brushwood and the thorns had been gathered. When all the other boys sat down together to eat, it was found that this boy had already eaten his food. Nadir ordered the boys to get up and beat the one who had disobeyed. The boys beat him until he died. They then sat down again and ate their food. When they had finished, they rose, each boy took his bundle of brushwood, and they returned to the town. The dead boy remained lying where he had fallen, near his pile of brushwood. All the children returned home, and Nadir, too, went to his mother. He said to her, "Such and such a thing did we do today, and the boy died. The boys will tell it to the family and to the *ḥākem* [the head of the town], and they will come and catch me. I want to escape. Give me two or three loaves of bread, and I shall go to another place."[8]

So Nadir left his town and fled to Chapushli, a big village at a distance of one *farsang* [about four miles] from Kona Gale. When he arrived at Chapushli, he went straightaway to the *ḥākem* of the place and said to him, "Such and such a thing has happened, and I have come to you to place myself under your protection." The *ḥākem*, who chanced to be the brother of the *ḥākem* of Kona Gale, accepted him. In the meantime, the news of the boy's death had spread through Kona Gale, and the *ḥākem* arrested Nadir's parents for interrogation. They said, "We know not where the boy is." Before long, however, it became known that Nadir was in the nearby village of Chapushli. So the *ḥākem* of Kona Gale sent messengers to his brother, the *ḥākem* of Chapushli, to demand that he deliver the boy and thus enable the kinsmen of the murdered boy to avenge his death upon Nadir. The *ḥākem* of Chapushli, however, answered the messengers, "Go and tell my brother that the boy came to me and honestly told me what had happened and asked my protection. I accepted him, and therefore as long as he is under my protection, I cannot give him up. If it be possible to persuade the dead boy's family to accept blood money, I am willing to put up the amount myself." The messengers went to and fro a number of times, and nothing could be settled. Both sides became angry and obdurate, and things reached such a point that a fight broke out between the followers of the two. The skirmishes between the contending sides lasted a year, and sixty of the men of Chapushli lost their lives. At last, the *ḥākem* of Chapushli called Nadir to him and said, "You are under my protection, and, as you know, we have fought for you and I have lost many of my fighting men. Should my brother, the *ḥākem* of Kona Gale, send fresh forces against us, we may find ourselves unable to face them. And if I should be taken prisoner, you, too, will be in his power. Therefore, it is my advice to you that you leave us and go to Abivard.[9b] I have there a friend with whom you will be safe."

So Nadir left the village of Chapushli, escorted by the *ḥākem* himself at the head of a band of his fighting men. The *ḥākem* entrusted Nadir to his friend in Abivard, and then returned with his men to Chapushli.

This friend of the *ḥākem* was the richest man in Abivard.[10] He possessed large herds of sheep. He took the eight-year-old Nadir to his chief shepherd to teach the boy to become a shepherd. Nadir would go out with the other shepherds to tend the flocks, and thus did he live for five years. When Nadir had attained the age of thirteen, the *ḥākem*'s friend gave into his care a flock of four or five hundred sheep. Now it was the wont of the shepherds in winter to let their sheep graze on the *gheshlagh* [winter grassland] near Abivard. As summer drew near, the *gheshlagh* became exhausted, and the flocks would be taken to the *yeylagh*ʿ [summer quarters], where the grazing was good. The *yeylagh* was situated some two or three *farsangs* from Abivard. Every two or three days, food and drink were sent from Abivard for the shepherds and their donkeys and dogs. Every month or two, the master himself would make the rounds of his flocks in their summer pastures to see if all was well. It was upon one such visit that the master, approaching the field where Nadir was pasturing his flocks, saw from afar that the sheep were scattered unwatched all over the countryside. In surprise, he hurried forward and soon came upon Nadir. Nadir stood perfectly still in the open field, with his eyes closed, his face turned upward, and his chin resting on the back of his hands, which lay clasped over his long shepherd's staff.[11] He stood there oblivious of everything about him, lost in reverie. "Some wild animal can attack the flock!" thought the master to himself, and he drew up to Nadir. Nadir did not hear him come. "What do you think you are doing?" shouted the master. "What do you mean by allowing the flock to scatter unwatched?" Nadir started, stared at his master, and then cried out in Turkic, *Even yükhülsun!*—"May your house be destroyed! In my thoughts, I had conquered the whole of Persia, and just as I was about to take Baghdad, you came and disturbed me!" "Never mind," said his master derisively. "When you have conquered all of Persia and only Baghdad will be left, call me and I shall come and take it for you." Nadir looked at him for a moment and said to him solemnly, "Do not forget what you have just said!"

Some months elapsed, and Nadir returned with the flocks to Abivard. His master began to notice strange things about Nadir that were not seen in other people. He would always get lost in thought and seem preoccupied with plans of his own. His master, watching him, began to fear him. One day, he said to Nadir, "I would like you to think well of me. Name what you wish, and I shall give it to you." Nadir said, "Give me a horse, a saddle, and a sword." His master said, "Choose any horse you wish." Nadir said, "Give me a good horse and a good sword." So his master brought him a fine horse, a good sword, and two saddlebags. Nadir filled the bags with bread and fodder. His master asked him, "Do you think well of me now?" Nadir said, "Yes, I do."

Nadir was eighteen when he thus left his master's service. What did he do now? He rode out into the fields, far away, came to a village, and stole two or three camels. He brought the camels back to Abivard and sold them there, and with the money thus acquired, he bought himself another horse. This horse he gave to one of his friends who was willing to join him in his adventures. However, he made one condition, that half of anything his friend should bring back was to belong to Nadir in payment for the horse. With this first follower, Nadir set out and carried off a number of camels. These he again sold in Abivard, and for the money he got, he bought horses. Then he made known that anyone who wanted to join him would receive a horse, for which he would have to give him half of his loot. Within twenty days, he had a following of ten riders. Nadir continued to receive half of anything they plundered in return for his horses. When he had twelve men, he raided Khiva,[d] the capital of the territory of Khorazm [Khwarizm], a big Turkoman town.[12] There they drove off two big herds of sheep. The sheep, however, could not be hurried and hampered the speedy retreat of the band. So what did Nadir do? He slaughtered one sheep, bound a rope around its legs, and gave the end of the rope into the hands of one of his horsemen. The rider dragged the slaughtered animal behind him, and the flowing blood formed a trail as he rode. All the sheep hurried after the trail and ran as fast as the riders rode.[13] So they all arrived back at Abivard, where Nadir sold the sheep and bought horses for the money. And once more he let it be known, as before, that whosoever would join him would receive a horse and in return would have to share his booty. Soon the number of his band reached fifty.

When Nadir saw that he had fifty riders, he said to himself, "The time has come for me to take Kona Gale, Chapushli, and all the land of Deregez!" So one day, he set out with his fifty horsemen, rode to Kona Gale, took the town, and then subjugated Chapushli also and all the land of Deregez. All this he accomplished with his band of fifty riders.[14] He appointed his former benefactor, the *ḥākem* of Chapushli, ruler of Kona Gale in place of his brother. Nadir himself set up his court in Chapushli and lived there like a king. When he had secured all Deregez, Nadir thought the time had come to be confirmed in his rule by the Shah. At that time, Shah Sultan Ḥusayn sat on the throne of Persia,[15] holding court at Isfahan, and he had a *vezīr* in whose hands the real power lay. It was to this *vezīr* that Nadir now wrote, or rather had a letter written in his name, for he himself could neither read nor write. In the letter, Nadir said, "I am not a rebel. I shall do what you tell me to do. The government in Deregez was not good, and therefore have I done what I have done." The letter was accompanied by appropriate presents to the *vezīr*, and Nadir was duly confirmed in his governorship.[16]

For three months, Nadir remained in Deregez, and in this time he gathered round him a cavalry a thousand strong. Every day, he went raiding the surrounding country. One day, he led his men against Quchan,[17] situated eight *farsangs* from Chapushli. Quchan was a town eight times the size of Kona Gale. They set out, all the thousand horsemen, in the afternoon. By nightfall, they had ridden three *farsangs*, and they rode throughout the night, so that they reached

Quchan with the dawn and quickly overpowered the city. In the six months that followed, Nadir's headquarters were at Quchan. From there, he organized his predatory expeditions, and in these six months he subjected to his rule Shirvan,[18] Böjnurt [Bujnurd], and Radkon [Radkan]—in fact, the whole area surrounding Quchan. Shah Sultan Ḥusayn's rule was weak, so that many towns revolted against him and declared themselves independent. Nadir occupied these towns, and he could always say that he only restored in them the rule of the Shah.

In Quchan, Nadir's army grew apace, until it reached the formidable number of five thousand horsemen. Nadir at that time was no more than twenty years of age. One day, he led his five thousand horsemen to Radkon, which, as mentioned before, he had already conquered, and stayed there with them for a few days. One evening, he set out with his troops, rode through the night, and toward dawn reached Meshhed.[19] He easily overran the city, occupied it, captured and killed its rulers and the heads of its army, and established his headquarters in the famous capital of Khorasan.[20] From there, he again sent a letter to the *vezīr,* saying, "I am not a rebel. The government in Meshhed was not good, and for this reason I conquered the city." The letter was accompanied by presents which surpassed everything he had sent to the *vezīr* up till then, and in due course the answer of the *vezīr* came, saying, "You have done well. You are to be from now the governor of Meshhed." So Nadir stayed in Meshhed for about five years.

The *vezīr* in the meantime plotted against the Shah, for he himself wished to be king. He could, however, do nothing, for he was always near the Shah, and though he had many adherents, many others in the court were faithful to the Shah. At that time, it happened that the city of Merv [today inhabited by Turkomans and belonging to Russia], which was at that time a part of Persia, rebelled against the Shah's rule. So the *vezīr* said to the Shah, "Let us organize an army, go to Meshhed, and from there we shall attack Merv and punish the rebels. But you yourself must lead the army, otherwise we shall not succeed." The Shah agreed, and sometime later, he arrived with the army and the *vezīr* at Meshhed, and camped one *farsang* from the town.

Every morning, the great ones of Meshhed, led by Nadir, came to the royal camp to pay homage to the Shah. The camp, however, was full of the adherents of the *vezīr,* so that anything the *vezīr* wished to do, he could do. The *vezīr* made plans to kill the Shah and to proclaim himself king in his stead. One day, when Nadir was received by the Shah in his tent, the Shah wanted to tell something to the *vezīr.* He said to a servant, "Go and call the *vezīr.*" The servant went and returned, saying, "The *vezīr* said he is busy now, and he will come when he has finished his work." The Shah became exceedingly angry, seeing that his *vezīr* did not obey him, and he said to Nadir with great wrath, "I do not know what to do with this *vezīr!*" Nadir said, "Give me your permission, and I shall be able to arrange things with the *vezīr.*" The king said, "Good." Sometime later, the *vezīr* entered, and the Shah immediately addressed him in wrath. "Why did you not come at the time I sent for you?!" The *vezīr* answered, "I had work to do. I cannot come any minute." Nadir then cried, "You wicked man! Is this how one speaks to the king?" And he drew his sword and cut off the man's head.[e]

Seeing this, the Shah became very frightened, for the *vezīr* had many servants and adherents in the camp. Nadir said to him, "Give me three hours and the guns." The king agreed. Nadir immediately ordered his men to take the guns to the nearby mountains and to direct them against the army. In the camp, there were some six thousand soldiers. They knew nothing of what had happened, and when they saw the big guns turned on them, they came to the Shah and asked, "What happened?" The Shah said, "The *vezīr* has been killed, and this was done so that the army should not be able to do anything against the Shah." Whereupon all said, "We are your faithful servants." Then Nadir gave orders to bring before him all the adherents of the *vezīr.* They were brought, and Nadir killed many of them, while others he let go free. Then Nadir said to the Shah, "It is not necessary that you should go yourself to Merv. Return to Isfahan, and I shall go with the army to Merv and capture it." So the Shah returned to Isfahan, and Nadir took Merv and put it again under Persian rule.

Before Nadir left Merv, he said, "If any one of you will do violence to anybody else, I shall come back and punish him." Sometime later, when Nadir camped with his army at a distance of many days' riding from Merv, a man came to him and told him that there was an old woman in Merv whose husband had died, and now one of the inhabitants of Merv had taken seven or eight of her sheep from her by sheer force. Nadir thereupon said to his officers, "I want to go somewhere, and shall be back in about two weeks' time. Stay here in the meantime with the army, and take care that I should find everything in order upon my return." No one of the officers dared to ask him, "Where are you going?" At midnight, when the whole of the army was asleep, Nadir set out on his horse, accompanied only by two or three riders. He rode with them to Merv, entered the house of the widow, and asked her, "Is it true that so-and-so took from you by force seven or eight sheep?" The old woman said, "Yes, it is true." Nadir then went to the man's house and took the sheep and returned them to the widow. Then he punished the man; he put him to death. Seeing this, all the inhabitants of Merv were very much afraid and did not dare again to do any violence. Nadir rode back, and a fortnight after he had set out from his camp, he came back there, again in the dead of the night.[21]

Again, a number of years passed, and seventeen towns in the Caucasus rebelled against Persia. The Shah wrote to Nadir to come and conquer the seventeen towns. Nadir came with his army from Meshhed and reached Isfahan. There the Shah gave him an additional army, and, thus reinforced, Nadir marched through Azerbaijan to the Caucasus. His conquest of the whole of the Caucasus was effected in about two and half or three years. But some months after Nadir had set out for the Caucasus or, at the utmost, after a year, the Afghans rebelled against Persia.[f] One of the great Afghan leaders collected an army twenty thousand men strong. He entered Persia from the east and proceeded, conquering and destroying everything on his way, until he reached the neighborhood of the capital, Isfahan. Shah Sultan Ḥusayn sent his son with an army of about five or six thousand men against him. The prince's army met the Afghan invader at a distance of some six *farsangs* from Isfahan, and there suffered utter defeat. The whole Persian army was scattered, and the prince himself was killed. The Afghans marched up to the city, surrounded it, and began to besiege it. The siege lasted for about forty days.[g] In the meantime, the Shah sent a letter to Nadir, saying, "Leave the Caucasus and come quickly to rescue Isfahan!" But Nadir did not obey the Shah and answered, "First I want to finish the conquest of the Caucasus; then I shall come and retake Persia."

When the forty days were up, the Afghans captured Isfahan. Within Isfahan, there was the *ark*,[22] the citadel, the fortified palace of the Shah. The Shah withdrew into it with the remnants of his men. A few days later, the *ark* also was taken by the Afghans. The Shah fled to the harem, where his own mother also lived, and he said to her, "Where shall I now go, where shall I flee?" His mother scornfully parted her legs, pointed to her privy parts, and said, "Go to the place from where you came! What sort of a king are you?" The Afghans entered and killed the Shah and all his family. Only one of the Shah's wives escaped. She was then pregnant. The Afghans remained in Isfahan about eight months.[23]

Six months after the Afghans killed the Shah, Nadir completed his conquest of the Caucasus and returned to Azerbaijan. He then proceeded into Persia and fought the Afghans. He conquered town after town until he reached Isfahan. The Afghans fled from Isfahan also, and Nadir pursued them, so that they had to flee the very way they came, until they reached the eastern borders of Persia. Nadir killed them all. He entered even into Afghanistan and conquered it, just as he had conquered the whole of Persia proper.

Then Nadir said, "Persia must have a king, and he must be from the royal family, the family of the Safavi." A man came and said, "There is a woman from among the wives of the late Shah who was pregnant and escaped death. She has in the meantime given birth to a son. This is the only one of the Shah's sons who has remained alive." The child was then about six months old. Nadir said, "This child must be the king!" So Nadir sent messengers to all parts of Persia to invite the nobles and the rulers of the people to come and elect the king. They all came. Nadir gave orders to bring in the child in his cradle, and they put the cradle on the *takht* [royal throne]. Above the child's head, they hung the crown on a string.

Nadir then turned to the great ones of the country present and said to them, "This child shall be our king!" And he fell upon his knees before the child and bid all the others do the same. Then he said, "Until the child grows up, I shall be the *nāyeb sultānī* [regent]." So all the rulers present fell on their knees, and then Nadir gave leave to them to return everyone to his place, and he himself stayed in Isfahan and was regent.[24]

Six months later, the child-king died. Who knows how this happened? He died. So all the great ones of Persia came and said to Nadir, "You must be Shah!" Nadir consented, and he was crowned Shah of Persia. He knew neither how to read nor how to write, and did not learn before he died.[25]

A year or two later, Nadir decided to go against Baghdad and to conquer it. He went with his army and fought against the Babylonians.[26] He reached the shore of the river Euphrates,[27] but the town was on the farther side of the river, and he was unable to cross in face of strong opposition on the part of the Babylonian army. Six months passed like this, and Nadir still could not cross the river. Suddenly, he remembered how he had dreamed, when he was still a simple shepherd in Abivard, that he had conquered all Persia, and how his former master came up to him and disturbed him in his dreams just as he was about to conquer Baghdad in his imagination. And he remembered what his former master had jokingly promised him: "When you shall have conquered the whole of Persia and only Baghdad will be left, call me and I shall conquer it for you!" So Nadir sent quick messengers to ride to Abivard and to fetch his former master. The man came; Nadir showed him some honor and said to him, "Do you remember what you promised me when I was your shepherd? Now I have conquered the whole of Persia, and only Baghdad is left. Now you must conquer Baghdad for me!" The man said, "Good, I will do it." And he stayed with the army. He said to Nadir, "We must do this by deceit. Give orders to bring five thousand big goats, ten thousand candles, and ten thousand big earthenware jars." Nadir did as he told him and prepared everything he wanted. The man said, "Good. How many soldiers have you got here?" Nadir said, "About forty thousand men."[28] The man said, "Order the five thousand best horsemen to leave the camp in the dead of the night quietly and ride along the bank of the river to a distance of about two or three *farsangs*. But let them do it so that nothing should be noticed from the other side." This was done at after midnight or one o'clock. Then the goats were brought, and two candles were tied to the horns of each. The candles were lit, and the goats were driven into the water by five thousand specially appointed men. The military bands also were brought up and ordered to play at full force. The men shouted and broke the jars, thus creating a terrible din.[29] When the Babylonian army from over the river saw the lights and heard the noise, they believed that the Persians were attempting a general attack by crossing the river at that point, and they concentrated all their strength opposite the goats. At the same time, word was given to the five thousand horsemen waiting two or three *farsangs* away to swim over on their horses. Horses can swim far better than men. The horsemen crossed, gained the other shore without any opposition, and attacked the unsuspecting enemy from an entirely unexpected quarter. In the confusion thus created, the rest of the Persian army could cross the river, and soon they were the lords of Baghdad.[30 h] After the conquest of Baghdad, Nadir conquered all the outer boundaries of Persia, from the Caspian Sea in the north to the Persian Gulf in the south.

In earlier days, India also formed a part of the Persian Empire, as it is written, "From India to Ethiopia."[31] So Nadir decided to reconquer this country. He set out on his expedition against India with ten thousand camels carrying ammunition, mainly lead cannonballs. After leaving Peshawar, between Afghanistan and India, they reached a mountain pass[32] so narrow that the heavy guns could not get through. The leaders of the army said, "What is to be done? It is impossible to pass." Nadir said, "Bombard the mountain with the cannons until it will be possible to pass." They did so and spent more than half the ammunition on it.[33] When the high officers saw this, they said to Nadir, "What are you doing? We are on our way to fight India, a mighty empire, and you waste all our ammunition on this mountain?" Nadir said, "You are fools! Do you think these cannonballs are aimed at the mountain? They are aimed straight at the heart of the king of India. When he hears that we are wasting so much ammunition on the mountain, he will think we have enormous reserves of ammunition, and he will not dare oppose us." And so indeed it came to pass.

On his way to India, Nadir reached a bridge. While crossing the bridge, Nadir suddenly turned to his learned *vezīr,* Mīrzā Mahdī Khān,[34] and asked him, "What is the best food which in one bite gives the most strength?" Mīrzā Mahdī Khān answered, "An egg." Many months later, on their way back from India, they again reached the bridge, Nadir remembered what he had asked Mīrzā Mahdī Khān on the same spot, and queried, "With what?" Without a moment's hesitation, Mīrzā Mahdī Khān answered, "With salt."[35]

From India, Nadir brought back rich treasures. Among them was a great diamond, round as a hill, which was called Kūh-i-Blūr, that is, "crystal mountain."[i] Another great brick-shaped diamond brought back by Nadir from India was called Deriā-i-Nūr, "sea of light."[36] When Nadir returned from India, he was so mighty and rich that he hung the Deriā-i-Nūr at the back of his saddle to serve as an ornament, so that it dangled over the hind legs of his horse. The kings who ruled Persia after Nadir were no longer so mighty, and they set the Deriā-i-Nūr in an armband [*bāzū band*]. The dynasty that followed, that of the Kajars, set it in their crown—that is, they were even less rich. Fatḥ-'Alī Shah had the Fātiḥa, the opening chapter of the Koran, engraved upon the diamond. In doing so, he lowered the diamond's value, so that it was worth only 50,000 pounds sterling. The kings who followed him no longer had the honor to wear the diamond and kept it in their treasure house under lock and key.

When Nadir returned from India, he fortified his old castle, Kalat Nadiri [Qal'at Nādirī], which lies north of Meshhed, with enormous blocks of hewn stones brought from a great distance. He paid special attention to reinforcing the natural caves in the mountain. He wanted to convert these caves into a treasury. Kalat is a natural fortress built by God. It is surrounded by a range of very high mountains in the form of an unbroken chain, the length of which attains twenty-four *farsangs.* There are but two mountain paths over which camels, horses, and carts can pass. Nine further paths can be traversed only on foot. Nadir did not trust the Persians, and therefore he wished to settle Jews in Kalat to serve as the guardians of his treasures. Accordingly, he gave orders to the town of Qazwin to send forty Jewish families to Kalat.[j] Owing to the difficulties of the way, the forty families could not travel together and divided into three groups. At the time of Nadir's death, only seventeen of the Jewish families had arrived in Kalat, and sixteen had got as far as Meshhed, while the remaining seven only reached Sabzawar. This, incidentally, was the beginning of the Jewish community of Meshhed, which exists there to this day.[37]

Nadir's trust in the Jews may have been connected with the following occurrence. One day, Nadir invited to him two Shī'a *mujtahids,* two popes (i.e., Christian priests), and two Jewish rabbis. He wanted to know which is the true religion, for he was a Sunnī and not a Shī'ī.[38] He said to them, "Sit down in one place and prepare yourselves to answer my questions." Then he asked them which of the books was the real one. First he asked the *mujtahids,* "What is written in the Koran?" They read out to him, and he saw that it spoke of Moses, Abraham, and others. Then he turned to the Christians and asked them, "What is written in the *Injīl?*"[39] They read out to him, and he saw that their book, too, was built on what had happened to the Jews previously. Then he asked the rabbis, "What is written in the *Tawrāt?*"[40] They read out to him from the beginning, and he saw that the book of the Jews begins from the creation of the world and goes on explaining what happened after then. So Nadir said, "This is the true book; this is the real book of God."[41]

When Nadir came back from India, he found that his son had collected an army around himself. This army consisted of ten thousand horsemen. A thousand had white garments and white horses, a thousand had black garments and black horses, a thousand gray garments and gray horses, a thousand yellow garments and yellow horses, a thousand brown garments and brown horses, and so on to ten thousand, according to each of the colors horses have. It was whispered to Nadir, "Maybe your son plans to revolt against you and wants to be king." Once his son came to him, and Nadir asked, "Who are you that you have made yourself all these horsemen, a thousand of each color?" His son answered him haughtily, "I am the son of Nadir Shah!" Then Nadir said, "But Nadir himself did not do the like!" His son said, "And whose son is Nadir?" To this question, Nadir could not answer, so he became very angry and gave orders to deprive his son of his two eyes. Mīrzā Mahdī Khān came and begged, "Do not do this; do not blind your son." Thereupon Nadir answered, "First your own eyes will be taken out, then the eyes of my son." And so it was done.[42]

Some years later, it happened that a letter came to Nadir from Europe, from one of the kings there. But nobody could read the letter. it was very shameful for the Persian government to admit that they could not read the letter. So they went to Mīrzā Mahdī Khān and asked, "Do you know if there is a man in Persia who can read the letter and understand it?" He answered, "No." They said, "What shall we do? The Shah must give an answer to the letter; he must know what is written in it." Thereupon Mīrzā Mahdī Khān said, "I can read the letter and translate it. Take me to the hot bath and bring there ice, and draw the forms of the letters on my naked back with ice, and in this manner I shall be able to translate the letter." This was done, and when the translation of the letter was presented to Nadir, he felt great regret for having blinded Mīrzā Mahdī Khān.[43 k]

Nadir was so mighty and powerful that each time before he attacked a town, he let the inhabitants know, "If you do not submit, I shall conquer the town, make slaves out of you, and take away all you have; the gold, the silver, and even the dust of your town I shall take away." So each time after he conquered a town, he said to his soldiers, "Take the dust of this town to Meshhed." Whereupon the soldiers took the sacks in which they used to give fodder to their horses, filled them with earth, and took them away with them. When they reached the neighborhood of Meshhed, they emptied their sacks so that large hills rose up. Such hills are to be found all over Persia. Between Meshhed and Quchan, there are two such hills at a distance of two *farsangs* from each other. These hills are called *tās teppe,* that is, "bowl hills." In Deregez, there are six or seven such hills. Other kings also used to build such hills, but the greatest number of them was made by Nadir.

After Nadir came back from India, he became very cruel. Once he said, "Tomorrow I shall take the eyes of my army until I have seven *rotls* of them." And he fulfilled his threat.[l]

It was his cruelty that made Nadir's commanders decide to kill him. Nadir camped with his army in Radkon, at a distance of eight *farsangs* from Meshhed. From Radkon, it was just barely possible to see the upper edge of the golden dome of the shrine of Imām Reza in Meshhed. The dome was covered with gold from before Nadir's time, paid for by foundations that had been established for the purpose of maintaining and embellishing the shrine. One evening, Nadir said, "Tomorrow I shall have the heads of so many soldiers cut off that from the top of the hill made of the heads, I shall be able to see the whole of the golden dome."[44] When his commanders heard this, they knew that Nadir had become mad, and they were afraid that he might kill a million in order to make a hill out of their heads, and, should he still not see the dome well enough, he might kill another million. So the nine commanders, among them the brother of Nadir's wife, decided to kill him the same night.

Nadir used to sleep in a tent within the camp. He would tell his wife to cross her legs, and he would rest his head in her lap, while in his hand he grasped a naked sword. As long as Nadir slept, his wife had to keep awake. He knew that in this position, he would be awakened by the slightest movement made by his wife, be it of fright or of anything else. In the dead of the night, the nine men set out jointly for Nadir's tent. But on the way there, they dropped off one by one, so afraid were they of Nadir. They were afraid even of his name. Finally, only the brother of Nadir's wife reached his tent. When he saw that he was alone, he was very much afraid. He slowly lifted the curtain covering the entrance to the test. His sister, Nadir's wife, when she suddenly perceived her brother standing in the tent opening with a drawn sword in his hand, started, and Nadir woke up. Nadir jumped to his feet, and his brother-in-law took flight. Nadir ran after him with the sword in his hand, but his foot got caught by the rope of the tent, and he fell. Thereupon his brother-in-law ran up to him and killed him with his sword.[45]

Nadir had had a beautiful garden laid out in Meshhed. This garden already was called the Garden of Nadir in his lifetime. He also gave expression to his wish to be buried in Meshhed. So after his assassination, they took his body to Meshhed and buried it in the Garden of Nadir.[46]

When Nadir was killed, a chronogram was composed, the numerical value of the letters of which give 1160, the date of his death by the Muslim year, 1747.

Nadir b'derek raft—"Nadir went to hell."[47 m]

14
THREE TALES ABOUT MULLAH SIMAN-TOV

Mullah Siman-Tov was a historical figure, a religious leader of the Jews of Meshhed, and a scholar of note who left behind quite a number of writings but of whose life practically nothing is known. If, as seems most likely, his death came about during the great cholera epidemic that struck Meshhed in 1830, the community enjoyed his leadership in the decades preceding the Allahdād of 1839.

That he must have been an impressive personality can be concluded from the fact that folktales were woven around his life and acts, including his last act of sacrificing his life for the benefit of his community, and were still part of the living folklore of Meshhedi Jews a century after his death.

The three stories here were told to me in Persian by Āqā Farajullah Nasrullayoff in Jerusalem in 1945, with his son Yoḥanan translating into Hebrew. They were published in my English translation in *Folk-Lore* 57 (December 1946): 179–84.

I

In the days of Mullah Siman-Tov, peace be upon him, the rule of Meshhed was in the hands of a descendant of Imām Reza, who was the Imām Jum'ah of Meshhed, a truth-loving and just man. When the Imām Jum'ah heard of the great wisdom of Mullah Siman-Tov, peace be upon him, he wished to talk to him and to discuss with him matters of religion. But the Jews were regarded as impure by the Muslims, and so it was impossible for the Imām Jum'ah either to invite Mullah Siman-Tov, peace be upon him, to his house, or to go and visit him. So the Imām Jum'ah had a small *madrasah*[1] built in the Jewish quarter, consisting of only three rooms, and in the innermost room of this *madrasah*, he would meet in secret Mullah Siman-Tov, peace be upon him, once or twice a week, with no one present to witness their meetings. The Imām Jum'ah would ask all manner of questions, especially concerning religious prescriptions in which the Muslim faith differed from the Jewish, and Mullah Siman-Tov, peace be upon him, would answer the questions by referring to the Bible,[2] and thus showing that the Jewish precept is the right one. Finally, the Imām Jum'ah felt that, not knowing the Bible, he was unable to argue with Mullah Siman-Tov, peace be upon him, or to catch him in making a mistake.

At that time, there came to Meshhed on pilgrimage[3] two converted Jews from Teheran, two brothers, Yitzḥaq and Moshe[4] by name. These two were learned men, well versed in the traditional Jewish lore, and they brought with them a letter of recommendation from the *mujtahid*[5] of Teheran, in which he asked the Imām Jum'ah of Meshhed to give all honor to the two converted *mullahs*, who were great scholars in the Bible, so that all the Jews might see it, and following their example might embrace Islam. The Imām Jum'ah rejoiced greatly at their arrival, for he thought, "These precisely are the people I need for my discussions with Mullah Siman-Tov," peace be upon him. So he took them into his house, and they were his guests of honor for six months.

After a time, the Imām Jum'ah began to take his two guests along with him to his secret meetings with Mullah Siman-Tov, peace be upon him, that they might see whether the answers Mullah Siman-Tov, peace be upon him, would give to his questions were correct. On these occasions, the Imām Jum'ah and Mullah Siman-Tov, peace be upon him, would sit side by side on a *dushak* (mattress) at the upper end of the room, while the two brothers would sit opposite them, near the door, holding between them a Hebrew Bible. Whenever Mullah Siman-Tov, peace be upon him, would answer one of the questions put by the Imām Jum'ah, the latter would turn to the two brothers. They would consult their Bible and reluctantly pronounce the answer correct.

Thus passed many weeks, and when the two brothers already had stayed with him for about six months, and the Imām Jum'ah saw that all *his* questions were always answered with the utmost precision by Mullah Siman-Tov, peace be upon him, he decided to let the two brothers question Mullah Siman-Tov, peace be upon him, and he said to them, "You know the Bible; therefore, next time, you ask him a question which he cannot answer." They agreed only too eagerly, and at the next meeting, they said to Mullah Siman-Tov, peace be upon him, "You Jews believe that all that God has created or ordained from the first day to the last day of the world is hinted at in the Song of Moses."[6] Said Mullah Siman-Tov, peace be upon him, "That is true." Then the two brothers said, "We two were Jews, learned persons, *mullahs*, and we left the Jewish faith and converted to Islam. Tell us, where in the Song of Moses is there any hint of that?" Mullah Siman-Tov, peace be upon him, answered without a moment's hesitation, "This is hinted at by the fifth verse of the Song of Moses, which reads, 'Corrupted are those who are not His children; it is their blemish, a perverse and crooked generation.'[7] The third letter of the word *banaw* [His children, spelled *bnyw*] is a *yod*, which is the first letter of the name Yitzḥaq, and you are called Yitzḥaq, while the third letter of the word *mumam* [their blemish, spelled *mwmm*] is a *mim*, which is the first letter of the name Moshe, and you are called Moshe."

When the two brothers heard this, they became exceedingly angry, took hold of the Bible which lay before them, and threw the heavy book at the head of Mullah Siman-Tov, peace be upon him. Thereupon the Imām Jum'ah cried out wrathfully and commanded the two brothers, "Come here immediately and kiss the feet of Mullah Siman-Tov," peace be upon him, "and ask for his forgiveness. You asked him a question, and he truthfully answered it; you should be thankful to him for the answer. And now that you have thus behaved, you will have to leave Meshhed within twenty-four hours, for one minute after the twenty-four hours have elapsed, I shall give orders to kill you."

II

In the days of Mullah Siman-Tov, peace be upon him, there lived in Meshhed a Jewish *zargar* [goldsmith]. One day, a Muslim came to this goldsmith and gave him five *miskal*[8] of gold, saying, "I am going to marry and should like you to make of this gold *gūshwāreh* [earrings] for my betrothed." At the time, no one was present in the workshop of the goldsmith excepting him and the Muslim. A few days later, the man came again to fetch the earrings and said, "Did you finish them? Give them to me!" But the goldsmith answered, "Who are you? I have never seen you! You never gave me anything to do for you!"

When the Muslim saw that he could not persuade the Jew to return his gold, he went to the Imām Jum'ah and brought his complaint before him. The Imām Jum'ah let the Jewish goldsmith come, but he could not extract from him an admission either. The deliberations lasted for six months,[9] and the goldsmith stuck to his denial. When six months had elapsed and the Imām Jum'ah saw that he was unable to bring a judgment, he decided to let his friend, Mullah Siman-Tov, peace be upon him, show his wisdom in this case, and sent the two litigants, accompanied by an official of his court, to Mullah Siman-Tov, peace be upon him, to present the case to him.

When the three men came before Mullah Siman-Tov, peace be upon him, the official began to relate to him the case in all detail, repeating what the Muslim said and what the Jew said, and not forgetting to stress that the case had already lasted for a full six months. When Mullah Siman-Tov, peace be upon him, perceived how things stood, he said—while the official was still talking—to the Jew in the Lo-Torai language,[10] *Nagāle, 'alīlah bemen!* ["Do not be afraid! Deny!"] And the Jew answered him back, quickly, *Menidam* ["I have denied"].

Immediately, Mullah Siman-Tov, peace be upon him, interrupted the official and said to him, "Take these two men back to the Imām Jumah, and tell him that the Jew has confessed his guilt before me. He is now ready to give back the gold to the Muslim."

When the official told the Imām Jum'ah how things happened and how Mullah Siman-Tov, peace be upon him, had decreed the guilt of the Jew even before he, the official, had finished explaining the case, the Imām Jum'ah was very much astonished and could not understand the matter. So when he met Mullah Siman-Tov, peace be upon him, the next time in the *madrasah*, he asked him, "Was it not out of fear that you pronounced the Jew guilty? Why did you do this, all I wanted was a true judgment!" Mullah Siman-Tov, peace be upon him, answered, "No, I did not fear you. when I am sitting on the chair of judgment, I cannot do aught but judge the case according to its merits." And then he proceeded to explain to the Imām Jum'ah how he was able to make what seemed to be a lightning judgment.

III

In the days when 'Abbās Mīrzā was governor of Meshhed,[11] there lived in the town some hundred Jewish families. In those days, a devastating *wabā* [cholera] swept over Meshhed and carried away within six months one-third of the population, Jews and Muslims alike. The old Jewish cemetery, situated within the 'Ēdgāh,[12] the Jewish quarter, was already disused at that time. This old cemetery was actually nothing more than a small courtyard surrounded by the houses of the Jews. No entrance door was left from any of these houses to the cemetery; only two cellars of two houses had small windows opening onto it. In the very middle of this old cemetery was the grave of Mullah Abraham, who had been many years previously the teacher of Mullah Siman-Tov, peace be upon him. As the Jews got no permission to establish another cemetery near the town, they had to bury their dead at a cemetery at a distance of some three miles from the city.

In the days of the plague, every day, one, two, or three people of the Jewish community succumbed to the cholera. The dead were placed in wooden coffins fastened to the back of donkeys or horses, and so, with great difficulty, transported to the distant cemetery. One day, twenty-seven Jews died of the cholera. Each one of the hundred families was already many times bereaved, and they were by then in such despair because of the plague that they did not find the courage to bring these dead to burial, not knowing whether they themselves would live to reach the cemetery. Some twenty to twenty-five people assembled, among them the heads of the community, and they decided to approach Mullah Siman-Tov, peace be upon him, and ask him to do something that the plague should cease. They came to the house of Mullah Siman-Tov, peace be upon him, and said to him, "Do something, if you can, that the plague should cease." He said to them, "Come with me, all of you." He led them to one of the cellars next to the old cemetery, opened the window, and remained there standing, facing the grave of Mullah Abraham which was visible from the window. All the people stood behind Mullah Siman-Tov, peace be upon him, waiting silently.[13] Suddenly, Mullah Siman-Tov, peace be upon him, said in a loud, clear voice, "Mullah Abraham! Go beneath the Seat of Glory and annul this *gezērah!*"[14] The people behind him listened but could hear no answer. A little later, Mullah Siman-Tov, peace be upon him, again cried out, this time still louder, "Mullah Abraham! Go beneath the Seat of Glory and annul this *gezērah!*" But still no answer was heard. Then Mullah Siman-Tov, peace be upon him, cried, "Mullah Abraham! If you cannot, I shall come!" And, again, there was neither a sound nor an answer.

Finally, Mullah Siman-Tov, peace be upon him, turned back to the people and said, "Let us go." When they left the cellar and stood in the street, he said, "Have no fear. From now on, no one will die of the plague. Go and gather your dead and bring them to burial. The plague has ceased." So the people went, and he returned to his house and said to his wife, "I am going up to my room. Do not let anybody come to me within one hour. Neither should you yourself disturb me. But after an hour, come and visit me."

Mullah Siman-Tov, peace be upon him, had his study on the second floor of his house, a room full of holy books, where he used to sit and learn. He now retired to this room, spread out a white linen sheet on the floor in the middle of the room, took off his clothes so that he remained clad only in his white linen shirt and underwear, neatly folded his clothes, and lay down on the sheet. With another sheet, he covered himself entirely, then stretched out his feet, stretched out his hands, closed his mouth, closed his eyes. . . .

An hour later, his wife came and entered the room. She saw Mullah Siman-Tov, peace be upon him, lying under the sheet. She called to him, but he answered not. She approached him, lifted up the sheet, saw that his eyes were closed, and touched his forehead. His forehead was cold like that of a man dead for an hour. She lifted up her voice and cried out, and the people came and saw that Mullah Siman-Tov, peace be upon him, was dead. Only then did they understand what he had meant when he said that he himself would come, that he himself would go to the Seat of Glory and annul the *gezērah.* For the cholera had really ceased, and from the moment that Mullah Siman-Tov, peace be upon him, died, no one, either Jew nor Muslim, died of the plague.

Mullah Siman-Tov, peace be upon him, was buried in the old cemetery beside his teacher, Mullah Abraham. Both graves can still be seen in Meshhed.

15
Two Stories about the Jews of Kalat

These two stories, contained in the reminiscences of Āqā Farajullah Nasrullayoff, describe the vicissitudes of the Jews in Kalat and the protection accorded them by Palang Tushkhan Jalāyir, the governor of Kalat.[1]

1. The Thieving Shaykh

Jews were first settled in Kalat by Nadir Shah to serve as guards of the treasure house he built there for his Indian loot in 1742.[2] In the course of years, the Jews built up a quarter for themselves, consisting of the same flimsy houses that were characteristic of the Persian villages and small towns, and their kitchen utensils were the same copper pots and pans that were used by the Muslims. As was the custom, the Jews, too, used to engrave their names on their vessels.

During the governorship of Palang Tushkhan Jalāyir, Kalat had no Imām to take care of the people's religious needs, until the religious authorities of Meshḥed sent to Kalat a scholar by the name of Shaykh Ibrāhīm to serve as its Imām. Shaykh Ibrāhīm took up residence in a house located next to the Jewish quarter of Kalat. Palang Tushkhan was a wise and considerate ruler and had sympathy for the Jewish community of Kalat. For every religious ceremony, he would invite also the elders and leaders of the Jews and honor them in public. By thus showing respect to the Jews, he warded off all open expression of hatred or contemptuous treatment the Muslims were inclined to accord to the Jews. He also made it known to the Jews that they could bring their complaints and problems to his court for consideration. One case that was brought before him, and in which he showed his strict adherence to justice, was the following.

Adjacent to the house of Shaykh Ibrāhīm was the house of a Jew, who noticed that with each passing day, several of his valued copper vessels would mysteriously disappear. He suspected that none other than the family of Shaykh Ibrāhīm could be guilty of the wrongdoing. However, he had no proof, and, apart from that, he dreaded the thought of accusing the leading Muslim clergyman. However, after another ten of his copper vessels disappeared, he became convinced that his neighbor was responsible for it.

Overcoming his fear and reluctance, he brought the issue to the attention of the governor. After listening to his complaint, the governor made it clear to him that for a Jew to bring a public accusation against a revered Muslim religious leader could prove quite dangerous to the small Jewish community of Kalat. He urged the Jew to investigate the matter further, examine his proofs most carefully, and refrain from accusations based merely on suspicion and speculation.

In the course of the following year, the number of missing vessels approached twenty. The thefts prompted the Jew to renew his complaint at the governor's court, and he again pointed to Shaykh Ibrāhīm as the only suspect. Finally, the Jew requested the governor to institute a search of the Shaykh's house, hoping that the missing vessels would be discovered. The governor agreed to send two of his men to carry out the search but warned the Jew that if the accusation proved false, and no copper vessels were found, it would have the gravest consequences for the Jew and his family. To accuse a highly revered Muslim religious leader of theft would be regarded as a terrible insult, and the Jew and his family would, in all probability, be faced with a death sentence. By that time, however, the Jew was so sure of the Shaykh's guilt that he nevertheless insisted on proceeding with the search.

The governor then summoned Shaykh Ibrāhīm and explained to him that eighteen copper vessels belonging to his Jewish neighbor had disappeared and that the Jew was accusing him of the theft. The Shaykh burst into a fit of rage, denying any wrongdoing and accusing the Jew of criminal contempt for Islam. Palang Tushkhan informed the Shaykh that he had authorized the Jew to enter his home, along with two government agents, in order to conduct an inspection of the premises. If no vessels were found, the Jew and his family would be executed for having insulted an honored Shaykh with false accusations. Shaykh Ibrāhīm had no choice but to agree, which he did very reluctantly and indignantly.

Instantly, two government agents were sent with the Jew to the Shaykh's house, and they carefully inspected every room, thoroughly combing through every shelf, drawer, nook, and cranny, inch by inch. The search uncovered no trace of any stolen vessel. By now, the Shaykh, members of his family, and even the government agents were showering the Jew with abusive language and curses. Before leaving the house, the Jew realized that he had forfeited his life, and, in his desperation, as he passed the brick wall of a new storage bin the Shaykh had built in a passageway, he gave a powerful kick to the wall. The bricks must have been loose, for they gave under the force of the kick, and grain began to pour out onto the floor of the courtyard. Following the grain, copper vessels also tumbled out into the open. One glance sufficed to show that they were all stamped with the seal of the Jew.

The government agents gathered the eighteen vessels and brought them back to the governor, who returned them to their rightful owner and dismissed the Jew. He then administered a furious tongue-lashing to the Shaykh, and dwelt at length upon the shame and infamy his action had brought upon Islam. There could be no greater disgrace than for a Muslim religious leader to be guilty of common theft. Then Palang Tushkhan decreed that Shaykh Ibrāhīm and his family would have to leave Kalat within the hour or face certain death. He ordered a few of his soldiers to escort the Shaykh and his household out of town, allowing them to take along only whatever possessions they could carry.

Comment

Although Farajullah Nasrullayoff told this story as a true account of what happened, and undoubtedly he had heard it told as such, in fact the story abounds in nonrealistic folkloristic features and reads more like a folktale than a true story. What is interesting in it, as well as in the following one, is that these stories about events that happened to the Jews of Kalat survived among the Jews of Meshhed. They can therefore be considered as testimonies to the Kalat origin of some of the Jews of Meshhed.

2. The Jews as Rainmakers

In the days of Palang Tushkhan Jalāyir, governor of Kalat, the Jews of Kalat almost fell victim to a vicious conspiracy. For three years, there was a severe drought in Kalat, with devastating effects on the agriculture of the town, which was almost totally dependent on rainfall. Only a small area of the Kalat fields had some means of irrigation for growing rice. The Muslims decided to make use of the calamity and make the Jewish community a scapegoat. Day after day, a mob would appear before Palang Tushkhan and complain that the Jews had provoked the wrath of Allah by their consumption of wine and alcoholic beverages, and thus caused the drought three years in a row. The mob demanded that the Jews be forced to convert to Islam and rid themselves of all alcohol or be annihilated. This was the only way to restore divine mercy and bring about an end to the drought.

At their daily appearances and demands before the governor, the mob fabricated all sorts of tales to give weight to their accusations. They cited various traditions in support of their claims. The governor felt that he had to do something in order to bring relief to the people in their dire predicament. This is the offer he made to them: Let the Muslims engage in intensive prayers for rain for forty days, in accordance with Muslim custom. If their supplications went unheeded, then he would order the Jews to pray for rain. If their prayers, too, remained unsuccessful, they would be dealt with according to religious law.

The Muslims prayed for forty days, as the governor had instructed them. When their prayers remained unanswered, on the fortieth day, they even separated the suckling infants from their mothers so that their cries should arouse divine mercy. But all was to no avail. Now it was the Jews' turn to pray. If their prayers caused rain to fall, that would be an indication of their innocence and piety. However, if their prayers went unanswered, it would be a sign that they were the cause of the drought.

The governor summoned the leaders of the Jewish community and told them of his decision. He warned them that if they were unsuccessful in their prayers for rain, he would be powerless to restrain the mob. They were to start their prayers right away and had three days to pray, during which they would have the governor's protection against attacks by the mob. The leaders of the Jews proclaimed a three-day fast for the entire community. The first two days were spent by all the Jews in the synagogue, immersed in prayer and begging for divine mercy. The third day happened to be a Jewish holiday, but looks of despair were on every face. They all knew that unless their prayers were answered, the Muslim mob would go on a rampage, kill every Jew in sight, and plunder all their belongings. In their desperation, they decided to take the male children over seven or eight years of age to the nearby hills, so that they should not be witness to the expected massacre of their loved ones, and the women should not have to see the killing of their sons. After bidding their spouses a final farewell, the men and their older sons set out, barefoot, for the mountains. All of them felt faint from their three-day fast, but, having reached the mountaintop, they began to recite the Minḥa prayers, crying and sobbing in despair.

Suddenly, a small cloud appeared over the horizon. It quickly grew and darkened and within a few minutes covered the entire land of Kalat. Then the rain began to fall; it turned into torrential showers and caused floods. The desperate prayers of the Jews were answered. God in his mercy brought an end to the drought and saved his people. The men and the boys tried to make their way down the mountain but were impeded by the slippery mud that instantly covered the slopes.

Meanwhile, as soon as the rain began to fall, Palang Tushkhan summoned all the Muslim religious leaders and the elders of the Muslim community and reproached them severely for their false accusations against the Jews. "You claimed all along," he rebuked them angrily, "that we Muslims are pious and that the Jews are infidels. You accused them of having caused the drought by their sinful acts. How then do you explain that all of you prayed feverishly for rain for forty days, and even separated nursing infants from their mothers' breasts, and yet not even a small cloud appeared, whereas on the very day on which the Jews ascended the mountain to pray, a rainstorm erupted? Doesn't this make it evident that the Jews are true servants of Allah? Now, let every Muslim man head for the mountain on which the Jews prayed for rain and bring them back to their families. Those of you who have horses or donkeys, take them and give rides to the Jews; those who have no animals must go and carry Jews on your own backs and take them to their families. If in the process any Jew is subjected to harm or mistreatment, I shall behead all your leaders. Any person who stays behind and does not join the effort to bring the Jews back to their homes will be subject to severe punishment."

Thus, all the Muslim men who resided in the vicinity of Kabud Gonbadeh [Gray Dome] of Kalat headed for the hills, either on foot or mounted on animals. The riders were the first to reach the hills. As they met the Jews struggling for footholds on the muddy slopes, they had them mount the animals, and the Muslim owners led the animals all the way back into town. Those who owned no animals gave the Jewish children piggyback rides across the rivers and flooded paths back to their families. Six hours after sunset, all the Jews were home safe and sound.

From that day on until the end of Palang Tushkhan's life, the Muslims of Kalat were unable to fabricate any more lies or to make false accusations against the Jews. However, the governor, sensing the deep-rooted Muslim hostility, hatred, and animosity toward the Jews, warned them of what could happen in the future, once he was no longer around to protect them. He advised them to consider moving away from Kalat before disaster struck. The Jews listened to his advice and started to leave Kalat. Most of them moved to Meshhed, others went to Bukhara, Samarkand, Kabul, and Herāt. Before long, all the Jews had moved away from Kalat. Even as I am recording these events in my memoirs, the synagogue in Kabud Gonbadeh lies in ruins.

16
How the Herāt Jews Were Saved

During and after the 1839 Allahdād attacks on the Jews of Meshhed, when they were forced to convert to Islam, some of them chose emigration rather than accept Islam even if only outwardly. Many of the latter sought refuge in nearby Herāt, capital city of the Herāt province of Afghanistan, a mere seventy-five miles from the Iranian border.

In the past, Herāt had been part of the Persian province of Khorasan, its governors were appointed by the rulers of Iran, and even the Persian mint was for a long time situated in Herāt. The kings of Persia could not easily resign themselves to the loss of such an important center, and in 1857, Naṣr al-Dīn Shah invaded Herāt with a large army. On the eve of Sukkoth, the Feast of Booths, of that year, the Persians took Herāt, and its Muslim inhabitants readily pledged allegiance to the Iranian conquerors. To curry favor with the Persians, they informed the Persian commander against the Jews, alleging that the Jews (most of whom had settled in Herāt less than twenty years earlier from Meshhed) were importing nails and horseshoes from Meshhed and selling these items to the Herātī forces, along with gunpowder and lead for their guns [thus helping them against the Persians].

The truth of the matter was that a handful of Herātī Jews actually did engage in such lucrative commercial endeavors, joining caravans plying between the two cities and importing all sorts of commodities into Herāt, including horseshoes and gunpowder. However, they did all this solely for business purposes and certainly had no intention of helping the Herātī forces against the Persians. Furthermore, their dealings in such commodities were quite insignificant, and probably did not add up even to 100 *toman*s during the entire period in question.

Nevertheless, on the fifteenth of Shevat 5617 [January–February 1857], the Persian authorities issued an edict charging the entire Jewish community of Herāt with treasonous activity and dealings in illegal arms trade, and arrested all the Jews—men, women, children, old inhabitants, as well as recent immigrants—and detained them in the walled section of the city, the Mosallah. Four days later, all the detained Jews were forced to march on foot, ahead of the Persian forces, all the way from Herāt to Meshhed, despite the bitter cold. During the twenty-day march, the cold and the lack of proper food and clothing claimed the lives of many among the elderly and enfeebled Jews. Those who could stand the rigors of the forced march reached Meshhed on the fifth of Adar. For two years, the prisoners were held in the Rabāt (caravanserai) of Baba Ghodrat (Qudrat) near the gates of the 'Ēdgāh, the Jewish quarter of Meshhed. During those two years, many of them died of malnutrition, disease, poor sanitary conditions, overcrowdedness, and lack of proper clothing.

The local Jews, who only eighteen years earlier had been forced to convert to Islam, were greatly handicapped in their efforts to help their imprisoned brethren, lest they fall under the suspicion of having secretly remained faithful to Judaism. Nevertheless, at every opportunity, they would bring food and clothing to the prisoners. They also appealed to the governor requesting the release of the captives. The governor initially demanded 100,000 *tomans* ransom for their release, and then reduced it to 70,000 *tomans*. However, the total wealth of all the Meshhedi Jews jointly amounted at that time to no more than 30,000 *tomans*, so that they were unable to meet the governor's demands.

The negotiations between the Jews and the governor dragged out for two years. In the meantime, a cholera epidemic struck the city, and more than half of the Rabātī prisoners fell victim to it. Finally, the governor announced his minimal demand: he would let the surviving Jews go against a ransom of 7,000 *tomans*. However, even the wealthiest Jewish family had not more than the equivalent of 1,000 *tomans*, so that despite the efforts of the leaders, the voluntary contributions added up to only one-third of the 7,000 *tomans* required. An appeal went out to each family to make a larger contribution, but even so, the goal of 7,000 *tomans* just could not be reached.

In this seemingly hopeless situation, Ḥajj Ismā'īl Levi took charge. He was a leader of the community, the founder of the Meshhedi synagogue in Jerusalem and of the Saré Heyté bathhouse in Meshhed. He gathered the heads of the families and made a passionate plea to them. He argued forcefully that all worldly possessions were worthless if they were not used to save the lives of their Jewish brethren. He said: "We will never be faced with a more dire predicament than this. You have requested that I give 100 *tomans* as my share in this ransom. I shall instead give 500 *tomans*, and my brother Ḥajj Yosef will match it with the same amount."

When the others saw the great sacrifice and generosity of Ismā'īl and Yosef Levi, they followed suit. Each family increased its share proportionately, and thus the entire 7,000 *tomans* were raised. On the twenty-fifth of Shevat 5619

[1859], the Jews paid over the ransom to the hands of the governor and gained freedom for their Herātī brethren after two years and ten days of captivity. They subsequently provided the Herātī Jews with transportation back to Herāt.

On the thirteenth of Teveth 5620 (1860), when they reached Herāt, a new power ruled in the city. Herāt was again in the hands of the Afghan forces, and the Jews were able to resume their lives in comfort and security, at least for the time being. Later on, some of them moved to Bukhara and remained there until the Russian forces occupied Merv. Although the Jews had established good commercial relations with the Turkomans, after the Russian occupation they no longer had any form of security in the territory. They therefore concentrated on local trade and opened stores in the bazaars of Merv, the Takhte Bazaar and the Yōlaton near Merv.

There was a marked difference between the attitude of the Afghans toward the Jews and that of the Persians. The Afghanis were Sunnī Muslims and considered themselves to be the descendants of the biblical tribe of Benjamin. They traditionally treated well the Jews who dwelt among them and bore no animosity toward them. The Persian inhabitants of Herāt, on the other hand, were Shī'ī Muslims who considered the Jews impure, did not associate with them in any way, and were always ready to inflict harm upon them. However, since the Shī'īs themselves were a minority in Herāt and were, in turn, considered impure by the Sunnī Afghan majority, they had no opportunity to vent their hatred upon the Jews of Herāt.

Comment

The story is not without a certain ambiguity. The events described took place less than twenty years after the forced conversion of the Meshhedi Jews, after which the Jadīdīm had to be extremely careful lest the Muslims discover that in secret they adhered to their ancestral religion. Many of the activities, arrangements, and observances described in this book had one common overriding purpose: to hide their Judaism from the Muslims of the city. And yet, in this story, they quite openly engage in a long bargaining process with the city's governor about ransoming Jewish captives brought to Meshhed from Herāt. There could be no doubt that the governor and his high officials were aware that the only possible explanation for the readiness of the Jadīdīm to sacrifice a major part of their fortune for ransoming the Herātī Jews was that they themselves had secretly remained Jews and thus retained their tribal solidarity with their coreligionists from Herāt. If they nevertheless tacitly tolerated the Jadīdī presence in their midst, the reason undoubtedly was that the Jewish commercial activity in the city redounded to the considerable financial benefit of both the government and the general population.

There is only one alternative explanation for the daring the Jadīdīm exhibited in entering into negotiations with the governor for the release of the Herātī Jews. As mentioned above, most of these Herātī Jews were refugees who had escaped from Meshhed in 1839 and their children. Given the close endogamy of the Meshhedi Jews, they were in all probability close relatives of the Jadīdīm who had stayed behind in Meshhed. Hence, the Jadīdīm could argue that even though they themselves had converted to Islam and were faithful Muslims, still they could not deny the ties of blood and were willing to sacrifice part of their fortune in order to save their brothers and cousins from what seemed slow but certain death in a miserable dungeon. To accept this explanation and to pretend that they believed it was saving face for the Muslims; for the Jews, it was, potentially at least, a matter of life and death, since a person who accepted Islam and then abandoned it was guilty of a capital crime.

17
The Story of the Woman Gohar

About 1893, an event occurred in consequence of which the Jews of Meshhed were freed from the duty of observing some of the Muslim funeral customs. A Jewish woman died. They washed her body in her house and sewed her shroud according to the Jewish custom. While they were busy doing this, one woman asked another, "Have you finished sewing the shroud?" This was overheard by Muslim women who were sitting on a roof of a neighboring house and watching. They went and told their husbands, "See, these Jews, to this very day, they have misled us!"

The reference to sewing the shroud, which the Muslim women overheard, was sufficient for them to conclude that the people who prepared the dead woman for burial acted in accordance with Jewish custom. According to the Muslim tradition, the first thing that was done with the body of a deceased was to wash it and then to place two twigs about two inches in length under the armpits. Then a packet containing a quarter of an ounce of soil from the tomb of Imām Reza was placed upon the chest of the deceased, together with a strand of prayer beads about a yard in length. Next, the deceased was wrapped in a shroud, which was not sewn in any way but consisted of strips of linen tied around the corpse. Finally, the body was placed in a coffin and taken to the great shrine, where they went with it around the tomb of Imām Reza. This was followed by further rites, and only thereafter was the body taken to the cemetery and buried.

The Jewish burial customs differed greatly from these Muslim rites. One of the most conspicuous differences was in the preparation of the shroud. The Jews sewed for the dead a shroud consisting of a long shirt and trousers. This is how the body of the woman, whose burial caused the incident described here, was dressed.

I

After the preparations were completed, ten men carried the woman's coffin to the mosque. In the meantime, the rumor had spread, and a large group of Muslims had gathered at the mosque and received the Jews with angry shouts: "You are Jews, and you will now die!"

"No, for we are Muslims," answered the Jews. The Muslims demanded that a Muslim woman examine the shroud, to see whether it was sewn according to the Jewish custom or followed the Muslim custom. But none of the Muslim women dared to go near the body, and the men were, of course, forbidden by their religion to touch the body of a woman.

Among the Jewish women, there was one who had accepted Islam, not only outwardly but wholeheartedly. There were such, although not many, among the Jews of Meshhed. This woman, named Gohar, was a widow who had not remarried. She was neat in her garb, good to look at, and pleasant in her speech, so that she was known and liked among the Muslims of Meshhed. When Gohar heard of the evil the Muslims were planning to do to the Jadīd al-Islām, she ran to the mosque, and when she arrived there, she started to shriek and shout, saying, "You despicable Jews, you have cheated us all these days. Now we shall kill all of you!"

While carrying on in this manner, she approached the coffin and said, "Let us see how the Jews did sew the shroud!" She reached in under the top sheet which covered the whole body and quickly pulled apart the sewing in the shroud until it was exactly like a Muslim shroud. Then she said, "Behold, she is a Muslim! Come and see!" Then others also stepped up to the coffin and saw that, in fact, the woman's shroud conformed to the Muslim custom. So they buried the woman in peace.

In this manner, the woman Gohar saved the whole Jewish community of Meshhed. And more than that: after this event, the Jews went to the mufti, complaining of the troubles and harassment they had to endure from the Muslims when bringing their dead to the tomb of the Imām Reza. They got permission from the mufti not to have to fulfill this duty any longer, except in the case of the burial of an important person, such as a *ḥajjī*, a man who had made the pilgrimage to Mecca and Medina. (Under pressure from the Muslims, every year, several of the rich Jadīdīm had to go on such pilgrimages.)

As for the woman Gohar, a few years later, she immigrated to Jerusalem, where she settled in the Bokharan quarter and lived in one of the rooms in the courtyard of the synagogue named after Ḥājjī Adoniya Kohen Aharonoff. In Jerusalem, too, Gohar continued her good works, in charity and aid to the poor, until her death in 1911. The informant who reported the event described above still remembered the day of her burial. It was on a Friday, on a cold winter day, when a heavy blanket of snow covered the whole city. A large crowd attended the funeral; before her coffin walked the pupils of the Talmud Torah school, and after it all the people of the quarter. Thus, they took her to the cemetery on the Mount of Olives, walking on foot back and forth.

Comment

The above story of how the woman Gohar saved the Jews of Meshhed was told to me by Farajullah Nasrullayoff in 1944 or 1945, in the course of one of my many interview sessions with him in his rug store in the Geulah quarter of Jerusalem. About the same time, at my suggestion, Āqā Farajullah began to write his reminiscences and included what he remembered about the incident with the woman Gohar, which had taken place when he was twenty years old. Evidently, after telling me the story, he was able to recall additional details and included them in his written version. What follows is the story as written by Āqā Farajullah in Judeo-Persian and translated for me into Hebrew by his son Yoḥanan Livian in New York in 1994. While preparing the English translation, I checked many of the phrases and expressions against the Judeo-Persian original with the help of Yoḥanan.

II

In my youth, I was witness to an incident that took place in the Jewish community of Meshhed. After the horrible Allahdād event, the Jews who had remained in Meshhed were considered Muslims. In the year 5653 [1893], the wife of Mardakh [Mordechai] Monghi, an elderly woman, passed away. All of her neighbors happened to be Muslims. One side of her house was in a ruinous state, and some Sayyids, who were also tobacco salesmen, lived there. The deceased was washed and prepared for burial near that part of the house that lay in ruins. The preparations for the burial were made in accordance with Jewish law.

The Jews of Meshhed always tried to observe their own burial rites but had to do it in secret. In accordance with them, the shroud was sewn, and nothing was placed in the coffin alongside the deceased. This is the manner in which the wife of Mardakh Monghi was prepared for burial. While she was being washed and readied, Muslim Sayyids, who lived next door, donned veils and stealthily watched the entire ceremony of the Jewish *levushah* [enrobing the dead] from over the wall. They observed that no twigs were placed under the deceased's armpits, no soil from the tomb of Imām Reza and no rosary beads were placed on her chest, and the shroud was sewn. The Sayyids hurried to the religious authorities who were in charge of the ritual circumambulation around the tomb of Imām Reza and informed them that the Jadīd al-Islām were about to bring the body of a woman who was prepared for burial according to the Jewish ritual. They demanded that the coffin should be seized and inspected. In this manner, the Jadīdīm would be exposed as Jews, and their entire community could be punished for their deception.

In conformity with the Muslim custom, the coffin of the wife of Mardakh Monghi was taken to the tomb of Imām Reza for the rite of circumambulation. Some seventy to eighty Jewish men accompanied the coffin. Once the coffin was brought to the main sanctuary which centered on the tomb of Imām Reza, it had to pass through the Gōharshad Mosque.[1] Only five or six men could carry the coffin around the tomb; all the others had to wait outside the sanctuary. I was among those who entered the main sanctuary.

Suddenly, seven or eight Sayyids, who were on duty, approached us and took hold of the coffin. They told us that the coffin had to be inspected in order to determine whether the deceased had been prepared for burial in accordance with the Muslim or the Jewish ritual. Word of what was transpiring quickly spread to the Jews who were waiting outside the mosque, and all of them fled in fear for their lives. Only the five or six of us who had carried the coffin into the sanctuary remained. Since the deceased was a woman, no man was allowed to cast an eye upon her body, and therefore a woman had to be found to inspect the coffin. Several women who entered the sanctuary were asked to do the inspection, but they were afraid to look upon a dead person. Farajullah Ghassāb [Qaṣṣāb] and I went out of the mosque to seek help. Suddenly, Āqā Ghassāb noticed that Karbalā'ī Gohar was approaching from a distance.

This Karbalā'ī Gohar had been the wife of a member of the Raḥmānī family. She was very intelligent, and had a manner of speaking very freely. After the death of her husband, she became a prostitute. She knew all the Meshhedi Jews, was talking to all of them. When talking to Muslims, she spoke in the Teherani accent, so that nobody suspected that she was a Meshhedi woman. With her talk, she attracted the men, and thus became well known all over the city. She always spoke with great sweetness and did not hide that she was a prostitute.

When Āqā Ghassāb saw that she was approaching, he ran up to her and told her about our predicament. He implored Gohar to enter the sanctuary and testify before the authorities that the deceased had been prepared for burial according to the Muslim ritual. Gohar assured us that she would take care of everything.

We returned to the sanctuary, and Gohar followed, sauntering in her usual manner. When the Sayyids saw her, they approached her and imposed upon her the task of inspecting the coffin. She agreed and sat down next to the coffin. She lifted up the lid of the coffin and inserted her arm to feel its contents. And then, with a convincing Teherani accent, she began telling the clergymen what her hand felt. "The shroud is not sewn," she said, "and here are the willow twigs under the armpits. Here is the soil on her chest, and also the strand of prayer beads. There is no question that this deceased has been prepared for burial according to Islamic law!"

The Sayyids were convinced and gave us permission to take the coffin for burial. We circumambulated the tomb of Imām Reza with the coffin and hastily left the mosque. All the way back to the Tousi bathhouse, we met not a single Jew in the streets who could have assisted us in carrying the coffin. At the bathhouse, we found a few Jewish men who had stayed behind, and they helped us to carry the coffin from there back to the 'Ēdgāh. As soon as we reached the home of Taghi Darvish, we took the deceased inside and proceeded to have her shroud replaced before the burial.

Thus, because of the courage of Karbalā'ī Gohar, the Jewish community of Meshhed once again escaped disaster and massacre. Despite her way of life, this woman never abandoned her Jewishness. Eventually, she migrated to Jerusalem, and she died there at a ripe old age.

Comment

There are major differences between the first (oral) and the second (written) versions of the Gohar story. The oral version states nothing of the Karbalā'ī title of Gohar but relates that she had converted wholeheartedly to Islam. This statement does not appear in the written version, which, on the other hand, states that she was a prostitute. No such comment is contained in the oral version. The oral version states that Gohar heard of the predicament of the Jews and volunteered her services, and loudly abused the Jews, calling them "despicable," which makes it clear that she played the role of a pious Muslim woman who hated the Jews. Of course, she did this only to make the clergymen in the sanctuary consider her a fervent Muslim whose testimony they would unquestioningly believe. According to the written version, she was asked by Āqā Ghassāb to help, and when she entered the sanctuary, the Sayyids demanded of her that she investigate the coffin. While doing so, she spoke to them in a Teherani accent to make them think that she was an outsider and had nothing to do with people in Meshhed, whether Muslim or Jadīdī.

According to the oral version, Gohar managed to unravel the sewn shroud under the lid of the coffin and then asked the clergymen to step up and look at it. This is illogical, because if the clergymen could look at the woman's body at that juncture, they could have themselves raised the lid of the coffin and looked into it before the appearance of Gohar. The written version maintains to the very end of the scene the prohibition for men to look at the body of a dead woman in her coffin.

Both versions date from some fifty years after the event. The oral one was recited spontaneously, on the spot, in response to my request that Āqā Farajullah tell me about mortuary customs in Meshhed, while he put down the written one probably several months later, after he had had ample time to delve into his memory. It is not improbable that this story, like the others told by Āqā Farajullah, contains its share of folkloristic embellishments or accretions that attached themselves to it in the course of half a century.

Yet another account of the incident with Gohar was obtained in 1946 by Yitzḥaq Kleinbaum, an official of the Jewish Agency for Palestine, who in that year visited Meshhed. His source was Āqā 'Abdul-Samad ben Yosef Dilmānī, a Meshhedi Jew, who supplied him with a copy of notes originally made in 1939 by Mullah Yosef ben 'Abdul-Samad Dilmānī, who seems to have been his father. The elder Dilmānī's notes recount briefly the well-known history of the settlement of the Jews in Meshhed in the days of Nadir Shah and dwell in particular on the periodic persecutions they suffered at the hand of the Muslims. After describing the 1839 Allahdād, Dilmānī recounts the incident with Gohar but gives as its date not 1893 (as does Āqā Farajullah) but 1870. Apart from this discrepancy, and the detail that Gohar is represented not as a widow or a prostitute but as the wife of a true Muslim, the incident itself is described largely as in Farajullah's oral version.

As an example of the rapid deterioration oral tradition experiences once its transmitters move away from the locality in which it originated (in this case, Meshhed), I present here, in conclusion of the Gohar story, the reduced form in which it survived in the memory of a descendant of Meshhedi Jews, born in Moscow in 1918. The parents of Mordekhai Ya'qovi left Meshhed sometime before he was born, and Mordekhai himself heard the story from them years later. After his *'aliya* to Israel, he told the story, one of several, in Hebrew, to an interviewer in Haifa in 1972.

> Once there was a beautiful woman, who fell into bad ways, and became assimilated. She went and became acquainted with many important people, people of the government. She came and went with them. This was in Meshhed, and the *goyim* [Muslims] in Meshhed were fanatics—they were waiting to catch Jews and to cause trouble.
>
> Once there was the burial of a woman, and they went to tell the Muslim neighbors that this was a Jewish burial, and that they wanted to bury her according to the Jewish custom. The Muslims bury differently from the Jews.

When the funeral got under way, they informed the Jews that they were waiting for them, and that they were accused of wanting to arrange a Jewish burial. They said to them, "On the way there will be a search; be careful!"

They did not know what to do. To go on or to return. After they had already prepared the shroud, they saw a very big crowd approaching them. Also the Shaykh and the judge and all kinds of big people came to see what the Jadīdīm were doing.

The funeral procession was stopped. They all came to this place and wanted to investigate how they buried. The people said, "This is a woman; how can we, men, uncover her?"

Suddenly, a women got up; she was that beautiful woman. She said, "You know that I am a Muslim. I shall investigate whether they are Jadīdīm or Jews."

They said, "Good."

She came and said, "Take the coffin aside." She put in her hand (she stuck a stick into the coffin) and said, "She is a Muslim. She is prepared for burial according to the Muslims."

Thus she saved the whole community.[2]

As we can see, in this atrophied version of the story, all the dramatic elements of the original story are lost. Not even the name of the heroine, Gohar, is remembered. What we see here is, in fact, the last faint echo of a folktale before it fades away.

18

THE DEATH OF ḤĀJJ ḤASAN EṢḤAQ

The story of the 1892 blood libel (see above, chapter 7) paints a picture of the conditions of the Meshhed Jadīdīm that shows them as a community whose adherence to Judaism was known and tacitly tolerated by the Muslims, and the identity of whose rabbi, Mullah Ibrāhīm by name, was also well known to the Muslim population. From the following story, also told by Farajullah Nasrullayoff, a different picture emerges: we learn that the Jadīdīm, who practiced their Judaism in strictest secrecy, were only one year later (1893) seriously endangered by being accused of observing Jewish religious customs, and they escaped annihilation thanks only to the quasi-miraculous death of their persecutor.

In the year 5652–53 [1893], one of the heads of the Shī'īs in Herāt, Ḥājj Ḥasan Eṣḥaq by name, immigrated from Herāt to Meshhed. He purchased a parcel of land near the 'Ēdgāh, the Jewish quarter, and built on it a house with an outer courtyard. Once the building was complete, he brought his wife and children to Meshhed and started a new life in his new residence. He established close association with the sages, clerics, and local authorities of Meshhed. Being a wealthy man, he soon became well known in the city. He sent gifts to all the clergymen and scholars and gave generous donations to their schools and institutions.

Ḥājj Ḥasan had always been an enemy of the Jews. Since he had lived in the vicinity of the Jewish quarter in Herāt as well, he was quite familiar with the way of life of the Jews and knowledgeable about their customs and traditions. The Jews of Herāt enjoyed greater religious freedom than the Jadīdīm of Meshhed and observed their feasts openly. They even discussed details of their customs with their non-Jewish neighbors. The Jews of Meshhed, on the other hand, were most secretive about their religious beliefs and observances. Outwardly they proclaimed their pious observance of the Muslim faith, but privately they adhered to the Jewish traditions. Even their children were warned against mentioning the Sabbath or any Jewish holiday in the marketplace or a public area, or referring to it in the presence of a non-Jew. They were taught proper responses to any question that might be addressed to them regarding their observances and were made knowledgeable of all Muslim holidays and customs. In this manner, the Meshhedi Jews managed to keep their Jewish identity well hidden and offered their Muslim neighbors no excuse to pick a quarrel with them. The fact that the Muslims in Meshhed knew very little about Judaism also helped the Jadīdīm keep their secret.

Now, however, that Ḥājj Ḥasan Eṣḥaq had taken up residence in the neighborhood, the Jadīdīm were faced with a difficult situation. Not only did Ḥājj Ḥasan harbor great resentment against the Jews, but he was also fully cognizant of all their customs and traditions. He kept taunting them with abusive language. Finally, three days before Passover, he delivered a stern warning to his Jewish neighbor Mishael Ḥakīm. "I know everything about you Jews," he said. "In three nights, you will be celebrating Passover. During that holiday, you don't consume any bread but eat only *maṣṣa* and rice. Therefore, on the very first night of your holiday, I shall assemble a group of ten to twenty Muslim scholars, and we shall conduct a search of your homes. I shall confiscate all your *maṣṣa,* and present them as evidence to the Muslim authorities. With that proof, I shall surely obtain a decree for the extermination of all of you!"

Mishael Ḥakīm hurried with the news of the threat to the leaders of the community. They in turn held an emergency meeting and discussed what action to take. They decided that in the privacy of two or three isolated inner houses, they would cook several big pots of pottage for the entire community. On the first night of Passover, each household would go and take a sufficient amount of this Passover meal for the entire family. During that first night, no one would wear new clothes [as was customary] or set a Seder table. Furthermore, each household would buy an amount of bread and store it in a corner of the house, in case Ḥājj Ḥasan carried out his threat and brought the Muslim scholars and clergymen to the houses. By taking these measures, no Jewish family could be held guilty of Ḥājj Ḥasan's accusations.

The Jewish community of Meshhed was greatly distraught and disturbed by this sad turn of events. The Muslim clerics in those days were very powerful, and often even the governor could not contain them. With their sermons, the clerics could always win the people to their position, and by doing so could undertake practically any action they desired. Ever since the forced conversion during the Allahdād, the Jadīdīm lived in fear of mob attacks and therefore took every threat most seriously.

In those days, the provincial government had set up posts of guards on the corners of some streets and major intersections. Each of these armed posts had a commanding officer (or sergeant), along with ten to fifteen soldiers who would patrol the neighboring streets. Every night, four hours after sunset, a curfew went into effect. At that hour, trumpets would be blown, signaling the beginning of the curfew. This was a form of military rule. Once the trumpets were sounded, no one was permitted to go out into the streets unless he knew the secret password. The password was sent down from the governor's office. If somebody ventured out after the start of the curfew and did not know the password, he was detained and held overnight at the command post. Next morning, he would be brought to army headquarters, where he would have to pay a fine [in effect, a bribe] to the commander in charge in order to be released. Once the curfew began, all shops and pharmacies had to be closed, and no physician would dare to make house calls. This was the situation when something like a miracle occurred to the Jews of Meshhed.

Ḥājj Ḥasan succeeded in obtaining a search warrant for twenty scholars from the Ḥājj Mīrzā Ja'far and the 'Abbās Golikhan schools to conduct a house-to-house search in the Jadīdī quarter on the first night of Passover. He intended to prove to the religious authorities that the Jadīdīm had not undergone true conversion to Islam. The night before the planned search, he gave a party to his friends and family in advance celebration of his victory over the Jews. He bragged about the way he managed to obtain a search warrant and assured his friends that once it was demonstrated that the Jews were lying about their acceptance of the Islamic faith, he would unfailingly obtain also a decree for their extermination.

Before the start of the curfew, the party broke up, and the guests returned to their homes. Ḥājj Ḥasan retreated to his bedroom, and at about eleven o'clock, he was suddenly seized with severe stomach cramps. His family tried to administer every type of home remedy they could think of in order to relieve his pain, but to no avail. If any of them was to go outside to summon a physician, he would surely be arrested. And even if he managed to bribe the soldiers on patrol, no doctor would agree to venture out into the streets after the curfew. And, assuming the physician was paid handsomely, did manage to come to the patient, and wrote out a prescription for him, there were no pharmacies open to fill it. The situation seemed hopeless, and all Ḥājj Ḥasan's family could do was wait helplessly for the end of the curfew in the morning. Two hours before sunrise, Ḥājj Ḥasan passed away.

In the morning, Mishael Ḥakīm heard cries of anguish and mourning from the house of his Muslim neighbor and soon discovered that Ḥājj Ḥasan had died during the night. Within a few hours, the entire Jewish community was aware of the news. As soon as the elders and leaders learned of the miraculous happening, they instructed the community to observe the Passover properly, in accordance with their ancient traditions. All bread was removed from the houses, and the Seder was conducted with renewed trust in the protection of God.

Comment

Although this story, like all the others presented by Farajullah Nasrullayoff, is told as the account of an event that actually did take place, it does not lack folktale elements. Most apparent is the folktale character of the warning Ḥājj Ḥasan delivers to his Jewish neighbor three days before the Passover. He puts Mishael Ḥakīm on notice that on the first night of Passover, he, with twenty Muslim scholars, would conduct a search of their houses, to see whether they observed the Passover ritual of removing all bread and having (and eating) only *maṣṣa*. By doing this, Ḥājj Ḥasan assured in advance that his search party would turn up no *maṣṣa* but would find bread instead in the Jewish houses. Only a fool would send such a warning, and Ḥājj Ḥasan is depicted as no fool but a shrewd, knowledgeable, and influential enemy of the Jews. It is definitely a folktale feature to depict the villain, whose downfall the story leads up to, as both evil and foolish.

Likewise folkloristic is the inability of the stricken Ḥājj Ḥasan to send a member of his family for a doctor because of the curfew. Ḥājj Ḥasan was an influential, rich, and generous man, known all over the city, and there is no question that a member of his family could have asked the commander of the nearest guard post to accompany him to the doctor and then, if need be, to rouse the pharmacist.

The death of Ḥājj Ḥasan is presented as a minor miracle (a big miracle from the point of view of the Jewish community), but, in fact, the cancellation of the search in consequence of his death, which the story tacitly assumes, redounded to the disadvantage of the Jews. Had the search been carried out, it would have resulted in finding bread and no *maṣṣa* in the Jewish houses, so that the Jews would have been vindicated: they did not observe the Passover, hence did not secretly maintain their allegiance to Judaism. However, since the search was called off, whether the Jadīdīm were secretly Jewish remained an open question and could be raised again anytime by new enemies of the Jews.

Finally, also folkloristic is the permission given for the search by the heads of Islamic religious schools in Meshhed, at a time when the city was controlled by a governor who instituted a curfew and put the city under something like military rule. Such a permission would have to be issued by the governor. Even more unrealistic is the decree Ḥājj Ḥasan planned to obtain (from whom?) for the extermination of the Jews or, rather, of the Jadīdīm if they were proven to observe Judaism in secret.

It appears that, like the other stories told by Farajullah Nasrullayoff, this one, too, is a folkloristic embellishment of what may have had a kernel of historic truth. Such a combination of history and folklore is characteristic not only of the traditions of the Jadīdīm but also of the Jews and Muslims of Iran in general.

III

CUSTOMS AND INSTITUTIONS

Introductory Note

As is the case with all Jewish communities, whether in the East or in the West, so with that of Meshhed, the customs observed and the institutions functioning in it evince a certain similarity to those of the non-Jews among whom the Jews constituted in each locality but a small minority. The most important factor of commonality between the Jews and the Muslims of Meshhed was unquestionably the language. The Jews of Persia had adopted Persian as their language many centuries before they first settled in Meshhed, and they spoke Persian in Meshhed as well. According to their own traditions, the language of their ancestors who first arrived in Meshhed was the Gilaki dialect of Persian, that of the province to the south and southwest of the Caspian Sea from where Nadir Shah ordered them to move to Kalat. (See above, chapter 1.) In the course of time, they adopted the local Meshhedi speech, speaking it, however, with certain dialectal differences, as well as with an admixture of Hebrew "culture words" needed to designate concepts nonexistent in the life of the Muslim Persian majority. That is, their language became the Meshhedi variant of what is known as Judeo-Persian. When writing this language, the Jews of Meshhed, like the Jews all over Iran, used the Hebrew alphabet.

The customs observed within the family circle on the occasion of the great stations of human life—birth, marriage, and death—were a mixture of traditional Jewish observances similar to those found in other Jewish communities in Iran and in other countries of North Africa, the Near East, and central Asia on the one hand, and of rites adopted from the Muslim majority on the other. In fact, the latter was more in evidence in Meshhed than in the other Jewish communities of the Muslim world, because of the fact that after the Allahdād, the Jadīdīm had to maintain the appearance of observing Muslim religious laws and customs, which meant not only that they had to be familiar with them but also that they inevitably adopted some of them. In the public aspect of family festivities and observances, especially of marriages and burials, they had no choice but to act as the Muslims did. When celebrating a wedding, two marriage contracts were written: one a traditional Hebrew *ketubba,* the other a Muslim marriage contract written in Persian. In the story of the woman Gohar (above, chapter 17), the secret observance of a Jewish burial custom that differed from that of the Muslims almost brought destruction to the Jews of Meshhed, but that story also shows that the local Muslim custom of taking the coffin before its burial to the shrine of Imām Riza had to be observed as a matter of course by the Jadīdīm as well.

The institutions in Jadīdī life in which Jewish tradition was most stringently observed, and on which depended the perpetuation of Judaism in the community were the synagogue and the school. For several decades after the Allahdād, synagogues functioned in the Jewish quarter in secret, and all kinds of precautions were taken to prevent Muslims from noticing their existence. Yet even in their religious life, the Jadīdīm could not entirely escape Muslim influence. Thus, Y'hoshu'a reports that the Muslim communal feast called *taqiyya* was observed by the Jadīdīm as well. The Muslim custom was to gather on the nights of the month of Muḥarram for festive meals in which hundreds participated, enjoying rice dishes, tea, cigarettes, and *narghīleh*s. The Jadīdīm held *taqiyya*s of their own, to which they invited Muslims as well, regaling them with choice but kosher dishes. The *ḥājjīs* (those who had made the pilgrimage to Mecca) and the *karbalā'īs* (those who had made the pilgrimage to Karbala) among them entertained the guests with stories of their religious experiences in those holy places of pilgrimage, and one of the invited Shaykhs spoke about the religious rites, the prophets of Islam, and the tragic chapters of Shī'ī history.

The secret school, established in a cellar, was not only the place where the young Jadīdīm learned Hebrew, the prayers, and the Bible but also the institution where Jewishness was inculcated into them. (See below, chapter 21.) And yet, even in this most Jewish institution (next to the synagogue, of course), some influence of the Muslim environment, or some similarity to it, could not be absent. The mnemotechnical words (*abgad* . . .) employed in learning the Hebrew alphabet were the same used by the Persians to learn the Persian (Arabic) alphabet; the *falak*, the wooden instrument used in punishing unruly pupils, was common to the Muslim and the Jewish schools. The girls' games described below in chapter 22 were played by Muslim girls just as they were by Jewish girls.

To the survival of Judaism in Meshhed, the most dangerous phenomenon was the attraction Ṣūfism exerted on some of the Jews both before and after the Allahdād, and the joint sessions Jewish and Muslim Ṣūfīs held under the guidance of Muslim Ṣūfī *murshid*s (guides). (See above, chapter 3.)

Another danger for the survival of Jewishness among the Jadīdīm was connected with their commercial activities, in pursuance of which many of their menfolk left their families in Meshhed and went to live for long periods in other cities (Merv, Deregez, etc.). While there, they neglected the most basic Jewish religious commandments, such as the observance of the Sabbath and the eating of kosher food. Āqā Farajullah's reminiscences include some interesting details about the non-Jewish way of life of Meshhedi Jews away from Meshhed and the efforts he himself, when still a teenager, made to remedy this situation. (See above, chapter 12.)

However, the Jadīdīm managed to survive all these dangers; in fact, some decades after the Allahdād, there was a definite revival of Jewishness among them, and still later their Jewish identification was strengthened by the burgeoning of Zionism among them and the relationship, however strenuous, established between them and the *yishuv* in Erez Israel.

What ultimately spelled the end of the Jadīdī community was the same phenomenon that brought about the disappearance of practically all Jewish communities from the Muslim world: emigration. This development is briefly sketched above in chapter 11. It did have a positive aspect. As a result of emigration, strong and vital Meshhedi communities became established in several parts of the world, especially Israel and America. Today, as a result of this new Meshhedi Diaspora, several thousands of Jews count themselves Meshhedis, many more than the number of those who ever lived in Meshhed itself. The members of these communities, including those of the youngest generation, evince serious interest in their past, are proud to be Meshhedis, identify themselves with their late mother community, maintain synagogues and communal institutions, publish books in English and Persian about this or that aspect of Jewish life in Meshhed, and have in this manner built for themselves a thriving Jewish existence in their new dispersion.

19
Birth Customs

In 1944–45, when I studied the Jews of Meshhed in Jerusalem, much of my attention was focused on family observances, such as marriage and death customs, the education of children, and the like. I wanted also to find out about customs surrounding childbirth and tried to locate an elderly Jewish woman from Meshhed who would be knowledgeable about those customs and whom I could interview. However, in those days, the life of the Meshhedi women in Jerusalem was still strictly confined to family and home. A typical Meshhedi home was a closed territory, to which outsiders were not admitted. Characteristic in this respect was that even though I was very friendly with Farajullah Nasrullayoff, and he was always prepared to spend hours with me in his rug store and to answer patiently all my questions, he never invited me to his home. Also, while I became friendly with his sons, I never as much as met his wife or any other female member of his family. Thus, while I got acquainted with quite a number of Meshhedi men, the only members of the female sex from Meshhed whom I met were two girls in their late teens who were "modern" and were willing to come to my house, where I always received them in the company of my wife and where they told me about girls' games in Meshhed. Girls of that age could not be asked about birth customs, of course. The only way I could have obtained information about birth customs would have been to ask my wife to visit one or two Meshhedi women and conduct interviews with them on the subject. However, my wife was more than busy taking care of our two infant daughters at that time, and no such visit materialized. Soon thereafter, I left Jerusalem without having obtained information on Meshhedi birth customs.

Fifty years later in New York, I tried to fill in the gap by asking my old friend Yoḥanan Livian (son of Farajullah Nasrullayoff) about the subject. However, as was the case fifty years ago, so in the 1990s Meshhedi men still had only limited access to and knowledge about the world of women, and the information he was able to supply was certainly far from complete. Nevertheless, even the little I learned from him is valuable, and I present here in summary form what I got from him in the course of several interviews conducted either in his home or in mine (both in Forest Hills, N.Y.), in March and April 1994.

At first, Livian stated flatly that he knew of no special methods resorted to in case a woman was barren. Upon further questioning, he remembered that the Jews of Meshhed did, after all, use certain things, such as cocaine, to render a woman warm (see below). When I told him that I had heard from informants from various other Oriental Jewish communities that barren women would swallow the foreskin of a newly circumcised boy so as to become pregnant, he remembered that this, indeed, was the case also in Meshhed. However, if a woman already had at least one child and thereafter could not become pregnant again, she did not swallow a foreskin but instead was given various substances to strengthen her. They gave her "warm" food to eat—foodstuffs and drinks were of two kinds, "warm" or "cold." Figs and nuts were "warm," oranges were "cold." Evidently, inability to conceive was considered a result of the "cold" nature of the woman, which could be remedied by giving her "warm" food and "warm" medicines. Other methods Livian remembered were to make the barren woman pass between the two trunks of a double-trunked tree or to ask a person who was traveling to Israel to take a thread and wind it around the tomb of Rachel near Bethlehem, and then they would wind the same thread around the body of the barren woman.

To make sure that a child would be a boy, the men recited the verse "If a woman be delivered and bear a man-child" (Leviticus 12:2) at the time of copulation. Or they smeared some oil, such as nut oil or *narbil* oil, on the husband's penis.

The birth itself took place on two stones or big bricks on which the woman sat, with the midwife behind her, holding her so that she would not fall backward. There were no special methods for helping a woman who had difficulties in childbirth. Immediately after the birth, they would give the woman one or two small glasses of almond oil, because they believed that almond oil was a very strong "warm" food and would not only make her quickly regain her strength after the birth but also enable her to become pregnant again soon. If the afterbirth was not expelled right away, they pressed the body of the woman, or the midwife even inserted her hand into the woman's body to remove it. The afterbirth was buried in a pit. The umbilical cord was tied and left alone until it fell off.

There were no special methods to induce abortion. But it was known that if a woman undertook very hard and exhausting work or if she suffered a hard blow, this could cause her to miscarry.

If the birth was easy, they did not use any charm or amulet. But if it was difficult, they tied to the woman's arm either a small copy of the Book of Psalms or an amulet made of metal or a piece of leather inscribed with kabbalistic names. Some people would tie a *khamsa*, a flat metal amulet in the shape of a hand, around the woman's neck.

They washed the child but did not put salt on its body (as was done in many Oriental Jewish communities). However, salt was used in various ways as a protection against the Evil Eye. No other measures were taken to protect the child during the first eight days of its life until circumcision.

After the child was born, but not before the birth, the parents and the grandparents consulted concerning the name to be given to the newborn. If the paternal grandfather wanted his name to be given to the child, they gave him that name, together with another name.

Circumcision was performed in the home of the child's parents. In the evening before the day of circumcision, the father of the child would invite friends and relatives to a meal (*s'udah*), at which the most important dish offered the guests was chicken soup. They also gave sweets to everybody. That night was called 'Aqedat Yiṣḥaq (the Binding of Isaac), after the title of the very popular book of philosophical homilies by Isaac Arama (c. 1420–1494; first published in Salonika in 1522 and frequently reprinted thereafter), from which sections were read during that night. There was also much singing and rejoicing.

The circumcision took place on "the Chair of Elijah," and occasionally they also used "the Staff of Elijah." For the circumcision rite itself, a big plate was heaped with red apples with layers of cotton wool in between. Immediately after the circumcision, the apples were distributed among barren women and women who were newly married and did not yet have children. (This custom was still being observed among the Meshhedi Jews in New York in 1994.) They also distributed bundles of sweets and cookies tied in handkerchiefs.

There was a custom in which the women would not hand over the child to his father to take to the circumcision ceremony until he promised them presents and a feast, called *shāl*.

There were several *mohel*s, ritual circumcisers, in the community. Farajullah Nasrullayoff himself was a *mohel*. He learned the skill from older *mohalim*, and he in turn taught younger ones. The work of the *mohel* was considered an important *miṣvah*, and he did not get paid for it. Everything done for the community was done "for the sake of heaven." "My father," said Yoḥanan Livian, "was circumciser, ritual slaughterer, he slaughtered even cattle, and never got a penny for it." Even the *shammashim* (sextons) in the synagogue worked voluntarily, without receiving any pay. However, if somebody was in need of money, they gave it to him, but in such a way that nobody knew about it, so that he should not feel that he was less than the others.

The foreskin, unless it was given to a barren woman to swallow, was buried in the earth.

After the newborn was washed, they straightened out its legs and arms and swaddled it, with the arms straight and next to its body, and put it into a cradle, called *gavoreh* (in literary Persian, kahvareh, basket). If it was a boy, they attached a pipe of about 12 to 15 inches to his penis and put the other end of the pipe into a bowl attached to the bottom of the cradle. In this manner, the child remained dry.

In general, it was customary for a woman to suckle her child for eighteen to twenty-four months. As long as a mother suckled her baby, she would not get pregnant again. If she did get pregnant, she stopped suckling. There was no difference in the duration of breastfeeding between a boy and a girl. In the meantime, of course, they began to give the child other food as well. They knew that the best food for an infant was mother's milk. If the mother had no milk, they took a wetnurse, a Jewish or Muslim woman.

There were a few exceptional cases in which a mother suckled a child for several years. Livian himself had an uncle, the youngest brother of his father, whom his mother suckled until he was seven years old. After him, his mother had no more children. He was the child of her old age. He would come home, and she would give him whatever he wanted. He ate and drank other things, too. Since she never stopped suckling him, she continued to have milk. But this was a very exceptional case.

Livian reported that there was no difference in the parents' attitude toward a child whether it was a boy or a girl. Of course, everyone wanted a boy, but if a couple already had a boy, they did not prefer to have another boy: "If all people would have only boy children, where would the next generation come from?" They did not go to the rabbi to obtain amulets to ensure that the pregnant woman would bear a son.

There was another custom. If within forty days, two children were born in the community, they observed a rite called *chehel-e bori,* "cutting the forty days." They made a small feast and sent gifts from one house to the other, so that neither of the two children should come to harm, and that they should not become childless when they grew up.

20
Jewish Names and Origins

It is a remarkable phenomenon that despite the Allahdād conversion in 1839 and the Marrano status forced upon the Jews of Meshhed for several decades, the city continued to attract Jewish immigrants. The names by which many of the Jewish families were known testified to the places of their origins. On this subject, Nasrullayoff writes in his reminiscences:

> Every Jewish family in Meshhed is known by a family name [he uses the Persian-Arabic term *laqab*, meaning agnomen, surname]. Those whose name is Kohen, Levi, Baṣṣālī, Qaṣṣābī, Zuqālī, Ḥakīmī, Siman-Ṭov, and Āq Raḥmānī are known to be the descendants of the original forty families who moved from Qazwin to Meshhed in accordance with the order of Nadir Shah. Also, the Kābulī and Aqlarī families belong to this group. However, the families known as Kāshī, Yazdī, Kermānī, Kurd, Kurdvānī, Gurjī, and Tehrānī are known to have immigrated to Meshhed at later times. All of these surnames refer to the town or province in Iran from where the families came to Meshhed. The Kāshīs came from Kāshān, the Yazdīs from Yazd, and so forth. Also, the ancestry of the Kermānīs can be traced to Yazd. Their ancestors moved from Yazd to Kermān about seventy to eighty years ago [ca. 1865–75], and that is why they are known as Kermānīs. From Yazd came also those known as Zār or Zārī. The families known as Kurd or Kurdvānī came from Sanandaj [in Kurdistan]. The Gurjīs came from Georgia in the Caucasus, the Tehrānīs from Teheran, the Lārīs from Lār in Shīrāz, and the Dilmānīs from Dilmān in Tabrīz. All these families came to Meshhed later.
>
> The Kābulīs hailed originally from Herāt. They included ten families who emigrated from Herāt [in Afghanistan] to Kābul [the capital of Afghanistan], and took up residence there in a caravansary. The time they spent in Kābul was a time of great hardship for them. When a person died, they had nowhere to wash and prepare the deceased for burial. They had no burial grounds, either. When a son was born, they had no *mohel* to perform the circumcision. Due to

> such hardships, after three years, they moved back to Herāt, and then went on to Bukhara and Samarkand. This is why they are called Kābulīs.
>
> There was in Meshhed a large family of Kohanim known as 'Azīz or 'Azarya'i. They were all descended from a Kohen family that was one of the original forty families who moved from Qazwin to Meshhed in the days of Nadir Shah. Those known as Qaṣṣābī descended from an individual who was a butcher [*qaṣṣāb*]. Those called Zuqalī, that is, "coal-like," were descended from an individual who always wore a large black cloak. The Ḥakīmīs were the offspring of a *ḥakīm*, that is, a physician. There was also a family in Meshhed known as Āqā Shavardi Zargar, who may have been the descendants of a goldsmith [*zargar*]. This family later converted to the Bahai faith.

The city of Lār is located not "in Shīrāz," but one hundred and seventy miles southeast of the city of Shīrāz, sixty miles to the north of the Persian Gulf coastline of Iran. Likewise, Dilmān is not located "in Tabrīz" but could refer to either of two towns by that name. One Dilmān, better known as Shahpur, is located some eighty miles to the west of the city of Tabrīz, near the northwestern corner of Lake Urmia. The other Dilmān is located some two hundred and twenty miles to the east-southeast of Tabrīz and some forty miles to the south of the southern coastline of the Caspian Sea. Since the Meshhedi Jewish tradition traces the origin of the Meshhedi Jews to the town of Qazwin, forty miles south of this second Dilmān (see above, chapter 1), it is more likely that the Dilmānī family hailed from this place. Such minor geographical inconsistencies aside, Āqā Farajullah's account of the origins of the Meshhedi Jewish families is remarkable for its details. It is also a testimony to the interest Meshhedi Jews had in their roots and genealogy.

On the occasion of a circumcision, a boy was given two names: a Hebrew-Jewish name and a Muslim Arabic-Persian name. Frequently, the name chosen was a biblical name that also had an Arabic-Persian form, so that the child was named Avraham (Hebrew), Ibrāhīm (Arabic-Persian); Yiṣḥaq, Iṣḥāq; Ya'qov, Ya'qūb; David, Da'ūd; Sh'lomoh, Sulaymān. Other names were similar in sound in the two languages, such as Levi, Vali; Shim'on, Sha'bān; Y'hudah, Yaḥya; R'fa'el, Rafi'; Nissan, Naṣrullah; 'Azariah, 'Azīzullah; Yirm'ya, Raḥmatullah; Binyamin, Amīn; R'uben, Raḥmān. Still other names did not sound alike in the two languages but had the same or similar meanings, such as Hebrew N'tanel, Persian Khudādād (meaning "God gave"); Mashiaḥ, Mahdī (meaning "Messiah"); Yonathan ("God gave"), Farajullah ("God comforted"); Ḥananel ("God graced"), Naṣratullah ("God's help"); Ḥananyah ("God graced"), 'Uzzatullah ("God's power"); Yoḥanan ("God graced"), Nematollah ("God's grace"); Mattityah ("God's gift"), Najatullah ("God's salvation"). Some people gave their children Hebrew and Muslim names without any correspondence between them, and some gave them purely Muslim names, such as 'Alī, Ḥasan, Ḥusayn, and so on.

The names Muḥammad and Reza, being the two names of the greatest sanctity for the Muslims of Meshhed and most closely associated with Islam, were not given to Jadīdī children. However, according to Tziyon Zabīḥī, there were Jews in Meshhed who were called Mumdusayn, a contraction of Muḥammad Ḥusayn.

21

The Secret School

(Hebrew Education)

In the days of the 1839 Allahdād, the inflamed mob destroyed the great courtyard, called *ḥavāli kenīseh* ("synagogue courtyard"), and the five or six synagogues that opened into it. It carried out a total "razing to the ground," *kūbīdan* in Persian, which was the symbol in Persia, as it had been centuries earlier in ancient Rome, of total destruction and the prohibition of rebuilding the ruins.[1] The stones and beams of the demolished buildings were carried off and used for the construction of a mosque.

Sometime later, the Jadīd al-Islām, as they were now called, proceeded to build rows of rooms around the courtyard, poorly executed simple structures, which were subsequently occupied by some twenty of the poorest families in the community. Beneath one of these buildings was a small cellar, *zīr zemīnī*, about three by thirty meters in size, which happened not to be filled in at the time of the destruction of the synagogues. The entrance to this cellar was through a trapdoor opening from one of the rooms, so that from the outside it was not at all possible to see that there was a cellar beneath that room. Some twenty years after the Allahdād (that is, around 1860), a *midrash*, or Jewish school, began to function in that dark and narrow cellar.

The twenty years between the forced conversion and the beginning of Jewish instruction in the cellar were the most critical period in the life of the Jadīdīm. The danger of assimilation and total disappearance was great. Part of the community, especially the poor who had nothing to lose, emigrated to Afghanistan, to the city of Herāt and other places. Those who remained had to observe all the commandments of the Muslim religion. To practice Judaism involved mortal danger. The children were forced to attend the *maktab*, the Muslim religious school, not as if there had been general compulsory school attendance but in order to demonstrate visibly that their parents had accepted Islam wholeheartedly.

In the *maktab*, they learned to read the Koran with the traditional cantillation, the prayers, and the Muslim religious customs, such as the washing of hands prior to the prayers. The teacher, *ākhūnd*, was a religious personage who was styled *mullah*. Around his cap, he wore a white turban, *'amāmeh,* of a length of several meters. (The Sayyids who officiated in the mosques wore green turbans wound around their caps.) The tuition fee in the *maktab* at that time was one *q'rān* or less per month, but this was a considerable amount since the total living expenses of a family were eight to ten *q'rān* per month. Well-to-do parents had to pay a full *q'rān,* the poorer ones half a *q'rān.*

Parents who observed in secret the precepts of Judaism had to hide this from their small children, lest their innocent prattle reveal to the Muslims their secret adherence to Judaism. Of course, the children who grew up in those twenty years knew nothing of Hebrew, Jewish prayers, or Judaism. As for the adults, many among them were suspected by their brethren of true adherence to Islam.

In these circumstances, the establishment of the *midrash* was a vital step indeed for the Jadīdīm. The heads of the community proceeded with all due caution, and the very existence of the *midrash* in the cellar was known in the first few years only to the most reliable members of the community. Accordingly, in the beginning, the number of pupils (sing. *shāgird*) in the *midrash* was very small, no more than ten to fifteen. The pupils were boys of twelve years or older who could be relied upon to keep the secret from the Muslims. These boys would first attend the Muslim *maktab* for three years or longer, and since at the time they began to attend the *midrash* they had already mastered Persian reading and writing, it was easy for them to learn how to read and write Hebrew. The Hebrew teacher, also called *mullah,* was one of the learned members of the community, who undertook the dangerous task voluntarily, without receiving any remuneration. The first teacher in the *midrash* after the forced conversion was Mullah Ḥizqiyah.

After a few years, the *midrash* was moved to the cellar of the house of Mullah Abba, who also was a volunteer teacher. The house of Mullah Abba was located at the edge of the 'Ēdgāh, the Jewish quarter, and the door to it opened from a street of the Muslims. This being the case, the children could not enter his house through the front door, lest they arouse the suspicion of the Muslims. They therefore went to a courtyard near Mullah Abba's house, within the Jewish quarter, climbed up to the roof of a neighboring house, from there crossed over to the roof of Mullah Abba's house, descended to its inner courtyard, and from there went to the cellar whose door and window opened into the courtyard. In Mullah Abba's cellar, a small group of ten to twelve pupils would get instruction. Among them was Farajullah Nasrullayoff, about the year 1884, after he had completed five years of study in the Muslim *maktab.* He attended the *midrash* only in the morning (from about eight to twelve), while other boys attended both in the morning and in the afternoon.

This *midrash* had no educational materials whatsoever. There were almost no Hebrew books in the possession of the community. Thus, when the *mullah* taught the children to read the Hebrew alphabet, he had first to write out for them each letter. Every pupil had to bring with him a few sheets of paper and a *qalamdān*, a small oblong box containing pens made of reed (*qalam ney*) with a small inkwell, *davāt*, containing viscous black ink, *murakkab*. The ink was made of gum Arabic, *ṣamagh 'arabī*. To make sure that the ink would not be spilled, they put a ball of cotton, *līqeh*, into the inkwell.

Scholars, physicians, and writers used to carry with them such a pen and ink holder in all the countries of the East, stuck slantwise into their girdle. Among the Meshhedi Jews, it was customary to present the bridegroom with a *qalamdān* of fine workmanship, made of silver or brass and decorated with intricate patterns of flowers in various colors. In order to write with the ink, which was all soaked up by the cotton ball, they had to add a little water. For this purpose, there was in the *qalamdān* a small, pointed spoon, *qāshuqak* (*qāshuq*), with a long and thin handle, occasionally made of silver. A few spoonfuls of water would be added, and then the ink would be stirred with the pointed end of the handle. A well-furnished *qalamdān* would contain three or four reed pens with points of varying thicknesses so that the writer would be able to produce a thin or heavier script. The *qalamdān* contained also a penknife, *qalam trāsh*, and a pair of scissors, *qeychī*, for cutting and sharpening the pens. The *qalamdān* of the schoolchildren was, of course, much simpler, made of a cheap material such as wood or tin.

The teacher sat on a cushion, *dūshakchih*, which was placed on the floor. The children sat facing him on mats called *ḥaṣīr* or *būryā*, or on goatskins. Before the *mullah* was a folding X-shaped bookstand, *lau*, upon which he placed his open book.

Some thirty to forty years after the forced conversion (1870–80), when the generation that had participated in the mob attack had passed away, the situation of the Jadīdim eased, and they enjoyed greater freedom in their activities and daily lives. One result of these improvements was that the number of children attending the *midrash* increased, reaching about one-fifth of the number of all the children in the community. In the 1890s, there were already two teachers. One was Mullah Khudādād (N'tanel, or "God gave" in Hebrew), the son of Mullah Ḥizqiyah, who continued the work of his father after the latter's death. The other was Mullah Yosef, the son-in-law of Mullah Abba, who taught a small group of children in his house during the day, while in the evenings and nights he taught the adults who had grown up without any Hebrew instruction because of the dangerous conditions in the years following the forced conversion.

Mullah Yosef was totally devoted to his work. He had two brothers, merchants, into whose hands he placed all his money, and they traded for him and gave him every month fifty *q'rān* for his livelihood.[2] In this manner, Mullah Yosef was free of the "yoke of livelihood" and able to devote all of his time to the service of the community. He served as a teacher and ritual slaughterer, without accepting any payment. Only for slaughtering sheep for the Jewish butchers did he receive a fee, which he distributed among the poor. At night, even on cold winter nights, he came to the houses of the people and taught them the Bible and prayers, one month in one house, the next in another.

To learn Hebrew was of especially great importance for the Jews of Meshhed, because knowledge of Hebrew was practically the only link between them and Judaism. He who knew Hebrew was a Jew; he who did not could as well have been a Gentile. The learning of Hebrew, that is, the prayers and the Five Books of Moses, was also the first step to the return to Judaism for those who had grown up without any Jewish education. Bringing these lost sheep back to the fold was the life's work of Mullah Yosef.

In the 1880s, there was in the community a woman whose husband had totally assimilated to the Muslims and wanted to know nothing of Judaism. (In telling me this story, Āqā Nasrullayoff insisted on not mentioning the man's name, out of consideration for the man's family and living descendants.) The woman had no son. One day, she went to Mullah Yosef and said to him, "I heard that you are a scholar and a saint. Give me an amulet, *dā'ah,* so that I should have a son." Mullah Yosef told her, "I can help you, but you, too, must do what I shall tell you." The woman agreed, and he said to her, "You must influence your husband that he should allow us to place the Torah scroll of the community in your house, and that we should come there to pray for forty days. Then, after the forty days are over, you will go to the *miqveh* [the ritual bath], and you will conceive and bear a male child." The woman went, spoke to her husband, and, although the matter was very dangerous, for it could become known to the Muslims, she managed to persuade him. She returned to Mullah Yosef and said to him, "My husband consented." In those days, the women, when they went out into the street, wore a large black wrap, *chādor,* which covered their bodies from head to foot. The woman would hide the Torah scroll under her *chādor* and take it from the house of Mullah Yosef to her house. On the same evening, the members of the community gathered in the house for the prayers, and they did so for forty days, in the mornings and in the evenings. Among those who attended the prayers were the pupils of Mullah Yosef, among them Farajullah Nasrullayoff. Mullah Yosef saw that the woman's husband did not enter the room with them at the time of the prayers. He said to the woman, "Your husband must be present and say 'Amen' after our prayers." On the third day, the husband came, sat there, and said "Amen." This went on for several days. Then Mullah Yosef copied out for him the Sh'ma' ("Hear, O Israel" Deut. 6:4 ff.) prayer in Persian script, and also the Ashrē (Psalm 84:5 ff., recited as part of the prayers), and ordered the man to read the Sh'ma' every morning and the Ashrē every evening. When three weeks had passed, Mullah Yosef wrote out for him the Hebrew alphabet with a Persian transliteration, told him that he must learn how to read Hebrew, and sat with him every evening for an hour and taught him. When the forty days were over, the man could read the prayer book and the Five Books of Moses, although not without difficulty. And then, just as Mullah Yosef had told the woman, after she went to the *miqveh* the next time, she conceived and gave birth to a male child. The woman's husband became one of the most religious Jews in the community, and to the end of his life he never missed a day going to the synagogue morning and evening. The son grew up, went to visit Jerusalem, and lives now (1944) in Meshhed as one of the leaders of the community. In this connection, Āqā Nasrullayoff remarked that Mullah Yosef never gave amulets to those who came to him for help but always helped them in a manner similar to this case.

Another important man whom Mullah Yosef taught Hebrew was Ḥājjī Y'ḥezq'el (Ezekiel). He, too, was of the generation that grew up in the years following the forced conversion, so that he did not know how to read Hebrew and how to pray and exhibited outwardly all the signs of Muslim religiosity. Every morning at four o'clock, he went to the mosque to pray, he fasted in the month of Ramaḍan (except on the Sabbaths), and he made the pilgrimage once to Mecca and twice to Palestine. Hence his title Ḥājjī. His Muslim name was Ḥājj Muḥammad Ismā'īl. But despite all this, Ḥājjī Y'ḥezq'el remained a faithful Jew in his heart. He was rich and had no children. He built at his own expense two bathhouses, *ḥamām*, for the Jews, one for men and one for women. Ḥājjī Y'ḥezq'el's house was near the house of Mullah Yosef. One evening, when Ḥājjī Y'ḥezq'el was about seventy years old, he went to Ya'qūb Ne'mat, the father of Farajullah Ya'qūboff, and divulged to him that he wanted to settle in Jerusalem. He handed to Ya'qūb Ne'mat the charity moneys he had in his possession. Thereafter, for a full month, Mullah Yosef went every evening to Ḥājjī Y'ḥezq'el and taught him Hebrew, Bible, and prayers. Then, having told the Muslims that he was going again on a pilgrimage to Mecca, Ḥājjī Y'ḥezq'el left for Jerusalem, where he bought himself a plot in the Bukharan quarter and built a big house with twenty rooms for his family and for the poor of the community. He also built a synagogue which to this day is named after him. He died in Jerusalem around 1906. Mullah Yosef died about the same time in Meshhed.

To return to the education of the children, the teachers of the *midrash* at first received no remuneration. Either they were supported by their families, or some other members of the community engaged in business on their behalf and gave them a share in the profits. In the 1890s began a system of gifts which, in the years preceding World War I, was replaced by regular payments. Under the gift system, the parents of the pupils gave the teacher whatever he needed (food, clothes, etc.). These gifts were given to the teacher before Passover and before the Jewish New Year, as well as on other occasions. Presents of food were given frequently.

After Mullah Khudādād, who toward the end of his life settled in Jerusalem and died there, the head of the synagogue was Mullah Murād (Mord'khai Aqlār, 1850–1936). He, too, died in Jerusalem.

In the years before World War I, an important change took place in the life of the Meshhed *midrash:* it was raised from the cellar and given two spacious rooms on the second floor of one of the houses in the Jewish quarter.

At about the same time, the cash payment of tuition fees to the *mullah* was introduced. Although the *mullah* was recognized as a teacher by the community, he was still not a public employee. He received the tuition fees directly from the parents of his pupils. A rich father paid more, a poor one less. After World War I, a well-to-do father paid ten to twelve *q'rān* per month.[3]

Up to the time of World War I, the Persian school system consisted of the traditional Muslim *maktab*, which provided primarily religious education. The *maktab*s required attendance all year round, except for the thirteen days of vacation at the 'Īd al-Naurūz (the Persian New Year),[4] and three days in the month of Muḥarram, the ninth, tenth, and eleventh days of the month. Every day, the children had to attend school both in the morning and in the afternoon, except for Fridays, when attendance was limited to the morning. Since the Jadīdī parents were anxious to appear to be good Muslims, they sent their sons to the *maktab* conscientiously, which meant that the Jadīdī children were able to attend the *midrash* only after finishing the years of their attendance at the *maktab*. There were only a very few boys, who were sent simultaneously to both schools, to the *maktab* during the day and to the *midrash* in the evenings. Such a double burden occasionally affected the health of the boys, so that they had to discontinue attendance at the Hebrew school.

In the 1880s, most of the Jadīdī boys attended the *maktab* of *ākhūnd* Mullah Ḥasan. His school was located in the Jewish quarter, and most of his pupils were Jadīdī children. Mullah Ḥasan was a learned man and a man of good will. He even learned from a Jew the Jadīdī alphabet, the specific Hebrew script used by the Jews of Meshhed. (See table below.) In return, he taught that Jew the Persian alphabet. Mullah Ḥasan did not know that the Jadīdīm faithfully adhered to the Jewish religion, and he considered the Hebrew script merely a kind of historical relic from their past. Until the years of World War II, whenever a Muslim asked about it, the Jadīdīm always gave this explanation for their interest in knowing the Hebrew script. In the 1890s, the Jewish children attended the *maktab* of Mullah Baqer.

In the years preceding World War I, government schools, *madrasah*, were opened in Meshhed. The tuition fee was five to ten *q'rān* per month. In these schools, the children followed an organized curriculum, and, most importantly from the point of view of the Jadīdīm, they were recessed for an eight- to ten-week summer vacation. The heads of the community instantly recognized that this gave them the possibility to begin Hebrew instruction of their children at a much earlier age. And since the fear of the Muslims' hatred had gradually diminished, they were no longer apprehensive of the consequences of the prattle of small children. An important factor in the abatement of the fear and tension in which the Jadīdīm had lived earlier was the development of intensive commercial contacts between members of the community and Russia, where they got acquainted with Jews possessed of a strong Jewish consciousness. In those years, the number of the children attending the *midrash* grew apace and reached four-fifths of the number of all the Jewish children.

In the government school, the children had a varied and well-rounded curriculum, including reading (*khvāndan*, pronounced *khondan*), writing (*nevesh-tan*), and arithmetic, in which they were taught two kinds of numerical notation. For all sorts of calculations, the Arabic numerals were used; this was called *ḥa-sāb.* For entering income and expenditure figures in a ledger (*rūz nāmeh,* "book of days") and for individual accounts (*daftar*) of customers, they used a system of notation called *siyāq* or *ruqum,* which was similar to the Hebrew numbers (where the letter *aleph* stands for one, *bet* for two, *yod-bet* for twelve, etc.), and in which special signs served for the numbers 1 to 9, other signs for 10, 20, and so on, and still others for 100, 200, and so on. Since with these symbols it was difficult to make additions and multiplications, they used an abacus, called *chotke* (from the Russian *s'chote*), which had ten to fourteen rows of beads and was imported from Russia. They were also taught grammar (*tajziyeh*), history (*tārīkh ayyām*), geometry (*hendeseh*), drawing (*naqāshī*), and, of course, most importantly, religion (*shar'iyāt*) and Koran, to which was devoted the first hour every day. At noontime, communal prayers were held in the school, and every day one pupil functioned as prayer leader (*pīsh numāz*), while another fulfilled the role of the *mu'azzin,* the crier who calls to prayer. The Jadīdī children had to participate in these religious exercises, of course, and it happened more than once that they excelled in the knowledge of the Muslim prayers and in the reading of the Koran in the traditional cantillation.

The Jadīdī children were generally good at their studies. During the first school year, the studies consisted only of Persian reading and writing. Many Jewish children learned how to read and write in half a year, and then they "jumped" to the next higher grade or occasionally even moved two grades ahead, so that in the second half of their first year at school, they attended the third grade.

Most characteristic of the improvements that took place in the situation of the Meshhedi Jews from the 1890s on was that they gradually reduced the age at which they divulged their Jewish identity to their children. In the 1890s, a child ten to twelve years of age who was in his third or fourth year of attendance at the Muslim *maktab,* still knew nothing of Judaism or of his family's adherence to it. Throughout the year, the children would be given lunches to take along to school consisting of bread, cheese, fruits in season, and, in the winter months, meat. During Passover, however, they would be given only rice and fruit. When the child would ask his mother why he was given only rice and no bread, she gave him some excuse, such as that the father was sick and she had no time to bake bread.

In the years of World War I, in contrast, the adherence of the Jadīdīm to Judaism was an open secret. After the reform of the school system with the introduction of government schools, the Jews no longer hesitated to begin the Hebrew instruction of their children when they were five or six years old.

The division of the children in the *midrash* into grades came about slowly. At first, all the children sat together in one class. As a result, the new pupils understood little of the instruction, while the older children sat around bored. Then the *mullah* began to separate the children into groups according to the degree of their knowledge. Three or four groups of children sat in the corners of the cellar; these were the different grades. One teacher taught all three or four classes. He was assisted by two or three helpers, advanced pupils who excelled in their studies. The *mullah* devoted his attention to one class for a period of time, then went on to a second class which sat in another corner of the cellar, and his place in the first was taken by the helper whose task was both to keep order in the group from which the teacher was absent and to go over the lessons with the pupils.

In the 1920s, the head of the *midrash* was Mullah Yosef Dīl, who was assisted by his brother Mūsā (Moshe). In those years, the *midrash* already occupied two rooms on the second floor of a house in the Jewish quarter. The number of pupils reached sixty or seventy. The class of beginners met in one room, while the other, larger room served several classes of advanced pupils. The studies took place from eight in the morning until noon and, after an intermission of one hour, from one to four or five in the afternoon. Between classes, there were recesses of fifteen to twenty minutes. The pupils who lived nearby went home during the noon interval; those who lived farther away brought food with them and ate their lunch at the *midrash.*

In the late 1920s, it was decided to equip the *midrash* with benches, *nīmkat,* so that at least some pupils sat on benches while others sat on the floor.

Some additional information on the conditions in the *midrash* about 1930 is available in an interview conducted in Jerusalem in 1966 by Naṣir Qamil Humayun with Tziyon Zabīḥī, quoted above in chapter 9. From the age of five to eight (1929–32) Zabīḥī was a pupil of the *midrash,* which he described as a large room in the private house of the teacher, who was also a wholesale merchant. He remembered that the *midrash* was far from his house, and that he had to go a long way along alleys and backstreets to reach it. It was in a hidden place, not far from the living quarters of the Muslims. In the southern part of the city, in many of the backstreets of the Jewish quarter, Muslims also lived among the Jews. However, they did not know that the school existed. In that room sat three or four groups of pupils, each forming a class, and what they studied were the reading of the prayers from a prayer book, the recitation of blessings, "and later, when we were advanced, also the weekly portion from the Bible." The children were not taught the translation of the texts; they were able to read them but did not understand what they read. "A boy who had a pleasant voice could go up on the Sabbath and read the book."

With the outbreak of World War II, and especially after the occupation of Meshhed by the Red Army in 1941, important developments took place in the educational efforts of the community. Contact with the Jewish community of Palestine increased. There was a growth in interest in the Hebrew language. In 1942, Daniel Nasrullayoff Livian, son of Farajullah Nasrullayoff, the head of the Meshhedi Jews in Jerusalem, visited Meshhed, and, upon his recommendation, modern textbooks for the study of Hebrew were sent from Eretz Israel to Meshhed. The youth department of the Jewish Palestine Office in Teheran organized a course for Hebrew instructors, which was attended by several young men from the Meshhed Jewish community who lived in Teheran. Others, who had spent some years in Eretz Israel, returned to Meshhed, and with their help evening courses for the study of Hebrew were instituted. In 1945, some fifteen pupils, ages six to twenty, took these courses.

In 1945, the *midrash* had ten classrooms on two stories of a house in the 'Ēdgāh. All the pupils sat on benches. The teachers had blackboards, chalk, and erasers at their disposal. The number of pupils (ages six to fourteen) was twenty to twenty-five in each class, or a total of some one hundred. The sessions took place, as a rule, only in the afternoon, from four or five to eight or nine o'clock, so as to accommodate pupils who studied in the government school or worked during the day. Only a few pupils attended morning classes at the *midrash.*

The pupils of the higher grades taught the lower grades. Some of the teachers of the *midrash* worked as volunteers and earned their livelihood during the day in shops or offices. Others received a salary from the community. In the courtyard of the *midrash* lived the *shammash* (caretaker), who was also a paid employee of the community.

Instruction began with the Hebrew alphabet, simple conversation in Hebrew, the Five Books of Moses, and prayers. Modern textbooks came from Erez Israel, such as *'Alēh* parts I and II, *Miqraot, Lashon vaSefer,* and *Sippurē haMiqra.* The textbooks were provided through the Palestine Office in Teheran, but they were not sent in a sufficient number of copies, so that in most cases two pupils had to share. The Hebrew pronunciation used gradually approximated that of the Yishuv (the Jewish community in Eretz Israel). The language of tuition was Persian,

Hebrew texts studied were translated into Persian, and the explanations were given in Persian. The reading exercises were carried on in groups: all the pupils in a class would read together as in a choir. The translation, explanation, and conversation were conducted individually between the teacher and the pupil.

During World War II, many Jews moved to the Darvaze Gennat ("Gate of Paradise") quarter, located in the new section of the city, and in 1945 several new classes were opened there. The teacher of three of these classes, among them one for girls, was Ya'qov Marash of Jerusalem, who worked in that year in Meshhed for the United Kingdom Commercial Corporation. This young Palestinian man was greatly respected by the heads of the community, who entrusted him with the tuition of their daughters, although it would have been entirely inconceivable to let a Meshhedi Jewish man conduct a class for girls.

Characteristic of the respect with which the teaching of Hebrew was regarded by the Jews of Meshhed is the following story, which was told me by Ya'qov Marash, a young Meshhedi Jew, who had spent several years in Palestine and returned to Meshhed, where Ḥājj Ibrāhīm Amīnoff, one of the heads of the community, wanted to persuade him to become a teacher of Hebrew. When the youth hesitated, Amīnoff promised him that if he undertook to teach Hebrew, he, Amīnoff, would exert his influence that the girl whom the youth wanted to marry should be given to him, although the girl's parents objected to the match because the family of the youth was not of sufficiently high standing for them. After Marash returned to Jerusalem, these classes had to be discontinued for lack of another teacher.

The method of teaching Hebrew in the *midrash* remained almost unchanged from the day it was founded until the reforms introduced during the World War II years. Since the only language the pupils knew when they started school was Persian, Hebrew had to be taught as a foreign language. When the child came to the *midrash,* he brought with him paper and the pen holder described above. The teacher would go from pupil to pupil and write on his paper the first four letters of the Hebrew alphabet. Then he taught them to read these four letters as if they were one word: אַבְגַ֫ד (*abjad*). A child had to learn the names of the four letters and be able to recognize them. Then the teacher continued in the same manner to teach the rest of the Hebrew alphabet. The following are the words into which the entire alphabet was grouped as a mnemotechnical device:

אַבְגַד הַוַז חַטִי כלַמַנ סַעְפַצ קַרַשַׁת.

(abjad, haważ, ḥuʼṭi, kalaman, sa'paṣ, qarashat)[5]

The final forms of the letters that had such forms were written above the letters in question:

ך ם ן   ף ץ

כלמנ   סעפצ

The names of the Hebrew letters used were as follows:

א	*alef*	ל	*lam*
ב	*bē*	מ	*mim*
ג	*gimel*	נ	*nun*
ד	*dal, dalet*	ס	*semakh*
ה	*hē*	ע	*'ayin*
ו	*vav*	פ	*pē*
ז	*zun*	צ	*ṣaṭ*
ח	*höt*	ק	*qof*
ט	*töt*	ר	*rosh*
י	*yod*	ש	*shin*
כ	*kaf*	ת	*taf*

The final forms of the letters ך. ם. ן. ף. ץ were called *kaf p'shuta* ("elongated *kaf*"), and likewise *nun p'shuṭa, pē p'shuṭa, ṣaṭ p'shuṭa,* and *mim s'ṭuma* ("closed *mim*").

The pupil had to memorize the letters by means of writing and reading exercises. After he knew the letters, he was taught the vowels. The vocalization (punctuation) was called *gāmeṣ-p'taḥ*. These are the names of the vowels preceded by their standard Hebrew names:

qamaṣ	*gāmeṣ*	*ḥolam*	*ḥolom*
pataḥ	*p'taḥ*	*qubuṣ*	*shuruq*
segol	*segol*	*shuruq*	*dagush*
ṣērē	*ṣarē*	*ḥireq*	*hiriq*
sh'va	*sh'va*	*ḥaṭaf pataḥ*	*sh'va p'taḥ.*

The Hebrew pronunciation taught and spoken in Meshhed was, in general, similar to the one spoken in Eretz Israel (the so-called Sephardi pronunciation), with a few minor differences: the *ḥet* was pronounced *hē;* the *'ayin* was pronounced like the *alef;* the *tṣade* like the *samekh;* the *qof* like the Persian *ghayn* (between *q* and *g*); the *qamaṣ* like the Persian long *fatḥa,* which sounds like the English *a* in *all.* All these phonemes received their specific phonemic values under the influence of Persian.

After the child had learned the individual letters and vowels, he was taught syllables and words. This phase of study was called *ḥibbur* in Hebrew, *hejigi* in Persian ("connection"). The teacher would write on the pupils' paper simple words and explain how they were pronounced (e.g., *sēfer, semakh; ṣavē, se; fe segol, fe; sēfe, 'im* [with] *rosh, sēfer;* or *shabbat, shin p'taḥ-sha; bē gāmeṣ-ba, shabba; 'im tav, shabbat.*

This phase of instruction lasted, in general, from three to four weeks. Older children, who had already learned to read and write in Persian, mastered the Hebrew reading in a shorter time. Some learned to read Hebrew within a single week.

The next step was to read a printed book. Since Hebrew textbooks were, in general, quite rare, they used for the first reading practices torn pages from old books, such as old prayer books or Bibles. The children brought these pages from home or got them from the teacher. Only after a child learned in this manner to read well did he begin to read the book of Genesis from its beginning. Copies of the Five Books of Moses were also rare; in general, three children would read from a single book.

After having learned the Hebrew "square" alphabet, the children were taught to write a form of Hebrew cursive script, which was referred to as Jadīdī script. The table that follows shows the form of this script. As one can see, in the Jadīdī script there are no final forms for the *pē* and the *ṣadē*.

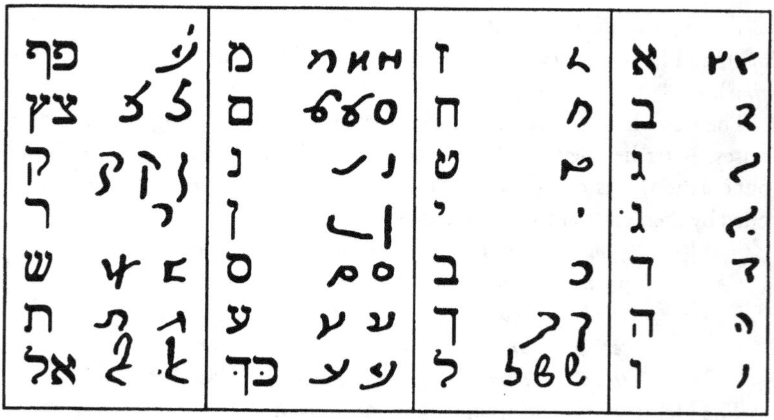

The children also learned to read the Rashi script, so that, in fact, they had to acquire three different types of Hebrew script.

As for the material read, students went through the book of Genesis from beginning to end, with many repetitions, until they could read it fluently. Together with the reading, they also learned the traditional cantillation, first of Genesis and later of the *Hafṭarot,* the weekly portions read from the prophets. At this stage, they were not taught the translation of the words and the sentences, so that all this time the children read without understanding. Most of the day at school was spent in reading exercises. The children read in unison, or the teacher asked one child to read five or six sentences, followed by a second child, and so forth, until all had their turn.

After they had acquired in this manner a sufficient fluency in reading, they went back to the beginning of Genesis and learned it again, this time with Persian translation, *tafsīl.*[6] For the study of *tafsīl,* each pupil brought along a copybook into which he entered the Hebrew words with their Persian translations.

Every day the pupils had to learn a certain number of words and translations. After Genesis, they continued in this manner to study the other books of the Bible. A very few even learned some Talmud.

The prayers, too, were taught at the *midrash,* although some of the children had already learned them at home from their parents or older brothers. About one hour every day was devoted at school to learning the prayers, which were read but not translated. The pupils who had acquired a good portion of the *tafsīl* of the Tora could, nevertheless, understand the prayers, more or less. However, most of the pupils stopped attending the *midrash* before they reached the *tafsīl,* and these, of course, understood not a word of the prayers which they nevertheless recited with fervor day after day.

In the advanced class of Mullah Yosef Dīl, there was a group of four or five pupils who studied *tafsīl.* All the pupils had to learn by heart certain basic prayers, such as the Sh'ma' ("Hear, O Israel"), Ashrē, and the like, and much time was spent at school every day reciting these prayers from memory.

Among those members of the community who had not studied *tafsīl,* it was customary to read the Persian translation of the Bible. The version used by the Jadīd al-Islām was the one prepared by the Muslim Persian scholar Fāzil (Fāḍil) Khān, which was printed by the British Bible Society in 1856.

In the 1920s, it was customary to have a small test at school every three months and a big examination once a year. The latter was given in the month of Ramaḍān, when the stores were closed until about ten in the morning. This enabled the fathers of the pupils and the heads of the community to go to the *midrash* several days in a row in the early-morning hours to listen to the examinations.

Two men from among the heads of the community were especially wont to attend the tests regularly and were always present during the ten or twelve days on which they were given. They were Mullah Farajullah Bur Elisha'off and 'Abd el-Karīm Yiṣḥaqoff. They would sit next to the teacher, while the parents of the pupils would sit on benches along the walls of the classroom. Mullah Farajullah Bur used to participate in the examinations by asking questions of the children, especially from the Torah.

Throughout the school year, the children would remain sitting in their places when answering questions put to them by the *mullah.* However, at the time of the tests, the pupil whose turn it was would come up front and stand before the teacher. The tests consisted of an oral and a written part. They were based on the entire material covered during the year: reading from the Torah and the prayer book, *tafsīl,* and recitation by heart of prayers, as well as dictation. The examination of each child took about half an hour; three to four children a day would stand for examination. This is why the tests lasted ten to twelve days.

When his examination was finished, the pupil would step up to the *mullah* and kiss his hand. Then he went to his father (or relatives) received from him a coin, smaller or bigger according to the father's fortunes. The child would drop the coin into a box next to the teacher. With the collected money, they would buy presents for the children.

The teacher would make a note of the mark the pupil earned. The highest mark was 20; a pupil who got 8 or less failed. These marks were the ones used in the Persian *madrasah*, where they represented the average of all subjects, and if it was 8, the pupil had to pass a second test in the subjects in which he was weak; if it was less than 8, he had to repeat the grade after the vacation.

After the exam, at the end of Ramaḍān, a celebration took place in which presents, especially sweets, were given to the children. The candy, *mampasi*, was usually imported from Russia.

For the children who completed their schooling in the *midrash*, a special feast was given. The well-to-do members of the community brought gifts, such as pocket knives, teapots, and cups. These objects were arranged on a long table in the courtyard of the *midrash*. The heads of the community, its honored members, and the children's parents were invited. The head of the community called the pupil who was best in his studies and told him to choose one of the presents on the table. Then came the turn of the pupil who finished second, then the third, and so on.

In order to increase the children's interest in learning the prayers and the benedictions, prizes were given to those who excelled. This method was introduced by Ḥājj Mullah Amīn, one of the heads of the community around the turn of the century, who served as ritual circumciser and donated all the money he received for his services to the purchase of presents for the pupils who were outstanding in knowledge of the prayers. If a child knew well the Sh'ma' or the Elohay the teacher would give him a note and send him to Ḥājj Mullah Amīn, who, in turn, would give the child a present: a menorah or a Book of Psalms or even a watch. The son of Ḥājj Amīn, Ḥājj Ibrāhīm Amīnoff, whose interest in education has been mentioned above, continued the tradition established by his father. He made it known that a pupil who learned the *Mode ani* or certain benedictions would receive from him a silver Star of David. Other members of the community also established various prizes and gave them to the teacher to use as rewards for outstanding pupils.

Several informants emphasized that there was a marked difference between the behavior of the pupils in the *midrash* on the one hand and the Muslim *maktab* and the government *madrasah* on the other. After the establishment of modern schools, the prestige of the traditional *maktab* declined, and with it the respect the pupils had for its teacher, the *ākhūnd*. The *ākhūnd* was able to keep order in his class only with great difficulty, and only by administering harsh physical punishments. No day would pass without several pupils being disciplined by beatings on the palm of the hand with the teacher's rod, *chūb ākhūnd*, or floggings with his whip, *shallāq*, a leather thong tied to the end of a rod. All kinds of infringements of the rules were punished by beatings. If a child spoke out of turn in class or did not prepare his homework or dirtied something in the school or did not behave properly while walking between his home and the school or while at home, he was given a beating. The beatings were so frequent that the children would comfort themselves by reciting a humorous Persian saying: *Chūb ākhūnd goleh—har kas nākhoreh kholeh.* ("The teacher's rod is a flower—he who does not receive it is stupid.")

Even though it was a "flower," the children were afraid of the teacher's rod and would make use of every opportunity to steal it. On the other hand, there were children who would present the teacher with rods found in the street or cut from a tree, in hopes of thus currying favor with him.

Occasionally, the children dared to exhibit cheeky behavior before the teacher, or even to play tricks on him. For instance, they would stick pins into the cushion on which the teacher sat on the floor of the classroom, so that he would be pricked as he sat down upon it. Someone even recalled that once the children made a small hole in the teacher's cushion and filled it with gunpowder.

Such tricks, as well as more serious transgressions such as thefts or unexcused absences, earned the most severe punishment, the *falak* or *falakeh.* This involved a stick to which were tied the two ends of a rope. The child receiving the punishment had to lie on his back, lift his legs, and place his two bare feet between the stick and the rope, whereupon the teacher twisted the stick around until the child's feet were held tightly by the rope. Then two children would hold up the two ends of the stick, immobilizing the feet of the culprit, and the teacher would beat the soles of the boy's feet with his rod. This punishment was an established institution in the *maktab,* and it would happen that parents who had a delinquent child would go to the teacher and ask him to treat their child to the *falak.*

In the years preceding World War I, greater attention to discipline and cleanliness was introduced in the schools. The pupils had to bring every week a note from their fathers to the effect that their behavior at home was satisfactory. The teacher examined every day the hands of the children to see whether their nails were clean. Every afternoon, when the classes were finished, the children had to line up in the schoolyard in front of the headmaster, and each child who was reported guilty of something received a beating. The headmaster decided how many stripes the culprit was to receive, and the actual beating was administered by the school caretaker. However, the children found it easy to protect themselves against this, for they could give *bakshish* to the caretaker, ensuring that his rod would touch them gently.

Once the beatings were over, the pupils would group themselves according to the quarters of the city in which they lived, and each group would start out for home under the supervision of a senior pupil who lived in the farthest part of the quarter, so that he was able to see that each child in his group entered the house of his parents and did not remain playing in the street. If a child disobeyed this prohibition, the supervisor gave his name next day to the teacher, and the culprit received a beating. At first, the older children walked ahead and the smaller ones behind them, but when the small ones could not keep up, they reversed the order.

The school had other means, in addition to beatings, of disciplining mischievous children and inducing them to do their study duties. One of these was the "long collar," *ṭōqe la'anat,* a kind of badge of shame that a child had to wear around his neck for a certain period of time. This practice was discontinued a long time ago, and the members of the community could not remember particulars about it.

Another, more modern method was to fix the seating order of the children in class according to their behavior and achievement in their studies. Half of the classroom was called "paradise," *behesht,* and the other half was "hell," *jahannam.* Within "paradise," the seating order was determined according to the degree of studiousness of the pupils. A child who did well in his studies was seated in front; those who did less well were placed in the back. To have a good record and to advance in the seating order became a matter of competition among the children.

The Jewish teacher, *mullah 'ivrī,* had a much easier task in keeping order and discipline in his class. The children in the classroom were, in general, quiet, even in a classroom in which pupils were divided into several groups, studying under the supervision of the *mullah*'s helpers. The most severe punishment consisted of strikes with the rod on the hand or the shoulder. *Falak* and the other severe disciplinary measures were unknown in the *midrash.* The *mullah 'ivrī* enjoyed great respect from his pupils. If they wanted to say or ask something, they raised a finger and spoke only after having been called upon by the teacher.

Next to the door of the classroom hung a little tablet, with the Persian word *raft* ("went") on one side and the word *āmad* ("returned") on the other. If a child wanted to go out, he did not have to ask permission from the *mullah* but got up quietly, went to the door, turned the tablet to the *raft* side, and went out. When he returned, he turned the tablet back to the *āmad* side, and then another child could go out. In this manner, the children were prevented from going out of the classroom in groups and from spending time outside in the courtyard playing. In the 1920s, the use of the tablet was discontinued.

As was the general rule in the entire traditional Middle East, so in the Meshhed Jewish community the school served only boys. Until the end of World War II, there was no communally maintained school for girls in Meshhed, neither among the Muslims nor among the Jews. This was the traditional situation, contrasted with the one in Merv, in Russian Turkestan, where there was an important community of Jews from Meshhed until the beginning of Soviet rule. There, both boys and girl studied in the same classroom in the school the Meshhedi Jews established for their children.

While in Meshhed most of the Jewish girls grew up without learning to read and write Hebrew, this did not mean that they remained altogether ignorant of Judaism. Quite to the contrary, their mothers taught them the benedictions, the prayers, and other religious matters that pertained to the lives of women and to the kitchen, so that the chain of Jewish tradition was not broken among the women, either. In fact, the Jadīdī women were most meticulous in the observance of the commandments, and it happened not infrequently that it was precisely because of them that Judaism was preserved in the family. The men, who in the course of their business dealings and other work had much contact with Muslims, were more inclined to assimilate, while the women watched assiduously over the observance of Jewish ritual.

A few learned women in the community could read and write Hebrew, and these women gathered groups of girls in their houses and taught them the Hebrew alphabet. The well-to-do among them did this as volunteers; the poor ones were given gifts or cash payments. There were in the community at all times women who could read the Torah and the prayer book.

Persian government schools for girls were opened in Meshhed around 1934, and the Jadīdī girls attended them.

22

GIRLS' GAMES

The girls' games described here were reported to me in Jerusalem in 1946 by two young Meshhedi women, Yafa Siman-Ṭov and Raḥel Raḥmānī, who had spent their childhood in Meshhed. Both stated that the same games were played by both Jewish and Muslim girls, which can be seen as a manifestation of the cultural communality between the Jadīd al-Islām and the old Muslims. The colloquial used by the Jadīdī girls, as by the Jadīdī community in general, was Persian.

Apart from enabling the girl children to acquire skills, these group games had an important role in developing sociability, group cohesion, solidarity, and character among the Jadīdī girls of Meshhed.

Qō'im Bāzī—Game of Hiding (Hide and Seek)

The game of *qō'im* (lit. *qāyim*) *bāzī* was played by ten to thirty girls ages four to nine, sometimes even older. Two girls were chosen, one to sit down and the other to bury her head in the seated girl's lap. All the others scattered and hid. The girl who had buried her head in the other girl's lap had to guess where each girl was hidden, without getting up and searching for them. She was aided in her task by the girls themselves, who from time to time would call out to guide her.

If she was unsuccessful, the girls came out of their hiding places and blindfolded her. She now had to try to catch one of them. They kept sufficiently close to her to be able to guide her by crying, *Albande! Albande!* ("The bound one!" or "The blindfolded one!"). If she succeeded in catching a girl, it was the latter's turn to sit down and bury her head in the other girl's lap, and the game started anew. This game was very popular.

Ghōb Bāzī—Game of Bones

The game of *ghōb bāzī* (lit. *qāb bāzī*), knuckle-bones game, was very popular with girls ages seven to thirteen, that is, with engaged girls, since most of the Jadīdī girls were engaged to be married before they were thirteen. The girls would meet every Sabbath at the house of one of them and would be engrossed in this game for hours. The five bones used in this game were from sheep ankles. Twenty to thirty girls would sit down in a circle on a big carpet. One of them would pick up the five bones, using only one hand, and throw them down on the carpet in front of her. Then she picked up one of the bones, threw it high up into the air, and tried quickly to gather the remaining four bones from the carpet before catching the first bone as it fell. Then she placed three bones on the carpet, flung up the other two, and quickly picked up the other three before catching the first two as they fell. Next, she placed two bones on the carpet, flung up three, and tried to gather up the two before catching the three. Then she did the same with only one bone left on the carpet.

Up to this point, she used only one hand. Now she began using both hands. One hand became the "gate": the fingertips were placed on the carpet, while the palm of the hand was raised. The gate was not moved throughout this part of the game. The other hand did all the playing. The girl gathered the five bones with her free hand and threw them down so that they should all fall close to the gate. She then picked up one of the bones, flung it high up, and, before catching it as it fell, she hastily pushed one of the bones on the carpet through the fingers of the gate. This done, she caught the falling bone. She repeated the same thing with the remaining three bones, whereby each of the bones had to be pushed through a different space formed by two neighboring fingers.

If the girl did not manage to catch a falling bone, or if she failed to pick up the requisite number of bones, or if a bone did not pass properly through its gate, the girl was "out," and another girl took her place and started over. If the girl succeeded in going through all the moves, she ceded her place to the next girl, and so forth, until all the girls had a turn.

This game was excellent practice for manual dexterity.

Halo Lombak—See-Saw

This game was played by groups of ten to fifteen girls, ages four to eight years. It was a modest little game in which girls who happened to live around the same courtyard would engage; in any case, the girls did not gather specifically for playing it, as was the case with the other games described here. A strong plank would be set across a big stone or a box, some of the girls would sit on one end of the plank, some on its other end, and they would swing up and down, singing *Halo Lombak* ("See-saw").

Ustāi Zanjīl Bof—Leader of the Chain

In this game (lit. *ustād zanjīr*), thirty to forty girls took part, ages five to ten. They stood in a straight line and held hands. Two girls were chosen to direct the game. One stood at the head of the line and was called *ustā* (leader), while the other stood at its end. It was the role of this second girl to ask the *ustā* questions. She began: *Ustā! Ustā!* The other answered: *Bale, bale* ("Yes, yes"). "Did you knit the chain?" The *ustā* answered: "Yes." "Did you throw it behind the mountains?" The *ustā:* "Yes." "May I go through?" The *ustā:* "By which way?" "Through the gate of the sheep."

The girl who asked the questions now proceeded to walk through between any two girls she chose, lifting their clasped hands to form a "gate," which now was considered "the gate of the sheep." As she went through the gate, all the girls followed her, bleating like sheep, *me-me-me.* As they went through, they lined up again, this time alternating, one of them facing this way, the other the opposite way. Next, the leading girl went through another gate, called "the gate of the cows," and all the girls following her mooing like cows: *moo-moo-moo.* Next followed the same procedure through "the gate of the cats" with the girls mewing, then through "the gate of the dogs" with all of them barking like dogs, then through "the gate of the frogs" with croaking like frogs, and so on. Each time they went through a gate, they arranged themselves in a line, facing in alternate directions and clasping hands.

When they had gone through all the gates, the leader said: "Father said we should beat the meat!" All the girl stamped their feet nosily. Then she said: "Father said we should beat the *ḥummuṣ* [chickpea]." They all again stamped their feet. This was followed by "Father said we should beat the salt," "we should beat the pepper," and so on, and the girls each time stamped their feet. Now the leader said: "Father said we should prepare the chicken," and all the girls started to crow like a cock: *ku-ku-ri-ku.* Finally, the leader said: "Father said we should loosen the ropes," whereupon the girls let go of one another's arm, and the game broke up.

This game was very popular, and much of the girls' time was spent in going through these motions.

'Arūsak Bāzī—Game of the Dolls

From five to ten girls took part in this game, sometimes up to fifteen, ages four to fifteen.

Each girl received from her mother a piece of beautiful cloth, needles, thread, scissors, and anything else that would be required, sometimes even a sewing machine. Many households had small sewing machines, turned by hand, so that even small girls could manage them. The girls would gather at the house of one of them and sit down to work, that is, to make dolls, stuffing them with cotton wool or small pieces of rags. They used real hair for the dolls' hair. They made eyes and eyebrows and painted the dolls' cheeks red. Then they sewed miniature underclothing, all made to measure, and dresses as beautiful as they could make them, embroidered with gold and silver threads and decorated with gilded buttons. The clothes were fashioned after those worn by adult women. Each girl tried to make her doll as beautiful as possible, and when she had difficulties, her mother helped her.

The girls would dress their dolls up as brides and proceed to arrange a wedding, all after the manner of real weddings in the world of the adults, and the excitement would indeed be great. Sometimes the dolls would be not brides but babies, and the girls would mother them, change their diapers, wrap them up, and put them to sleep.

This game was much loved by the girls and was also of considerable educational value, for everything was done in exact imitation of what the adults did. Incidentally, it also took the place of sewing lessons and practice and was an introduction to the care of babies. Most girls began playing it at a tender age, so that by the time they married, they were quite familiar with these womanly duties.

Angushtar Bāzī—Ring Game

From ten to fifty girls took part in this game, ages five to fifteen. The girls divided themselves into two groups, which sat down facing each other on a big carpet spread on the floor. Each group chose a leader, and after deciding which group should have the ring first, they began to play.

The leader of the group that got the ring held it in her hand until all the girls had hidden their hands beneath a big blanket. Then she slipped the ring under the blanket into the hands of one of the girls, who, in turn, passed it on to her neighbor, and so the ring went from hand to hand. When the ring reached the hand of the girl who was supposed to hold it, they all pulled their closed fists out from under the blanket, and the leader of the opposing group had to guess which girl had the ring. The number of permitted guesses was fixed in advance. The leader would point to the girl who she believed had the ring and say: *Fush ya gol?* ("Full or empty?") If she guessed correctly, the ring passed to her own group, and the game started over again. If none of her permitted guesses proved correct, the first group kept the ring, and the game started again.

This game was played as a rule on rainy days when the girls could not go out to play in the courtyard. Occasionally, some girls brought along their small brothers, ages six or seven, to participate in the game. However, when the boys grew a little older, they were no longer allowed to play with the girls.

Yak Anor De Anor—One, Two

This game, too, was played on rainy days when the girls could not go out. At least nine girls would take part, their ages ranging from five to nine. They would sit with their legs stretched out before them. One girl would be chosen to do the counting, and she would begin by counting the legs from one to nine, and leg number nine would be out. She would continue to count, again from one to nine, and again the ninth leg would be out. She would go on until only one leg remained. This leg they would now proceed to "cook." They would wrap it up in blankets to "heat" the food, and when it was sufficiently "cooked," they would begin to "taste" it, each girl making some comment on its taste: it "lacked salt" or "lacked pepper," and so on. The girls would vie with each other in thinking up funny comments to the delight and laughter of everybody. When the "food" was deemed fit to be eaten, they took the blankets off the leg and proceeded to "eat" it by pinching the leg not at all gently, as if they were helping themselves to a morsel of food. The game was accompanied by much laughter, squealing, and merriment. When the "eating" was done, the game began all over again.

Piq Piq—Pinching

This game was identical to the previously described one, except that instead of legs, arms figured in it.

Ōtesh Dōri?—Have You Fire?

Two to five girls, ages five to twelve, took part in this game. Each held one hand before her, with the fingers spread out, so that the thumb of one girl touched the small finger of her neighbor, and so on. One girl was chosen as the questioner. She placed her finger between the first two fingers in the line and asked: *Ōtesh dōri?* (lit. *ātesh dāri;* "have you fire?"). The owner of the fingers would answer: *Bola taraq,* ("A little higher!"). The questioner now slipped her finger between the second and third fingers of the same hand, repeated the question, and received the same answer. When she reached the last two fingers and put the same question, the answer would be: "Don't go further, because the cat will eat you!" Despite this warning, the questioner tried to proceed, but the girls, with loud mewing and squealing, broke into a general scuffle, attacking each other playfully, amid general laughter. When they had enough of this, they began the same again, with another girl as the questioner, and would continue until each of the girls had filled the questioner's role.

23
Ritual Observances

Observance of the dietary laws and the other religious *mitzvoth* (commandments) posed difficult problems for the Jadīdīm. The fulfillment of many commandments involved the acute danger of being discovered and unmasked as false Muslims. The Dilmānī document (quoted above, chapter 7) contains a brief overview of these difficulties:

> In the early period after the forced conversion, the Jews were unable to observe the laws of eating kosher meat. He who wanted to obtain kosher meat would give his wife a chicken, and at nighttime she would carry it under her *chādor* to the *shoḥēṭ* [the ritual slaughterer], have it slaughtered, and then take it back home and cook it the same night. There were such who, in the middle of the night, would slaughter a sheep in secret, and in the same night would distribute the meat to sick people and to women in childbirth who did not eat *ṭ'rēfa* [non-kosher] meat. They did this amidst great trepidation and with great precautions.
>
> In that early period, the Jews did not gather on weekdays for prayer, and only on the Sabbath and the holidays did they get together in three or four secret places, in cellars that could accommodate ten to fifteen men. They locked the doors and posted guards outside, so that nobody should know that they were praying inside. As guard, they would have a woman with uncovered head sit in the courtyard or the entrance corridor, to make sure that no stranger would enter. [If a stranger saw an unveiled woman sit in the courtyard of a house, the strict rules of segregation prevented him from entering.]
>
> For the feast of Passover, every family prepared for itself ten to fifteen *sīr* [about 75 grams per *sīr*] of flour, and at night, behind closed and well-guarded doors, they baked the *matzoth* on a *sāj* [a big, upturned iron pan], and with much fear and trepidation, they would hide the *matzoth* in a secret place, so that their presence should not become revealed. In order to mislead the Muslims, on the Passover, the Jews would buy bread in the marketplace, and on the way back home, they would distribute it among poor Muslims. Throughout

the Passover, they would eat mainly rice. Wine for the Passover they could obtain only with great difficulty.

On New Year's Day and the Day of Atonement, they did not blow the *shofar,* because of the fear of the Muslims. On the Day of Atonement, all the Jews fasted and gathered to pray in secret in the houses. On the feast of Sukkoth, they did not sit in booths, but as far as it was possible, they did obtain two *lulabhs* and *ethrogs,* and all the Jews of the city would pronounce the blessings over them.

Circumcisions were performed according to tradition. For the wedding ceremony, they first went to the Muslim sages and wrote everything according to their customs, but on the same day, after dark, they gathered ten to fifteen men in the house, closed the doors, and performed the *ḥuppa* [Jewish wedding] and wrote the marriage contract according to the religion of Israel. They observed the laws of *niddah* [menstrual impurity] and of childbirth, but they had no *miqveh* [ritual bath]. But since in the general baths in those days there were basins of warm water, they took baths in them as in a *miqveh.*

Prayer books and the Holy Scripture were preserved in great secrecy. On the Sabbath and the holidays, they kept their stores open but sold nothing.

The Dilmānī document also contains some information about improvements in the conditions of the Jadīdīm from 1895 on. In that year, Jadīdī families began to move to Turkestan and to Russia, and "since then the *gālūt* [exile] no longer oppressed the Jews as much." As a result of this emigration, the number of the Jews in Meshhed decreased in the course of the ensuing two decades, but when the Russian Revolution broke out in 1917, many of the Meshhedi Jews who had emigrated to Russian Turkestan returned to Meshhed. Under the rule of the Kajar Shahs, the situation of the Meshhedi Jews was tolerable, and then, "recently, when the shining star appeared, his glorious highest majesty, the esteemed Shah of Shahs, Reza Shah Pahlavi, father of the Iranian kingdom, may his days be long! one can say that the exile of the Marranos came to an end, and good days dawned on the Jews."

In 1928, military service was introduced, Dilmānī informs us, and thereafter, until 1939 some three hundred men were recruited from among the Jadīdīm to the army, each serving two years. None of them had officer's rank, but some were subalterns, up to the rank of sergeant, and some worked as storekeepers, "for they were trusted."

The situation with regard to ritual observances in the 1930s was vividly recalled by Tziyon Zabīḥī in an interview in Jerusalem in 1966. Even though, according to Zabīḥī, in his childhood and youth the situation of the Jews was much better than in the years immediately after the Allahdād, still the Jadīdīm were considered unclean and were not allowed to enter the Muslim holy places or walk along the public thoroughfares that led across them. If one of them nevertheless entered and was recognized, "he was beaten, or worse. In the course of several decades of *gālūt* [exile], and very hard *gālūt* at that, the Jews got used to this life, they got used and taught the children to avoid contact, as far as possible, with the Muslims."

The problem of having kosher meat was solved, according to Zabīḥī, in this manner:

> I heard this being discussed in our house more than once. They would go to a Muslim butcher and buy meat. That meat, of course, was *t'rēf* for us. They would carry the meat home in their hands, so that the neighbors should see that they were buying meat outside. Once they reached home, they destroyed that meat, or gave it to the cat, or threw it away. All the time they observed the rules of ritual kosher slaughtering. How did they do it? Almost all the houses of the Jews in one alley were connected with secret doors, so that they could cross over from one house to the next. They slaughtered a lamb in one house, and distributed the meat among the neighbors so that nobody from the outside could notice it.

Another problem the Jewish merchants who had stores in the bazaar had to cope with was how to observe the Sabbath and the Jewish holidays. The way they did this in the 1930s, according to Zabīḥī, was as follows:

> I remember that the store of my father was in a kind of passage called in Persian *kāravān serah,* or in brief *serah.* There were three or four Jewish stores there; the rest belonged to Muslims. On the Sabbath, and even on Yom Kippur, in the morning, I as a boy, and my brother, went there, opened the outside door, and closed the glass door (for every store had two doors: an external door and an internal, glass door), and returned home. If we were asked what happened, we said that Father was sick or gave some other excuse. In the evening, we returned to the store and locked the outer door. Or else, on the Sabbath, in order not to give reason to the people to say that we don't want to work, we went, opened the store, and then sat down at some distance in the sun or, in the summer, in the shade, and conversed. If somebody came to buy something, we said that it was not ready, or we did not have it and expected to get it tomorrow, and used all kinds of other excuses. Thus, we tried, as far as possible, not to do any business on the Sabbath, but postponed everything to next day. Of course, at lunchtime on the Sabbath, we went home to have our meal, which we did not do on weekdays. Thus, we spent an hour or more, and then returned and closed the store early. I remember that up to thirty years ago [1936], this was the situation. But gradually the Muslims, as if they felt that this was merely for appearances' sake, ceased [to try to buy anything on the Sabbath].

24
Marriage

The Age of Marriage

In Persia, as in all the countries of the Middle East, boys and girls were married off at a very tender age. Especially in well-to-do families, where the considerable expenses involved constituted no obstacle, the weddings were celebrated well before the onset of puberty. Among the Jews of Meshhed, marriages were arranged at an even earlier age than among their Muslim neighbors. This especially was the case with a girl, out of fear lest a Muslim come and ask for her hand in marriage for his son. For this reason, they arranged the engagement of their daughters at the age of four to six years, and when the girl reached the age of nine or ten, they celebrated the wedding (Persian *'arūsī*, or Hebrew *qiddush*).

Occasionally, a father would betroth his daughter on the very day of her birth, as was practiced in talmudic times.[1] The same custom was practiced in other Middle Eastern Jewish communities, too, such as among the Jews of Afghanistan,[2] as well as among the Arabs, such as the *fellahin* of Palestine.[3] It also was customary among the Muslims in Persia to betroth children while they lay in their cradles, or even before birth.[4] Among the Jews of Meshhed, such an engagement of a girl on the day of her birth had no legal validity unless both the girl and the boy to whom she was betrothed consented in later years. Occasionally, if a father was downcast because a daughter instead of a son was born to him, a relative would comfort him, "Don't worry, she will be for my son." If the daughter objected after she grew up, the engagement was null and void, but usually the children did not refuse to follow their parents' wishes, and when the time came, they were duly wedded to each other. The father of one of my informants betrothed his daughter in this manner on the day she was born. The boy who became her bridegroom was six years old at the time. After the children grew up, they married.

The general rule was to celebrate the wedding several years before the bride reached puberty, so that it did not signify the beginning of cohabitation but had only legal and social significance. After the wedding, the bride moved from her parents' house to that of the bridegroom's parents. The Jews of Meshhed believed that the girl must mature in the house of her husband's parents rather than in her own parents' home. If a girl reached puberty (about thirteen years of age) and was still in her parents' house, she was considered an old maid, a girl who "has remained in the house" (*khānah māndeh*).

It often happened that immediately after the wedding, the young husband would embark on a lengthy commercial trip to other Persian cities or abroad (especially to Russia) and return only several years later, and only then did the couple begin to live together as man and wife. And even if the husband did not go on a voyage, regular sexual cohabitation began, in most cases, a few years after the wedding.

The arranging of a marriage (*numzad* [lit. *nāmzadi*] *dāri* or *numzad kardan*) for a girl at the suitable age was a concern not only of the parents and close relatives but of the community as a whole. Discussions with a Muslim who came to ask for the hand of a Jadīdī girl could have caused unpleasantness and even brought danger for the whole community. Therefore, if the heads of the community saw that the parents procrastinated in arranging a marriage for their daughter, they would visit them, inquire into the situation, urge the father to arrange for the marriage as soon as possible, and, where needed, give him financial aid. When the sister of one of my informants was about eight years old, the head of the community, Mullah 'Abdallah Amīnoff, came one evening to his father's house and said to him, "You must have the wedding right away, lest the Muslims come and ask for your daughter for one of them!" Before the girl reached her ninth year, she was married. Her bridegroom was seventeen years old. This young woman gave birth the first time when she was sixteen. The passage of several years between engagement and marriage, and again between marriage and the first birth, was the general rule in the community.

The Choice of a Match

Marriages between close relatives, and especially between children of two brothers, which are customary among the Persian Muslims as well as in the entire Middle East,[5] were practiced even more frequently among the Jews of Meshhed. The closest female relative (beyond, of course, the forbidden first degree) was considered the natural match for a young man. A father who wanted to find a wife for his son would, first of all, look to a daughter of his other son or the daughter of his own brother. The same factors that made for arranging the engagement and wedding at an early age induced them to choose a wife within the closest family. It was obligatory to maintain and strengthen the family ties so that the community constituted a strong, self-contained unit in the face of the constant dangers threatening it from the outside. In addition, the choice of marriage partners reflected the class differences that characterized not only the Meshhed Jews but Persian society in general: rich people married only among themselves.

Housing conditions played a considerable role in these endogamous marriages. The young men remained living in their parents' houses after their marriages, so that paternal cousins and other paternal relatives who could become marriage partners grew up together. Moreover, members of the same extended family knew one another well, and the boy's parents were thoroughly familiar with the character and manners of the girl they considered a match for their son. Financial arrangements also were easier for the parents of both the boy and the girl, for any assets that had to change hands as a result of the marriage would remain within the same extended family. In addition to all this, they subscribed to the view that a bride from the same family would be more devoted and faithful (*najīb*) to her husband than one from a strange family.

Several of my informants, when I asked them the reason for marriages between close relatives, replied with the same word that was their answer to my question concerning the reason for early marriage: *gālūt*—"exile." An old woman quoted a proverb in reply: "Home-baked bread is better than bread from the marketplace."

If the engaged couple lived in the same house or, more precisely, in rooms opening into the same courtyard, certain modifications, albeit not significant ones, took place in the engagement and wedding ceremonies. These changes were required by the fact that the two families lived in close proximity.

The Engagement

In rich or well-to-do families, the mother began to prepare clothes and jewels for her daughter soon after she was born. A rich bride got from her parents a great number of dresses and other apparel made of velvet and silk embroidered in gold and silver. The preparation of these embroidered dresses proceeded slowly, over the course of several years. It was generally held that the respect a woman would enjoy from her husband and his family was directly related to the amount of property she brought with her as dowry (*jehāz;* see below). For this reason, the women of the family busied themselves assiduously with the preparation of the dresses that constituted the main part of the *jehāz*.

Engagement among the Jews of Meshhed, as among the Jews and Muslims of Persia in general, was in fact a long series of ceremonies and rites, all of which had to be carried out before the engagement acquired legal validity and the couple was considered actually engaged to be married.

Zīr Dandāne: Under the Tooth

When the parents of the boy found a girl whom they wanted to become their daughter-in-law, they would send one of their own relatives, either a man or a woman, to her parents in order to sound them out. This emissary was never a professional matchmaker, as was the *delāleh* among the Muslim Persians,[6] but always a member of the family, usually an old man who was used to doing good works, or an old and respected woman. With the first visit of this emissary began a long series of visits and ceremonies whose purpose was to bring the two families closer together. The first visit was supposed to find out how the girl's parents felt in general about her marriage, and whether they would reject the matter with some excuse, such as the tender age of their daughter. Only after several visits, with decent intervals between them, did the girl's parents finally give a definite answer about their willingness to give her as wife to the youth in whose name the emissary acted. As a token of his consent, the father of the girl gave the emissary a small lump of sugar; this custom provided the name for this phase of the engagement: *zīr dandāne,* the giving of a lump of sugar "under the tooth" of the emissary.

Baleh Giri: Taking Yes

When the emissary came and informed the father of the boy that he had received the *zīr dandāne,* the father got together a small group of people—two, three, or more respected male relatives—and this delegation proceeded to the girl's parents in order to "obtain yes," that is, to get their explicit consent to the marriage. Only after this, too, had been accomplished did the task of the matchmaker (*khāzandeh*) begin. The *khāzandeh* was either a man or a woman who mediated between the two families to arrange of all the details pertaining to the marriage.

Shīrnī Gīrān and *Shīrnī Dādan:* Taking Sweets and Giving Sweets

One of the tasks of the *khāzandeh* was to set the date for the first meeting between the families of the bride and the bridegroom and to arrange all the particulars connected with this important event. This meeting took place in the bride's parents' home, and their name for it was *shīrnī* (lit. *shīrīnī*) *dādan,* "giving sweets," while from the point of view of the groom's parents it was called *shīrnī gīrān,* "taking sweets." On the date set, ten or twenty men from the boy's family paid a group visit to the parents of the bride. The latter prepared a large quantity of candy and sweets, as well as a sugar cone (*kaleh qand*) for the occasion, keeping all this in an inner room so that when the guests arrived, they saw no traces of any preparations made for their reception.

If the families involved were rich and respected, the heads of the community also participated in the *shīrnī dādan*. The master of the house received the guests in a friendly but dignified manner and, first of all, greeted the head of the community with all the respect due his position. The initial conversation touched upon various subjects—for it would not have been seemly to broach the purpose of the visit right away—and then the head of the community would say to the father of the girl, "So-and-so, the son of so-and-so, sent us to ask for the hand of your daughter for his son." These words touched off a play of refusal whose form was firmly set by age-old custom. The expected first answer of the father was, "I cannot engage my daughter, she is too young." An additional request elicited the response, "I must, first of all, ask my father who is at present out of town," or "I must ask my uncle who lives in Teheran," or "my elder brother who is now in India," and the like. Each excuse of this kind had its proper answer delivered by the head of the community or another member of the delegation.

The opinion of the elder women also had to be heard in the *shīrnī dādan*. The bride's father, for instance, would say, "I must ask my mother." Then the old lady would be brought into the room and would be asked whether she consented that her granddaughter become engaged to so-and-so. Her usual answer was, "I do not know the young man." In a like manner, all the relatives of the bride would be asked, and all would give a negative or non-committal answer. This gave the relatives of the groom ample opportunity to praise his looks, his fine nature, his intelligence and learning, and so on. At last, the bride's father said yes, whereupon tablecloths were brought in and spread upon the rugs on the floor, and then the *shīrnī* was fetched and offered the guests. In addition to sweets, there were various kinds of candied nuts, such as peeled and sugar-coated almonds (*noqlō bādām*); round *ḥalvah* with *manna* (*ḥalvā-ī-gaz*),[7] and more of the like. The sugar cone was sent to the bridegroom's house.

Neither the bridegroom nor the bride was present at the *shīrnī dādan*. When the guests finished enjoying the sweets, the two families fixed the date for the official engagement ceremony, and then the guests took their leave.

Shīrnī Khōran: Eating Sweets

The official engagement ceremony was called *shīrnī khōran*, "eating sweets." This, too, took place in the house of the bride's parents, and the bride and groom were again absent. The period of time between the *shīrnī dādan* and *shīrnī khōran* was not fixed. They could take place one after the other, on the very next day, or several months could elapse between them. The latter was the case if the parents of the bridegroom needed time to prepare the presents, or if the father of the bride had to go out of town on a business trip.

On the morning of the day fixed for the *shīrnī khōran,* the bridegroom or, more precisely, his parents in his name set a *khāncheh,* a square tray as big as a tabletop, laden with all kinds of gifts for the bride. The gifts, attractively arranged, included dresses, a coat, shoes, stockings, and the like, as well as gold and silver ornaments and the inevitable sweets. The parents of the bride, on their part, prepared a meal of sweets for the guests and also invited a group of musicians (*sāzendeh*). The musicians were Muslims, and their instruments consisted of drum (*dā'ireh*), tambourine (*dombak,* lit. *tanbak*), flute (*nay*), and six-stringed violin (*tār*).[8] The large orchestras were ten to fifteen men strong. The flutist occasionally played a solo piece.

The rejoicing at the *shīrnī khōran* reached its peak with the recitation of Psalm 121, "A Song of Ascents": "I will lift up mine eyes unto the mountains. From whence shall my help come?" The *mullah* was honored with the reading of this psalm, with which the engagement became a legally accomplished fact.

Although the engagement was also called by the Hebrew name *qinyan* (pronounced *gönyan*), no formal *qinyan,* a binding agreement between the parties by the handing over of an object, was made. Nor were *t'naim* (literally, "conditions")—a formal wedding agreement or nuptial contract—written.

The joyful company did not break up until late at night, when some of the sweets were sent to the bridegroom's house so that he, too, should be able to enjoy them. The party that took the sweets to the bridegroom was accompanied by lanterns (*shām lāleh*), which were candles within lily-shaped glass enclosures.

Most of the details of the *shīrnī khōran* as described above also were observed by the Muslim Persians, so that the Jadīdīm were able to celebrate it openly, without having to hide anything from the Muslim servants who worked in their houses, or from their Muslim neighbors. The main difference between the Muslim and the Jadīdī *shīrnī khōran* lay in the sex of the participants. Among the Muslims, only the women of both families participated in it,[9] while among the Jadīdīm both men and women took part, although they sat separately, as was the general custom on all festive occasions. In another version of the *shīrnī khōran* found among the Jadīd al-Islām, even this difference had disappeared, and only women participated in it, while for the menfolk a second *shīrnī khōran* was given on another day, at which the bridegroom and his friends also were present. In days past, a game of dolls was held at the *shīrnī khōran* in a women's room.

Dāmād Khān Barān: Invitation of the Bridegroom

Sometime after the *shīrnī khōran,* the parents of the bride invited the bridegroom to their house. This was the first time that the bridegroom entered his bride's house. This visit, too, was the occasion for a festive meal attended by a large group of men from the bridegroom's side. The bride's parents gave the bridegroom a present, in most cases a tray laden with suits of clothes and a gold watch. There were some who, instead of suits, gave the bridegroom fine material, from which he had a suit custom-made.

From Engagement to Wedding

According to a custom observed all over the Middle East, the bridegroom was not allowed to see the bride until the day of the wedding. Among the Jadīd al-Islām, the bride was even forbidden to speak with any of the groom's male and female relations. The observance of this custom was considered a matter of honor for the bride. However, it presented some difficulties in the normal routine of life if the families of the bride and the groom were related and dwelt in one courtyard. If the bride sat in the courtyard and saw, for instance, that the groom's mother came out of her door, she had to hide, and in most cases she fled in confusion into her own house, to her mother's room.

It often happened that the bridegroom left for another city or went abroad in connection with his business immediately after the *shīrnī khōran* or the *dāmād khān barān*. In this case, of course, no incidental encounter could take place between him and his bride. One of my informants, for instance, went to Russia after his engagement (he was fourteen years old at the time, and his bride was seven) and remained there, with short interruptions, until his wedding, which took place seven years later, when he was twenty-one and the bride fourteen. In the course of those seven years, he returned to Meshhed only once in a year or in two years for short visits.

Immediately after the *shīrnī khōran,* the bride, even though still a child, had to begin to wear the veil (*maqna'ah*) with which the Meshhed women covered themselves while at home. However, modesty demanded that the bride should not show herself to the groom even when covered by the *maqna'ah,* and that she hide from him so that he should not see even the clothes she was wearing.

Custom also required that during the long years between engagement and wedding, the bridegroom send the bride, for every holiday, and especially for Purim, Passover, and the fifteenth of Sh'vat, a large round tray (*majmu'eh*) (lit. *majma'ah*) with clothes, ornaments, and sweets.

Ōtāq Kardan and *Numzad Bāzī:* Making Room and Bride Play

On a few rare occasions between the engagement and the wedding, the bride and groom were given an opportunity to spend a few minutes together, and to do so without the presence of a third person. The parents of the bridegroom would invite the family of the bride once, and on that occasion they "made room" for the two young people. At other times, one of the relatives invited both families, and the bride and groom were enabled "to make room" in his house. The manner in which this brief ritualized togetherness took place was as follows. They put the bride and the groom in a room, locked the door, and left them alone in it for about a quarter of an hour. During that time, the couple sat side by side, the groom gave the bride the present he had brought for her (for each *ōtāq kardan,* the groom had to bring a gift of jewels or gold coins), and he asked her to remove the veil that covered her face, or, if he had enough courage, he lifted it himself. Modesty and good manners required that the bride sit all the time without making any movement, with her eyes closed, and without uttering a single word. If the groom dared to kiss the bride, and she, in her childish innocence, later told it to her mother, no more *ōtāq kardan* was allowed, and the bride's parents did not let the groom even see her until the wedding day. But if the groom behaved properly, he could meet the bride in this way several times.

Occasionally, the bridegroom would ask the bride to look at him and to answer his questions, but only rarely did he succeed in persuading her to behave contrary to custom. These first attempts at approach between bride and groom were called *numzad bāzi,* "bride play."

If the couple did not come out of the room on their own initiative after the fifteen minutes were over, the parents of the bride would knock on the door and say, "Come out, quickly!" The young couple then had to emerge from the room shamefacedly and in confusion, to the merriment of the assembled guests. Rich families also invited musicians for the *ōtāq kardan.*

Although the *ōtāq kardan* was an established custom, the parents of the bride usually gave it the appearance of a special favor they did for the bridegroom. This being the case, the groom used to bring presents not only to the bride herself but also to her parents. In most cases, these were sweets, but occasionally some silver object, which he would give, for instance, to her grandmother as an inducement to let him meet the bride.

The practice of the *ōtāq kardan* among the Jews of Meshhed was symptomatic of the generally less stringent restrictions among them on contact between men and women in comparison with the rules obeyed by their Muslim neighbors. While among the Jews this custom enabled bride and bridegroom to meet at least occasionally in an approved fashion during the long period between the engagement and the wedding, no such possibility was available to Muslim engaged couples. For example, Nurullah Khan describes quite enthusiastically in his autobiographical notes that after he became engaged in 1877, on one single occasion his mother made extraordinary arrangements to enable him to see his betrothed through a hole in a curtain.[10] Only in the very week of the wedding (when, according to the rules, the groom was still not allowed to see the bride) was he able, with her help, to sneak in to her occasionally. The Muslims called this *nāmzad bāzi,* that is, "play of the engaged (couple)."[11] Both the Jewish and the Muslim customs are reminiscent of the old Jewish custom that was practiced, according to the Talmud, in Judea but not in the Galilee in tannaitic times. Rabbi Y'huda said, "In Judea, at first they let groom and bride be together alone for a short while [prior to their entering the *ḥuppa,* i.e., prior to the wedding ceremony], so that he should not be shy toward her, but in the Galilee this was not practiced."[12]

Bāshlaq Barān: Sending the Bride Price

When the parents of the bridegroom decided that the time had come for celebrating the wedding, they informed the bride's parents by sending them a special present. This was done one or two months before the wedding. This present was called *bāshlaq,* "gift" or "donation."[13] The *bāshlaq* was, in fact, the bride price which the groom paid to the bride's parents. According to my informants, this custom was adopted by the Jadīdīm from the Muslims after the forced conversion of 1839. Among the Muslims, the *bāshlaq* was considered a payment rendered to the bride's mother for having suckled her as an infant. In accordance with this view, the Muslim Persians termed the bride price *shīr bahā,* "milk price."[14]

Soon after the custom of *bāshlaq barān* became established among the Jadīdīm, the heads of the community issued a decree limiting to 150 *q'rān* the amount the parents of the bridegroom, whether rich or poor, could send to the parents of the bride.[15] The regulation was, in general, obeyed, and if it nevertheless happened that a rich bridegroom sent a larger amount, the family of the bride considered it an insult, as if it would indicate that they were poor and needed the money. In the late 1890s, when an elder brother of one of my informants got married, his parents sent 250 *q'rān* instead of the 150. The bride's parents became angry, for they looked at this as a slight on their honor, and the quarrel over the matter lasted several months. After World War I, however, the regulated *bāshlaq* fell into disuse, and every family sent as much as it wanted.

On the other hand, if the parents of the bridegroom sent no *bāshlaq* to the parents of the bride, the latter refused to celebrate the wedding. They would say, "You sent us no *bāshlaq;* how can we have a wedding?"

The gold wedding ring which was part of the *bāshlaq* was wrapped in a thin silk handkerchief (*dastmāl kasari*) made in Yezd. The little bundle was placed in the middle of a large copper plate (*b'shqāb*). Around it were arranged sweets, especially candied sugar and a sugar cone, as well as other sweets and fruits. All these were covered by a tray cover (*khāncheh pūsh*), and the tray was sent to the bride's house. According to one of my informants, they sent four plates full of candy, cookies, tea, and other things.

In the richest families, the mother would distribute the *bāshlaq* money, or part of it, among the poor. The less well-to-do used it to defray the expenses of the wedding, such as payment to the seamstresses who sewed dresses for the bride from the materials sent by the groom, the purchase of jewelry for the bride, and the like. From part of the money, the bride's father used to buy a suit, or material for a suit, for the bridegroom. He would invite the groom to go with him to the bazaar to choose a piece of material he liked, and then bought it for him and gave it a tailor to sew.

Ṣalāḥ Binān: Consultation

A week or two before the wedding, the father of the bride would invite several of his relatives for a consultation (*ṣalāḥ binān*) concerning all the particulars of the wedding. Since several hundred guests were invited to the wedding feast, the house of the family was not always suited to accommodate such a large-scale banquet. Therefore, the first thing to be decided at the *ṣalāḥ binān* was where the banquet was to be held. In most cases, the solution was to decide on the house or the courtyard of one of the rich relatives. It was also necessary to prepare a list of those to be invited. The list was written with black ink (*murakkab*), and hence its name, *si'ī*, from *si'ah*, "black." The list would occasionally contain two hundred or even more names.

At the same time, the women would hold a consultation concerning the invitation of women. Since the women were unable to write, they called in an old woman of the family and asked her to be the inviter—*ādam talk,* literally, "people inviter." If the woman accepted the task, she brought along with her yellow peas (*nokhōd*) tied in her veil. The women of the house called out names to her, saying, "Invite so-and-so, her daughter, her sister, etc." After listening to each name, the inviter would transfer one pea to another place in her veil or, temporarily, to her hand. When all the names were enumerated, the woman would repeat them, returning one pea with each name. In this manner, she knew that she remembered all the names. When she went from house to house to deliver the invitations, she took the peas along with her, and after each invitation, she put one pea in a different part of her veil. When all the peas were transferred, she knew she had delivered all the invitations without forgetting any.

A third important matter to be decided in the men's consultation was the date of the wedding. Not at any time and any hour could a wedding be celebrated. First of all, there were certain periods in the year in which Jewish law did not allow weddings, such as the 'Omer days between Passover and Pentecost (with the exception of the new moon of Sivan and the thirty-third day of 'Omer) and the days of mourning from the seventeenth of Tammuz to the ninth of Av. In addition, no weddings could take place, according to Muslim law, during the whole two months of Ramaḍān and Muḥarram. If no suitable place could be secured for the wedding, one also had to take the weather into account: in the summer, weddings could be celebrated in a courtyard in the open air, but in the winter, the tables had to be set inside the house. For this reason, the poor people preferred to have weddings in the summer, while the rich, whose houses were spacious enough, had weddings in the winter as well. Finally, it was customary to have the wedding in the middle of the week, on a Tuesday or a Wednesday, but not on a Friday or on the eve of a holiday. In the following description, in order not to confuse the days, we shall assume that the wedding ceremony was held on a Tuesday. It must also be mentioned that, in contrast both to the Muslim custom and to that of the Kurdish Jews in the past,[16] it was not customary among the Jews of Meshhed to consult an astrologer for choosing a lucky day for a wedding, or for any other undertaking for that matter.

'Aqd Bandān: Gentile Wedding

The family conference also had to decide on the manner in which the Muslim wedding, the *'aqd,* would be celebrated. In general, rich families invited the *mujtahid,* the Muslim clergyman, as well as several Shaykhs and other Muslim religious functionaries, to officiate at the wedding. The poor went to the mosque of Imām Reza and had the wedding there. The date for the Muslim wedding was, as a rule, three days before the Jewish wedding. (In this connection, it is interesting to recall that among the Spanish Marranos in the Middle Ages, the order was reversed: first they had the Jewish wedding and then went to the Christian church to celebrate the Christian nuptial.) For the Muslim wedding, both the bride and the groom appointed a *vakīl,* a representative, and these two persons took care of the wedding formalities for and in the name of the couple. The Muslim wedding ritual was considered a ridiculous thing by the Jadīdīm, and when they described it to me, they did so amid much laughter and merriment.[17] The witnesses, who of course were of the Jadīdī community, signed their names on the Muslim marriage contract in Hebrew letters.

From the days of Reza Shah (r. 1925–1941), the authorities were no longer satisfied with a Muslim religious wedding but required the couple to appear before a notary in the marriage bureau (*maḥḍar izdavāj*).

Dīm Vardārān: Taking of Face

Two days before the wedding—that is, on Sunday if the wedding was set for a Tuesday—the women of both families gathered in the bride's house in order to carry out the *dīm vardārān,* "taking of face." This ritual involved beautifying the bride by the removal of all hair, even the faintest and thinnest, from all over her body, and especially from her face and forehead. The women who came over from the bridegroom's house brought along the bath tray (*khāncheh ḥamām*), which was a present of the bridegroom to the bride, to be used by her the next day when she went to the bath. The bath tray contained about fifty pieces of fragrant soap, for the bride and for all the women who accompanied her to the bathhouse; a large quantity of henna; perfumes; face powder; a richly decorated comb; a pair of wooden shoes; all kinds of utensils for the beautification of the body; and money for the expenses of the bath. All this, as well as sweets, was beautifully arranged on the bath tray and tied with a large kerchief (*khāncheh pūsh*).

The process of *dīm vardārān* was carried out by the *dīm vardār,* the "face taker," a woman who had this as her profession. In the Meshhed Jadīdī community, there were some four or five such women. They took care not only of the preparation of the bride on that day but also of her beautification after the wedding, by removing the hair from her face, forehead, and body once a month, after her menses and before she went to immerse herself in the bathhouse.

To begin with, the *dīm vardār* tied a kerchief around the bride's head, pulling it tight over her hair. Then she took a small knife, and with it she scraped downward the thin and short strands of hair that grow over the forehead just at the hairline. Then the groom's mother stepped up to the bride with a gold coin in her hand, pinched one of the short hairs between her nail and the coin, and plucked it out. Then she threw the coin into the lap of the bride and kissed her on the forehead. The coin then was given to the *dīm vardār.* The same act was performed by the other women after the groom's mother, and only after they all had their turn came the time for the *dīm vardār* to get to work seriously on the removal of the superfluous hair from the bride's body. She did this with the help of a thin thread. She first wetted it with water and then made of it a large loop which she twisted around several times. Next she pulled it along the bride's face, so that all the hairs that got caught between the two sides of the loop were plucked out. After the forehead and the face came the rest of the body, from which all hairs were thus removed, except, of course, the hair of the head, which was covered by the kerchief. Lucky was the bride who at the time of this operation had not yet reached puberty, for otherwise the *dīm vardārān* would have caused her considerably more pain.

In order to make the procedure easier for the bride, they gave her candy to eat, while the assembled women performed dances in front of her to entertain her.

The removal of all of the bride's body hair was practiced by the Muslim Persians as well. The account of it given by Nurullah Khan also apprises us of the belief underlying the custom: the bride was taken to the bath, and there they painted her hair, hands, and feet with henna, and removed all her body hair very meticulously, because they believed that there was one single hair of the Angel of Death on the body of the woman, and if that hair remained in its place, bad luck would come upon the whole family.[18]

Harzeh Vazān: Rude Things

The same day (Sunday) in the evening, they gave a meal in the house of the bride in which only women participated, especially the young friends of the bride. This meal was called *harzeh vazān*, "rude things," because there was great merriment as they cheered up the bride with all kinds of games and pranks, and there was no lack of licentious language. The latter, however, was more in evidence at the *harzeh vazān* given at the same time in the bridegroom's house for men and his young friends. In the course of this gathering, the more experienced relatives of the bridegroom made him understand, with hints and joking comments, the meaning of married life. The bride's relatives did the same for her at her meal.

'Arūsi Ḥamām: Bath of the Bride

Next day, Monday, at two or three o'clock in the afternoon, the bride was taken to the bathhouse for the ritual immersion. Before she left her parents' house, her fingernails were carefully cleaned.

Until Ḥājj Y'ḥezq'el built them a bathhouse in the Jewish quarter, the Jadīdīm used one of the Muslim baths that were suitable as a *miqveh* (ritual bath; also called *khazīneh*) from the Jewish halakhic point of view. Rich Jadīdīm would rent the whole bathhouse for the special use of the bride and her entourage, so that they should be able to perform all the rites of the immersion without being disturbed by the presence of strangers. This renting of the bathhouse was called *qoroq*, "special." The poor Jadīdīm who could not afford a *qoroq* sent the bride with her women companions to the bathhouse at a time when it was open for other women as well. Of course, in such a situation, the Jadīdī women had to be more careful about how they acted and what they said than in the presence of the female bath attendants alone, for the latter could be relied upon to keep quiet against the payment of sizable *bakshish*.

The bride was taken to the bathhouse in a festive procession accompanied by musicians, and especially by players on a *dombak*, or tambourine, and a *dā'ireh*, a round drum. Many women from the families of both the bride and the groom were invited to participate in this ritual procession. The women of the bride's family prepared and brought along all kinds of sweets, fruits, cakes, and milk dishes, as well as *kōkō sabzī*, a vegetable omelette, and *sherbet*, sweet drinks. The women's company spent at least three to four hours at the bathhouse, eating, drinking, and bathing, and returned home after sunset.

The bathing itself consisted of several phases. The first was to wash in a tub full of warm water. Then came the immersion in a pool of cold water, which was the ritual *kasher miqveh*. The water in the pool was very cold; in the winter, it was even frozen over, and it was necessary to break the layer of ice in order to be able to submerge oneself.

After this submersion, the *kīseh māl* went to work on the bride. She used a small bag (*kīseh*), with which she smeared a fragrant, pasty cream called *lakhlakheh*, made of a powder mixed with water, all over the body of the bride. This rubdown took some fifteen or twenty minutes, after which the bride again entered the tub to remove the paste. As a result of this treatment, her whole body became clean, soft, and sweet-smelling. The fragrance of the *lakhlakheh* remained and enveloped her body for several days. (It should be mentioned here that the men, when they went to the bathhouse, were similarly treated by a male *kīseh māl*. This treatment, and the *mushtu māl* that followed it, were integral parts of every thorough bathing.) After this bath, the bride proceeded to the other room in the bathhouse in which she had left her clothes, and there, before she could get dressed, she had to undergo a treatment by the *mushtu māl* (masseuse).

After the massage was finished, they painted the soles and the feet of the bride with henna, as a kind of preliminary to the elaborate painting with henna to which the whole night following that day was devoted.

Apart from this visit to the *ḥamām*, which was obligatory for the bride from the point of view of her ritual purity, there was a custom of taking her to the bath (*ḥamām barān*) about a month prior to the wedding. This was a way in which the groom's mother honored the bride. She invited the bride and several women from both families to the *ḥamām* for a joint bath. This ritual was observed only by the rich, who would rent the whole bathhouse for the occasion as a *qoroq*.

According to one of my informants, the bride went twice to the *ḥamām*: once on the day before the wedding (i.e., on Monday), when she was washed thoroughly, as described, and a second time on the wedding day itself (Tuesday), in the morning, for a simple immersion.

For comparison, let us describe briefly the customs attendant to the bathing of the bride among the Muslim Persians. They made the bride sit on a saddle in the bathhouse, with her face turned toward Mecca, and with all the knots in her clothes loosened. In front of the bride they placed a mirror and a comb, and before the mirror they put two lighted candles. A white sheet was draped over her head, sweets were put into her mouth, and two lumps of sugar were rubbed together over her head so that the powder should fall on it. In order to increase her luck, a woman would take a needle and thread it with seven thin colored threads twisted together, and with this thread she would sew back and forth several times through the sheet with which the bride's head was covered. Spices were strewn into the fire which was lit in the *ḥamām* in order to fill the place with a good fragrance.[19]

Dāmād-i ḥamām: Immersion of the Bridegroom

On Tuesday, in the morning, the bridegroom would go to the *ḥamām* in the company of his friends. The men, too, were given sweets, and the bridegroom underwent a treatment by a male *kīseh māl* and a male *mushtu māl,* in a manner similar to that of the bride.

Ḥanā Bandān: Henna Tying

The night before the wedding day (i.e., the night between Monday and Tuesday) was the night of the *ḥanā bandān,* "henna tying." The long and dark corridor that led from the street to the courtyard of the houses of the Jadīdīm was lighted up for that occasion with many candles and lamps. A watchman was seated before the gate of the house on a low chair, with a lamp in his hands in order to show the way to the approaching guests. Men and women did not mingle in this festivity, either, and the father of the bride arranged for suitable places for men and women to gather in separate groups. The whole courtyard was illuminated with lamps (*lāleh*). Musicians, too, were invited, as well as a group of two or three comedians or actors (*muqallad* or *lūṭī*), who occasionally would bring along a monkey, to the greater merriment of the people. These musicians and actor-comedians were Muslims. In past times, they also had a performance of a puppet theater, in a manner similar to that of the engagement night.

The henna had been brought by the women from the house of the bridegroom to that of the bride on the previous day, together with the bath tray. Red henna was used, and the fingertips of the bride were painted with it all around. Then white bandages were tied around her fingers—hence the name "henna tying"—and left there until the morning of the next day. Occasionally, the bridegroom would send a round tray filled with small bags containing henna and candy to the bride's house on the very night of the henna. This gift was called *ṭabaq barān*, "sending of a tray."

On the other hand, on the night of the henna, the family of the bride would send a large number of plates with sweets and candy to the groom, as well as material for a suit of clothes and a pair of shoes. This gift was accompanied by some henna. The young man who carried the trays to the groom's house would dance with them. While this was going on, the bridegroom sat in a place of honor, surrounded by the elders of the community. He was considered a king. The gift-bearers also danced before him in the house. The center of the bridegroom's palms were painted with henna. The festivities of the *ḥanā bandān* lasted at least until midnight.

The Clothes of Bride and Groom

No special clothes were worn for the wedding. Only the fact that both the bride and the groom wore new and luxurious clothes, made especially for the wedding, indicated that this was a great day in their lives. However, the same clothes were worn thereafter on the holidays of the Jewish year.

The bride wore a *yāl,* a short jacket made of dark blue or red velvet (these two colors were the favorites in velvet clothes), with sleeves decorated with gold *guldūzī* (embroidery) with flowery patterns, and with beautiful buttons called *dogmeh* (lit. *dukmeh*). From the hips down, she wore a *shelvār,* a short skirt, also of velvet, which reached to the knees. From the knees to the ankles, the *nezūmi* (trousers) were visible, likewise made of velvet and richly embroidered in gold around the legs. On her feet, she wore *qorjeh sa'rī* (shagreen shoes), in the Gruzinian (Gurji) fashion, made of green, rough, granular leather and shaped like slippers. They covered only the front part of the feet, had high tapering heels, and pointed toes bent up and back in a semicircle. These were the best and most expensive shoes, the like of which were no longer produced by 1945. The head of the bride was covered with a golden kerchief (*chārqad zarī*), to which were sewn small, round, shiny sequins called *pūlak* (literally, "fish scales"). Over all her clothes, the bride wore the "prayer wrap" (*chādor numāz* or *maqna'ah*), which covered her body from the top of the head to her feet.

Of all the clothes worn by the bridegroom, only the hat, the outer coats, and the shoes were visible. The hat (*kulāh*) was tall and conical, made of the black fur of unborn lambs. Under the *kulāh,* he wore a skullcap (*'araqchīn*). At his neck, the shirt (*pīrāhan,* pronounced *pirhan*) could be seen. A sleeveless cloak (*'abā*) descended from his shoulders, open in front, or a cloak with sleeves (*chūkhā*). Under this, the bridegroom wore a long kaftan (*qabā*), also open in the front. Under the *qabā,* he had on a smooth undershirt (*alkholoq;* literally, *alhkāleq*), with a broad and many-colored linen or silk hip belt (*shāl-ī kamar*). On cold days, the bridegroom (and men in general) wore also a *labādeh,* a long overcoat with sleeves, lined with cotton wool and quilted. The *labādeh* was worn under the *'abā* of the *chukhā* but over the *qabā.* At the bottom, under these coats, one could see the trousers (*tanbān*). The bridegroom, too, was shod in *qorjeh sa'ri.*

'Arūsī: The Marriage

On the wedding day, both the bride and the groom fasted until after the ceremony under the wedding canopy, the *ḥuppa.* In the morning, the bandages were removed that had been tied on the evening before around the bride's henna-colored fingers. Then the bride was dressed in her festive red and blue velvet clothes with the rich embroidery. (After World War II, they began to use, instead of these traditional clothes, a white dress.) The bride's hair was braided into thirty to forty thin braids, around which colored papers were tied. On her forehead, they pasted small, round, shiny, confetti-like metal disks (*zarak*) of various colors and sizes. They were to remain in place for several days. These disks were fixed to her forehead with wood glue (*zönj*) and were left until they fell off by themselves. Often, they caused small irritations on the bride's sensitive skin. The application of the *zarak* was carried out by an old woman, who undertook it as a special task.

The *ḥuppa* was set up in the house of the bride about the time of the Minḥa (afternoon prayer). Since the *ḥuppa* was the most visible *Jewish* ritual in all the wedding festivities, it was conducted in secret, in the presence of only a few invited guests. Until the guests assembled, the bride and the groom sat side by side. One of the guests approached them, held out a mirror in front of the bridegroom, and said to him, "Look, what do you see in the mirror?" or words to this effect. The bridegroom looked into the mirror and saw in it his veiled bride.

After a *minyan* (ten adult men) gathered, they locked the door so that no non-Jew should be able to witness the proceedings, and spread a *ṭallit* (prayer shawl) over the heads of the bride and the groom. When the couple stood under the *ḥuppa,* they threw coins (*shābāsh*) at them. These coins were later given to the musicians. Four to six men held the corners of the *ṭallit* over the head of the couple. The *mullah,* the person who functioned as a rabbi, recited the traditional Seven Benedictions and the blessing over the wine. Then the groom and the bride each took a sip of the wine, after which the wine glass was wrapped in a kerchief and the groom threw it to the floor and thus broke it. Since in many

Hebrew marriage contract from Meshhed, dated 5544 (i.e., 1784). Size $23\frac{1}{2}$ x 27 inches. Courtesy of Farajullah Aminoff, Jerusalem.

cases the floor of the room was covered with rich rugs, the groom did not throw the glass on the rugs but hurled it through the window into the courtyard. But if a non-Jewish serving woman happened to be in the courtyard, the bridegroom did not throw the glass there but broke it in the room, near the wall, next to the broom. The moment the glass broke, the people present cried, *Mazzal tov*—"Good luck!" Some of them added, "Thus should break your enemies and the enemies of Israel!"

After the breaking of the glass, the *mullah* read out the text of the *ketubba*, the marriage contract.[20]

The *ṭallit* under which the wedding ceremony was held was a present from the bride to the groom. The bride embroidered its four corners with gold thread.

هو المؤلف بين القلوب
جامع المحب والمحبوب

بسم الله الرحمن الرحيم

Persian Muslim marriage contract of a member of the *Jadīdī* community of Meshhed, dated 1306 H. (1888–89). The signatures of the witnesses are in Hebrew. Size 17 x 26 inches. From the collection of Raphael Patai; gift of the Nasrullayoff family, Jerusalem.

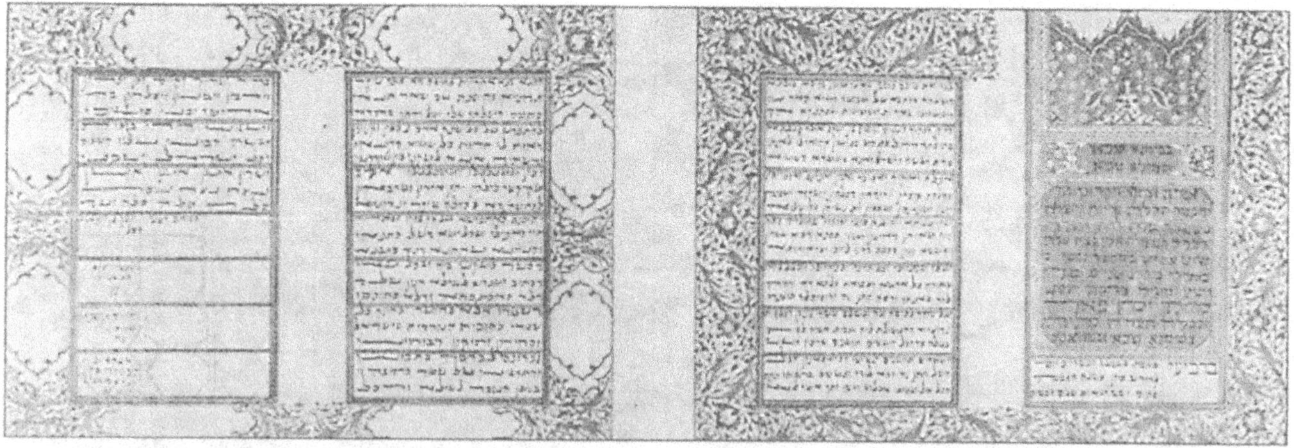

Hebrew marriage contract, dated 5662 (i.e., 1902). Size 26½x 9 inches. Courtesy of Farajullah Ya'quboff, Jerusalem.

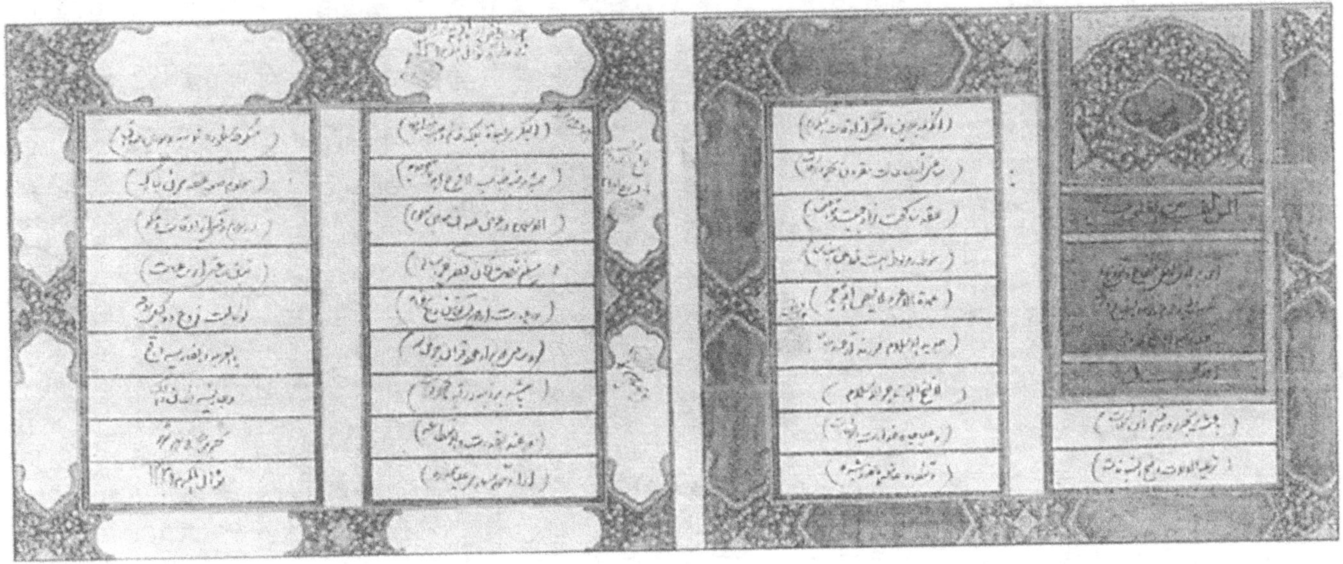

33 Persian Muslim marriage contract of a member of the *Jadīdī* community of Meshhed, dated 1339 H. (1920–21). The signatures of the witnesses are in Persian. Size 23 x 9¾ inches. Courtesy of Farajullah Ya'guboff, Jerusalem.

When the couple moved out from under the *ḥuppa*, those present showered them with candy and sweets. Then the bride and groom, who had fasted up to that time, had a meal consisting of chicken and meatballs, and then some of the assembled guests accompanied the groom to his house.

Immediately after the wedding ceremony, a printed copy of the Five Books of Moses was brought to the bridegroom's house on a tray which also held a jar full of water, candy, and a mirror. At the same time, they also sent, from the bride's house to that of the groom, the bedding the young couple was to use in the first night of their married life.

Majles: Banquet

Now came the main banquets of the wedding, one in the bride's house for the women and one in the groom's for the men. If the wedding took place in the summer, they spread rugs on the brick-paved courtyard of each house and upon them placed mattresses as seats. In front of the mattresses was spread a long white piece of linen, measuring thirty or more meters long and one meter wide, taking up practically the whole length of the courtyard. This linen, called *sufreh*, served as both table and tablecloth. If the number of guests was great—and there were Jewish weddings in Meshhed in which several hundred guests were invited to the banquet—they either set up two rows of mattresses with a *sufreh* in front of each or arranged two rows of mattresses with one *sufreh* between them, with one row of mattresses along the wall. In this case, the elders and honored members of the community would be seated next to the wall so that they could lean against it, while the youths and children sat opposite them on the other side of the *sufreh*. Along the whole length of the tablecloth, they placed large numbers of colored candles, both for light and for decoration. Above the heads of the guests, they stretched a long rope across the courtyard, from which were hung glass-enclosed lamps and paper-covered lanterns.

The preparation of a sumptuous meal for a hundred or more guests required careful planning. For several days before the banquet, large-scale food purchases were made by the two parental couples, each for its own banquet. They bought meat, rice, vegetables, fruits, sugar, and many more ingredients needed for the dishes and the sweet drinks. A task of considerable difficulty was to collect enough pots, pans, plates, and tableware from relatives and friends for the large number of guests invited. The serving, too, had to be organized. The cooking itself was entrusted to expert cooks (*āshpaz*), who labored for several days. The *āshpaz* were non-Jewish men, and their number, for a large banquet, reached ten to fifteen. In the large houses of the Meshhedi Jews, there was no lack of space—the entire ground floor was taken up by kitchens and storerooms—so that there was enough room for the cooks and for a requisite number of servant girls, also non-Jewish, whose task it was in the main to wash the used dishes while the meal was going on and to do other cleanup jobs. The vegetable dishes were prepared in their entirety by the non-Jewish cooks, but the meat reached their hands only after the women of the house had rendered it kosher in the traditional Jewish manner.

A large group of young men from both families undertook the important task of serving the food to the guests in the groom's house and of removing the used plates from the tablecloth to the kitchen. In the bride's house, the same tasks were taken care of by young girls. Thus, both banquets were strictly one-sex affairs. The groom's father directed the voluntary waiters, assisted by five or six men from among his closest friends, issuing an incessant flow of instructions about whom and what to serve. When the waiters saw that the plate in front of a guest was empty, they instantly filled it again from a large perforated ladle (*kafgīr*). In the bride's house, her mother and her friends managed the banquet in a similar manner.

The food was taken from the kitchen to the tablecloth on large copper trays. In front of every two guests, a joint plate (*da'uri*) was placed. It was filled with a mixture of cooked rice and chicken meat (*pelau; pilau*), with half a chicken per *da'uri*, as well as mutton. The *pelau* was eaten with the fingers, without any utensils. After the *pelau*, the waiters served the *sherbet*, a cold drink made with sugar, *hel* (cardamom seeds), which gave it a pleasant aroma, various fruits, such as lemon and melons, saffron, and so on. In the summer, they also put pieces of ice into the *sherbet*, which was served in wide and deep cups (*ṭās*), from which it was spooned up with wooden ladles (*qāshaq chūbī*), two of which were provided for each *ṭās*. They also served *araq*, a strong drink made of raisins. After the *sherbet*, they served seven *khōroshi*, which were dishes of vegetables with meat—whence the name of the wedding banquet menu, *pelau hafkhōroshi*, *pelau* with seven *khōroshi*. The *hafkhōroshi* were served as seven separate dishes, each of which consisted of meat and a different kind of vegetable or fruit, as follows:

1. *Khōrosh nokhōd*, with peas.
2. *Khōrosh qormeh sabzī*, small pieces of fried meat with fried vegetables and onions.
3. *Khōrosh bādenjān*, eggplant.
4. *Khōrosh beh*, quinces.
5. *Khōrosh sīb*, applies.
6. *Khōrosh ālū*, plums.
7. *Kōrosh līvās* (literally, *rīvās*), a kind of rhubarb described as "juicy and sour; sweet at the bottom near the roots and sour at the top, and very widespread in Iran."

Occasionally, instead of the *khōrosh līvās*, they served *khōrosh kangar* (artichokes). These were described as "similar to lettuce, have thorns, and only the thick central part is eaten."

If the seven *khōroshi* were served, no mutton was added to the *pelau* but only the half of a chicken for each *da'uri*. The same dishes were served at weddings among the rich Muslims, except that they used butter and *leben* (a kind of sour milk) for cooking.

Musicians were invited to this banquet, too, and in an even greater number than to all the preceding rites. Usually, they hired a drum band (*sāzeh balabān*) consisting of at least twelve men. Accompanied by this band, the young friends of the bridegroom executed dances in one corner of the courtyard in order to cheer him up. The adult men and the elders said words of moral instruction and delivered homilies, and the whole company sang wedding songs. Only after this had been going on for quite a while did the groom's father announce that the serving of the meal was about to begin, and at that time the last-minute preparations for serving the *pelau* were made in the kitchen. These preparations took, in general, about half an hour, after which the servers began by bringing jars of water with large bowls and towels, holding them for each guest to enable him to wash his hands. Then the *pelau* was brought out, and the meal began.

'Arūs Kashān: Bringing the Bride (or *Lāleh Kashi:* Bringing the Lamp)

When the banquet was finished at about midnight, the father of the bridegroom sent the musicians, together with twenty to thirty young men, to the house of the bride to fetch her. As this deputation was arriving at the bride's house, the members of her family brought her out, surrounded by a crowd of women. Then the procession set out with many lamps and torches, especially around the bride. When the sound of music indicated that the procession was approaching the bridegroom's house, he, too, left his house in the company of his family and friends, so as to meet the bridal procession in the street.

When the two processions had approached to a distance of about a hundred meters, they seated the bride and the groom on chairs in the middle of the street, while the guests lined up along the two sides. The bridegroom's parents then said to the bride's group, "Bring the bride a little nearer!" The answer was, "No, you bring the bridegroom nearer!" One side pushed the chair with the bride a step forward, and the other side did the same with the chair on which the bridegroom sat, and so the bridal couple was gradually brought nearer, step by step. Suddenly, when they were quite near, the company of the bride (or of the groom) would say, "You did not bring the bridegroom (or the bride) near enough," and thereupon they would move the bride (or the bridegroom) back a little distance. When the company of the bridegroom (or the bride) saw this, they, too, took him (or her) back, until the distance between the couple was again as great as in the beginning. This game was repeated several times, until finally they let the bride and groom approach each other. Then both would get up from their chairs, and at that moment the guests, and especially the young men and the children, began to fire toy guns, send up firecrackers, and let go colored balloons under which there were lamps with cotton wool.

Now the father of the bridegroom stepped up to the young couple, took the bride's hand, put it into the hand of the groom, and pronounced a blessing, "Be happy, be good, have much luck." And since it was always possible that Muslims were nearby, since Muslims lived even in the 'Ēdgāh, the Jewish quarter itself, one of those present would remember and say, "Recite a *ṣalāt*," a brief Muslim prayer. Also, when they passed by the house of a Muslim, they would say in a loud voice, "He who loves the religion of Muhammad should mention his name."

The bride and groom kissed the hands of their parents, and then the groom again took the bride's hand in his and led her into the house, followed by the guests. At the moment when the couple reached the door of the house, a lamb or chicken was slaughtered as a *kapparah* (atonement) for the bride who entered the bridegroom's house for the first time. The blood of the animal was allowed to flow to the floor so as to make a line in front of the threshold, and the couple stepped over the line as they entered the house. This sacrifice was called *qodom* (*qadam*, foot), for it served as an atonement for the foot of the bride, the entrance of the bride into the groom's house. The meat was distributed among the poor.

There were some who, for fear of the Muslims, carried out the game of approach and withdrawal not in the street but in the courtyard of the bridegroom's house, after the procession bringing the bride had arrived there. In any case, it was customary to shoot with toy guns and to let fly fireworks similar to bombs at the moment the procession arrived at the groom's house. They also set off *āftau māhtau* (lit. *āftāb-māhtāb*, "sunlight moonlight"), which were firecrackers of various colors and shapes, and let several *fānūsi franji* (European lamps) rise up slowly into the air over the guests' heads. These lamps were paper globes under which they lighted a candle, so that as the air in them warmed up, they rose up, like miniature hot-air balloons. All these fireworks were tended by a special expert. In the courtyard, they also lighted a *hīzam* (bonfire) of dry twigs and danced around it. The groom's party stood on one side and the bride's on the other, with the bonfire in between. Here, too, they took the bride and the groom back and forth, to and from each other, with many jocular requests and refusals. Many of the young men would leap across the fire in their exuberance.

As a comparison to the Jewish custom, let us again refer to Nurullah Khan's description of the Muslim wedding procession. The men gathered in a hall in the bride's house, and the women in the women's rooms. *Sherbet* was served, and then tea and a *narghīleh* (water pipe). When the bride was ready to go, the men formed a procession, after which came a second procession of the women of both families, who surrounded the bride seated on a richly caparisoned Bahrein donkey. However, the bride's father and mother remained at home. The moment the bride left the house, her youngest brother gave her some bread, salt, and cheese tied in a kerchief. Before the bride walked a man who held in his hands a mirror turned toward her face. On the way, women of her family repeatedly held up the procession demanding presents, which had to be given to them by the groom's family. When the bride approached the groom's house, the women in her entourage stopped and declared that they would not go on until the bridegroom appeared. The groom, upon hearing the approaching sound of music and the noise of the fireworks, would leave his house and go to receive his bride. When the women saw him, they cried, "We have received you! You have made great exertions!" Then the bridegroom turned around and thus led the bridal procession back to his house. When the procession reached the street in which the groom's house was located, his family sacrificed five lambs in order to avert the Evil Eye, and the procession passed between the lambs' bodies on one side and their heads on the other. The meat was distributed among the watchmen, the musicians, and others.[21]

The Union

To return to the marriage customs of the Meshhedi Jews: when the bride and the groom entered the room in which their union and first cohabitation was to take place, the groom tried to step on the foot of the bride. If he succeeded, it was believed he would realize the words of the Bible, "and he shall rule over thee" (Gen. 3:16). But the bride, who was warned in advance by her mother and older girlfriends, tried to prevent him from doing so. Nurullah relates that his bride tried to step on his foot, but he avoided her and managed to step on her foot, so as to rule over her all his life.[22]

In the wedding chamber, the groom and the veiled bride sat down side by side, but they were still not alone. Several of the family members entered with them; they took the mirror that was brought to the groom's house, together with the cup of water and the printed copy of the Torah, and held up the mirror before the couple. Then it was time for the bride to lift her veil, and she and the groom looked at each other for the first time in the mirror—so that their lives might be as bright and shining as the mirror. This custom was called *ayneh* (lit. *ā'īneh*) *Torah*, "mirror Torah."

The groom's father then opened the Torah at random and read a few lines from the top of the page. Next, the groom's mother opened the book the same way, and since women in general could not read, again the groom's father read a few lines for her at the top of the page. This rite was a kind of augury, in order to know what sort of life awaited the young couple. But almost every passage in the Torah could be given a favorable meaning.[23]

This was followed by a presentation of various sweets, especially sugared almonds, to the bride. She took the sweets into the palm of her hand, and the groom picked one candy directly out of her hand with his mouth and ate it. Then the mother of the groom took a candy in the same fashion from the bride's hand, and, following her, the other relatives of the groom did likewise. This custom was called *kaf dasi nabāt* (sugar from the palm of the hand), and its purpose was to make sure that the bride would bring sweetness into the house of the bridegroom. From the moment the groom's relatives ate the sweets from the hand of the bride, she was again allowed to speak to them. Then the bridegroom, too, took sweets into his hand, and the bride ate one candy from his hand. Everybody stood up while this eating went on. A few minutes later, all those present would leave the room, and bride and groom were finally left alone.

Some ten or twenty experienced women from both families, however, would sit down in front of the closed door of the wedding chamber. They were termed *yengeh* (witness, actually bridesmaid), and they incessantly emitted the high trilling sound of *lu-lu-lu-lu-lu,* the typical Middle Eastern sound of female jubilation, produced by the rapid vibration of the tongue or the uvula. The stated purpose of this noisemaking was to prevent any sound from the wedding chamber from being heard outside. The women also had a popular tradition according to which women had uttered this sound—or, more precisely, *Leah-Leah-Leah-Leah*—ever since Laban brought Leah, instead of Rachel, into the tent of Jacob. On that occasion, the women wanted to warn Jacob by trilling *Leah-Leah-Leah-Leah,* but he did not understand them.

Since, in general, the bridegroom was a young boy without any sexual experience—even though both he and the bride received some jocular instruction at the *harzeh vazān* meal—the women witnesses had, in most cases, to wait until the morning for the bridegroom to emerge from the wedding chamber. Thereupon they would enter in order to see whether any blood was visible on the sheet or on the bride's gown. Often it happened, especially in times past, that because the bride was so young, the first intercourse did not take place on the wedding night but only much later, even several years later. Because of the very early marriages and the extremely strict supervision of the daughters, it never happened—according to the unanimous testimony of all the informants—that a bride should be found not to be a virgin. The bloodstained sheet or gown was shown by the women to all the guests, and then the bride's parents would keep it.[24]

The custom of placing a mirror before the bridal couple was practiced among the Muslim Persians as well, and it is possible that the Jews of Meshhed adopted it from them. Nurullah Khan describes how he and his bride saw each other in the mirror placed before the bride. However, before she let him see her visage in the mirror, he first had to give her an expensive present, a ring with a pearl set into it.[25] The same custom was followed by the Muslims in Meshhed: on both sides of the mirror in which the bride and groom caught the first glimpse of each other, there were burning candles, and in front of the mirror was placed a copy of the Koran with dishes of sweets around it.[26]

The Day after the Wedding

Next morning (Wednesday), two or three friends of the bridegroom came to his house and took him first to the bath and then to the synagogue. In the synagogue, all those present rose when the bridegroom entered, and they sang special songs in his honor. In general, they treated him as if he were a king, for the bridegroom was considered a king, a Shah. If he knew how to pray, he functioned as the prayer leader both on that morning and at the services on the Sabbath three days later. If he was not versed in the art of the prayers, each of which had its own special melody, his father or another relative took his place. On the Sabbath, he was also called up as third to the reading of the Torah (after the Kohen and the Levite, who always have the first two places), and as he went up to the reading desk, the people threw candy and sweets at him.

On the day after the wedding, the *jehāz* (dowry) was sent from the bride's house to that of the bridegroom. This was done in a procession, with as much pomp and circumstance as the family could manage. Many porters carried the bride's belongings and the dowry she received from her parents. This was an occasion for the bride's parents to parade the riches and variety of presents they gave their daughter and to show them demonstratively to the bridegroom and his family. For this reason, they employed a large number of porters, each of whom carried much less than what he would have been capable of. At the head of the *jehāz* procession, they sent the bride's clothes which had been prepared in the course of many years, and the clothes they had sewn for her from the fabrics given her by the bridegroom. Gold and silver jewelry was, of course, an integral part of the *jehāz,* which also contained all kinds of kitchenware, cooking utensils, tableware, and bedding (in addition to the set of bedding that was sent in advance for the wedding night). Furniture and furnishings, rugs, boxes to keep the clothes in, and so on, also were sent. The porters usually were Muslims whose wives worked in the Jewish houses as maids, cooks, and servants. They were mostly from Seistan, for the people of Seistan were known to be good, quiet, and patient.

Among the Muslim Persians, the *jehāz* was sent to the bridegroom's house on the very day of the wedding, before the arrival of the bride herself. Nurullah Khan relates that this was done on the afternoon of his wedding day. The procession of porters passed all the major streets of the town, so that everybody should see the riches of the presents. There were many pieces of furniture, such as cushions and featherbeds, gold-embroidered velvet curtains, lamps, candlesticks, copper and china vessels, cups and saucers for tea and coffee, and many other objects of utility and luxury. All this was carried by the porters on large trays. The rugs and boxes full of the bride's clothes were carried by richly caparisoned mules, with bells hanging from both sides of their necks.[27] Jakob Polak, who spent several years in Persia in the 1850s, describes the *jehāz* in great detail. He remarks that these things remained the property of the wife, and the husband could in no way dispose of them. He comments also on the artificial lengthening of the procession of porters, by, for example, loading empty boxes on the backs of the mules.[28]

Shab Sūr: The Night of the Repast

This day (Wednesday) came to a close with a *majles* (festive meal) in the groom's house. This meal was called *shab sūr* (night of the repast), and the main course was *chlau nokhōdau,* a rice and vegetable soup. In the course of this meal took place the *jehāz numai* (exhibition of the dowry). In a separate room, they would set out everything sent from the bride's house, lifting up each object in turn to show it to the guests, and the groom's parents and other relatives would come to view each piece and to estimate its momentary value.

The Seven Days of the Feast

Among the Muslim Persians, it was customary for the bridegroom to refrain from touching the bride for three days after the first cohabitation. When the three days were up, the bride went to the *ḥamām* to immerse herself, and then she was again permitted to the bridegroom. In the beginning of their Marrano existence, the Jadīdīm adopted this custom and considered the bride unclean for three days only. Only occasionally did it happen that the bridegroom's mother warned him on his wedding day, "For seven days you are not allowed to touch the bride!" During World War I, a *ḥakham* (a learned man, rabbi) came to Meshhed from Samarkand in Turkestan, one Mullah Ḥazqi by name (he died in 1944 in Jerusalem), and he introduced a very strict rule, prohibiting the bridegroom from touching the bride for fourteen days after the first cohabitation; that is, there were seven days of uncleanness and seven days of purification, exactly as observed at the time of the regular menses. The Jadīdīm, who always set store by family purity, accepted this stricture.

For seven days after the wedding, the bride and groom were not allowed to leave the house without a retinue. In general, they rarely went out of the house during that week, and if they did, a group of relatives and friends would accompany them. According to the Meshhedi view, the reason for this was the fear of demons.

During those seven days, the bride and groom also were forbidden to do any work. Every day, they put on new clothes, and the clothes they wore they did not return to the *boqche* (lit. *baghcheh*), the bundle tied in a large kerchief in which clothes were usually kept, but hung them from a rope in the room, because to fold up the garments and to tie them in the *boqche* was considered work.

After the festive week was over, workaday life began for the young couple, and the bridegroom often left immediately on a long business trip to another city or abroad. Nevertheless, for a whole year after the wedding, the young wife was referred to as a "bride." During that year, she wore the festive dresses in which she was clad during the wedding ceremony.

Polygyny

Although polygyny was permitted according to both Muslim and Jewish law, only a very few Jews in Meshhed had more than one wife simultaneously. Only if the first wife was barren, or sick and bedridden for a long time, did the heads of the community occasionally give their consent to a man to marry a second wife. In those instances, each of the two wives had to have a separate room of her own.

One of my informants told me that, having had no children from his first wife, he wanted to marry a second one, but the leaders of the community did not permit it. And although this lack of consent had only a moral force, it was strong enough to keep him from marrying a second wife despite his deep desire to have children.

Divorce

While polygynous marriages were very rare, divorce did not exist at all in the community. For more than a hundred years that were remembered firsthand or known secondhand by the old people in the community, there had not been a single case of divorce. Mullah Ḥazqi of Samarkand wanted to allow divorce, but a veritable storm of protest arose, and the *mullah* had to back down. His attempt to permit divorce was held against him, and he had to leave Meshhed and move to Jerusalem.

A Jewish Wedding Song from Meshhed

The language of the song below is typical of the Judeo-Persian spoken by the Jews of Meshhed. The italicized words are Hebrew terms and expressions, several of them taken from the Hebrew liturgy. The spelling of these words in the Meshhedi Jadīdī script is entirely phonetic in the manuscript I had at my disposal; ***ḥtn*** (bridegroom) is spelled ***ḥātān; Ysral*** (Israel) is spelled *Yṣrā'īl,* etc. The expression *Ya'qūb nabī* (or *navi:* "the prophet Jacob") shows Muslim influence; in Jewish sources, Jacob does not have the title "prophet."

WEDDING SONG

Shodi *ḥātān,* mubārak bād,
Hashem poshto panāhat bād,
Tavīle omr hamrāhad bād,
Benik nāmi dar *Yisrael*
Shlaḥ go'el shlaḥ go'el!
Z'khut ne'eman Y'qutiel.

You became a bridegroom, be blessed,
God behind you be your shield,
Long life be with you,
With a good name in Israel.
Send the Redeemer, send the Redeemer!
The merit of faithful Y'qutiel.

Hashem bāshad b'tō yāvar,
Shavand khoshnūd pedar mādar,
Modām bāshi saro sarvar
Miyāne qom *Yisrael.*
Shlaḥ . . .

God be your helper,
Let father, mother rejoice,
Be always head, prince
In the people of Israel.
Send . . .

Nedā āmad ke yā Musa:
B'gīr dar dast to in āsā,
Boro dar Mesr b'kon *nēs*-hā
Barāye qom *Yisrael.*
Shlaḥ . . .

A vision came, O, to Moses:
Take the staff in your hand,
Go to Egypt, make miracles
For the people of Israel.
Send . . .

Alām vāri bolandam kon,
Agar zeshtam pasandam kon,
Agar talkham chun qandam kon,
Miyāne jāme *Yisrael.*
Shlaḥ . . .

Like a flag raise me up,
If I am ugly, choose me,
If I am bitter, make me like sugar,
In the people of Israel.
Send . . .

Qadat chun sarv āzādast,
Rukhat chun māh khodā dādast,
Chun Yusef shākh shemshādast,
Shavi jabbār dar *Yisrael.*
Shlaḥ . . .

Your stature like a free cedar,
Your face like the moon which God gave,
Like Joseph, a cypress branch,
Be a hero in Israel.
Send . . .

Khodā bāshad negāh dārat,
Dehad pirūz dar har kārat,
Bovad mādām sar dārat,
V'ham bar qom Yisrael.
Shlaḥ . . .

God be your guardian,
Let Him give success in all your deeds
Let Him always watch your head,
And also the people of Israel.
Send . . .

Shavad omrat chun *Ben Amram*,
Shavi del shād zefarzandān
Chun Yaqub *navi* pordān,
Bekāme del dar *Yisrael.*
Shlaḥ . . .

Let your life be like the son of Amram,
Let your heart rejoice in sons
Wise like Jacob the prophet,
With heart's desire in Israel.
Send . . .

Hame yāran qam khārān,
Bebazm āyid sar dārān,
Sarūd khanīd sad hazārān,
Jamī qom *Yisrael.*
Shlaḥ . . .

All my friends and well-wishers,
The banquet guests and the princes,
Sing a hundred thousand songs,
The community of the people of Israel.
Send . . .

Z'khut Moshe uSh'mu'el,
Dar ayāmat shavad *go'el,*
Dar *bet hamiqdāsh shirā hādāsh*
Dar *Yisrael shlaḥ go'el.*
Shlaḥ . . .

The merit of Moses and Samuel,
In your days let the Redeemer be,
In the Temple a new song
To Israel send the Redeemer.
Send . . .

B'siman tov shodī *ḥātān,*
Shavad yāvar tora soltān,
Shavi qāleb tovar shaytān,
Qavi bar din(e) *Yisrael.*
Shlaḥ . . .

In a good sign you become a bridegroom,
May the Sultan [God] be your shield,
Be victorious over Satan,
Strong in the religion of Israel.
Send . . .

Besho khosh (nūd) behamzādat,
Nesībat in khodā dāde
Torā hamrāh, ferestāde
Hamān soltān *Yisrael.*
Shlaḥ . . .

Rejoice in your spouse,
The noble one, whom God gave
To be your spouse: she was sent
By the Sultan [God] of Israel.
Send . . .

Dar in haft rūz to āzādi,
Ba bazm eysh bepardāzi,
Valī khod rā nayandāzi
Zerasme dīn(e) *Yisrael.*
Shlaḥ . . .

In those seven days you are free,
Them you shall spend in joy,
But let yourself not fall away
From the law of the religion of Israel.
Send . . .

Zahokme qādere yaktā
Ke tā yek sāl bā hamtā
Shavīd mashqūl bar eysh'hā,
Bebīnīd khēr dar *Yisrael.*
Shlaḥ . . .

At the command of the only omnipotent
For one year with your spouse
Be busy with rejoicings,
See the good of Israel.
Send . . .

Khodā bāshād nazīre to,
Behamrāhe vazīre to
Shavad dōlat asīre to,
Shavī nāmdạr dar *Yisrael.*
Shlaḥ . . .

Ayā *ḥātān,* tōī qābel,
Omīdhāyat shavad hāsel,
Dar ayāmat shavad vāsel
Daru *shefa b'Yisrael.*
Shlaḥ . . .

Arūsat kāmdārat bād,
Shavad az qam delat āzād,
Khānahat rā konad ābād,
Benīk nāmī dar *Yisrael.*
Shlaḥ . . .

Hame kāmi ziyek digar
Bebīnītān dar barābar,
Eysho eshrat ham sarāsar;
Honarmandān dar *Yisrael.*
Shlaḥ . . .

Shavid lāyek befarzāndān
Khodā tarsān vehūshmandān;
Bebārad bar to chun bārān
Nemate haq dar *Yisrael.*
Shlaḥ . . .

Agar mā khod gonahkārīm
Shafā'at khāh basī dārim,
Chun Mūsā pishe ḥaq dārim,
Nemitarsim zehīc *mamzer.*
Shlaḥ . . .

Darān ayām ke ū āyad,
Dar(e) *shefā* begoshāyad,
Digar *gālūt* nafarmāyad,
Kesi bar qome *Yisrael.*
Shlaḥ . . .

Bet hamiqdāsh shavad ābād,
Azīn *gālūt* shavim āzād,
Ravīm khāne shavīm del shād,
Zenūre khāse *Yisrael.*
Shlaḥ . . .

God be your guard,
With your *vezīr* [i.e., wife]
Let riches be captive to you,
Be a man of name in Israel.
Send . . .

O bridegroom, be capable,
May what you hope come to you,
In your days let there be and received
A gate of plenty in Israel.
Send . . .

May your bride give you satisfaction,
Let your heart be free of sorrow,
She will build your house,
With a good name in Israel.
Send . . .

All the wishes of one from the other
May you see [fulfilled] in each other,
Joy and happiness all the time;
Be nimble in Israel.
Send . . .

Be worthy of sons
Who will fear God and will be wise;
May descend upon you like rain
The blessing of the God of Israel.
Send . . .

Even if we commit sins
We have many mediators,
Like Moses before God we have,
We shall not fear any bastard.
Send . . .

In that time, when he [the Messiah] will come,
The door of plenty will be opened,
Exile will not be decreed again,
By anybody upon the people of Israel.
Send . . .

The Temple will be rebuilt,
Of this exile we shall be free,
We shall go home with a joyful heart,
From a special light of Israel.
Send . . .

Hame āyim bedel khāhi,	We shall come with a willing heart,
Bedō cheshmāne bīnāī,	With two eyes [we shall] see,
Shekhīnā rā biyāvarāni,	Bring the Shekhina for us,
Tamāme qom(e) *Yisrael.*	All the people of Israel.
Shlaḥ . . .	Send . . .
Hame khānīm khodā lāhu,	We all say thanks to Him,
Hazaq barukh. Anjām shod.	Be strong and blessed. Finished.[29]

Postscript

Although by the early twentieth century, the customs of betrothing a newborn girl and of actually celebrating the wedding of a girl at the tender age of ten or eleven were no longer observed, their memory survived as something that was practiced "in the good old days." In 1966, Tziyon Zabīḥī related:

> Once I asked my mother: "How old were you when you got married?" She said: "Ten years old. Other girls, too, were married at that age fifty years ago." I asked her: "Why? A ten-year-old girl still wants to play with dolls; what is this?" She explained: "They married off the girls so early so as not to marry them to a Muslim. If the girl remained in the house [of her parents] until the age of fifteen or sixteen, the Muslims could come and ask to marry her to a Muslim youth. . . ." Moreover, on the very day a girl child was born, they announced that she was engaged to so-and-so, a nephew or a cousin, or the like. This was done so that in case a Muslim should come and ask for her hand, they should be able to say that she was already engaged. This could be done because the Meshhedi Jews were like one big family who were all intermarried among themselves. Very few Jews of Meshhed married non-Meshhedi Jews. This was still the situation about twenty years ago [in the 1940s]. Thereafter, of course, they started to move away, to travel to other places, and gradually they began to intermarry with others. Still, for a while, this custom continued even in Jerusalem, where the Jews of Meshhed married only among themselves, but it no longer exists. My little sister, for instance, is married to a Jewish youth from Poland.

25
Burial Customs

The following account is based on oral information supplied by Farajullah Nasrullayoff, head of the Meshhedi Jewish community in Jerusalem, and by M. Gohari, a member of the same community.

In Qazwin

In the city of Qazwin, the previous hometown of the Jews of Meshhed, it was the custom that as soon as a person died, they laid him on the floor with his feet pointing to the west, the direction of Hēkhal Zion (the Temple of Zion). Although the direction was westward, toward Jerusalem, they called it *mizraḥ* (East), just as later, until the very end of their sojourn in Meshhed, the Jews used to hang *mizraḥ* tablets (indicating the direction of prayer) on the west side. At the head of the deceased, they put an oil lamp and watched it carefully lest it go out. They covered the body with a white sheet, on top of which they put all his possessions, including his silver and gold and the legal documents pertaining to any immovable property he owned.

All members of the family, young and old, would sit down on the floor around the body. The richer the deceased, and the more important the family to which he belonged, the greater were the wailing, mourning, and crying over his death. Each of those present would hold two pebbles in his hand and beat them together according to the rhythm of the dirges. This was a custom that, according to their tradition, the Jews of Qazwin had brought with them from Babylonia.[1] When a visitor entered the house, they began the wailing anew. This order of wailing and reciting dirges was continued until the deceased was taken to the cemetery and the mourners returned to their homes.

The ceremonial washing of the dead was performed as follows. Next to the spring outside the city, they pitched a tent,[2] into which they placed the box or casket on which the body was laid for the washing. The deceased was brought into the tent, and they washed the body with pure water taken from the spring.

They used a special soap, called "Zion" because it was made of pure olive oil imported for this specific purpose from the holy city of Jerusalem, which they referred to as Zion. With this soap and the spring water, they washed the body seven times. After the last thorough rinsing of the body, they plugged all of its orifices with clean cotton wool. They did not shave the hair of his head,[3] nor did they pare his fingernails.[4] If the deceased was a woman, they did not even comb her hair.

The shroud was made of fine and expensive white linen.[5] It consisted of a shirt, long trousers, a vest in the shape of a small *ṭallit* (prayer shawl), and over all this a long coat. The head of the deceased was covered with a cap and wrapped in a turban. When all this was done, the body was wrapped in a sheet tied over his head, at his hip, and at his feet.

The coffin was made of polished nut-tree wood. They made sure that the coffin should not become wet, because any wetness would again render the body unfit until after the *ṭahara* (ritual washing) was completed. However, if the coffin became wet from rain, this was not considered to cause impurity.[6] The deceased was eulogized in the tent, and then they took him in a procession to the cemetery.

In the cemetery, a two-cubit-deep grave was dug. Since the Persian cubit was a double cubit, it corresponded to about one meter; the depth of the grave, therefore, was about two meters. The grave was referred to as *serdabeh* (cold room, crypt). It actually was given the shape of a room, into which the body was introduced from the side, and not from the top, through an antechamber, a ramp that slanted downward from the ground level. In order to be ready for any eventuality, they always had ten to fifty such "cold rooms" prepared in advance. After the body was placed in the grave, they closed its side entrance with bricks. On top of the grave, they set a large tombstone, which also was prepared in advance. After the burial, they chiseled into the tombstone a brief elegy in Hebrew Rashi script.

Thus far Gohari's account. According to Nasrullayoff, the custom of burial in the *serdabeh* continued in Meshhed until the middle of the nineteenth century. He explained that the *serdabeh* was a sort of artificial cave dug into the slope of a mountain, or in a place where the ground was slanting, and it served as a family tomb. The dead were laid one beside the other on the floor of the cave, which then was closed up. The cave remained closed until the next death in the family, when it was opened to receive the new body. According to him, this was a Muslim custom, and in the courtyard of Imām Reza's tomb, there were several such caves.

To return to Gohari's description of burials in Qazwin: as long as the Jewish community was small, not only the members of the deceased's immediate family but all those who accompanied the dead to the cemetery would perform the rite of *qri'ah,* making a cut or a tear in their outer garment as a sign of mourning upon their return from the interment. Then they all sat in mourning until the following day.[7]

The mourners sat on the floor, and over their heads they spread a black linen covering. A bowl full of food was placed before them, which was replaced by a new one for every meal. The black covering was called "mourning screen," and the mourners sat under it from morning to evening for seven days. This screen prevented the mourners from seeing anybody, and the visitors who came to comfort them could neither see them nor hear their wailing and crying. Only the mourning children were exempt from sitting under this screen. All the visitors who entered the house of mourning would themselves wail and cry, and in the course of the seven days of mourning, all the members of the community would come to participate in the sorrow of the mourners.

Since the visitors had to be offered a meal, the mourning family had to bear great expenses during the seven days of mourning. For this reason, if the bereaved family was poor, the members of the community, each according to his means, participated in the expenses. Also, on the thirtieth day after the burial and on its anniversary, meals were given in the mourners' house for all members of the community. However, two or three generations later, when the number of the Jews in Qazwin had grown, the custom of tearing the garments of all the participants in the burial was confined to the mourners themselves. A change was also introduced in connection with the mourning screen. Although the mourners continued to sit under it, it was arranged so that they could see the faces of those who came to comfort them. They were also allowed to raise their voices in wailing and crying.

A short time prior to the transfer of the Jews from Qazwin to Meshhed, a great change took place in the mourning customs: the screen was abolished altogether, and the shiny, polished nut-wood coffin was replaced by a simple one made of rough eucalyptus planks. Opposition to the participation of nonfamily members in the mourning rites grew, and the tearing of garments and the sitting on the floor by outsiders came to be considered a sin that would bring about a death in the families of those who performed them. Because of the growth of the community, all members were no longer invited to the mourning meals, but only the rich and the leaders. On the other hand, the custom developed of purchasing 100 cubits of linen, from which they made the shroud for the deceased as well as mourning shirts for the relatives and acquaintances who wore them on the day of the burial. Those who came to comfort the mourners would take some ashes from a bowl prepared for this purpose and put it on their foreheads. They would be given a cup of black coffee without sugar. Visitors would read a few chapters from the Book of Psalms and then leave without the customary greeting.

In Meshhed

When somebody died, all the members of the community participated in the traditional death rites. They washed the body in the cellar of the house. Except for this change and for the abolition of the use of Zion soap, the washing and the burial continued according to the old customs. However, the shroud was no longer made of expensive fine linen but rather of simple "Arab cloth." The dead were buried in the Jewish cemetery, the land for which was acquired by the Jews soon after their arrival in Meshhed. The cemetery was located within the city, near the Jewish houses. Since the cemetery was small, they reduced the size of the graves to the minimum, about two meters long and three-quarters of a meter wide. In place of the mourning shirt which they had used in Qazwin, they gave a kerchief to each of those who accompanied the dead to the cemetery.[8] The old tombstone inscriptions were in most cases written in faulty Hebrew.

During the decades after the 1839 Allahdād, the death customs observed were partly of Jewish and partly of Muslim origin. When they saw that a person was about to die, they were careful lest he or she notice anything that could be interpreted as a preparation for his or her demise. Only in the very last minute did the nearest relative put his hand over the eyes of the dying person, and the latter, if he was able to, would recite the Sh'ma' Yisrael, "Hear, O Israel, the Lord our God, the Lord is One."[9] Immediately after the dying person gave up his soul, they lifted him from the mattress and blankets on which he lay and placed him on the floor, with his head under the niche that was in the eastern wall of the room, so that his feet pointed to the west, toward Jerusalem. On the ledge of the niche, above the head of the deceased, they put a lighted oil lamp. Placing a second candle at the feet of the deceased was discontinued in the years prior to 1944.[10] Then a white sheet was placed over the body, including the face. All the water found in the house, in any jar, pot, or vessel, was poured out, because it had become defiled. But if there was water in the *miqveh* (ritual bath), one did not have to pour it out, for it remained pure.[11]

It was customary to provide oneself well in advance with white linen for sewing the shroud in case of death. When death occurred, one member of the family immediately notified those people in the community who made it their voluntary task to take care of the burial rites. While these were busy washing the body, women volunteers began to sew the shroud.

The body was washed in the courtyard of the house. The community had in its possession a tent and a box for washing the dead. The tent was set up in the courtyard, the box placed in it, and the body was laid out on top of the box. There it was washed three times with warm water and soap from Jerusalem and then rinsed with cold water. (In the Persian Jewish community in Jerusalem, the use of soap was given up.) With the help of a tube, the body was cleansed on the inside as well. Burning candles were placed at its head and feet. According to Gohari, a custom taken over from the Muslims was to sprinkle the washed body with clear water, with water mixed with *sadr v'kāfūr* powder, a kind of lemon salt, or to strew this powder on it in a dry form. The property of this powder is that he who eats of it loses his sexual desire. They sprinkled the dead with it so that his heart should be able to tear itself away from this world and that he should not yearn for his family. According to Nasrullayoff, *sadr* is a white powder similar to salt, which they put into the water with which they wash the body. This *sadr* is not identical with *sedr*, which is an unguent made of lotus leaves and similar to henna, with which the Persians used to anoint themselves after bathing.[12] *Kāfūr* is, of course, camphor. According to Nasrullayoff, they used to sprinkle *kāfūr* powder—which is a very cold substance and a remedy for a hot nature—upon the body of the dead after it was washed.[13] Plugging the orifices of the body was practiced by both Jews and Muslims. Contrary to their former custom, the Jadīd al-Islām used to pare the nails and cut the hair of the dead.[14]

After the washing, the rabbi of the community circumambulated the body seven times. Each round was accompanied by the breaking of a small earthenware jar full of water, which had been placed for this purpose upon the box next to the body.[15] At each round, moreover, one of those present would throw a coin into the air so that it should fall outside the tent. If a Muslim happened to be nearby, they omitted the rounds altogether. But if there was no fear of being observed, others participated in the round walk in addition to the rabbi. After the washing, the sons of the deceased sprinkled some dust into his eyes, which it was believed would cause the eyes, which had been open until that moment, to close by themselves. This was in accordance with the saying frequently quoted by both Jews and Muslims, "Only earth satisfies the eyes of men."[16] Thereafter, pads of cotton wool were placed upon the eyes of the deceased.

If there were Muslim houses near enough to the courtyard in which they set up the tent for the Muslims to see what was going on, they clothed the deceased in the shroud inside the tent. If there was no such danger, they carried the body out of the tent, put him on a rug, and then dressed him.

The shroud was made of cotton cloth which the deceased had purchased for himself while still alive. Part consisted of a pair of long trousers that reached below the soles of the feet. Each leg of the trousers was tied in a knot under the feet, like a sack. Another part was a long shirt that reached to the feet, made of a square of cotton cloth of about two by two meters. In its middle, they made an opening, and thus it was draped over the head of the deceased. This shirt was called "the dress of Adam, the first man." Over the shirt, they put on a coat about as long as the body; this coat opened in the front, and its two sides were folded over the chest. The hands of the deceased were placed over his belly, so that one palm rested on the other. The head was covered with a turban. The mouth, nose, and ears were wrapped in a white veil. On the chest, they put a seal made of clay brought from one of the Muslim holy places. They also placed upon the body the beads he used during his lifetime in order to know whether his endeavors would succeed or were doomed to failure. These two rites were executed in accordance with the Muslim custom. Under each armpit, they put a staff, which was to serve him as a support in the hour of the resurrection of the dead. This, too, was adapted from the customs of the Muslims, who put two green willow twigs under the armpits of their dead.[17] Over the entire shroud came a white sheet, tied above the head and under the feet, and fastened with a belt tied over the navel.

The men who washed and dressed the dead were allowed to look into his face. The relatives of the deceased who wished that he would appear to them in a dream did not look at his face. If they did not want him to appear, and in order that they should not yearn for him too much, they uncovered his face and looked at it.[18]

When all the preparations were finished, the deceased was placed in a coffin that was wider at the head and narrower at the feet. This coffin, in which the dead rested only on the way from his house to the cemetery, had four or six legs. It was carried on the shoulders,[19] and the bearers often changed places on the way. Sons accompanied their dead father to the cemetery.

The coffin was wrapped in a white cloth, and on top of it they placed an embroidered blanket of varying colors. If the deceased was a man, they put a turban on the middle of the coffin and tied it on; if it was a woman, they wrapped her coffin in a large woman's veil. All this was in accordance with the Muslim custom, since the coffin had to be carried through streets inhabited by Muslims. If the deceased was a greatly respected man, a rabbi, or a scion of a leading family, they covered his body with a *ṭallit* inside the coffin, but not on the outside, lest it be recognized that he was a Jew.

After the Allahdād, for about fifty years (from 1839 to about 1890), the Jadīdīm had to follow the Muslim custom in the public religious part of the burial. They washed the body in the house, in secret, and put the shroud on it according to the Jewish custom, but from the moment they left the house until the actual interment, they had to observe the Muslim burial customs. Following the Muslim custom, if the deceased was an important person, they organized a great procession in which large crowds participated. A group of men would beat their chests according to the rhythm of the dirge; another group would take up iron chains tied to the ends of sticks and whip their own backs with them, over the right and left shoulders alternately, this according to the rhythm. In the funeral procession of a woman, they would lead a white horse covered with beautiful cloths and colored shawls, with two swords hanging on its two flanks. For the funeral of a man, they would place a turban and two swords on the back of the horse which was led in front of the coffin, while the people participating in the procession followed the bier. In this manner, the procession went from the house of the deceased to a *ziyāra* (visitation; lit. *ziyārat,* pilgrimage) at the shrine of the Imām Reza. There the deceased was eulogized, parts of the Koran were read for him, and the coffin was taken around the tomb of Imām Reza. Finally, they moved on to the cemetery (after a number of years, the Jadīd al-Islām were again able to purchase a separate cemetery for themselves). But even in the grave, they were forced to orient the body toward Mecca, that is, to the south of the direction of Jerusalem.

The shapes of the grave and the tombstone were like those in Qazwin. On the sixth day after the funeral, both the Muslims and the Jadīdīm would go to the cemetery, to take a meal and stay there until the evening.

In the cemetery, there was a spacious house, and in it was a table upon which they would place the body. Next to it they put seven coins, and, accompanied by prayers, they threw the coins one by one to the outside.[20] In some cases, it was only in the cemetery that they sprinkled dust into the eyes of the deceased; for this purpose, they opened the topmost sheet which covered his face after they had placed him in the grave.

The body was put in the grave without the coffin. Over the body, they left a space, and somewhat higher, upon a ledge in the grave, they placed stone slabs that effectively closed the grave. Over these slabs, they poured earth, until the grave was completely filled up.

On the way to the cemetery and back, they recited Muslim prayers. If no Muslims were present at the interment, they recited the Kaddish, the Jewish prayer for the dead, over the grave. If a Muslim was present, they omitted it and recited it after they returned to the house of the mourners. The Muslim custom demanded that the mourners make a rent in their shirts, mourn for the dead three days, and then sew up the rent shirts; therewith the mourning ritual was actually finished. Not so among the Jadīdīm. When the company returned from the cemetery, they washed their hands at the entrance to the house,[21] but they did not dry them with a towel. Instead, they held them out in the air and wind until the hands dried by themselves. After entering the house, each mourner performed the "rending" for himself.[22] The rending was done by hand (that is, not with a razor, knife, or scissors), at the neck opening of the shirt which they wore next to their skin. If somebody was unable to make a rent with his hands, he used scissors to make a cut. They wore the same torn shirt during all seven days of mourning. Thereafter they sewed up the rent and continued to wear the shirt until the end of the thirty-day mourning period. After the thirtieth day, they gave the shirt to an indigent. The first meal after the return from the cemetery consisted of a hardboiled egg and some bread. For thirty days after the burial, the mourners did not go to the bathhouse, cut their hair, or pare their nails.[23]

During the first seven days of mourning, the mourners sat on the floor on rugs, in the very room in which the departed had breathed his last.[24] There they would recite the afternoon (Minḥa) and evening (Ma'ariv) prayers in a *minyan,* in the company of ten adult males. However, for the morning prayer (Shaḥarit), part of which on Mondays and Thursdays is a reading from the Torah, they would repair to the synagogue in the company of friends, for the mourners were not allowed to go out alone during those seven days.[25]

Relatives came to comfort them every day, although friends and acquaintances came only once. The comforters read to the mourners chapters from the Book of Psalms, and the bereaved family served them tea or coffee (a Muslim custom). When the visitors left, they did so without saying good-bye.

During these seven days, day and night, many people were invited to meals in the mourners' house.[26] The food was cooked and prepared by the relatives, and the expenses were borne by the community. Since it was considered a great *mitzvah,* a religious commandment and good deed, to participate in these expenses, there was never any lack of means to defray them. Meals were given on the thirtieth day and on the day of the anniversary, but the mourners had to bear the expenses for these.

The mourners wore dark garments.[27] They had a candle lighted in the house of mourning for thirty days. At the end of the year, the mourners' relatives gave them new clothes. The members of the family did not use the clothes of the deceased but gave them to the poor. On the seventh, thirtieth, and anniversary days, it was customary to visit the grave of a deceased father or mother. Each time somebody visited the grave, he put a stone on the tombstone. They also would visit the graves of the parents before leaving the city for a long voyage. On the anniversary day of a father's or a mother's death, they would fast until the evening meal.[28]

If parents lost a second child within thirty days after the death of the first one, they slaughtered a cock (for a son) or a hen (for a daughter), and buried the bird together with the deceased child. This was believed to prevent a third death in the family.[29]

The tombstone was inscribed with a few lines in accordance with the age and character of the deceased. There were always some people in the community who knew how to write poetry, and they undertook the task of composing these brief elegies, as well as longer dirges that were recited in the house of the mourners.[30] Thus according to Gohari. According to Nasrullayoff, the tombstones were divided into two parts: the upper part was inscribed in Persian with the Persian name of the deceased, and the lower part with his Hebrew name in Hebrew characters.

Conclusion

In conclusion, I turn to a brief consideration of the place of the Jadīdī community and its history in a global Jewish perspective. Statistically and demographically, and even historically and from the point of view of their religious-scholarly-literary contribution, the Jadīdīm constituted a very small, not to say insignificant, community overshadowed by the larger, longer-lived, and culturally more productive Jewries of Europe, Asia, and North Africa. The total history of the Meshhed community spanned only some two centuries, about half of it before, and half after, the Allahdād. Its numbers never exceeded a few hundred families, and its religious-literary output consisted of not more than a dozen or so books of a liturgical and exegetic character, written in Judeo-Persian and of no special significance beyond their function of providing moral support to the Jadīdī community itself. And yet, despite these limitations, the Meshhed community was (and still is, because its traditions survive in the Meshhedi Jewish communities functioning in several places in the world) of unique significance among the communities of the Jewish Diaspora.

The uniqueness of Meshhed becomes evident if we compare it to the other Jewish group that experienced expulsion and forced conversion—that of the Jews of Spain. While a certain parallel does exist between the fate of the *anusim* (forced converts) in Christian Spain and those in Muslim Meshhed, a comparison of what happened in the two places points up the differences between them. In Spain, some forty thousand Jews preferred acceptance of Christianity to emigration, which was chosen by about a hundred thousand: they became *conversos*, New Christians, in order to be allowed to stay. Many of these tried to remain faithful to Judaism in secret and to live as Marranos, crypto-Jews. However, before long, they began to be hunted down by the Inquisition; many perished in *autos-da-fé*. Others managed to flee the country and sought refuge in places where they could openly return to Judaism, especially in the Muslim realm and the Protestant countries of Western Europe. In Spain itself, as Howard M. Sachar, the most recent historian of the Sephardim, put it, "nearly four decades later [that is, by ca. 1530] any lingering Jewish identity among this remnant was all but extinguished."[1] Sachar's reference is to individual Jewish identity. As far as Jewish communal life was concerned, that had become totally extinct. We know of not a single synagogue or prayer room in which, after the expulsion and the attendant forced conversion, services were held, of no school in which children of Marranos were given a Jewish education, of no other communal institution that served those who in secret remained, or wanted to remain, faithful to Judaism. Judaism is a religion whose functioning requires a framework of communal institutions, in the absence of which individual Jewishness is doomed to wither away. And this is precisely what happened in Spain.

In Meshhed, developments took a different turn. True, the events of the Allahdād of 1839 paralleled in many respects those of the Spanish expulsion of 1492: both forced the Jews to choose between conversion and exile, and in response to both, some Jews opted for the first, some for the second of the two bitter alternatives. But in contrast to Spain, where within about a generation after 1492 Jewish identity was all but extinguished, in Meshhed, individual Jewish identity continued to be vigorously maintained after the Allahdād. In the privacy of their homes, the Jadīdīm continued to observe their traditional Jewish way of life, and even Jewish communal functions continued in the secrecy of cellars and walled inner courtyards. One generation after the Allahdād, as its memory gradually faded from the Muslim consciousness, the Jadīdīm felt that they could relax their vigilance to some extent, that they no longer had to be quite as fearful of discovery and as careful to hide their Jewishness as they had had to be in the first few years after the forced conversion.

Several factors played a role in this gradual and moderate easing of the situation. One was the absence in Iran of anything paralleling the Spanish institution of the Inquisition. In Spain, the Inquisition was a powerful and ruthless organization, maintained and supported by both the ecclesiastic and the secular authorities for the purpose of rooting out heretics, in particular Marranos who secretly Judaized. The official state policy in Spain, introduced and sponsored by the "Catholic kings" and carried out by the Inquisition, was to ferret out suspected Judaizers, to arrest them on the merest hint of suspicion, to subject them to torture in order to extract confessions, and to secure from them the indictment of others, ultimately to condemn them to death by being burned alive or, mercifully, if they "repented," to execute them by garroting. For more than a decade prior to the 1492 expulsion, and for a long period after it, much of the energy of state and church was concentrated on inquisitorial investigations and proceedings. The Inquisition was omnipresent and made the lives not only of the Marranos but also of those *conversos* who had wholeheartedly embraced Christianity, and even of their children, a nightmare of fear and trembling. The number of victims, whether true *conversos* or secret Marranos, burnt alive or garroted, ran into thousands. In one generation after the expulsion, Spain became *judenrein.*

In Persia, there was never anything even remotely resembling an organized body whose task would have been to track down, expose, punish, and publicly execute Jadīdīm who secretly adhered to Judaism. Once a Jew accepted Islam—which could be done by simply pronouncing the succinct Muslim confession of faith, *La Ilāha ill' Allah waMuḥammad Rasūl Ullah* ("There is no god but Allah, and Muhammad is the Messenger of Allah")—he counted as a Muslim, and, in general, as long as he attended prayers in the mosque and performed a few other Muslim religious duties, no effort was made to check what he did in the privacy of his home. This meant that the Muslim religious environment was more favorable to secret, private Judaizing than was that of Christian Spain. Whatever attacks against Jadīdīm suspected of Judaizing did take place were occasional mob actions, engaged in by members of the underclass who were envious of the relatively well-to-do New Muslims and were easily incited by false rumors of Jewish ritual murders or desecrations of Muslim rites. The outbreaks that did occur at varying intervals were, as a rule, instigated by a few fanatical *mullahs* but were short-lived and were disapproved, opposed, stopped, and occasionally even punished by the higher authorities. The position of both the religious and the governmental leaders, in general, while it was one of dislike and disdain of the Jadīdīm, was characterized also by their grudging tolerance and by an unwillingness to take action against them, unless it became apparent and could be proven that they had actually practiced Judaism in secret. This laisser-faire attitude of the authorities was carefully nurtured by "gifts" the Jadīdīm were expected, and did not fail, to give to those in power and control.

In Spain, as a result of inquisitorial thoroughness, within a generation after the expulsion, Jewish presence had become a thing of the past. What remained, because it was more difficult to get rid of, was an almost neurotic anxiety about the lingering traces of Jewish blood in the veins of the Spaniards. The country seemed to be obsessed with the elusive quest of *limpieza de sangre* ("purity of blood"), which in practice meant the absence of Jewish blood, even though to try to establish it was a very difficult and hazardous undertaking in view of the widespread intermarriages between Spaniards and converted Jews, which had been going on for centuries.

This issue of purity of blood simply did not exist in the Muslim world. There, descent was so emphatically patrilineal that the identity of a person's mother or grandmothers did not count at all and often was not merely ignored but not even remembered. Many of the rulers and potentates, beginning with the Shah himself, had Jewish women among their wives, but this fact made the sons born of such unions no less "pure" descendants of their father's line. It so happened that Aḥmed 'Alī Mīrzā, the prince who was governor of Meshhed in the early nineteenth century, was himself a son of the ruling Shah by one of his wives who was Jewish.[2] In the days of the Allahdād, when several Jewish girls were abducted, some members of the clergy took the attractive ones among them into their harems and made them their wives or concubines.[3] As far as is known, no Muslim suffered any discrimination because his mother was Jewish. The Muslim view was succinctly expressed in the adage "The woman is a vessel that empties," meaning that the fact that a man's seed is incubated in the body of a woman before his child is born is of no significance at all: the child is considered purely and exclusively the offspring of his father.

Another factor that made the preservation of Judaism easier for the Jadīdīm in Meshhed than for the Marranos of Spain was the structure of Persian society, in which each ethnic group, even each origin group—that is, any group that traced its descent to a common ancestor or a common locality—was expected to, and actually did, maintain its separate identity. The Muslim inhabitants of the city of Meshhed, which, with its shrine of great sanctity, attracted pilgrims from all parts of the Shī'ī Muslim world, many of whom settled in the city, made up several such separate ethnic and origin groups, each inhabiting a separate quarter, having its separate mosque, practicing group endogamy, distinguished by its garb and speech, and maintaining its own customs. The Jadīdīm of Meshhed, having accepted Islam, came to be considered yet another of these groups, and nobody found it unusual that they should keep to themselves and differ in all these features from the other groups. This greatly facilitated for the Jadīdīm the preservation of their traditional Jewish life and the maintenance of their communal customs.

A third factor was the general character of traditional Muslim society and social life. In the Shī'ī world (as well as in the most traditional Sunnī Muslim countries), there was a strict separation between men and women, the veiling of womenfolk was insisted upon, and consequently there was an absence of mutual visiting and entertaining among unrelated families. For a man to approach or talk to a woman who was not one of his wives or first-degree relatives was unheard of. The home of a man was taboo territory for other men, entry into which required elaborate preparatory arrangements. Typical in this respect was a custom to which informants and sources frequently refer: when the menfolk in a house engaged in some Jewish religious function in which they did not want to be surprised by a Muslim visitor, they had some of their women sit at the entrance door—veiled, of course—and their presence there was sufficient to prevent the entrance of any stranger. It was certainly easier for the Jadīdīm to observe Jewish religious rites in the safety of their homes than it was for the Marranos in Spain.

The last difference to be considered is the greater homogeneity and cohesion within the community that characterized the Jews of Meshhed as compared to those of Spain. Spain was a big country, with the Jewish element scattered in many cities and with a considerable internal heterogeneity within the Jewish population of each locality. In these circumstances, joint action for the preservation of Jewish community life was practically impossible. The Meshhed Jewish community was small, emphatically endogamous, hence closely interrelated, largely homogeneous as far as religious observance was concerned, and, beyond all this, possessed of a strong sense of cohesion among its members, of mutual responsibility, of obligation to help one another. In this situation, the determination of a few rabbis, respected and recognized as leaders of the community, to maintain Jewish life in the secrecy of the 'Ēdgāh was sufficient to produce among the overwhelming majority of the Jadīdīm a positive response and a willingness to go along with whatever their *mullahs* decided had to be done. This is how it came about that secret synagogal services could be held, that the Sabbath and the holidays could secretly be observed, that Torah schools could function in secret, that ritual slaughterers could secretly continue to supply kosher meat to members of the community, that secret circumcisions, weddings, and funerals according to Jewish rites could be carried out, and that, as a result of all this, a full Jewish individual, familial, and communal life could be maintained.

It was this internal cohesion, coupled with an iron determination to remain Jewish, both individually and communally, that proved to be the most important factor in the survival of the Jadīdī community. Judaism for them was not merely a religion but a total way of life, which, although the Allahdād forced certain external modifications upon it, they managed to maintain in essentially the same form it had had prior to that catastrophic event. This is how the Jadīdī community of Meshhed survived as an intensely Jewish community for some four generations after the forced conversion, until its mass emigration following the establishment of Israel.

However, the passing of the Jewish community in Meshhed did not mean the end of Meshhedi Jews. For a long time prior to it, a gradual emigration had been under way, so that by the time the Jadīdīm evacuated Meshhed, they could join vital Meshhedi communities established in Jerusalem, New York, London, and other places, where they had created a veritable Meshhedi Diaspora, in which the memories and traditions of Meshhed are maintained, fostered, and passed on to new and future generations.

Notes

Introduction

1. Bernard Lewis, *The Jews of Islam*, Princeton, 1984, p. 34.
2. Salo W. Baron, *A Social and Religious History of the Jews*, New York and Philadelphia, 1952, vol. 1, p. 131.
3. See *Encyclopaedia of Islam*, 2nd ed., s.v. *Dhimma*, and literature there.
4. Lewis, pp. 33–34, and sources on p. 98, note 38.
5. *Encyclopaedia Judaica*, Jerusalem, 1972, s.v. Persia.
6. Wilhelm Bacher, "Les Juifs de Perse aux xviie et xviiie siecles d'aprés les chroniques poétiques de Babai b. Loutf et de Babai b. Farhad," *Revue des Etudes Juives* 51 (1906): 121–36, 265–79; 52 (1906): 77–97, 234–71; 53 (1906): 85–110.
7. Ibid.
8. George N. Curzon, *Persia and the Persian Question*, London, 1892, vol. 2, pp. 510–11.
9. Walter J. Fischel, "The Jews of Persia: 1795–1940," *Jewish Social Studies* 12 (1950): 119–60; Laurence D. Loeb, *Outcaste: Jewish Life in Southern Iran*, New York, 1977, p. 288.
10. See the detailed article on Meshhed in the *Encyclopaedia of Islam*, s.v. Mashhad.

Chapter 1. Early Times

1. Amnon Netzer, "Qorot Anusē Meshhed l'fi Ya'aqov Dilmanian" (The History of the Forced Converts of Meshhed according to Jacob Dilmanian), in *Pe'amim* 42 (1990): 127–56.
2. Ibid., p. 132.
3. Laurence Lockhart, *Nadir Shah*, London, 1938, pp. 51–52, 54, 89, 91.
4. Ḥabīb Lēvī, *Tārīkh-ī Yahūd-ī Īrān* (History of the Jews of Iran), Teheran, 1339/1960, vol. 3, pp. 589–91, as quoted by Netzer, p. 132.
5. Netzer, "Qorot," pp. 132–33.
6. I published the above account of the beginnings of the Jewish settlement in Meshhed in 1945 in a Hebrew article titled *Massorot Historiyot uMinhagē Q'vurah Ētzel Y'hudē Meshhed* (Historical Traditions and Mortuary Customs of the Jews of Meshhed). My article formed part of a small volume titled *Dappē Zikkaron liR'fa'ēl Aharonoff Z"L* (Memorial Pages for Raphael Aharonoff), published by the Simon Raphael Aharonoff family in Jerusalem in 1945. My summary of the beginnings of the Jewish community of Meshhed was reproduced in 1960 in a hectographed treatise in Persian titled *Tārīkh-ī Isrāīlhā-ī Meshhed Az Varūd b'Meshhed Dar Zamān-ī Nādir Shāh-ī Afshār Ilā Muhājarat Az Meshhed* (The History

of the Israelites in Meshhed from Their Arrival in Meshhed in the Times of Nādir Shah Afshār until Their Emigration from Meshhed) by Ya'aqov Dilmanian, a Meshhedi Jew, without crediting the source. The relevant paragraph was translated by Amnon Netzer into Hebrew, in his study on the history of the forced converts of Meshhed, from which I present it here in my literal English translation:

> The late Farajullah Nasrullayoff wrote that Nadir Shah, in order to guard his treasures, ordered to take forty families from Qazwin to Kalat. When Nadir Shah was killed, seventeen families had reached Kalat, sixteen families remained in Meshhed, seven families had reached Sabzawar, and the soldiers left them in the city. Of these seven families, some went to Meshhed and others to Bukhara. Those who had arrived in Kalat remained there and became owners of synagogues and dwellings, but because of the evil behavior of the local inhabitants, some of them went to Meshhed and the rest went to Samarkand, Herat, and Bukhara.

I am not aware that Āqā Farajullah "wrote," that is published, any writing on the history of the Jews of Meshhed prior to 1987. Netzer adds that "Dilmanian accepts the version of Nasrullayoff as correct" and that Nasrullayoff "served in the 1940s as head of the Meshhed community in Jerusalem" (p. 136).

Chapter 2. Before the Allahdād

1. From document S25/5291 in the Central Zionist Archives, Jerusalem, as quoted by Ben-Zion Y'hoshu'a-Raz, *MiNidḥē Yisraēl b'Afganistan l'Anusē Meshhed b'Iran* (From the Lost Ones of Israel in Afghanistan to the Forced Converts of Meshhed in Iran), Jerusalem, 1992, pp. 102–3.
2. *Encyclopaedia of Islam,* 2nd ed., s.v. al-'Āmili. I wish to thank Ben-Zion Y'hoshu'a-Raz for calling my attention to the relationship between the two nineteenth-century lists of restrictions and those in the *Jāmi'-ī 'Abbāsī* (letter dated Nov. 12, 1994). See also Ḥanina Mizraḥi, *Toldot Y'hudē Faras uM'shor'rēhem* (History of the Jews of Persia and Their Poets), Jerusalem, 1966, pp. 36–37. The English translation of the *Jāmi'ī 'Abbāsī,* of the list of discriminatory measures against the Jews imposed a few years later at the initiative of the renegade Jewish butcher Abū Ḥasan Lārī, and of the anti-Jewish restrictions issued in the second half of the nineteenth century, is given by Loeb in *Outcaste,* pp. 292–94. See also Bacher, "Les Juifs en Perse," 52:237.
3. M. Truilhier, "Mémoire descriptif de la route de Téhran a Meched," in *Bulletin de la Société de Géographie,* 2nd series, no. 9, Paris, May 1838. Reprinted Paris, 1841, ed. by P. Daussy.
4. Baron Yegor Fiodorovich de Meiendorf, *Voyage d'Orenburg a Bouhara . . . 1820,* St. Petersburg, 1826, p. 173.
5. James B. Fraser, *Narrative of a Journey into Khorasan in the Years 1821 and 1822,* London, 1825. Reprinted New York, 1984, p. 467.
6. Arthur Conolly, *Journey to the North of India . . . ,* London, 1834, vol. 1, pp. 267, 303.
7. Ibid., pp. 252–47, 303–8. On the office of the *darogha* (lit. *darūgha*), see *Encyclopaedia of Islam,* vol. 2, p. 162.
8. Joseph Wolff, *Researches and Missionary Labours among the Jews, Mohammedans, and Other Sects,* London, 1835.

9. Ibid., p. 136.
10. Fraser, *Narrative*, p. 467; Conolly, *Journey*, p. 257; Wolff, *Researches*, p. 131.
11. Sources in 'Azarya Lēvi, "'Ēduyot uT'udot l'Toldot Y'hudē Meshhed" (Testimonies and Documents on the Jews of Meshhed), *Pe'amim* 6 (1981): 62–63.
12. J. P. Ferrier, *Caravan Journeys and Wanderings in Persia . . .*, London, 1856; new edition, 1976, p. 488.
13. Sources in Levi, "'Ēduyot," p. 65.
14. See Ezra Spicehandler, "A Descriptive List of Judeo-Persian Manuscripts in the Klau Library of the Hebrew Union College," *Studies in Bibliography and Booklore* (Spring 1968): 114–36.

Chapter 3. The Sūfī Lure

1. See R. Nicholson, *The Mystics of Islam*, London, 1975, p. 103; *Encyclopaedia Judaica*, Jerusalem, 1971, vol. 15, pp. 486–87, s.v. Sufism, and literature there. A somewhat different translation of Muḥyi 'l-Dīn's lines is found in William Stoddart, *Sufism*, New York, 1986, pp. 51, 82.
2. See *Encyclopaedia of Islam*, 2nd ed., vol. 4, p. 62.
3. See Wilhelm Bacher, *Zwei jüdisch-persische Dichter—Schachin und Imrani*, 2 vols., Budapest, 1907–8; Walter J. Fischel, "Shahin," in *Encyclopaedia Judaica*, vol. 14, p. 1258.
4. Myron M. Weinstein, "A Hebrew Qur'ān Manuscript," *Studies in Bibliography and Booklore* 10 (Winter 1971–72): 1–2.
5. Wolff, *Researches*, p. 127.
6. See Louis Ginzberg, *Legends of the Jews*, Philadelphia, 1909–46, vol. 1, pp. 421–22.
7. E.g., in *Midrash Tanḥuma, Aggadat B'reshit, Yalqut Makhiri*. See Ginzberg, vol. 5, p. 322, note 319.
8. See sources in Ginzberg, *Legends*, vol. 6, pp. 407–9.
9. See Raphael Patai, *Sex and Family in the Bible and the Middle East*, New York, 1958.
10. Wolff, *Researches*, p. 137.
11. Ibid., pp. 133–34.
12. Ibid., p. 177.
13. Ibid., p. 132.
14. Ibid., p. 147.
15. Ibid., pp. 131–32.
16. Ibid., p. 133
17. Ibid., p. 134.

Chapter 4. Allahdād!

1. Joseph Wolff, *Narrative of a Mission to Bokhara in the Years 1843–1845*, London, 1845, 1846.
2. Ibid., p. 394.
3. Ibid., p. 177.
4. Ibid., pp. 394–95.
5. Ibid., p. 394.
6. Ibid., pp. 394, 396.

7. Ibid., p. 396.
8. Ibid., pp. 396–98, 408.
9. J. P. Ferrier, *Caravan Journeys*, pp. 121–23.
10. Central Zionist Archives, document S25/5291.
11. Persian text and Hebrew translation in Netzer, "Qorot," p. 138. A less complete text of this inscription is found in Yitzḥaq Ben-Zvi, *Meḥqarim uM'qorot* (Studies and Sources), Jerusalem, 1966, p. 325; and Y'hoshu'a, *MiNidḥē*, p. 109.
12. Walter J. Fischel, *HaY'hudim b'Hodu* (The Jews in India), Jerusalem, 1960, pp. 176–203; as cited by Ben-Zion Y'hoshu'a, *Diyoqnah shel Q'hillat ha'Anusim b'Meshhed sheb'Iran* (Portrait of the Community of Forced Converts in Meshhed, Iran), Jerusalem, 1980, p. 19.
13. Sir James Abbott, *Narrative of a Journey from Herat to Khiva* . . . , 1842, vol. 1, p. 35, as cited in Lēvi, "'Ēduyot," p. 66.
14. Cited by Netzer, "Qorot," pp. 139–40.
15. Y. Ben-'Ami, "Yahaduth b'Maḥteret" (Judaism Underground), *Qol Sinai* 1 (Kislev-Teveth 5722 [1962]).
16. Published in Ben-Zvi, *Meḥqarim.* Preserved in the library of the Hebrew University of Jerusalem, Joel Catalogue no. 502.
17. Sources in Lēvi, "'Ēduyot," p. 66; Netzer, "Qorot," p. 141.
18. Lēvi, "'Ēduyot," p. 66.

Chapter 5. After the Allahdād

1. Lēvi, "'Ēduyot," p. 68, citing British Foreign Office documents.
2. Ibid., p. 67, quoting Wolff, *Researches*, p. 126; Āqā Muḥammad 'Alī Yishqaft (Ashkabadi), letter to the British Ambassador, Foreign Office 60-87, Mashhad, April 1842.
3. Lēvi, "'Ēduyot," pp. 67–68, quoting Foreign Office 60-87, no. 59, 29.4.1842.
4. Ibid., p. 68, quoting Fischel, *HaY'hudim*, pp. 189 ff.
5. Ibid., p. 68, note 42, citing Fischel, *HaY'hudim*, pp. 189 ff.
6. Ibid., pp. 69–70, quoting Foreign Office 249-34, 21.10.1843.
7. Ibid., pp. 68–69, quoting Foreign Office 60-106, 30.11.1844.
8. See above, chapter 4.
9. Ferrier, *Caravan Journeys*, p. 488.
10. Israel Joseph Benjamin, *Acht Jahre in Asien und Afrika*, Hannover, 1860, pp. 189–90.
11. Ephraim Neumark, "Massa' b'Eretz haQedem" (Travel in the Land of the East), *HeAsif* 5 (1889): 39–75; reedited with annotations by Abraham Ya'ari, Jerusalem, 1947.
12. Netzer, "Qorot," pp. 141–42.
13. His tract was published by R. Kashani, "Qorot Z'manim l'haRav Mattityahu Garji mēAfganistan" (The History of the Times by R. Mattityahu Garji of Afghanistan), *Shēveṭ v'Am* 1 (1971): 136–59.
14. Ibid., pp. 143–44, as quoted by Y'hoshu'a, *MiNidḥē*, pp. 110–11.
15. Y'hoshu'a, *MiNidḥē*, pp. 125–26, citing D. Muradi, "HaRav Mord'khay Aqlar, Rabbam shel ha'Anusim baMaḥteret" (R. Mordechai Aqlar, Rabbi of the Forced Converts in the Underground), *Qol Sinai* 8:1 (1962): 174–75.
16. Lēvi, "'Ēduyot," pp. 70–72.
17. Ibid.
18. Netzer, "Qorot," p. 144.

Chapter 6. Conversions to the Bahai Faith

1. Tajan, Yamut, and Gurgan (probably an error for Guklān) were Turkoman Sunnī tribes located around the southeastern corner of the Caspian Sea.
2. It is not clear whether Āqā Farajullah refers to Turbat-i Haydari or to Turbat-i Shaykh-i Jam, both of which lie about eighty miles from Meshhed, the first to the south-southwest, the second to the south-southeast.
3. Birjand is a district and town to the south of Meshhed. The town lies two hundred and twenty miles due south of Meshhed.
4. Sayyid Muḥammad Bāb: This is how Āqā Farajullah refers to Sayyid 'Alī Muḥammad, known as al-Bāb, the founder of the Bahai faith.
5. In Āqā Farajullah's Judeo-Persian text, he is called Jabrā'īl al-Muballegh.
6. In the books and studies on the Bahai faith to which I had access, I found no trace of this temporary prohibition of alcohol, tobacco, and spices.

Chapter 7. A Decade of Blood Libels and Other Incidents, 1892–1902

1. Gōharshad (Gawhar Shād) mosque in Meshhed was built in commemoration of Gawhar Shād, grandmother of Yādgār Muḥammad, who was accused by the Tīmūrid Sultan Abū Sa'īd ibn Muḥammad of intelligence with Ibrāhīm ibn 'Alā' al-Dawla ibn Baysunghur and executed in 1457.
2. Nāyeb (deputy) Muḥammad was the Muslim official placed in control of the Jewish quarter.
3. Dilmani's account (in Hebrew) is preserved in the Central Zionist Archives in Jerusalem (document S25/5291). A copy of it was kindly put at my disposal by the Archives.
4. Netzer, "Qorot," p. 146.
5. Y'hoshu'a, *MiNidḥē,* pp. 114–15.
6. Lewis, *Jews of Islam,* p. 147.
7. Ibid., p. 148.
8. *Encyclopaedia Judaica,* s.v. Damascus Affair.
9. Lewis, *Jews of Islam,* p. 158, and sources there.
10. Charles Stuart, *Journal of a Residence in Northern Persia,* London, 1854, pp. 325–26.
11. Loeb, *Outcaste,* p. 72; D. Littman, "Jews under Muslim Rule: The Case of Persia," *Wiener Library Bulletin* 49–50 (1979): 12–14.

Chapter 8. Zionism and Early *'Aliya*

1. R'fa'ēl Ḥayyim Hakohen, *Avanim baḤomah* (Stones in the Wall), Jerusalem, 1970, p. 48, as quoted in Loeb, *Outcaste,* p. 263.
2. Mizraḥi, *Y'hudē Faras,* as quoted in Loeb, *Outcaste,* p. 263.
3. B. Gili, *Dappē 'Aliya* (Immigration Pages), Jerusalem, 1951, p. 28; Loeb, *Outcaste,* p. 264.
4. Y'hoshu'a, *MiNidḥē,* pp. 140–41.
5. Mizraḥi, *Y'hudē Faras,* pp. 206–12; and Ben-Ami, "Yahaduth baMaḥtereth," p. 37.
6. *Encyclopaedia of Zionism and Israel,* new ed., 1994, s.v. Iran, Zionism in.

7. Dīlmānī's report, Central Zionist Archives, Jerusalem, doc. S25/5291.
8. Y'hoshu'a, *MiNidḥē,* between pages 126 and 127.

Chapter 9. Disturbances in the 1940s

1. I wish to thank Professor Haim Avni, head of the Avraham Harman Institute of Contemporary Jewry, Hebrew University, Jerusalem, for putting a copy of the document at my disposal.
2. Zāhedān is an Iranian town near the Afghanistan-Pakistan border.
3. Darra Gaz (colloquially Deregez) is a district and town in Iran to the north of Meshhed, near the Turkmenistan border.
4. Bajnurd (or Bujnurd) is a town in Iran, one hundred and sixty miles northwest of Meshhed.
5. Al-Zahrā, "the Shining One." Title given to Fāṭima, the daughter of Muhammad, all over the Muslim world. However, it was primarily among Shī'īs that she was glorified and venerated. Fāṭima became the wife of 'Alī and the mother of Ḥasan and Ḥusayn; she died shortly after the death of Muhammad. Several Muslim feasts are dedicated to Fāṭima: the feast of Mubāhala on the twenty-first, twenty-fourth, or twenty-fifth of the month of Dhu 'l-Ḥijja; the celebration of her birth on the twentieth of Ramaḍān; and the commemoration of her death on the third of Jumāda II and the second of Ramaḍān. See *Encyclopaedia of Islam,* vol. 2, pp. 841–50. None of these dates falls in the middle of the lunar month, which would have to be the case if Soliman Muradi's identification were correct.
6. *Chādor* is the traditional outdoor garb of Persian women. It is a black or white sleeveless, flowing robe covering the body from head to foot.
7. The reference here is to the old Jewish quarter, the 'Ēdgāh, located next to the old walls of the city of Meshhed, near the southwestern corner of the city. It was inhabited mainly by the poor elements of the Jewish community, while the well-to-do moved to a new quarter, called Janāt.
8. Mujtahid Ayatollah Nihāwandī was a top religious leader of the Meshhed Muslims.
9. The reference to the Jews as Jadīd al-Islām indicates that the Muslim leadership of the city considered the Jews converts to Islam.
10. By 1946, there was a sizable Jewish community in Teheran.
11. Yitzḥaq Kleinbaum, an official of the Jewish Agency, was stationed in 1946 in Teheran and visited Meshhed in the spring of that year. The report he obtained of the disturbances in Meshhed is presented below, in chapter 10.
12. A. Landstein, stationed in Teheran, was an emissary of the Keren Kayemeth leYisrael, the Jewish National Fund.

Chapter 10. A Picture of Jewish Life

1. Kleinbaum's report is preserved in the Central Zionist Archives in Jerusalem, no. S25/5291.
2. I wish to thank Rabbi Benjamin Amoyelle, executive vice president of Ozar Hatorah in New York, for information on the work of the Ozar Hatorah in Persia.

Chapter 11. Emigration, *'Aliya,* Dispersion

1. The correspondence presented in this chapter is preserved in the Central Zionist Archives in Jerusalem, no. S25/5291.
2. The text of the two chief rabbis' opinions is reprinted in Y'hoshu'a, *MiNidḥē,* pp. 143–44.

Chapter 12. A Meshhed Jewish Family

1. Farajullah (Jonathan): Among the Jews of Meshhed, it was customary to have an "official" or public Persian (or Arabic-Persian) name, as well as a Hebrew name used internally, in the synagogue, etc. The Persian and the Hebrew names usually had either the same or similar meanings, e.g., Arabic Farajullah ("Allah comforts"), Hebrew Yonathan ("God gave"); Persian Khudādād ("God gave"), Hebrew Nethanel ("God gave"); or were similar in sound, e.g. Arabic Nasrullah ("Allah saves"), Hebrew Nissim ("marvels").
2. Karb. Short for Karbalā'ī, the designation given to Muslims in Persia who had made the pilgrimage to Karbala, the famous Shī'ī holy place in Iraq where Ḥusayn ibn 'Alī was killed and buried, located some fifty miles south-southwest of Baghdad. Some of the Marranos of Meshhed, wishing to appear pious Muslims, assumed the title if they stopped at Karbala on their way to or from Jerusalem, or even if they never set foot in Karbala. A similar religious title was Meshhedī, abbreviated as Meshdī, claimed by those Muslims (and Jews) who made the pilgrimage to Meshhed. Also, the title Ḥajjī or Ḥājj, given to those who made the pilgrimage to Mecca and Medinah, the most holy places of Islam, was assumed by some of the Jews of Meshhed.
3. Āqājān: Title meaning something like "dear man," derived from *āqā,* the Persian form of the originally Turkish title *agha,* meaning brother, uncle, sir, master, Mr., etc. Among the Jews of Meshhed, the title was used in the form of *āqā,* as well as *āq.*
4. Nadir Shah Afshar (1688–1747) ruled Persia from 1736 to his death in 1747. After his return from his Indian campaign, in 1741, he put Indian craftsmen to work on building for him a fortress in Kalat, some seventy miles north of Meshhed, where he deposited the loot brought home from his campaign.
5. Farajullah's reference to Nadir Shah's distrust of the Muslims of Persia has a basis in historical fact: Nadir's declared policy was to restore a form of Sunnī Islam to Persia, which brought him in conflict with the leadership of the dominant Shī'ī Islam of the country and its adherents. He may actually have been hesitant to entrust the guarding of his treasure house to Persian (Shī'ī) Muslims.
6. Qazwīn: City located about ninety miles northwest of Teheran, south of the Caspian Sea. The Persian form of the name is Qazvin.
7. Sabzawar: City located some 110 miles west of Meshhed.
8. According to Āqā Farajullah's account of Nadir's life story, Nadir was killed in Radkon. See below, chapter 13.
9. Rādkān (Radkon): Town in Khorasan, located about fifty miles northwest of Meshhed.
10. 'Am(o): Paternal uncle. In most cases, the translator substituted the Hebrew *dod* ("uncle") for this Persian word.
11. Merv, lit. Marw or Marw Shahijan ("Royal Marw"). City in Turkmenistan, important commercial center, about 180 miles to the northeast of Meshhed. Under the 'Abbāsids part

of Khorasan, Merv was occupied in 1884 by the Russian army and became in 1924 part of the Turkmenistan S.S.R. The Jews of Meshhed had lively commercial connections with Merv, and many of them lived in Merv for years.

12. Geber, lit. *gabr:* Name generally used in Persian literature to designate the Zoroastrians. On the history and position of the Zoroastrians in Iran, see *Encyclopaedia of Islam,* s.v. Madjūs.
13. The detailed account Āqā Farajullah gives of the purchase and maintenance of the bathhouse by his great-grandmother Bemōnī and her son Simḥa (his grandfather) shows what importance he (and the Jadīdīm in general) attributed to the availability of a ritual bath (a *miqveh*) for the community. This emphasis on the ritual cleanliness of both men and women, obtainable only by immersion in a *miqveh,* seems to have been greater among the Jadīdīm than in other Jewish communities, perhaps under the influence of a similar importance attached to ritual purity by the Shīʿī Muslims.
14. Part of the traditional Jewish mourning ritual is for the first-degree relatives of the deceased to make a cut (*qriʿah*) in their upper garment at the time of the burial, and then, seven days later, upon conclusion of the first deep mourning period, to sew up the cut.
15. The custom of providing food for a whole year to the family of the deceased, referred to in Āqā Farajullah's narrative, did not obtain in other Jewish communities. It can be considered a manifestation of the great inner cohesion of the Jadīdīm.
16. Jadīdī (Rashi) writing: The Jews of Meshhed wrote both Hebrew and their own Judeo-Persian (Jadīdī) language in a Hebrew cursive script they called Jadīdī or Rashi script. See below, chapter 21.
17. *Abgad* or *abjad:* The first of six mnemonic acrostics composed of the letters of the Hebrew alphabet, which were taught the Jadīdī children to enable them to memorize more easily the Hebrew alphabet. The six acrostics were: *abgad, hawaz, ḥuṭī, kalaman, saʿpaṣ, qarashat,* i.e. *aleph, beth, gimel, daleth; he, waw, zayin; ḥet, ṭet, yod; kaf, lamed, mem, nun; samekh, ʿayin, pe, ṣade; qof, resh, shin, tav.* See below, chapter 21.
18. Seray Nasriyyah: A commercial quarter in Meshhed.
19. Ḥājjihā Street: A street in Meshhed.
20. *Kal:* Colloquial abbreviation of Karmeli (Hebrew), "of the Carmel."
21. Āqā Farajullah uses the word *plastiq* in his original text.
22. Āqā Farajullah mentions this dish as an example of the utter disregard of Jewish religious laws by the Meshhedi Jews in Deregez: they made fire and cooked on the Sabbath, and ate non-kosher food, *ṭ-rēf* meat, which, in addition, was cooked in butter.
23. Kakistar: A locality not far from Meshhed.
24. People slept on mats or quilts that were spread on the floor in the evening and were again rolled up and laid aside in the morning.
25. In Persian (as in Arabic), the word for "children" usually designates boys only.
26. General Kropotkin was governor of Merv, in Russian Turkestan.
27. Dushakh: Turkmenistan town, sixty-five miles north of Meshhed, ten miles north of the Turkmenistan border.
28. Chashme Bilan: Iranian town, fifty miles north-northeast of Meshhed, on the Turkmenistan border.
29. Because of the great heat during the day, the caravans would start out in the evening, march all night, and then stop the next morning at a point where they could take a rest. In this case, Farajullah's caravan did not reach Chashme Bilan until noon of the next day. Such a

strenuous night journey was usually followed by one or more days of rest. The pace at which the camels proceeded was slow enough to enable people to keep up with them on foot.

30. *Fayton* or *faytun:* Arabic-Persian form of the French *phaeton*, a light four-wheeled carriage.
31. Qara Tuqan: Iranian town forty-five miles northeast of Meshhed, on the Turkmenistan border.
32. Sarakhs: Iranian town ninety miles to the east of Meshhed, on the Turkmenistan border. Qahqeh, or Kaakhka: Town eighty miles north of Meshhed, across the Turkmenistan border. Qazal Arwad or Kizyl Arvat: Town in Turkmenistan, two hundred and fifty miles northwest of Meshhed.
33. Bazār Také: A bazaar in Merv.
34. The illness Farajullah describes here took place in 1890, when he was sixteen years old.
35. The opinion of the Turkoman physician (or, rather, healer) that "the Jews have soft flesh" and therefore should not be given the painful treatment with the hot iron is of considerable interest. It shows that the Turkomans, even though Jews had lived among them for many generations and were assimilated to them to a considerable degree, yet considered the Jews a different, less hardy people, whose sensitivity required special consideration. The opinion of the "second old Turkoman" healer was that by treating the Jewish patient mercifully, the first healer "killed him," that is, allowed the disease to kill him. When Farajullah's condition worsened, the Turkoman physicians concluded that, after all, hot iron would have to be applied. The painful treatment ultimately proved effective.
36. Meaning "Better that he should cry of pain than that we should cry over his death."
37. Muslim religious laws require that animals should be slaughtered according to ritual rules in order to be *ḥalāl,* that is, lawful, permissible for consumption. Muslim ritual considers the meat sold by a kosher butcher as *ḥalāl,* but the Jews did not consider *ḥalāl* meat to be kosher.
38. Ashkhabad: City in Russian Turkmenistan, near the Iranian border, 140 miles northwest of Meshhed.
39. Yultan (Iolotan): Town in Russian Turkmenistan, about forty miles southeast of Merv.
40. Luṭfabād: Iranian city on the border between Russian Turkmenistan and Iran, eighty miles north of Meshhed.
41. Chahar Ju (Chārju, formerly Āmu): Town in Turkmenistan, 140 miles northeast of Merv.
42. Artoq or Artok: Turkmenistan town fifteen miles north of Deregez, about ninety-five miles north of Meshhed.
43. Bayram 'Alī: City in Turkmenistan, fifteen miles east of Merv.
44. On the role of an orchestra in the Jewish wedding in Meshhed, see below, chapter 24.
45. *'Arus kashan:* Accompanying the bride. A wedding rite. See below, chapter 24.
46. *Shiv'ah:* Seven, designation of the seven days of deep mourning for a close relative.
47. *Gāl* or *shter zanak:* According to Yoḥanan Livian, a scorpion-like black insect, whose sting can cause a dangerous poisoning to the body.
48. In Āqā Farajullah's memory, each of the three major illnesses he suffered in his youth lasted forty days. One wonders whether he was not influenced by the forty-day period that figures frequently in the bible as the duration of important events; see Gen. 7:4, 12, 17, 8:6, 50:3; Ex. 24:18, 34:28; Num. 13:25; Deut. 9:9, 18, 25, 10:10; 1 Sam. 17:16; 1 Ki. 19:9; Ezek. 4:6; Jonah 3:4.

    As for the sting and its treatment, I consulted my daughter Jennifer Patai Schneider, Ph.D., M.D., and in her opinion, Āqā Farajullah's account of the incident "is very descriptive of the bite of a spider of the *Lactrodectus* genus, a widow spider. . . . After a momentary sharp pain at the bite site, there is a cramping pain that begins locally within fifteen to sixty minutes and may spread to involve all extremities and the trunk. The abdomen is boardlike, and the waves of pain become excruciating, causing the patient to turn, toss, and cry out. Respiration is often labored and grunting. There are also nausea, vomiting, headache, sweating, salivation, twitching, tremor, paresthesias (numbness and tingling) of the hands and feet, and occasionally elevated blood pressure. Many patients have fever. Because the bite itself is not prominent, victims are often thought to have some abdominal catastrophe such as perforated ulcer. Widow spiders tend to stay in dark places. It is very likely that when Farajullah lowered his trousers, the spider in the lavatory was disturbed and moved into the pants. Then, when he pulled up his trousers, the spider, again disturbed, bit his leg. Current treatment consists of pain medication, drugs against muscle spasms, and antivenin. The spinning and the milk treatment administered to Farajullah were undoubtedly a response to the belief that because there was abdominal cramping, there was something wrong with his stomach and vomiting had to be induced. Maybe they also thought that the spinning would relieve generalized muscle cramping."

49. Siman Maretoff, a Jew, and Mashdi Rustam, a Muslim, were business partners of the Nasrullayoff family. The title Mashdi is contracted from Meshhedi, the title of a man who had made the pilgrimage to the sanctuary of Imām Reza in Meshhed.
50. Bone setter: Āqā Farajullah's Persian text has *sh'kasteh band.*
51. Kalateh and Khonjeh: Names of two estates.
52. Kalachah: Name of an estate.
53. Kurchashmeh: Name of an estate.

Chapter 13. A Popular "Life of Nadir"

(A somewhat different version of this chapter was originally published in *Edoth* 3 (1948): I–XX.)

1. Laurence Lockhart, *Nadir Shah,* London, 1938.
2. Deregez: See chapter 9, note 3. Here and in the following, I give the popular phonetic forms of place names. On first mention, I add the literary form of the name in parentheses.
3. Muḥammadābād: Iranian city on the Turkmenistan border, the main city of the district of Deregez. Āqā Farajullah habitually refers to this city as Deregez.
4. Lockhart, *Nadir Shah,* pp. 18, 20.
5. *Mullah,* "master," "teacher," is the title of religious personages in Persia.
6. Herodotus reports the same to have occurred in connection with the birth of one of the remote predecessors of Nadir on Persia's throne, Cyrus. Astyages dreamed that his daughter Mandane urinated and the water filled not only his town but the whole of Asia. Again, when his daughter was pregnant with Cyrus, he dreamed that a vine grew out of her womb and covered all of Asia. The dreams were interpreted by the magi: his daughter's son would reign in his stead (Herodotus 1.107–8).
7. The period of six months recurs frequently in the narrative; see chapter 14.
8. Again, we are reminded of what Herodotus tells about the childhood of Cyrus. when Cyrus had reached the age of ten in the house of the poor shepherd, his foster father, he played with the children in the streets of the village, and they chose him to be their king. One of

the children disobeyed him, and he commanded the others to beat him with whips. The beaten child complained to his father, and in consequence Cyrus's identity was discovered (Herodotus 1.114–16).

9. Abivard, according to my informant, lies six *farsangs* (about twenty-four miles) east of Chapushli.
10. This is the first instance where we are able to check the veracity of the folktale. It does seem to be a historical fact that in his youth, Nadir entered the service of Baba 'Alī Beg Kusa Aḥmadu, chief of the Afghans of the town of Abivard (Lockhart, *Nadir Shah*, p. 21).
11. Upon reaching this point in his narrative, my informant got up from his chair and went through Nadir's movements in the scene he was describing.
12. East of the Caspian Sea, near the Oxus River. Today the whole territory is called Khiva. It is, of course, impossible that Nadir should have raided Khiva, at a distance of 320 miles from Deregez, with twelve horsemen. We may perhaps attribute this story to a muddled reminiscence of Nadir's Turkestan expedition in 1740, when he took Khiva with a force many tens of thousands strong (Lockhart, *Nadir Shah*, pp. 193–95).
13. According to my informant, this method was still used in the 1940s, and it is in the nature of sheep to behave like this.
14. It is a fact that Nadir, after having first served and then opposed Malik Maḥmud of Meshhed, fled back to Abivard, where he raised a force of horsemen with which he raided the Deregez district (Lockhart, *Nadir Shah*, pp. 22–23).
15. My informant knew only of Shah Sultan Ḥusayn as having been the king of Persia during the whole period of Nadir's ascent. According to him, Shah Sultan Ḥusayn was followed on the throne by the infant king, and then by Nadir himself. Actually, however, Shah Sultan Ḥusayn ruled only from 1694 to 1722, when he was deposed; he was finally put to death in 1726. In 1722, his third son, Ṭahmāsp, proclaimed himself Shah. Ṭahmāsp was crowned in 1729 and was deposed by Nadir in 1732. From 1732 to 1736, nominally at least, the infant Abbas III, son of Ṭahmāsp, was Shah.
16. In 1726, Ḥasan Ali Beg, the "assayer of the kingdom," appointed Nadir deputy governor of Abivard on Ṭahmāsp's behalf (Lockhart, *Nadir Shah*, p. 24).
17. Quchan: Iranian city, about ninety miles northwest of Meshhed.
18. The town of Shirvan lies between Radkon and Bujnurd. All three towns lie southwest of the district of Deregez.
19. The actual distance between Radkon and Meshhed is some forty-eight miles.
20. In fact, Nadir took Meshhed in 1726, when he was thirty-eight (Lockhart, *Nadir Shah*, p. 27).
21. A raid on Merv actually figures among Nadir's early exploits (ibid., p. 23).
22. *Ark*, lit. *arg:* Small citadel.
23. The whole story is legend. Isfahan was besieged by the Afghans in 1722, and Ṭahmāsp, after having been elected crown prince, escaped. Some months later, his father surrendered the city. In 1729, Nadir recovered Isfahan for Ṭahmāsp, who was then and there crowned Shah. Nadir's Caucasian campaign did not take place until 1741 to 1743, that is, even after the invasion of India (ibid., pp. 39, 197–211).
24. In 1732, Nadir arranged for the deposition of Shah Ṭahmāsp and for the investiture of the Shah's eight-month-old son as 'Abbās III. A chronicler in Nadir's service, Muḥammad Muḥsin, relates that the infant's cradle was brought forward and Nadir laid the *jiqa*, the aigrette of sovereignty, by his head and placed a shield and sword beside him. Nadir was made regent on the same occasion (ibid., p. 63).

25. Actually, Nadir's coronation took place in 1736, four years after the coronation of 'Abbās III. Nadir sent the child-king to Khurasan to join his father, Ṭahmāsp. Both father and son were put to death in 1740 by Reza Quli, the eldest son of Nadir Shah, during the latter's absence in India (ibid., pp. 104, 176–77).
26. The Hebrew name of both Iraq and Baghdad is *Bavel,* Babylon. Actually, Nadir's opponents in this campaign were the Turks who ruled Iraq.
27. Actually, of course, Baghdad lies on the banks of the Tigris, not the Euphrates.
28. In this point, the folk story falls behind reality. The number of Nadir's army was much greater than forty thousand (ibid., pp. 69–70).
29. One can feel in this story a clear reminiscence of the biblical story of Gideon's tactics with the pitchers and torches against the Midianites (Judg. 7:16ff.).
30. Nadir's Baghdad campaign took place in December 1732. He crossed the Tigris over a floating bridge with twenty-five hundred men, was followed the next day by another fifteen hundred, and thus blockaded Baghdad. The city suffered from famine, but a Turkish army was sent to relieve it, and Nadir's forces were defeated in July 1733. Nadir reorganized his army, again besieged Baghdad, and in December 1733, he signed a treaty with Aḥmad Pasha, the Turkish governor of Baghdad—which did not, however, include the surrender of the city (ibid., pp. 65–75). It is thus only in the folktale that Nadir conquered Baghdad.
31. Esther 1:1. This, of course, is a personal addition by my informant; the Persian peasants of Moḥammadābād are most unlikely to have quoted the Bible.
32. Actually, Peshawar lies some fifty-five miles west of the Indus River, that is, beyond the mountain passes leading from Afghanistan into India.
33. This was the only part of the story in which my informant's second version differed from his first. The second time, he said, "They came to a very steep hill. They could not draw up the guns. There was no way around the hill. So Nadir commanded that the hill be leveled by artillery fire."
34. Mīrzā Muḥammad Mahdī Kaukabī Astarābādhī was appointed by Nadir at his coronation in 1736 to serve as official historiographer. His *Tārīkh-i Nādirī* is judged by Lockhart to be the most important contemporary source of the history of Nadir. Mīrzā Mahdī actually accompanied Nadir to India. His title was Munshī al-Mamālik, "secretary of the kingdoms" (ibid., pp. 292, 293).
35. This anecdote has been attributed to many historical figures.
36. Lockhart, *Nadir Shah,* p. 152, mentions only the famous Kohinor diamond as having been brought back by Nadir from India.
37. Historical sources do not refer to this order. However, M. Truilhier, who was in Meshhed in 1807, reported that there were about a hundred Jewish families there whom Nadir Shah had gathered with a view to activating commerce, and whose situation had deteriorated greatly after Nadir's death ("Mémoire descriptif," p. 273. Lockhart wrote to me on June 19, 1946, "In view of Nadir's habit of transferring large numbers of tribesmen from one place to another for purposes of defense, I think that it is quite probable that he did in fact give orders for these Qazvini Jews to be moved to Kalat."
38. See Lockhart, *Nadir Shah,* pp. 278–81.
39. The Evangelion, the Gospel.
40. The Torah, the Pentateuch.
41. This legend, of course, has a distinctly Jewish coloring. However, it seems to be a fact that Nadir ordered the Old and New Testaments as well as the Koran to be translated into

Persian, and that he assembled the priests of the respective religions to make the translations (Lockhart, *Nadir Shah*, p. 280).

42. Actually, Nadir's eldest son, Reza Quli, was made viceroy of Persia by his father when the latter set out on his Indian campaign. Reza Quli "formed a special corps, 12,000 strong, of Khorasani *jazayirchis*, whom he equipped with gorgeous uniforms of cloth of gold and silver." When Reza Quli met his father on his return from India in 1740, the latter ordered his son's fancy troops disbanded. The blinding of Reza Quli took place in 1742, more than two years later. Nadir suspected his son of having hired an assassin who tried to kill him, and it was for that reason that he blinded him. History knows nothing of the blinding of Mīrzsâ Mahdī. On the contrary, it is said that Nadir put to death many of his nobles who were present when the sentence was carried out for not having offered to undergo the punishment in place of his son (ibid., pp. 126, 174, 180, 207–9).
43. It is a fact that Mīrzā Mahdī drafted several letters, manifestos, and treaties for Nadir. He was well versed in Persian, Turkish, and Arabic (ibid., pp. 60, 293, 295, 296).
44. This has a legendary flavor. It is, however, a fact that in 1747, "wherever he halted he had many people tortured and put to death, and had towers of their heads erected" (ibid., 259).
45. This account of Nadir's assassination largely corresponds to that given in ibid., p. 262.
46. Actually, Nadir had built himself tombs in Kalat and in Meshhed in the Khiabian-i-Bala, the Upper Avenue (ibid., p. 198).
47. The chronogram is not quite correct, for it gives 1161, while Nadir was assassinated in 1160. If, however, we take Nadir's name written not in its full form (with an alif after the *N*), which was assumed only at his coronation, but in its original form without the alif, we reduce the number by one and thus get 1160. It is very possible that the hatred felt toward Nadir was expressed in the original form of the chronogram not only in the words but also by referring to him by his original humble name, Nadr.

Notes by Laurence Lockhart

It is unfortunate that so little authentic information has been preserved regarding Nadir's early life. It is possible that, if ever the missing first volume of Muhammad Kazim's work is found, we may learn a good deal more, but that is mere conjecture. I must regret that I have, so far, been unable to visit the Darragaz-Abivard country, so as to collect for myself any local tradition that may still be current.

a. I have not seen any reference elsewhere to Nadir's baldness and regard this statement as improbable.
b. Abivard. For position, see map on p. 19 of Lockhart, *Nadir Shah*.
c. *Gheshlagh* and *yeylagh:* I suggest that the spellings *qishlaq* and *yailaq* are preferable.
d. Raid on Khiva. There is confusion here with the early raid on Merv, as stated in note 12.
e. There seems to be some confusion here between (1) Fatḥ 'Alī Khan Daghistani, who was disgraced and blinded for his alleged plot to deprive Shah Sultan Ḥusayn of his throne, and (2) Fatḥ Ali Khan Qajar of Astrabad. There seems, however, to be very little doubt that Nadir was responsible for the death of his rival Fatḥ 'Alī Khan Qajar.
f. The chronology here is, of course, faulty, as the Afghan invasion took place in 1722. Nadir's Caucasian campaigns took place nearly twenty years later.
g. Shah Sultan Ḥusayn sent word to Vakhtang, the viceroy of Georgia, asking him to march to the relief of the capital, but Vakhtang refused.

h. The story of the capture of Baghdad is pure fantasy.
i. Kuh-i-Blur: Kuh-i-Bulur, "mountain of crystal."
j. This is certainly very probable. It will be recalled that Shah Abbas the Great moved many Armenians from Julfa on the Aras to "New" Julfa, just south of Isfahan, in order to foster trade in his capital. Nadir may well have decided to imitate him. He had often transferred tribesmen from one district to another for purposes of defense.
k. There is no truth in the statement that Nadir blinded Mīrzā Mahdī.
l. There is no doubt whatever about Nadir's terrible cruelties in his later years, but the story of the eyes reminds me of Agha Muhammad's wholesale blinding of the people of Kirman after his capture of that city in 1794.
m. I agree that in order to make this chronogram correct, the alif in Nadir's name should be dropped, causing it to revert to its original form.

Chapter 14. Three Tales about Mullah Siman-Tov

1. A *madrasah,* "school," is a religious college for studious adults, as distinguished from the *maktab,* the Muslim religious school for children. See below, chapter 21.
2. This took place at a time when no Persian translation of the Bible was yet current. The translation by the Persian savant Fazil Khan was published by the British Bible Society in 1856, and became popular among the Jews of Meshhed who could not read the Hebrew Bible because they were ignorant of the Hebrew alphabet and language.
3. The pilgrims who went to Meshhed in the 1940s to visit the shrine of Imām Reza numbered about sixty thousand annually. A man who has made the pilgrimage to Meshhed assumes the title Meshhedi, just as a pilgrim to Mecca and Medina receives the title Ḥājjī.
4. Or Isḥāq and Mūsā in Persian.
5. The Persian equivalent of mufti.
6. Deut. 32.
7. The text of the verse evidently is corrupt in the original Hebrew and defies all attempts at translation.
8. *Miskal* is the smallest measure of weight, equivalent to twenty-four *nakhud* (peas). See Jakob E. Polak, *Persien, das Land und seine Bewohner,* 2 vols. (Leipzig, 1865), vol. 2, p. 157.
9. Note the recurrence of six months as the duration of anything critical; see above and also below, in the third tale.
10. The Lo-Torai, i.e., "not Toraic," is a secret language of the Jews of Meshhed, containing Hebrew, Persian, anagrammatical, and other elements.
11. It is characteristic of the reliability of the historical traditions as remembered by my informant that all the data that can be verified by historical sources are corroborated by them. My informant knew that 'Abbās Mīrzā was the governor of Meshhed, that he was the crown prince, the son of Fatḥ 'Alī Shāh, and that he did not succeed his father to the throne, as he died before him. All of these are correct historical facts, as is the occurrence of a severe cholera plague in Meshhed (as well as in all Persia) in 1830. See *Encyclopaedia of Islam,* s.v. Meshhed; George Fowler, *Three Years in Persia,* London, 1841, vol. 1, p. 31.
12. 'Ēdgāh, "place of festival." This was the original name of the gardens just within the city walls, where the Jews bought land and built their houses in the middle of the eighteenth century.

13. When he reached this point in his narrative, my informant, overcome by emotion, had to interrupt his account.
14. *Gezērah* is an evil decree, a natural or social catastrophe ordained by God.

Chapter 15. Two Stories about the Jews of Kalat

1. Palang Tushkhan Jalāyir, who figures as the governor of Kalat in Āqā Farajullah's stories and is remembered as "a wise and considerate ruler," seems to have been a late descendant of the Mongol Jalāyir dynasty that held sway over parts of the defunct Ilkhanid Empire in the fourteenth century and survived in Lower Mesopotamia until 1432. See *Encyclopaedia of Islam,* vol. 2, pp. 401–2.
2. See above, chapter 13.

Chapter 17. The Story of the Woman Gohar

1. See above, chapter 7, note 1.
2. Interview conducted by Tamara Tkhornitzki with Mordekhai Ya'qovi in Haifa in December 1972. Transcript in the Israel Folktale Archives, Haifa, no. 9697. I wish to thank Professor Haya Bar-Itzhak and Edna Hechal for providing me with a copy of that transcript.

Chapter 21. The Secret School

An earlier version of this chapter was published in Hebrew, in *Edoth* 1:4 (July 1946): 213–26. This chapter is based on information supplied in 1944–45 by members of the Meshhedi Jewish community and of the Meshhed youth club in Jerusalem. I am especially indebted to Farajullah Nasrullayoff, head of the community, and his three sons, Daniel, Ḥananiah, and Yoḥanan, as well as to Farajullah Ya'quboff, Mr. and Mrs. Yiṣḥaq Ya'qubi, Eliyahu Ben-Moshe, and Ya'qov Marash, all members of the Meshhedi community in Jerusalem.

1. See Polak, *Persien,* vol. 1, p. 50.
2. The value of the currency constantly decreased in Persia. While in the 1880s, as mentioned above, 8 to 10 *q'rān* were sufficient for the monthly expenses of an average family, by the end of World War I, these expenses had increased to 150 to 170 *q'rān.*
3. At that time, a *man* (about 3 kilograms) or 6.5 pounds of bread cost 1.20 *q'rān.* A pair of shoes in European style cost about 30 to 35 *q'rān.* A pair of Persian shoes cost 8 to 12 *q'rān.*
4. See Polak, *Persien,* vol. 1, p. 367ff., for a detailed description of the New Year (Naurūz) festivities.
5. Such mnemotechnical words were in use in other Jewish communities as well, such as among the Jews of Kurdistan, in the town of Arbil (Eric Brauer and Raphael Patai, *The Jews of Kurdistan,* Detroit, 1993, p. 242); and among the Yemenite Jews (according to oral information supplied by Y'hudah Ratzhabi). It was used also among the Arabs (oral information supplied by Irene Garbel).
6. The correct literary form of this word is *tafsīr,* but in the colloquial, the final *r* has become an *l.*

Chapter 24. Marriage

An earlier version of this chapter was published in Hebrew in *Edoth* 2 (April–July 1947): 65–92.

1. M. Qid. 3:5; B. Qid. 62b; Maimonides, *Mishne Torah*, Hilkhot Ishut 7:16.
2. Erich Brauer, "The Jews of Afghanistan," *Jewish Social Studies* 4 (1942): 127; Y'hoshu'a, *MiNidḥē*, p. 392.
3. Yosef M'yuḥas, *HaFallaḥim*, Jerusalem, 1937, p. 57; Moshe Stavsky, *HaK'far ha'Aravi*, Tel Aviv, 1946, pp. 237–38; Klein, *ZDPV* 6:81 ff.
4. Polak, *Persien*, vol. 1, p. 200; A. Donaldson, *The Wild Rue*, London, 1938, p. 49.
5. Polak, *Persien;* Raphael Patai, *Golden River to Golden Road: Society, Culture, and Change in the Middle East*, 3rd ed., Philadelphia, 1969, pp. 135–76.
6. Polak, *Persien*, vol. 1, p. 206; Nurullah Khan, *The Glory of the Shia World*, translated and edited by P. M. Sykes, London, 1910, p. 66. Nurullah Khan was a Persian nobleman born in 1859, and his book contains autobiographical material. His own engagement was arranged in 1877, when he was eighteen.
7. The *gaz* is the *manna* tree and also candy made of *manna*. According to Farajullah Nasrullayoff, *gaz* can be found only in Isfahan. *Ḥalvah* is made of wheat flour, oil, and sugar, and various substances to improve the taste.
8. Polak, *Persien*, vol. 1, p. 221.
9. Nurullah Khan, *Glory*, p. 70.
10. Ibid., pp. 67–68.
11. Polak, *Persien*, vol. 1, p. 211.
12. Tos. Ketubbot 1:4, ed. Zuckermandel, p. 261; Y. Ket 25a mid. The words in brackets are added in B. Ket. 12a.
13. Farajullah Nasrullayoff explained to me that *bāshlaq* is a Turkish word that literally means "for the head," that is, a payment through which the head of the bride is acquired.
14. Polak, *Persien*, vol. 1, p. 200.
15. In 1880, this sum still sufficed for the living expenses of an average family for at least a year. A similar decree limiting the bride price to 130 *q'rān* plus jewelry was issued in 'Amadiyya, in Kurdistan, about 1890 (Erich Brauer and Raphael Patai, *The Jews of Kurdistan*, Detroit, 1993; p. 91).
16. Ibid., p. 98; Nurullah Kahn, *Glory*, p. 71.
17. On the Persian wedding ritual, see Polak, *Persien*, 1:210ff.; Nurullah Khan, *Glory*, p. 75; Donaldson, *Wild Rue*, pp. 48ff.
18. Nurullah Kahn, *Glory*, p. 79.
19. Ibid., pp. 72–75.
20. Several *ketubbot* from Meshhed were published by Y. Yoel in *Kiriath Sefer* 21 (1944–45): 302, 303, 306.
21. Nurrulah Khan, *Glory*, pp. 78–80.
22. Ibid., p. 76.
23. The same rite also was performed before entering a new house or setting out on a trip.
24. Similar customs were practiced in many other places in the traditional Middle East.
25. Nurullah Khan, *Glory*, p. 76.
26. Donaldson, *Wild Rue*, p. 50.

27. Nurullah Khan, *Glory*, pp. 77 ff.
28. Polak, *Persien*, vol. 1, p. 212.
29. Nassim Bassalian, a member of the Meshhedi Jewish community in Kew Gardens, N.Y., helped in transliterating this wedding song.

Chapter 25. Burial Customs

This chapter was originally published in Hebrew in *Dappe Zikkaron liR'fael Aharonoff* (Jerusalem: Heshvan, 1945), pp. 39–54, and as an offprint, part of *Historical Traditions and Mortuary Customs of the Jews of Meshhed* (Jerusalem: Palestine Institute of Folklore and Ethnology, 1945), pp. 9–24.

1. In other communities it was the custom to leave a pebble in the house of the mourners. Thus, e.g., among the Jews of Kutais in the Caucasus, who considered the stone "a symbol of lifelessness, since the body had become lifeless." Yosef Y'huda Chorny, *Sēfer haMassa'ot b'Eretz Qavqaz* (St. Petersburg, 1884), p. 188.
2. Ibid., p. 117, about the Jews of Mogo in the Caucasus: "They took him [the deceased] to the field, where they pitched a tent *fun layvint* [of linen] and placed the deceased into it." See S'maḥot 8:2, ed. Higger, p. 149, and the term "The *ḥuppa* [canopy] of the dead" in the *Baraitot of Ēvel Rabbati*, ed. Higger, p. 231, and parallel passages there.
3. In contrast to B. Mo'ed Qatan 8b, where it says, "They cut his hair." See Maimonides, *Mishne Tora*, Hilkhot Evel 4:1. The Yemenite Jews shave the hair of the deceased. Erich Brauer, *Ethnologie der jemenitischen Juden* (Heidelberg, 1934), p. 222.
4. Eighteenth-century German Jews used to pare the nails of the dead. Johann C. G. Bodenschatz, *Kirchliche Verfassung der heutigen Juden*, 4 vols. (Erlangen and Coburg, 1748), 4:171.
5. Shroud of white linen: B. Mo'ed Qatan 27b; see Tos Nid. 9:17, ed. Zuckermandel, p. 651; B. Ket. 8b; *Sēfer Maharil* (1858), p. 240. This is the general Jewish custom to this day; cf. *Sēfer Z'khira v'Iny'nē S'gullot* (Wilmersdorf, 1729), p. 53b: "The *s'gulla* [virtue] of white linen for the dead and the quick."
6. See B. Sanh. 47a: "If rain streams down upon his bier, this is a good sign for the dead."
7. The same custom was observed in medieval Germany; see *Kol Bo* (Lvov, 1860), p. 88a [*Hilkhot Ēvel*]: "And the comforters likewise sit on the floor."
8. See Rabbi David Ibn Abi Zimra [RaDBaZ], pt. 2, par. 94. Similarly among the Jews of Calcutta, India; see Ya'qov Sapir, *Even Sapir*, pt. 2 (Mainz, 1874), p. 101: "In the days of their mourning they wear a white kerchief around their necks hanging down to the chest."
9. According to one of my Meshhedi informants, not a relative but an old man would close the eyes of a dead man and an old woman the eyes of a dead woman.
10. Among the Jews of Kutais, Caucasus, the custom of placing a candle at the head and the feet of the deceased was observed by Chorny, *Sēfer haMassa'ot*, p. 188.
11. The Bene Israel of India poured water upon the body of the deceased from seven clay vessels, one after the other, and then broke the empty vessels. Haeem Samuel Kehimkar, *The History of the Bene Israel of India* (Tel Aviv, 1937), p. 154. The breaking of vessels is performed when the body is removed from the house in various Jewish communities; see Abraham M. Luncz, *Y'rushalayim* (Vienna, 1882), 1:13; Y'huda Bergmann, *HaYahadut, Nishmatah v'Hayyehah* (Jerusalem, 1938), pp. 76, 83; Johannes Buxtorf, *Synagoga Judaica*

(Basel, 1643), p. 630; Bodenschatz, *Kirchliche Verfassung,* 4:173; Paul C. Kirchner, *Jüdisches Zeremoniell*. . . (Nürnberg, 1724), p. 217; Max Grunwald, "Aus Hausapotheke und Hexenküche," *Jahrbuch für jüdische Volkskunde* (1923), p. 219.

12. Nevertheless, one should not exclude the possibility that originally it was the lotus that was used in connection with washing the dead, since in Egypt they used to wash the dead with water in which lotus leaves (*nabq* or *sidr*) had been boiled. Edward W. Lane, *Manners and Customs of the Modern Egyptians,* Everyman's Library ed. (London, n.d.), p. 518.
13. The belief that camphor diminishes sexual desire is found among many peoples; see Hovorka and Kronfeld, *Vergleichende Volksmedizin,* 2 vols. (Stuttgart, 1909), 2:166.
14. Thus according to Gohari. According to Nasrullayoff, they pared the nails but did not touch the hair.
15. One cannot fail to notice the similarity between these burial rites and the bride's circumambulation of the bridegroom, the breaking of a glass at the wedding, between the tent and the *ḥuppa*.
16. Similarly among the Bene Israel of India: they sprinkle earth from Jerusalem into the eyes and mouth of the dead. Kehimkar, *History of the Bene Israel,* p. 155.
17. However, there are similar customs also among the Ashkenazi Jews. They put a wooden fork in the hand of the deceased (Bodenschatz, *Kirchliche Verfassung,* 4:174) or into his coffin, to serve him as a support on his way to Jerusalem in the days of the resurrection. A. M. Spoer, *Folk-Lore* (London), 42 (1931): 73. According to Luncz, *Y'rushalayim,* 1:12, "The custom of putting branches into the hands of the dead . . . is not practiced here [in Jerusalem]." The Jews of India put a branch into the deceased's right hand (Kehimkar, *History of the Bene Israel,* p. 155).
18. However, see *Sēfer Maharil,* p. 241: "He warned his sons that they should not look into the coffin when they opened it in order to lay the dead into it in a proper manner." Among the Jews of Morocco also it was forbidden to look at the face of the dead. Lancelot Addison, *The Present State of the Jews*. . . (London, 1675), p. 223.
19. In accordance with the old custom: "The deceased is carried on the shoulders" (*Baraitot of Ēvel Rabbati,* ed. Higger, p. 246).
20. Thus according to Gohari. According to Nasrullayoff, this rite was performed in the tent set up in the deceased's house. The custom continued to be observed among the Meshhedi immigrants in Jerusalem. Similar customs with coins were found also among other communities in Jerusalem (Bergmann, *HaYahadut,* p. 76). Among the Jews of Basra, Iraq, see Grunwald, "Aus Hausapotheke," p. 219.
21. In the Ashkenazi custom of medieval times: "They should wash their hands prior to entering their houses" (*Kol Bo,* Hilkhot Evel, chap. 10, p. 2). The general Jewish custom is to wash the hands when leaving the cemetery.
22. Thus according to Gohari. According to Nasrullayoff and a third informant, they made the tear after washing the body but before they took it to the cemetery. See also S'maḥot 9:8, ed. Higger, p. 171; and in general, S'maḥot, chap. 9 on the rules of the *qri'a* (rending).
23. This conforms to the general Jewish custom; see S'maḥot 6:1, ed. Higger, pp. 130–31; 6:11, pp. 140–41, and other sources there; also 9:11. See also R. Abraham ben Natan ha Yarḥi, *Sēfer haManhig,* Warsaw, 1885, pp. 174, 178.
24. In Germany, the mourners used to sit in the place where the deceased lay (Kirchner, *Jüdisches Zeremoniell,* p. 220).
25. Gen Rab. 96:5; haYarḥi, *Sēfer haManhig,* p. 178; *Kol Bo,* Hilkhot Evel, 88a. Similarly

among seventeenth-century Moroccan Jews: Addison, *Present State of the Jews*, p. 218. In Jerusalem: *Sēfer Taqqanot* (Jerusalem, 5602 [1842]), p. 68a, par. 83.

26. Similarly among the Jews of Calcutta: Sapir, *Even Sapir*, 2:100. "The mourners spend a lot of money in the days of mourning, for every day during the seven days of mourning they give ample repasts to the poor and the rich, like the meals at circumcisions and weddings, with many desserts and all kinds of fruits, so as to give occasion to many benedictions. This is done to honor the dead, for the exaltation of the soul of the deceased. And thus they do on the thirtieth day, and again on the first anniversary. And the expenses of mourning are as high as those of the weddings, except that at the mourning meals the invited guests do not sit on chairs at tables, but sheets are spread for them on the floor, and so they eat." Also among the Caucasian Jews: Chorny, *Sēfer haMass'ot*, p. 117; also Leon de Modena, who says in his *History of the Present Jews*, London, 1707, p. 229, that in the East and in many other places, the relatives and friends have the custom of sending, in the evening and in the morning of the seven days of mourning, grand and sumptuous repasts to the deceased's relatives, and eating with them in order to comfort them. As for banquets after the conclusion of the seven days of mourning, see Flavius Josephus, *Wars of the Jews* 2.1.1. Among the Yemenite Jews: Brauer, *Ethnologie*, p. 227.
27. On the mourners' garments: Joseph Perles, "Die Leichenfeierlichkeiten im nachbiblischen Judenthume," *MGWJ* 10 (1861): 393; A. Marmorstein, "Beiträge zur Religionsgeschichte und Volkskunde, II," *Jahrbuch für jüdische Volkskunde* 2 (1924–25): 257, n. 1.
28. This custom is attested elsewhere as well: see *Sēfer haTashbetz*, Lemberg, 1858, par. 427; *Sēfer Maharil*, p. 238. Among seventeenth-century Moroccan Jews: Addison, *Present State of the Jews*, pp. 223–24.
29. Similarly in Jerusalem: "If two should die in one courtyard, they will slaughter a cock for a man and a hen for a woman. They bury the head and the feet of the birds and distribute the meat among the poor" (Moshe Reischer, *Sēfer Sha'arē Y'rushalayim*, Warsaw, 1879, p. 91).
30. Likewise among the Jews of North Africa: cf. Benjamin II (Israel Joseph Benjamin), *Sēfer Massa'ē Yisraēl* (The Book of the Travels of Israel), Lyck, 1859, p. 129: "The dirge contains those things which are befitting the value and works of the deceased, and they compose new dirges for almost every person who dies."

Conclusion

1. Howard M. Sachar, *Farewell España: The World of the Sephardim Remembered*, New York, 1994, p. 169.
2. See above, chapter 2.
3. See above, chapter 4.

Judeo-Persian Vocabulary

This vocabulary lists those Persian and Hebrew words used by the Jadīdīm in their Judeo-Persian colloquial which appear in this book. The Hebrew words are set in *italics,* the Persian in **boldface.** The abbreviation "JP" (for "Judeo-Persian") appearing after a Persian word indicates that the word, or that particular form of it, is (or was) used by the Jadīdīm of Meshhed but is not part of the literary (or standard) Persian language. The abbreviation "lit." stands for "literary form" or "literal meaning." The well-known fact that many of the Persian words are derived from the Arabic is left unmentioned—it has no relevance for Judeo-Persian. Of the Judeo-Persian wedding song contained in chapter 24, only the few Hebrew words appearing in it are listed here.

Pronunciation Guide

In the pronunciation of the words given in transliteration in the text and in this vocabulary, the following should be taken into account:

With a few exceptions, all the words, whether Hebrew or Persian, are accented on the last syllable.

' stands for glottal stop, as in *mu'azzin.*

¯ (macron) over a vowel indicates that it is long.

ʿ stands for the *ʿayin* in Hebrew or the *ʿayn* in Persian, which, however, usually remains unpronounced, as in Hebrew *ʿālīlah,* pronounced *ālīlah;* Persian *ʿabā,* pronounced *abā.*

The vowels are pronounced as follows:

a as in bUt	i as in Is	ö as in French pEU
ā as in tAll	ī as in m*EE*t	u as in lOOk
e as in tEn	o as in lOt	ū as in tOOl
ē as in Ape	ō as in gO	

As for the pronunciation of the consonants, the following should be noted:

ch as in CHin

g as in Go

gh guttural g (as in Arabic غ)

ḥ emphatic h but usually pronounced h

j as in Joy

kh as in German naCH (Arabic خ)
q a deep emphatic k (Arabic ق)
r lingual r, as in Italian
ṣ a somewat guttural s (Arabic ص)
sh as in SHe
ṭ emphatic t (Arabic ط)
th as in THin
ẓ palatal z
The remaining consonants are pronounced more or less as in English.
'abā, sleeveless cloak.
abgad or *abjad,* etc., mnemotechnical words composed of the letters of the Hebrew alphabet.
ādam, man, person, people.
āftau (lit. **āftāb**), sunlight.
Akhālī, Turkoman tribe.
ākhūnd, teacher.
albande (JP), slave, the tied one, the blindfolded one.
alchin, length unit, about one quarter of a meter.
'alijeh, a textile.
'alīlah, false statement, denial.
'alīlah **bemen** (JP), make a denial.
'aliya, immigration to Palestine or Israel.
alkholoq (lit. **alkhāleq**), undershirt, vest.
Allahdād, "Allah gave," term for the 1839 attack on the Jews of Meshhed.
ālū, plum.
āmad, came; from **āmadan,** to come.
'amāmeh, turban.
āmbār (ānbār), dung.
āmbār pāzan (JP), dung preparer.
'amo, uncle.
angushtar, ring.
anār, pomegranate.
anusim, forced converts.
āq, short for **āqā.**
āqā, sir, Mr., master.
'aqd, wedding.
araq, raisin brandy.
'araqchīn, skullcap.
ark (lit. **arq**), citadel.
'arūs, bride.
'arūs kashān, "accompanying the bride," a wedding rite.
'arūsak bāzī, doll game, a girls' game.
'arūsī, wedding, marriage.
āshpaz, cook.
Ashrē, a Hebrew prayer.
'Ashūrah, "tenth," the feast of the tenth of Muḥarram.
Ayatollah, high religious dignitary.
ayneh (lit. **ā'īneh**), mirror.

ayyām, pl. of **yawm.**
Azharōt, liturgical poems.

bādām, almond.
bādenjān, eggplant.
badiyah, pot.
bahā, price.
bakshish, tip, gratuity.
bal, bale, large bundle.
balabān, musical instrument played with the lips.
baleh, yes.
baleh giri, "taking yes," an engagement rite.
bandān, to bind, tie, fasten.
barān, to send, carry.
barukh, blessed.
bāshī, head, chief.
bāshlaq, hood, cowl, a gift for the bride.
bāshlaq barān, "gift sending," a wedding rite.
Bast, place of refuge, name of the sanctuary in Meshhed.
bāṭin, internal, interior.
bāzī, game.
bāzū band, arm band, armlet.
beh, quince.
behesht, paradise.
bemen (JP), make.
Bet hamiqdash, the temple of Jerusalem.
binān, to see; see **ṣalāḥ binān.**
bot (lit. **bāf**), weaving.
bolā (lit. **bālā**), upward.
bolā taraq, see **ṭaraq.**
boqcheh (lit. **baghcheh**), bundle.
bori (lit. **borra**), cutting; from **baridan,** to cut.
b'shqāb (lit. **bashqāb**), plate, dish.
bul (or **gul**) **hand,** heating place of a bath.
būryā, mat.

chādor, veil.
chādor numāz, prayer wrap, women's overall cloak.
chārqad, kerchief.
chehel-e bori (lit. **chehel-i borra**), "cutting forty," a feast forty days after the birth of a child.
chlau (lit. **chulāv, chilo**), plain boiled rice.
chlau nokhōdau (lit. **chulav nokhōdāb**), rice and pea soup; see **nokhōd.**
chotke (from Russian *s'chote*), abacus.
chūb, chōb, stick, rod.
chudan, cast iron, metal pot.
chūkhā, coat with sleeves, overcoat.

dā'ah (lit. **dō'ā**), blessing, amulet.
dādan, to give.
daftar, ledger.
dagi (lit. **daghi**), a disease.
dā'ireh, dayreh, tambourine, drum.
dāmād, bridegroom.
dandāne, tooth.
dāri (from **dārā,** having), to have, make, arrange.
darogha, officer.
Darvāzeh Jennat ("Gate of Paradise"), the new Jewish quarter in Meshhed.
dasi (lit. **dast**), hand.
dastmāl, handkerchief.
da'uri (lit. **dūrī**), plate, dish.
davāt, inkwell.
dayyan, judge, assistant rabbi.
de (lit. **do**), two.
delāleh, matchmaker.
derek, hell.
dīm, face.
dīm vardārān, "face taking," facial treatment in a wedding rite.
dogmeh (lit. **dukmeh**), button.
dombak (lit. **tanbak**), tambourine.
dōri (lit. **dāri,** from **dārā,** having), you have.
dūdī, smoky.
dushak, mattress.
dūshakchih, cushion.

'Ēdgāh, "feast place," name of the Jewish quarter in Meshhed.
Elohay n'shamah, Hebrew prayer.
Englestan, England.
'erev rav, mixed multitude.
ethroq, citron, used in Sukkoth ritual.
even yükhülsun (Turkic), "May you be destroyed!"

falak, falakeh, contraption for bastinado.
falqī, camel litter for women.
fānūs, lamp.
fayton (from French *phaeton*), carriage.
fayub, basin, cistern.
franji, "Frank," European.
fūsh (lit. **fāsh**), open.

gāl, scorpion-like black insect.
gālūt (lit. *galut*), exile.
gavōreh (lit. **gahvāreh**), cradle.
gaz, confectionery made of manna.
gezērah, evil decree.

ghazāl, a poetical form.
gheshlagh (lit. **geshlāq**), winter grassland.
ghōb Lit. **gāb**), knuckle-bones.
giri (from **giraftan,** to take, catch), taking, catching.
go'el, redeemer.
gol (lit. **gāl**), deceit, empty.
gōleh, flower.
goleh (JP), fear.
gōnyan (lit. *qinyan*), acquisition.
gov (lit. **gav**), ditch.
gov āmbār, heating place of a bath.
gōyecheh (JP), container of clothes.
goyim, gentiles.
gūd, gōd, (lit. *kud*), cattle dung, manure
guldūzī, embroidery.
gulhand (lit. *gulkhan*), fireplace of a bath.
gūshwār(eh), earring.
gvir, lord, chief.

hādāsh (lit. *ḥadash*), new.
haf (lit. **haft**), seven.
Hafṭarah (pl. *hafṭarot*), prophetic passage read in the synagogue.
hajigi (lit. **hijī**), spelling.
Ḥājj or **Ḥājjī,** title of a person who has made the pilgrimage to Mecca.
ḥākem, headman.
ḥakham, learned man, rabbi.
halo lombak, see-saw, a children's game.
ḥalutz, pioneer.
ḥalvāh, sweemeat, halvah.
ḥamām, bathhouse.
ḥanā, henna.
Ḥaram-i Sharīf, Noble Sanctuary, in Meshhed.
harzeh vazān, "frivolous or rude things," taught to bride before the wedding night.
ḥas v'shalom, "God forbid!"
ḥasāb, arithmetic.
Hashem, "the Name," i.e., God.
ḥaṣīr, mat.
hātān (lit. *ḥatan*), bridegroom.
ḥavāli kenīseh, synagogue courtyard
hazaq (lit. *ḥazaq*), "Be strong!"
Hēkhal Zion, temple of Zion.
hel, cardamom seed.
hendeseh, geometry.
ḥibbur, spelling.
hīzam, bonfire.
ḥummuṣ, chickpea.
ḥuppa, wedding canopy.

'Īd al-Naurūz, New Year's Feast.
Ilāha, God.
Imām, religious leader.
Imām Jum'ah, "Community Imām," chief Imām.
Imāma, Imāmate, the office of the Imām.
Injīl, Enjīl, Evangel, Gospel.
'ivri, Hebrew, Jewish.
izdavāj, marriage.

Jadīd al-Islām, "New One of Islam," designation of a person who converted to Islam, "New Muslim."
Jadīdhā, Persian plural of Jadīd.
Jadīdīm, Jadīd with the Hebrew plural *-im.*
jahannam, hell.
jehāz, dowry.

Kabūd Gonbadeh (lit. **ganbad**), "Dark-blue Dome," part of Kalat.
Kaddish, prayer for the dead.
kaf dasi, palm of the hand.
kafgīr, ladle, skimmer.
kāfūr, camphor.
kalām, "talk," the formula of conversion to Islam.
kaleh qand, big sugar loaf.
kamar, belt.
kangar, artichoke.
kapparah, atonement.
Kāravān-bāshī, leader of the caravan.
kāravān serah, caravansary.
Karbalā'ī, title of person who has made the pilgrimage to Karbala.
kardan, to do, make.
kasari, fine cotton, silk.
kashān, kashi (from **kashīdan,** to draw, pull, haul, carry), bringing.
kasher, kosher, ritually clean food.
kavareh, big basket.
kazad bashi, chief emissary.
ketkhoda (lit. **kadkhoda**), chief, chieftain.
ketubba, marriage contract.
khadkhuda, see **ketkhoda.**
khajāwa (lit. **kajābeh**), saddle-like conveyance, camel litter for women.
khākister be ser-esh, "Ashes on his head!" a malediction.
khān barān, invitation.
khānah māndeh, "remained in the house," old maid.
khāncheh, a painted tray.
khārīz, cistern.
khāzandeh, matchmaker.
khazīneh, ritual bath.
kholeh, stupid.

khondan (lit. **khvāndan**), reading.
khōrān (lit. **khāran**), to eat.
khōrosh, vegetable and meat dish.
khosh nawīs, "fine writer," calligrapher.
khoshāve, "good water," a fruit drink.
kīseh māl, a masseur, masseuse in a public bath.
Kobehī, Turkoman tribe.
kōkō, omelette.
kōkō sabzī, vegetable omelette.
kosher, see *kasher.*
kūbīdan, to raize to the ground.
kulāh, hat.
kūr sheved, "May he be blind!" a malediction.

labādeh, overcoat with sleeves.
lakhlakheh, jelly, cosmetic cream for the face.
lāleh, lamp, lantern.
lāleh kashi, "bringing the lamp," a wedding rite.
lau, fold, an X-shaped bookstand.
leben, sour milk.
levushah (from *l'vush,* clothing), enrobing the dead.
līvās (lit. **rīvās**), rhubarb.
Lo Tōrāī, "not Torahic," term for the JP colloquial of the Jadīdīm.
lulabh, palm branch, used in Sukkoth ritual.
lūṭī, comedian, actor.

Ma'ariv, evening prayer.
madrasah, Muslim governmental school.
maḥallah, city quarter, ghetto.
maḥḍar, bureau, office.
maḥḍar izdavāj, marriage bureau.
Mahdī, Muslim equivalent of the Jewish Messiah, also proper name.
māhtau (lit. **mahtāb**), moonlight.
mahūt, velvet-like textile.
majles, gathering, banquet.
majmu'eh (lit. **majma'ah**) tray.
makhshir, instrument, conveyance
maktab, Muslim religious school.
mapasi (from the Russian), candy.
mamzer, bastard.
man, pl. **manāt,** weight unit, about 3 kilograms or 6 pounds.
manāt, Persian name of the Russian ruble, equalling 100 kopecks.
mappah, map, chart
maqna'ah (lit. **miqna'ah**), veil, woman's cloak.
Mashiaḥ, Messiah, also proper name.
maṣṣa, pl. *maṣṣot,* unleavened Passover bread.
mathnawī, poem in rhyming couplets.

matzoth (*maṣṣot*). See *maṣṣa*.
mazzal ṭov, good luck!
midrash, Jewish school
Minḥa(h), afternoon prayer.
minyan, quorum of ten adult men.
miqveh, ritual bath.
Mīrzā, prince, lord.
miskal, small weight unit.
mitzvah (*miṣwah*, pl. *mitzvot*, *miṣwot*), religious commandment.
mizraḥ, east.
möghallad muqallad, actor.
mohel, ritual circumciser.
moshav, *moshav shiṭufi*, two forms of cooperative settlement.
mu'azzin, prayer caller.
mujtahid, high religious functionary.
mullah, master, teacher.
murakkab, ink.
murshid, Ṣūfī spiritual guide.
Musā'ī, Jew.
mushtahed, see **mujtahid.**
mushtu māl (lit. **mushtmāl**), a rubbing with the hand, masseuse.

nabāt, sugar.
naft, gasoline.
nagāleh (JP), "no fear!" see **goleh.**
najīb, faithful, chaste.
nakhud, peas. See **nokhōd.**
nāmeh, book.
naqāshi, drawing, sketching.
narghīleh, water pipe.
nasī, prince.
naurūz, new year.
nay, flute.
nāyeb, deputy.
nāyeb sultānī, regent.
nēs, miracle.
neveshtan, writing.
nezūmi (lit. **nezāmi**), women's trousers.
niddah, menstruating woman.
nīl, indigo.
nīmkat, bench.
nishtar, nail, needle.
niss (lit. **niṣf**), half.
nokhōd, pea.
nokhōdau (lit. **nokhōdāb**), pea soup, see **chlau nokhōdau.**
noqlō (lit. **noql**), sugarplum, comfit.
noqlō bādām, sugar-coated almonds.

numai (lit. **namāi**), exhibition.
numāz (lit. **namāz**), prayer.
numzad (lit. **nāmzad**), bride, marriage.

ojāq, oven, hearth, fireplace.
omer, the days between Passover and Shavu'ot.
ōtaq (lit. **oṭāq**), room.
ōtaq kardan, "room making," a wedding rite.
ōt bāsh (Turkic?), a disease.
ōtesh (lit. **ātesh**), fire.

palang, leopard, panther, commander, also proper name.
pālkī or **pālqī,** litter, palanquin.
pazan or **fazan** (JP), to tread.
pelau, pilau, pilav, pilaw, plaw, rice and meat dish.
piq (JP), pinching.
pirhan (lit. **pīrāhan**), shirt.
pīsh, front, before.
pīsh numāz, prayer leader.
piyyuṭ, liturgical poem.
posh'ē Yisraēl, apostate.
p'ri'ah, uncovering, part of the circumcision ritual.
pūl, penny.
pūlak, sequins; literally fish-scales.
pūsh, cover, tarpaulin.

qabā, long caftan.
Qadi (lit. **qāḍī**), religious judge.
qalam ney, reed pen.
qalam trāsh, penknife.
qalamdān, pen case.
qal'at (also **kalat**), fort.
qalyūn (**narghīleh**), water pipe.
qāshaq, qāshuq, spoon, ladle.
qāshaq chūbī, wooden ladle.
qaṣṣāb, butcher.
qeychi, scissors
qiddush, wedding.
qiddush haShem, sanctification of the Name (of God).
qinyan (pronounced *gönyan*), acquisition, a marriage rite.
qodom (lit. **qadam**), foot.
qō'im (lit. **qāyim**), hide, hiding.
qorjeh (JP), shoe.
qorjeh sar'ī (JP), shagreen shoe.
qormeh, preserved meat.
qoroq, reserved, special.
q'rān, monetary unit.

qri'ah, cutting the upper garment as sign of mourning.
Qurbān Bayrām, "sacrificial feast," also called *'Īd al-aḍḥā,* celebrated on the tenth of the month Dhu 'l-Ḥijja.

raft, went (from **raftan,** to go).
rasūl, messenger.
riḍa, satisfaction, also proper name.
Rosh haShanah, New Year.
ruqum (lit. **raqm,** figure), numerical notation.
rūz, day.
rūz nāmeh, ledger.

sabta, grandmother.
sabzī, vegetable.
sadr, lotus.
sadr v'kāfūr, powder applied to the body of a deceased.
ṣaḥarā, sand, desert.
sāj, pan.
ṣalāḥ, goodness, advice.
ṣalāḥ binān (lit. "to seek advice"), consultation.
ṣalāt, prayer.
ṣamagh 'arabī, gum arabic.
Sareh Heyteh, "Head of the Places," a place name.
sar'ī, shagreen, rawhide.
Sayyid, title of a religious functionary who claims descent from Muhammad.
sāzeh (lit. **sāzī**), instrumental music.
sāzeh balabān, drum band.
sāzendeh, musician.
S'domi, Sodomite.
sedr, unguent made of lotus leaves.
serah, seray, see also **kāravān serah.**
serdabeh, "cold room," crypt, grave.
s'gullot, "precious things."
shab sūr, "repast night," a wedding rite.
shābāsh, coins thrown at weddings.
shāgird, pupil.
Shaḥarit, morning prayer.
shāl, scarf, shawl, in JP the name of a feast at which gifts, such as scarves, were given to the guests.
shāl-ī kamar, hip belt.
shallāq, whip.
shām lāleh, lamp, lantern.
shame', candle.
shammash, sexton, synagogue servant.
sharḥ, commentary.
shar'iyāt, (study of) religion.
shawl, see **shāl.**

shefa', plenty, abundance.
Shekhīna, divine spirit.
shelvār, short skirt.
sherbet, sweet drink.
shevāvil (JP, also *shekhakhil*), a devastating disease, cancer.
Shī'a, the dominant Muslim sect of Iran.
Shī'ī, an adherent of the Shī'a.
shīr, milk.
shīra(h), song.
shīrnī (lit. **shīrīnī**), sweets.
shīrnī dādan, "sweets giving," an engagement rite.
shīrnī girān, "taking sweets," an engagement rite.
shīrnī khōran, "eating sweets," engagement ceremony.
shish pareh, "six sides," Persian term for the Magen David, the Star of David.
shiv'ah, "seven," the seven days of heavy mourning for a close relative.
sh'kasteh band, bone setter.
shlah (lit. *shlaḥ*), send.
Sh'ma' Yisrael, "Hear, O Israel."
shoḥēṭ, ritual slaughterer.
shter zanak (lit. **shutur zan**), a large kind of spider.
sīb, apple.
si'ī (from **si'ah,** black), list of invitees.
siman ṭov, good sign, good omen.
sīr, weight unit, equalling ca. 75 grams.
siyāq (lit. order, style), a numerical notation.
s'liḥot, penitential poems.
s'udah, feast, festive meal at a circumcision.
Ṣūfi, Muslim mystic.
sufreh, tablecloth.
Sukkoth, Feast of Booths, tabernacles.
Sunnī, a member of the major Muslim sect.

ṭabaq, tray.
tafsīl (lit. **tafsīr**), translation.
ṭahara, ritual washing of the dead.
Tajānī, Turkoman tribe.
tajār (sing. **tājir**), merchants.
tajār bāshī, chief of merchants.
tajziyeh, grammar.
takht, throne.
talk, inviter.
ṭallit, prayer shawl.
tanbān, trousers.
Taqiyya, Muslim feast, celebration.
tār, six-stringed violin.
taraq (lit. **taraqi**), progress, ascent, see also **bolā taraq.**
tārīkh, history.

tārīkh ayyām, history.
ṭās, brass plate, cup.
tās teppe, "bowl hill."
Tawrāt or **Tōrāt,** Torah.
tefillin, phylacteries.
tīzāb, nitric acid.
t'naim, "conditions," nuptial contract.
ṭōqe la'anat, "long collar," a badge of shame.
toman, monetary unit, equals 10 *q'rān.*
totzereth ha'aretz, product of Palestine, later of Israel.
t'rēf, t'rēfa, ritually unclean food.
tzaddiq, ṣaddiq saintly man.

ustā (lit. **ustād**), teacher.

vakīl, representative.
vardār (lit. **bardār**), taker, treater, the woman who treats the bride's face.
vardārān, to take, treat, see **dīm vardārān.**
vezīr, minister.

wabā, cholera.

yak, one.
yāl, jacket.
yaum, yawm, day.
yengeh, bridesmaid.
yeylagh (lit. **yeylāq**), summer quarter.
yishuv, the Jewish community of Palestine, later of Israel.
Yom Kippur, Day of Atonement.

ẓāhir exterior, external
zanjīl (lit. **zanjīr**), chain.
zar, Persian measure of length, ca. 108 cm.
zarak, "of gold leaf," confetti-like metal disks.
zargar, goldsmith.
zarī, golden.
zemīn, earth, ground.
zemīnī, terrestrial, of the ground.
zhīd, Jew (derogatory).
zīr, under.
zīr dandāne, "under the tooth," an engagement rite.
zīr zemīnī, "underground," cellar.
ziyāra (lit. **ziyārat**), visitation, pilgrimage.
z'khut, merit.
zönj (lit. **zinj**), gum wood glue.
zumeh (lit. **zamā**), rock alum, vitriol.

Bibliography

Note: Sources used in connection with a comparative discussion of Jadīdī tales and customs are not listed. They can be found in the notes. However, included here are several titles consulted but not cited in the book.

Abbott, Sir James. *Narrative of a Journey from Herat to Khiva . . .* , 2 vols. London, 1842.

Adler, Elkan Nathan. *Jews in Many Lands.* Philadelphia, 1905.

———. "The Persian Jews: Their Books and Their Rituals." *Jewish Quarterly Review* 106 (1898): 584–625.

Aqlar, Mullah Mord'khai. *Siddur T'filla lYmē haḤol k'Minhag S'faradim uM'turgam b'Lashon Parsit w'Nigra 'Avodat haTamid* (Prayer Book for Weekdays according to the Custom of Sephardim and Translated into the Persian Language and Is Called Perpetual Service). Jerusalem, 1906.

Bacher, Wilhelm. "Les Juifs de Perse aux xviie et xviiie siècles d'aprés les chroniques poétiques de Babai b. Loutf et de Babai b. Farhad." *Revue des Etudes Juives* (1906), 51:121–36, 265–79; 52:77–97, 234–71; 53:85–110.

———. *Zwei jüdisch-persische Dichter—Schachin und Imrani,* 2 vols. Budapest, 1907–8; Strassburg, 1907.

Baron, Salo W. *A Social and Religious History of the Jews,* vol. 1. New York and Philadelphia, 1952.

Ben-'Ami, Y. "Yahaduth b'Maḥteret" (Judaism Underground). *Qol Sinai* 1 (Kislēv-Tēvēt 5722 [1962]): 34–37, 39.

Benjamin, Israel Joseph. *Acht Jahre in Asien und Afrika.* Hannover, 1860.

———. *Sēfer Mass'ē Yisraēl* (The Book of the Travels of Israel). Lyck, 1859.

Ben-Zvi, Yitzḥaq. "'Alilot Dam uG'zērot Sh'mad b'Meshhed, b'Salamas uv'Herat baMēah ha19" (Blood Libels and Forced Conversions in Meshhed, Salamas and Herat in the 19th Century). *Meḥqarim uM'qrot* (Studies and Sources). Jerusalem, 1966. Pp. 319–34.

———. *Meḥqarim uM'qorot* (Studies and Sources). Jerusalem, 1966.

———. *Nidḥē Yisraēl* (The Forgotten of Israel), 3rd ed. Tel Aviv, 1956, 1963.

———. "T'udot b'Farsit-Y'hudit 'al Gērush Tze'etza'ē Anusē Meshhed Mē'Ir Herat b'1856" (Documents in Judeo-Persian on the Expulsion of the Descendants of the Forced Converts of Meshhed from the City of Herat in 1856." *Zion* 3 (1939): 254–57.

———. *Zion* 4 (1938): 250–57.

Bernblum-Cohen, T. "Histaglut Anusē Meshhed 'Esrim Shanah l'Aḥar 'Aliyatam" (The Adjustment of the Forced Converts of Meshhed Twenty Years after Their Immigration). *Sa'ad* 1 (1959): 45–46.

Brauer, Erich, and Raphael Patai, *The Jews of Kurdistan*, Detroit, 1993.

British Foreign Office. Documents 60–87: Mashhad, April 1842. Documents 60–106, November 30, 1844.

Conolly, Arthur. *Journey to the North of India—Overland from England through Russia, Persia and Afghanistan*. London, 1834, 1838.

Curzon, George N. *Persia and the Persian Question*. London, 1892.

Dilmānī, Mullah Yosēf ben Āqā 'Abdul-Samad. Unpublished document in the Central Zionist Archives, Jerusalem. Doc. No. S25/5291.

Dilmanian, Ya'aqov. *Tārīkh-ī Isrāīlhā-ī Meshhed az vorūd biMeshhed dar-ī Nādir Shāh-ī Afshār ilā muhājirat az Meshhed* (History of the Jews of Meshhed from Their Arrival in the Days of Nadir Shah Afshar until Their Emigration from Meshhed). Multigraphed document. Teheran, 1966 (?). As summarized by Amnon Netzer, in his "Qorot," see below.

Edoth: A Quarterly for Folklore and Ethnology. Ed. by Raphael Patai and Joseph J. Rivlin. Vols. 1–3. Jerusalem, 1945–48.

Elhanani, Y. "Anusē Meshhed b'Yisraēl" (The Forced Converts of Meshhed in Israel). *Maḥanayim* 93–94 (1964): 124–27.

Encyclopaedia Hebraica. s.v. "Anusim" (Forced Converts).

Encyclopaedia of Islam, 2nd ed. In progress.

Encyclopaedia Judaica. Jerusalem, 1972.

Encyclopaedia of Zionism and Israel, new ed. 1994.

Erlich, Y. "Anusē Meshhed 'Olim" (The Forced Converts of Meshhed Immigrate). *Sh'luḥot* (Sivan-Tammuz 1950): 6–9.

Ferrier, J. P. *Caravan Journeys and Wanderings in Persia, Afghanistan, Turkestan and Beluchistan . . . 1845*. London, 1856, 1976.

Finkel, Joshua. "A Judaeo-Persian Tale." *Jewish Quarterly Review* 21 (1930–31): 353–64.

Fischel, Walter J. *HaY'hudim b'Hodu* (The Jews in India). Jerusalem, 1960.

———. "HaY'hudim b'Iran baMē'ot 16–18" (The Jews in Iran in the 16th–18th Centuries). *Pe'amim* 6 (1980): 5–32.

———. "Israel in Iran." In Louis Finkelstein, ed., *The Jews*, vol 3. Philadelphia, 1949. Pp. 817–58.

———. "Q'hillat ha'Anusim b'Faras" (The Community of the Forced Converts in Persia). *Zion*, n.s. 1 (October 1935): 49–74.

———. "Secret Jews of Persia." *Commentary* 7 (1949): 28–33.

———. "Shahin." *Encyclopaedia Judaica* 14, p. 1258.

———. "The Jews of Persia: 1795–1940." *Jewish Social Studies* 12 (1950): 119–60.

———. "Toldot Y'hudē Paras bYmē Shoshelet haSafavidim baMēah ha17" (History of the Jews of Persia in the Days of the Safavid Dynasty in the 17th Century). *Zion* 3 (1937).

———. Article in *Yidisher Kemfer*, March 21, 1952.

Fowler, George. *Three Years in Persia*. London, 1841.

Fraser, James B. *Historical and Descriptive Account of Persia*. New York, 1836.

———. *Narrative of a Journey into Khorasan in the Years 1821 and 1822.* London, 1825. Reprinted New York, 1984.

Gili, B. Dappē 'Aliyah (Immigration Pages). Jerusalem, 1951.

Ginzberg, Louis. *Legends of the Jews.* Philadelphia, 1909–46.

Ḥakīmī, M. *Jadīd al-Islām: Anusē Meshhed* (New Muslims: The Forced Converts of Meshhed). Multigraphed, 1966.

Hakohēn, R'fa'ēl Ḥayyim. *Avanim baḤomah* (Stones in the Wall). Jerusalem, 1970.

Ish-Hurwitz, Ch. "Muslimim baShuq—Y'hudim b'Sēter" (Muslims in the Marketplace—Jews in Secret). *'Al haMishmar* (Passover supp., April 1986): 32–33.

Kashani, R'uvēn. *Anusē Meshhed* (The Forced Converts of Meshhed). Jerusalem, 1979.

———. "Qorot Z'manim L'haRav Mattityahu Garji mē Afganistan" (The History of the Times by R. Mattityahu Garji of Afghanistan). *Shēveṭ v'Am* 1 (1971): 136–59.

Kleinbaum, Yitzḥaq. Report on the Jews of Meshhed, 1946. Typescript preserved in the Central Zionist Archives, Jerusalem.

Kohēn, Aharon. "M'gillat Anusē Meshhed b'Faras" (The Scroll of the Forced Converts of Meshhed in Persia). *Yeda' 'Am* 5 (1958): 56–62.

Lazarus-Jaffe, H. *P'raqim b'Toldot ha'Aravim v'ha'Islam* (Chapters in the History of the Arabs and of Islam). Jerusalem, 1967.

Lēvi, 'Azarya. "'Ēduyot uT'udot l'Toldot Y'hudē Meshhed" (Testimonies and Documents on the History of the Jews of Meshhed). *Pe'amim* 6 (1981): 57–73.

———. "Gērush Herat" (The Expulsion from Herat). *Pe'amim* 14 (1983): 77–91.

Lēvī, Ḥabīb. *Tārīkh-ī Yahūd-ī Īrān* (History of the Jews of Iran), vol. 3. Teheran, 1339/1960.

Lewis, Bernard. *The Jews of Islam.* Princeton, 1984.

Littman, D. "Jews under Muslim Rule: The Case of Persia." *Wiener Library Bulletin* 49–50 (1979): 12–14.

Lockhart, Laurence. *Nadir Shah.* London, 1938.

Loeb, Laurence D. *Outcaste: Jewish Life in Southern Iran.* New York, 1977.

Malkov, Tzippi. *Yahadut Iran: Sippurah shel 'Ēdah* (The Jews of Iran: The Story of a Community). Jerusalem, 1979.

Meiendorf, Baron Yegor Fiodorovich de. *Voyage d'Orenburg a Bouhara . . . 1820.* St. Petersburg, 1826.

Mizraḥi, Ḥanina. *Toldot Y'hudē Faras uM'shor'rēhem* (History of the Jews of Persia and Their Poets). Jerusalem, 1966.

Muradi, D. "HaRav Mord'khay Aqlar, Rabbam shel ha'Anusim baMaḥteret" (R. Mordechai Aqlar, Rabbi of the Forced Converts in the Underground). *Qol Sinai* 1, 8 (Tammuz 1962): 174–75.

Nasrullayoff, Āqā Farajullah "Levi." *Gōrshehā-ī az Tārīkh Jāmi'a-mā* (Notes on the History of Our Community). New York, 1987. Written in Jerusalem, 1930. With a foreword by Harun Kohanim.

Netzer, Amnon. *Tārīkh-ī Yahūd dar 'Aṣr Jadīd* (History of the Jews in Modern Times). Tel Aviv, 1982.

———. *Otzar Kitvē haYad shel Y'hudē Faras b'Makhon Ben Zvi* (Treasury of Manuscripts of the Persian Jews in the Ben Zvi Institute). Jerusalem, 1988.

———. "Qorot Anusē Meshhed l'fi Ya'aqov Dilmanian" (The History of the Forced Converts of Meshhed according to Jacob Dilmanian). *Pe'amim* 42 (1990): 1127–56.

———. "R'difot uSh'madot b'Toldot Y'hudē Iran baMēah ha17" (Persecutions and Conversions in the History of the Jews of Iran in the 17th Century). *Pe'amim* 6 (1980): 33–56.

———. *Y'hudē Iran* (The Jews of Iran). Ḥolon-Tel Aviv, 1988.

Neumark, Ephraim. *Massa' b'Eretz haQedem* (Travel in the Land of the East). Jerusalem, 1947. Originally published in *HeAsif*, 1889.

Nicholson, R. *The Mystics of Islam*. London, 1975.

Patai, Raphael. "Anusim fun Persie Tzurikgekert tzum Yidishen Gloyben" (Forced Converts of Persia Return to Jewish Faith). *Unzer Vort*, Paris, January 15 and 16, 1964.

———. "How and Why Judaism Survived in Meshhed." *Alliance Review* (Winter 1964): 6–9.

———. *On Jewish Folklore*. Detroit, 1983.

———. *Sex and Family in the Bible and the Middle East*. New York, 1958.

Polak, Jakob E. *Persien, das Land und seine Bewohner*, 2 vols. Leipzig, 1865.

Sachar, Howard M. *Farewell España: The World of the Sephardim Remembered*. New York, 1994.

Shoshani, H. "'Olē Meshhed bYrushalayim" (Immigrants from Meshhed in Jerusalem). *Hēd Hamizraḥ*, March 15, 1946, p. 14.

Shoshkes, H. Article in *Jewish Journal*, April 27, 1951.

Siman-Tov, Yaffa, and R. Raḥmani. "Misḥaqē Y'ladot b'Adat Y'hudē Meshhed" (Girls' Games in the Meshhed Jewish Community). *Edoth* 3 (1948): 88–92.

Siman-Tov Melamed, Mullah. *Sēfer Ḥayāt al-Rūḥ* (Book of the Life of the Spirit). Jerusalem, 1898.

Spicehandler, Ezra. "A Descriptive List of Judeo-Persian Manuscripts in the Klau Library of the Hebrew Union College." *Studies in Bibliography and Booklore* (Spring 1968): 114–36.

Stoddart, William. *Sufism*. New York, 1986.

Stuart, Charles. *Journal of a Residence in Northern Persia*. London, 1854.

Truilhier, M. "Mémoire descriptif de la route de Téhran a Meched." *Bulletin de la Société de Géographie*, 2nd series, no. 9, Paris, May 1838. Reprinted Paris, 1841, ed. by P. Daussy.

Vámbéry, Armin. *Reisen in Mittelasien*. Leipzig, 1865. Reprinted Nürnberg, 1979.

Weinstein, Myron M. "A Hebrew Qur'ān Manuscript." *Studies in Bibliography and Booklore* 10 (Winter 1971–72): 1–2.

Wolff, Joseph. *Journal of the Rev. Joseph Wolff . . . Missionary to the Jews* . . . London, 1839.

———. *Narrative of a Mission to Bokhara in the Years 1843–1845*. London, 1845, 1846.

———. *Researches and Missionary Labours among the Jews, Mohammedans, and Other Sects*. London, 1835.

———. *Travels and Adventures of the Rev. Joseph Wolff*, 2 vols. London, 1860–61.

Y'hoshu'a, Ben-Zion. *Diyoqnah shel Q'hillat ha'Anusim b'Meshhed sheb'Iran* (Portrait of the Community of Forced Converts in Meshhed, Iran). Jerusalem, 1980.

———. *MiNidḥē Yisraēl b'Afganistan l'Anusē Meshhed b'Iran* (From the Lost Ones of Israel in Afghanistan to the Forced Converts of Meshhed in Iran). Jerusalem, 1992.

Zabīḥī, Tziyon. Interview, 1966, Jerusalem. Unpublished manuscript in the archives of the Avraham Harman Institute of Contemporary Jewry, Hebrew University, Jerusalem, no. 813.

INDEX

Abba, Mullah, 206, 207
'Abbās I, 27, 31
'Abbās II, 15–16, 27
'Abbās III, 289*n*15, 289*n*24
'Abbās Kulī Mīrzā, 48, 292*n*11
Abbott, J.: *Narrative of a Journey from Herat to Khiva,* 61
'Abdallah, Mullah, 30–31
Aberdeen, Lord, 67
Abraham: *Kiyāfat al-'Ābidīn* (Directions for the Servants [of God]), 41
Abraham, Mullah, 28, 189
Abū Ḥamīd Muḥammad ibn Muḥammad al-Ghazālī, 41
Abū Ḥasan Lārī, 280*n*2
Abu 'l-Qāsim 'Abd al-Karīm (Hawāzin al-Qushayrī), 45
Achaemenid empire, 14
Afghanistan: attitude toward Jews, 180; British invasion of, 52; English invasion of, 52; historical traditions concerning held by Jews of Meshhed, 50; Jews of, 231; rebellion against Persia, 162
Aḥmed 'Alī Mīrzā, 37, 275
'Ali al-Riḍa (Imām Reza), 19–20
'Alī ibn Abī Tālib, 11, 12, 83
'Alī Muḥammad (al-Bāb), 76, 77, 283 *n*4
Allahdād, 18, 27, 51–64; capture of Jewish women by Muslims during, 61; date of, 53, 56, 57; destruction of synagogue courtyard, 205; Muslim envy of Jewish wealth as motive for, 57
Alliance Israélite Universelle, 17, 87, 106
al-Qazwīnī, 14
al-Yahūdiyya ("the Jewish city"), 14
Amani, 42
Amīn, Ḥājjī (Mullah Benjamin), 37
Amīn, Mullah, 218
Angushtar Bāzī (Ring Game), 225–26
Aqājān, Karb, 113, 116, 124–25
'Aqd Bandān: Gentile Wedding, 241
'Aqedat Yiṣḥaq (the Binding of Isaac), 200
Aqlar, Mullah Murād (Mordechai), 73–74, 87, 210; *'Avodat ha Tamid* (The Perpetual Service), 74; *'Olam Shabbat* (Sabbath World), 74
Aqlar, Rafi, 74
Artaxerxes II, 14
'Arūsak Bāzī (Game of the Dolls), 225
'Arūsī: the Marriage, 231, 247–52
Arūsi Ḥamām: Bath of the Bride, 243–45
'Arūs Kashān: Bringing the Bride, 254–56
Avraham Harman Insitute of Contemporary Jewry, Hebrew University of Jerusalem, 92
Ayatollah, 12
Ayneh Torah, 256

Babai ibn Farḥad, 16, 25, 27
Babai ibn Luṭf, 25, 27; *Kitāb-i Anusi* ("Book of the Forced Converts"), 16
Baba Qudrat (Baba Ghodrat), 152, 179
Babylonian Geonim, 14

Babylonian Talmud, 14
Bahai faith, 76, 283*n*6
Bahā' Ullah (Mīrzā Ḥusayn 'Ali), 76
Baḥya ibn Paquda: *Duties of the Heart*, 39, 41
Baleh Giri: Taking Yes, 234
Bāshlaq Barān: Sending the Bride Price, 239–40
Ben-'Ami, Y., 61
Benjamin, Joseph, 68
Bey, Ragheb, 66
Bible, Persian translation of, 216, 217
Birth customs, of Jews of Meshhed, 198–201; customs during birth, 199; customs for barren women, 199; customs for circumcision, 200; customs for difficult births, 199–200; customs for naming, 199–200; customs for suckling, 201; customs to insure a boy-child, 199
Blood libels, 79–82, 83–85, 92–94, 94–97, 189
Bolsheviks, 137, 138–39
Bukhara, 32, 65, 66, 67, 75, 124, 135, 136, 144
Bukhara, Jews of, 49
Burial customs: of Ashkenazi Jews, 296*n*17, 296*n*21; of Bene Israel of India, 295*n*11, 296*n*16; of German Jews, 295*n*4; of Jews, 295*n*5, 296*n*23; of Jews of Calcutta, 295*n*8, 297*n*26; of Jews of Kutais, 295*n*10; of Jews of Meshhed, 265–72; of Jews of Morocco, 296*n*18, 297*n*28; of Jews of North Africa, 297*n*30; of Yemenite Jews, 295*n*3

Caliphs (khalīfa), 11
Chādor, 94, 284*n*6
Chehel-e bori, 201
Cohen, David, 43
Conolly, Arthur, 36, 67; account of Jews of Meshhed, 33–35, 38
Curzon, George N.: *Persia and the Persian Question*, 16–17
Cyrus, 288*n*6, 288*n*8

Dāmād-i Ḥamām: Immersion of the Bridegroom, 245
Dāmād Khān Barān: Invitation of the Bridegroom, 236–37
Daoud Cohen, Mullah, 53
Darius II, 14
Dastgird, 156
Deregez (Darra Gaz), 155, 284*n*3; Jewish community in, 113, 122, 136–37, 286*n*22
Deriā-i-Nūr, 164–65
dhimmīs, 13, 14, 15
Dietary laws, observance of by Jews of Meshhed, 228–29, 230, 287*n*37
Dīl, Mullah Yosef, 212, 217
Dīlmānī, Mullah Yosef ben Āqa 'Abdul-Samad, 57, 81, 82, 88; folktale of Gohar saving Jews of Meshhed, 187–88
Dīlmānī, Samad Āqā ben Yosef: account of Allahdād, 57–59
Dilmanian, Ya'aqov, 60–61, 63, 71, 75, 82, 90
Dilmanīs family, 74
Dīm Vardārān: Taking of Face, 242–43
Divorce, 260–61
Du Ryer, André, 43

'Ēdgāh, 18, 28, 115, 206, 284*n*7, 292*n*12
Edoth, 22, 94
Elyashar, Eliyahu, 109
Esther, book of, 14
Ezra, book of, 13

Fatḥ-'Alī Shah, 164, 292*n*11
Fāṭima al-Zahrā, 94, 284*n*5
Fāzil (Fāḍil) Khān, 217, 292*n*2
Feast of Bairam, 53
Ferrier, J. P., 67–68; on the Meshhed Allahdād, 55–57
Firdawsi, 42
Fischel, Walter J.: *Encyclopedia Judaica*, 15, 39
Folk-Lore 57, 168
Folktales and legends, of Jews of Mesh-

hed: about Jews of Kalat, 152, 173–77; about Mullah Siman-Tov, 152, 168–72; about rescue of Jews of Meshhed by Gohar, 182–88; about the Thieving Shaykh, 173–75; deterioration of oral tradition, 187–88; oral *versus* written tale of Gohar saving the Jews of Meshhed, 186–87; popular "Life of Nadir," 154–67; story of death of Ḥājj Hasan Eshaq, 152, 189–92
Fraser, James Baillie; account of Jews of Meshhed, 32–33, 38

Gafuri, Ḥabab, 90
Games, of Meshhedi Jewish girls, 222–27
Garden of Nadir, 167
Garji, R. Mattityahu, 72, 73
Ghazāl, 43
Ghōb Bāzī (Game of Bones), 223
Gilaki dialect, 27, 72, 195
Gilan, 25, 27
gittim, 57
Glazemaker, Ian Hendrik, 43
Gohar: story of rescue of Jews of Meshhed by, 152, 182–88
Gohari, M., 265

Ḥājjī Y'ḥezq'el Synagogue, 87
Ḥakīmī family, 60, 61, 74, 78, 90
Hakohen, Ḥājjī Adoniyah, 87
Halo Lombak (See-Saw), 223–24
Ḥanā Bandān: Henna Tying, 245–46
Haram-i Sharīf (Bast), 20
Harzeh Vazān: Rude Things, 243
Hasan Eshaq, Ḥājj: story of death of, 152, 189–92
Hayyim, 40
Ḥazqi, Mullah, 259, 260
Hebrew Union College (Cincinnati), 39
Heim, Shemuel, 88
Herat, 32; Jews of, 72–73, 152, 178–81, 189; Persian conquering of, 152, 178
Heratis, 64
Herodotus, 288*n*6, 288*n*8
Herzog, Rabbi Yitzḥaq Halevi, 110–11
Ḥāfiẓ: *Dīwān*, 43
Ḥizqiyah, Mullah, 206
Hoshea Rabbah Kohana, 59–60
Humayūn, Nāṣer Kamil (Naṣir Qamil), 92, 212
Ḥuppa, 247
Ḥusayn, 12, 83
Ḥusayn, Shah Sultan, 16, 159; and Nadir, 160–61
Ḥusayn Beg, 155
Ḥusayn ibn Manṣūr al-Ḥallāj, 41

Ibn Tufayl: *Risālat Hayy ibn Yaqẓān* (Treatise of the Living, Son of the Wakeful One), 41
Imām al-Ma'mūn, 19–20
Imāmate (Imāma), 11
Imām Jum'ah of Meshhed, 58, 62, 63, 168–71
Imām Reza, 19–20; mosque of, 71; tomb of, 182, 185, 186
Iran. *See* Persia
Iran-Iraq War, 12
Iran-Turkmenistan (U.S.S.R.)–Afganistan border area, map of, 12
Isaac Arama, 200
Isfahan, 14
Ismā'īl, Shah, 20
Ismā'īliyya, 11
Israel: opinions of chief rabbis on religious status of Jews of Meshhed, 110–11, 285*n*2a
Ithnā 'Ashariyya ("Twelver") Shī'īs, 11–12

Jacob ben Joseph Tavus, 37
Jadīd al-Islām (Jadīdīm). *See* Jews of Meshhed
Jadīdī script, 216
Jāmi'-i 'Abbāsī (The 'Abbāsian Collector), 31–32, 280*n*2
Jehāz, 233
Jewish Exilarch *(Resh Galutha)*, 14

Jewish Ṣūfīs of Meshhed, 41–45, 46–48; confusion in religious concepts of, 44–45; contact with Muslims, 46; familiarity with traditional Jewish literature, 45–46
Jews of Bukhara, 49
Jews of Herat, 189; folktale about saving of, 72–73, 152, 178–81
Jews of Kalat (Qal'at): folktales about, 152, 173–77; as rainmakers, 175–77
Jews of Khiva, 49
Jews of Meshhed: abandonment of pretense of Islamic conversion, 82–83, 106–7, 211–12; aid to Jews of Herat, 152, 178–81; Allahdād, 18, 27, 51–64; arrival of in Meshhed, 25–27, 165; attitudes and traditions in early 19th century, 49–50; attitude toward Reza Shah Pehlevi, 89, 229; birth customs, 198–201; blood libels against in late nineteenth century, 79–82, 83–85, 189; blood libels against in 1940s, 92–100; and British, 26, 65–68; burial customs, 265–72; cohesion within community, 113–14, 276–77, 286*n*15; communal charity among, 88; community life in 1936, 88–91, 101–11; community life in 1946, 101–6; cultural influences upon, 90–91; custom of childhood betrothal among, 90; customs and institutions, 195–97; Diaspora, 17–18, 89, 197, 277; distribution of Persian translation of Torah among, 75; education of girls, 220–21; effect of Allahdād upon, 54; efforts to arrange for mass emigration to Israel, 108–11; emigration after Khomeini revolution, 111; emigration after the Allahdād, 72; emigration to Afghanistan, 205; emigration to and commerical activity in India, 90; emigration to Palestine, 87, 91; emigration to Turkestan, 229; emphasis on ritual cleanliness, 286*n*13; endogamy among, 46; engagement in international commerce, 70–71, 124, 211; ethnic separatism, 64; factions after the Allahdād, 71–72; familiarity with traditional Jewish literature, 45–46; flight of some to Herat, 178; folktales and legends, 151–97; forced attendance of children at *maktab,* 205–6; ghetto *(maḥalleh),* 102; girls' games, 222–27; heads of community, 49; Hebrew pronunciation of, 215; historical traditions concerning Afghans, 50; importance of learning Hebrew to, 208, 214; influence of Ṣūfism on, 41–45, 46–48, 53, 196; interest in classical Persian poetry, 53; interest in the Koran, 44; Islam inclination of some, 48–49, 74–75; as Jadīd al-Islām, 16, 17; Judeo-Persian language of, 195; Kalat origins of, 175; knowledge of Hebrew, 74, 102; life before the Allahdād, 29–40; marriage customs, 231–64; memoirs of Nasrullayoff family, 112–47; military conscription of, 88–89, 229; names and origins, 202–4; non-Jewish way of life of those away from Meshhed, 196–97; observance of dietary laws, 228–29, 230, 287*n*37; observance of Sabbath and Jewish holidays, 230; observance of *takiyya,* 196; opinion on religious status of by chief rabbis of Israel, 110–11, 285*n*2a; Persian and Hebrew names, 285*n*1; place in global Jewish perspective, 273–77; reestablishment of schools and baths after Allahdād, 72; refugees from Russia among, 89–90; reimmigration from Erez Israel, 103–4; relationship with local governors, 114; relationship with Turkomans, 114, 129; religious and national education of, 102–3, 106; religious Zionism among, 91, 102, 197; resentment against Jews who triggered Allahdād, 61; rites adopted from Muslims, 195–96; ritual observances, 228–30; role of women among, 198; secret adherence

to Judaism, 18–19, 189–92; secret school of, 196, 205–16; in Shī'ī Muslim environment, 11; sources of history of, 21; story of rescue of by Gohar, 152, 182–88; story of those who moved to Herat rather than convert, 72–73; strengthening of Jewish consciousness through travel, 75; synagogues of, 196; titles, 285*n*2, 285*n*3; visits to Jerusalem, 87. *See also* Allahdād
Jews of Persia: after Muslim conquest, 14; attitude toward treatment accorded them, 17; emigration, 17, 86, 87; forced conversions to Islam, 15–16; history of, 13–15; limitations imposed on by Pact of 'Umar, 15; under Nadir Shah, 16; persecution of in 17th and 18th centuries, 16–17; reaction of Europeans to treatment of, 16–17; religious Zionism among, 86, 87–88
Jews of Qazwin, 26–27, 64, 115, 265–68
Jews of Spain. *See* Marranos
Jews of Yazd, 49
Jews of Yemen, 31
Jizya, 14
"Joseph and Zulaika," Judeo-Persian version, 42–43
Joseph ibn Aknin, 41

Kabul, 50
Kajar dynasty, 16, 164, 229
Kalām, 66
Kalat Nadiri (Qal'at Nādirī), 165
Kalat (Qal'at), 26; folktales about Jews of, 152, 173–77
Khānah māndeh, 232
Khāzandeh, 234
Khiva, Jews of, 48–49
Khomeini, Ayatollah, 13, 15
Khorasan (Khurāsān), 19, 20, 155; folk traditions about Nadir in, 154; role of British agents in, 38
Khudādād, Mullah, 207, 210
Khiyābān, 20
Kleinbaum, Yiṣḥaq, 60, 88, 108, 187, 284*n*11; report to Jewish agency on Jews of Meshhed, 98–100, 101–6
Kohen, Mullah Aharon, 87
Kohen, Nissan Azariah, 37
Kohinor diamond, 290*n*36
Kona Gale (Kohnah Qal'ah), 155–56
Koran, 42
Kurdvānī, Ḥājjī Mullah Amīn, 75

Lāleh Kashi: Bringing the Lamp, 254–56
Lēvī, Habīb, 25
Levi, Ismā'il, 179
Levi, Yosef, 179
Lewi, Rabbi Isaac, 106
Lewis, Bernard, 84
"Life of Nadir," 154–67
Livian, Daniel Nasrullayoff, 213
Livian, Fatḥullah, 90
Livian, Yoḥanan, 81, 112, 168; on birth customs of Meshhedi Jews, 198–201; memoirs, 145–47
Lockhart, Laurence, 154, 155, 290*n*36, 290*n*37, 291*n*a–m
Lo-Torai, 292*n*10

MacNeil, John, 65, 66
Madrasah, 210–11, 292*n*1
Mahdī, Mullah. *See* Mashiaḥ Ajun (Mullah Mahdī)
Maimonides, 41
Majles: Banquet, 252–54
Maktab, 205–6, 292*n*1; discipline in, 218–20
Marash, Ya'qov, 214
Marranos, 16, 241; comparison to Jews of Meshhed, 273–76
Marriage customs, of Jews of Meshhed: age of marriage, 231–32; *'aqd bandān:* gentile wedding, 241; arranging of a marriage *(numzad dāri* or *numzad kardan)*, 232; *'arūsī:* the marriage, 247–52; *arūsi ḥamām:* bath of the bride, 243–45; *'arūs kashān:* bringing the bride (or *lāleh kashi:* bringing the lamp), 254–56; *baleh*

Marriage customs (*cont.*)
giri: taking yes, 234; *bāshlaq barān:* sending the bride price, 239–40; choice of match, 232–33; clothes of the bride and groom, 246–47; *dāmād-i ḥamām:* immersion of the bridegroom, 245; *dāmād khān barān:* invitation of the bridegroom, 236–37; date of marriage, 240–41; the day after the wedding, 258–59; *dīm vardārān:* taking of face, 242–43; divorce, 260–61; engagement, 233–34; from engagement to wedding, 237; *ḥanā bandān:* henna tying, 245–46; *harzeh vazān:* rude things, 243; *jehāz,* 258–59; *majles:* banquet, 252–54; marriage contracts (ill.), 248–50; *ōtāq kardan* and *numzad bāzī:* making room and bride play, 237–39; polygyny, 260; *ṣalāh binān:* consultation, 240–41; the seven days of the feast, 259–60; *shab sūr:* the night of the repast, 259; *shirni girān* and *shirni dādan:* taking sweets and giving sweets, 234–35; *shirni khōran:* eating sweets, 235–36; the union, 256–58; wedding song, 261–64
Mashiaḥ Ajun (Mullah Mahdī), 33, 37; familiarity with Rabbinic literature, 45; influential position in Meshhed after the Allahdād, 68; interest in Ṣūfī mysticism, 37, 42, 47–48; interest in the Koran, 43–44; involvement with British agents, 38, 51, 67–68; wealth of, 38
Mathnawī, 42
Mattityahu Garji, Rabbi, 39
Mawlana Shāhin, 43
Mazenderan, 27
Mehmed II, Sultan, 84
Meiendorf, Baron Yegor Fiodorovich, 32
Merv (Marw), 20, 285*n*11; Jewish community in, 113
Meshhed, 19–21; arrival of first Jews in, 25–26; cholera epidemic of 1830, 28, 171, 292*n*11; community life before 1929, 88–89; 1942 disturbance, 92–94; 1946 disturbance, 94–100; occupation by Red Army, 213; power structure, 83–84
Meshhed Allahdād. *See* Allahdād
Meshhed Jews. *See* Jews of Meshhed
Mesopotamia: Jewish community of, 14
Mibuna, Efrayim ben Yitzḥaq, 39
Midrash, 45
Midrash, of Jews of Meshhed, 205–16; in 1930, 212–13; in 1945, 213, 214; discipline in, 220; examinations, 217–18; feast for completers of, 218; instructional practices in, 213–14; method of teaching Hebrew in, 214–17, 286*n*17; prizes, 218; teachers of, 209
Miqvehs, 72, 243
Mīrzā 'Askarī, 54
Mīrzā Hadāyat Ullah, 48
Mīrzā Ḥusayn 'Ali (Bahā' Ullah), 76
Mīrzā Mas'ūd, 63
Mīrzā Muḥammad Mahdī Kaukabī Astarābādhī, 164, 166, 290*n*34, 291*n*42, 291*n*43
Mohels, 200
Moses of Narbonne, 41
Muhammad, 11
Muḥammadābād, 155, 156, 288*n*3
Muḥammad al-'Āmilī, 31
Muḥammad 'Alī, 42, 48
Muḥammad 'Alī Yishqaft, 66
Muḥammad Shah, 63
Muḥyi 'l-Dīn Ibn al'-Arabī, 42, 281*n*1
Mujtahids, 11–12
Muqaddasī, 14
Murādī, Solimān, 94
Murshid, 42, 44, 46; duties of, 47–48
Mushtāq-Fars (Dervish), 47
Muslims. *See* Shī'ī Islam; Sunnī Islam
Muslims of Meshhed: plots against Jews after Allahdād, 79–85
Muslims of Persia: marriage customs, 231, 232, 233, 236, 239, 243, 245, 258; nonexistence of issue of blood purity among, 275–76
muṭ'a marriages, 13
Muzaffar al-Din, Shah, 17

Nadir's Fort (Qal'at Nādiri), 26
Nadir Shah Afshār, 20, 50, 285*n*4, 285*n*5, 289*n*10, 290*n*41; and arrival of first Jews in Meshhed, 25–26, 115, 151, 165, 173, 292*n*j; birthplace, 156; blinding of Mīrzā Mahdī Khān, 166, 291*n*42, 292*n*k; blinding of son, 165–66, 291*n*42; childhood illness, 156; conquering of Afghanistan, 162; conquering of Baghdad, 163–64, 290*n*30, 292*n*h; conquering of Deregez, 289*n*14; conquering of India, 164; conquering of Merv, 161, 289*n*21; conquering of Meshhed, 160, 289*n*20; conquering of Quchan, 159–60; conquering of the Caucasus, 161–62; coronation, 162–63, 290*n*25; cruelty, 151, 166–67, 291*n*44, 292*n*l; death, 167, 285*n*8, 291*n*45; diamonds brought from India, 164–65, 290*n*36; father, 156; garden of, 167; invasion of India, 154; Jews of Persia under, 16, 165; mother, 156; popular life of, 154–67; as a shepherd, 157–58; taking of Baghdad, 154–55
Namdarīs family, 74
Names and origins, of Jews of Meshhed, 202–4
Naṣr al-Dīn Shah, 178
Nasrullayoff, Āqā Farajullah, 15, 18, 21–22; account of arrival of Jews in Meshhed, 26, 27; account of burial customs of Jews of Meshhed, 265; account of Herat Jews, 73; on danger posed by Bahai faith to Jews of Meshhed, 76–78; death of, 147; death of brother and father, 119–20, 125; education, 120, 121; family chain of descent, 114, 115–18; folktale of death of Ḥājj Ḥasan Eṣḥaq, 183–87, 189–92; folktales about Mullah Siman-Tov, 39, 168–72; great-grandmother of, 116, 118–19; illnesses and medical treatment of, 129–35, 141–42, 287*n*34, 287*n*35, 287*n*48; immigration to Israel, 146; on Jewish Meshhed community life, 88; life in Israel, 146–47; loans to local Muslim officials, 145; memoirs, 112–47; as a *mohel,* 200; on names and origins of Jews of Meshhed, 202–4; personality, 112–13; popular "Life of Nadir," 155–67; religious conviction, 113, 122–23, 136
Nathan, Ibrāhīm, 66
Nathan, Mūsā, 66
Nāyeb Muḥammad, 80–81, 283*n*2
Nebuchadnezzar, 14
Nethanel, Israel, 39
Netzer, Amnon, 25, 60, 71, 279*n*6
Neumark, Ephraim, 68–71
Nihāwandī, Mullah Ayatollah, 93, 96, 97, 284*n*8
Numzad dāri (numzad kardan), 232
Nurullah Khan, 294*n*6

Obadiah, 45
Ōtāq Kardan and *Numzad Bāzī:* Making Room and Bride Play, 237–39
Otesh Dōri? (Have You Fire?), 226–27
Ottoman Empire, blood libels against Jews in, 84–85
Ouziel, Rabbi Ben-Zion Meir Ḥay, 111
Ozar Hatorah, 87, 90, 106, 107

Pact of 'Umar, 14–15
Palang Tushkhan Jalāyir, 173, 174, 175, 176, 293*n*1
Palestine Institute of Folklore and Ethnology, 94
Palmerston, Lord, 65
Panizhel, Rabbi Eliyahu M., 74
Parthians, 14
Pe'amin, 60
Pelau hafkhōroshi, 253
Pentateuch, Judeo-Persian translation, 37
"People of the Book," 14, 83
Persia (Iran): Allied conquest of, 88; blood libels against Jews in, 85; cholera epidemic of 1830, 28; forced conversion of Jews in, 29; Jewish history in, 13–15; Khomeini revolution,

Persia (Iran) (*cont.*)
111; limitations imposed on Jews after the Allahdād, 30–32; limitations imposed on Jews before the Allahdād, 29–30; marriage customs in, 231; Muslim conquest of, 14; prohibition against Zionism, 88; recognition of Israel, 88; school system, 210–11, 221; structure of society, 276
Pinḥas, Mullah, 46, 48
Piq Piq (Pinching), 226
Piyyut, 39, 74
Poll tax *(jizya),* 14
Polygyny, 260

Qajars, 17
Qalamdān, 207
Qal'at Nādiri (Nadir's Fort), 26
Qazwin, 25, 285*n*6; Jews of, 26–27, 64, 115, 265–68
Qinyan, 236
Qō'im Bāzī (Game of Hiding—Hide and Seek), 222–23
Qoroq, 243, 244
"Qorot Anusē Meshhed l'fi Ya'agov Dilmanian" (The History of the Forced Converts of Meshhed according to Jacob Dilmanian), 25

Raḥman, Efrayim, 65–66
Raḥman, Mullah, 65
Raḥmānī, Raḥel, 222
Raḥmānī family, 60, 61, 74
Rainmaking competition stories, 175–77
Raphael, Yitzḥaq, 110
Rashi script, 216, 286*n*16
Responsa, 14
Reza Quli, 290*n*25, 291*n*42
Reza Shah Pahlavi, 26, 88, 229
Ritual impurity, 13, 15
Ritual observances, of Jews of Meshhed, 228–30
Russia, bombardment of Meshhed, 20
Russian Revolution, 229

Sabzawar, 26, 27, 285*n*7
Sachar, Howard M., 273
Safi, Mullah, 65
Ṣalāh Binān: Consultation, 240–41
Samuel ben Reuben, 39
Sanabad, 20
Sarakhs, 89, 287*n*32
Sassanids, 14
Schneider, Jennifer Patai, 287*n*48
Sēfer haYashar, 45
Sephardi pronunciation, 215
Shab Sūr: the Night of the Repast, 259
Shahin of Shiraz: *Sēfer Sharḥ 'al ha Torah* (The Book of Shahin's Commentary on the Torah), 37
Shalem, Yosef, 65
Shauloff, Mullah Binjamin, 39, 87
Shaykh Ibrāhīm, 173–75
Sheil, Justin, 67
Shī'ī Islam (Shī'ī 'Alī): attitude of contempt toward Jews, 13, 29, 83; differences from Sunnīs, 11–13; forced conversion of Jews to Islam in, 13; Ithnā 'Ashariyya ("Twelver") Shī'īs, 11–12; recognition of *muṭ'a* marriages, 13; role of ritual impurity in, 13; sects, 11
Shiraz, 85
Shirni Girān and *Shirni Dādan:* Taking Sweets and Giving Sweets, 234–35
Siman-Ṭov, Yafa, 222
Siman-Tov Melamed, Mullah, 28, 39; *Azharot in the Holy Tongue and in the Persian Tongue,* 39; folktales about, 152, 168–72; *Sefer Ḥayāt al-Rūḥ* (Book of the Life of the Spirit), 39; unpublished works, 39; writings of, 39–40
Simḥa Bemōnī, 116, 118–19
Spain, Jews of: *See* Marranos
Spanish Inquisition, 274
Stoddart, Charles, 36, 66, 67
Ṣūfīs, Jewish, of Meshhed, 41–45, 46–48
Ṣūfism, 41; Jewish influence on, 41; principles of, 47

Sukkoth, 178
Suleiman, 16, 84
Sunnī Islam, 11; differences from Shī'īs, 11–13

Tafsil, 216, 217, 293*n*6
Ṭahmāsp, 289*n*15, 289*n*16, 289*n*23
Tās teppe, 166
Tawḥīd, 63
Teheran, Jews of, 89, 284*n*10
Thieving Shaykh, folktale about, 173–75
Tobit, book of, 14
Torah, Persian translation of, 75
Truilhier, M.: account of Jews of Meshhed, 32, 290*n*37
Turbat, Jewish emigrants in, 72
Turkomans, and Jews of Meshhed, 114, 129
Tus, 20
Twelvers (Ithnā 'Ashariyya), 11–12
Tzaddiq, 152

'Umar I, 14
"Unbelievers," 13
Ustāi Zanjīl Bof (lit. ustād zanjīr—Leader of the Chain), 224

Vámbéry, Arminius, 68, 154
Van Dort, Immanuel Jacob, 43

Wedding song, of Jews of Meshhed, 261–64
Weinstein, Myron M., 43
Wolff, Joseph, 35–37; on the adherence of Meshhed Jews to Judaism after Allahdād, 54; claim to have baptised Mullah Mahdī, 67; on history and life of Meshhed Jews, 49–50; on Jewish Ṣūfīs of Meshhed, 42–48; on the Meshhed Allahdād, 51–55; missionary letter to Jews of Meshhed, 51–55; on Muslim knowledge of Jadīd al-Islām adherence to Judaism, 54–55; *Narrative of a Mission to Bokhara in the Years 1843–1845,* 51; *Researches and Missionary Labours among the Jews, Mohammedans, and Other Sects,* 35, 36–37, 38

Yak Anor De Anor (One, Two), 226
Ya'qovi, Mordekhai, 187
Yāqūt, 14
Yazd, Jews of, 49
Yemen, Jews of, 31
Yezdis, 64
Y'ḥezq'el ben Ya'aqov Halevi, Ḥājjī, 87
Y'ḥezq'el (Ezekiel), Ḥājjī, 209, 243
Y'hoshu'a, Ben-Zion: *MiNidḥē Yisraēl b'Afganistan l'Anusē Meshhed b'Iran,* 90, 111
Y'hoshu 'a-Raz: *MiNidḥē Yisraēl,* 32
Yiṣḥaq Gōhari, 26
Yosef, Mullah, 207–9
Yūsuf Khān (Muhammad 'Alī Shah), 20

Zabīḥī, Tziyon, 92, 94, 204, 212, 229, 264
Zakariyya al-Qazwini, 27
Zaydiyya, 11
Zion Zabīḥī, 108

Raphael Patai also edited these works:

Mivḥar haSippur haArtzi Yis'reli (with Zevi Wohlmut)
(In Hebrew: *Anthology of Palestinian Short Stories)*
EDOTH (Communities): A Quarterly for Folklore and Ethnology
(with Joseph J. Rivlin) (In Hebrew and English)
Sifriya l' Folqlor v'Etnologia (with Joseph J. Rivlin)
(In Hebrew: *Studies in Folklore and Ethnology)*
Meḥqarim Ḥevrutiyyim (with Roberto Bachi) (In Hebrew and English: *Social Studies)*
Erich Brauer: Y'hude Kurdistan (In Hebrew; translated and edited by R.P.)
The Hashemite Kingdom of Jordan
The Republic of Syria
The Republic of Lebanon
Herzl Year Book
The Complete Diaries of Theodor Herzl
Angelo S. Rappoport: Myth and Legend of Ancient Israel
Women in the Modern World
Encyclopaedia of Zionism and Israel
Thinkers and Teachers of Modern Judaism
(with Emanuel S. Goldsmith)
Events and Movements in Modern Judaism
(with Emanuel S. Goldsmith)

www.ingramcontent.com/pod-product-compliance
Lightning Source LLC
Chambersburg PA
CBHW070750230426
43665CB00017B/2313
* 9 7 8 0 8 1 4 3 4 0 7 5 2 *